ALSO BY D. PETER MACLEOD

The Four Wars of 1812

The Canadian Iroquois and the Seven Years' War

Northern Armageddon

Northern Armageddon

The Battle of the Plains of Abraham
and the Making of the American Revolution

D. Peter MacLeod

ALFRED A. KNOPF NEW YORK 2016

THIS IS A BORZOI BOOK
PUBLISHED BY ALFRED A. KNOPF

Copyright © 2008, 2015 by D. Peter MacLeod

www.aaknopf.com

Library of Congress Cataloging-in-Publication Data

Names: MacLeod, D. Peter, [date] author.
Title: Northern Armageddon : the Battle of the Plains of Abraham and
the making of the American Revolution / Peter MacLeod.
Description: First United States edition. | New York : Alfred A. Knopf, [2016] |
Includes bibliographical references.
Identifiers: LCCN 2015015893 | ISBN 9780307269898 (hardcover : alk. paper) |
ISBN 9781101946954 (ebook)
Subjects: LCSH: Quebec Campaign, Quebec, 1759. | Plains of Abraham,
Battle of the, Quebec, 1759. | Canada—History—To 1763 (New France)
Classification: LCC E199 .M17 2016 | DDC 971.01—dc23
LC record available at http://lccn.gov/2015015893

Front-of-jacket image: *French Fireships Attacking the English Fleet off Quebec,
28 June 1759* by Dominic Serres © National Maritime Museum,
Greenwich, London
Back-of-jacket image: *A View of the Launching Place Above the Town of Quebec,
Describing the Assault of the Enemy, 13 September 1759* by Francis Swaine.
Library and Archives Canada
Jacket design by Carol Devine Carson

Manufactured in the United States of America
First United States Edition

For Caitlin, Meghan, Simon,
Rory, Brenna, and James

I come from New England with a company of volunteers to serve His Majesty in the reduction of Canada.

—MIDSHIPMAN ASHLEY BOWEN,
speaking to Major General James Wolfe, July 15, 1759

Contents

Maps

Illustrations

The People of 1759

ADAMS, WILLIAM—commander, Royal Navy; captain of HMS *Hunter*

AILLEBOUST DE CERRY, PHILIPPE-MARIE D'—captain of the port of
    Quebec; advised Ramezay to surrender Quebec to the British

ALBERGATI-VEZZA, FRANÇOIS-MARIE BALTHAZARA D'—ensign, *troupes
    de la marine;* organized a force of militia and *troupes de la marine*
    to cover the retreat of the French army at the Battle of the Plains of
    Abraham

AMHERST, JEFFERY—major general, British Army

ANSON, GEORGE—First Lord of the Admiralty

ARGALL, SAMUEL—admiral of Virginia; led the first British attack on New
    France in 1613

ARNOUX, ANDRÉ—Quebec surgeon; owner of the house where Montcalm
    died

AVÈNE DES MÉLOIZES, NICOLAS RENAUD D'—captain, *troupes de la
    marine;* recorded the dialogue between a French lookout and a
    British officer who persuaded the sentry that the flotilla carrying
    Wolfe's army to the Anse au Foulon was a French provision convoy

BARRÉ, ANNE—refugee from Gaspé

BARRÉ, ISAAC—major, British Army; Wolfe's adjutant general

BARRÉ, JEAN—officer, Canadian militia; merchant marine captain from
    Gaspé

BEAUJEU, DANIEL-HYACINTHE-MARIE LIÉNARD DE—captain, *troupes de la
    marine*

BELCOURT, THISBÉ DE—lieutenant, French navy; commander of a
    company of militia cavalry at the siege of Quebec

BELL, THOMAS—captain, British Army; aide-de-camp to James Wolfe

BERNETZ, FÉLICIEN DE—lieutenant colonel, Royal Roussillon Regiment;
    second-in-command of the Quebec garrison

BERNIER, BENOÎT-FRANÇOIS—captain, *troupes de terre;* Montcalm's
    commissaire ordonnateur des guerres (deputy quartermaster general)

BERNIER, MADAME—resident of L'Islet; forced to flee when George Scott's troops burned her home

BERTHOU-DÛBREÜIL—Quebec merchant whose warehouse was destroyed by Williamson's bombardment

BIARD, PIERRE—Jesuit priest; author of "Nostre prinse par les anglois" (Our capture by the English)

BIGOT, FRANÇOIS—intendant of New France

BLAND, HUMPHREY—lieutenant general, British Army; author of *A Treatise of Military Discipline*

BOISHÉBERT, CHARLES DESCHAMPS DE—captain, *troupes de la marine*

BOTWOOD, NED—sergeant, Forty-Seventh Regiment; author of "Hot Stuff"

BOUCHERVILLE, AMABLE DE—volunteer, *troupes de la marine;* wounded twice at the Battle of the Plains of Abraham

BOUCHETTE, JOSEPH—surveyor general of Lower Canada; author of *Description topographique de la province du Bas Canada* (*A Topographical Description of the Province of Lower Canada*)

BOUGAINVILLE, LOUIS-ANTOINE DE—colonel in the *troupes de terre;* senior aide-de-camp to Louis-Joseph de Montcalm

BOURLAMAQUE, FRANÇOIS-CHARLES DE—brigadier, *troupes de terre;* third in command of the *troupes de terre* in Canada

BOWEN, ASHLEY—New England sailor; served aboard HMS *Pembroke* during the siege

BROWNE, HENRY—lieutenant, Twenty-Eighth Regiment; helped to carry the dying James Wolfe off the battlefield

BULLAU, ANTOINE—ensign, Canadian militia; left Canada after the British conquest

BURTON, RALPH—lieutenant colonel, Forty-Eighth Regiment

CADET, AUGUSTIN—Quebec butcher; uncle of Joseph-Michel Cadet

CADET, JOSEPH-MICHEL—*munitionnaire général* (purveyor general) of Canada; responsible for supplying the French armed forces with provisions

"CADET'S CRITIC"—author of the "Mémoire du Canada" (Memoir of Canada)

CALCRAFT, JAMES—captain, British Army

CAMERON, EWAN—private, Seventy-Eighth Regiment; rumored to have killed nine French soldiers with his claymore at the Battle of the Plains of Abraham

CARLETON, GUY—lieutenant colonel, British Army; Wolfe's quartermaster general

CARRON—Menominee warrior; fought at the Battle of the Plains of Abraham

CHADS, JAMES—commander, Royal Navy; captain of HMS *Vesuvius;* commanded the boats that carried Wolfe's army to the Anse au Foulon

CHAREST, ÉTIENNE—captain, Canadian militia

CHARLEVOIX, PIERRE-FRANÇOIS-XAVIER DE—Jesuit priest; author of the *Histoire et description générale de la Nouvelle France* (*History and General Description of New France*)

COATS, EDWARD—lieutenant, Royal Navy; author of *A Private Journal of the Siege of Quebec*

COOK, JAMES—master, HMS *Pembroke;* charted the St. Lawrence River

CRÈVECOEUR, MICHEL-GUILLAUME-SAINT-JEAN DE—lieutenant, La Sarre Regiment; author of *Letters from an American Farmer*

CUISY D'ARGENTEUIL—ensign, *troupes de la marine;* wounded three times at the Battle of the Plains of Abraham

DAINE, FRANÇOIS—Quebec's senior magistrate; leader of a group of Quebec notables who asked Ramezay to surrender the city to the British

DELAUNE, WILLIAM—captain, light infantry; recorded Wolfe's orders to his junior officers on the Plains of Abraham

DESANDROUINS, JEAN-NICOLAS—captain, Ingénieurs du Roy (King's Engineers); told Samuel Holland that one French battleship could have saved Canada in 1760

DESAULNIERS, THOMAS-IGNACE TROTTIER—captain, Canadian militia; killed a French grenadier in a duel

DOLBEC, ROMAIN—Quebec butcher; godfather of Augustin Cadet

DOMAS, FRANÇOIS—sergeant major of Quebec; responsible for training the militia of the government of Quebec

DOUGLAS, FRANÇOIS-PROSPER DE—captain, Languedoc Regiment; commander of the Samos battery, which guarded the Anse au Foulon

DREW, GEORGE—premier of Ontario and companion of the Order of Canada; called French Canadians a "defeated race" who had only the rights that English Canadians chose to give them

DUMAS, JEAN-DANIEL—captain and adjutant general of the *troupes de la marine;* commanded the Canadian militia, Native American warriors, and regulars of the *troupes de la marine* attacking Wolfe's northern flank during the Battle of the Plains of Abraham

DURELL, PHILIP—rear admiral, Royal Navy; third in command of the British fleet at the siege of Quebec in 1759; failed to intercept a French provision convoy in the spring of 1759

EASTBURN, ROBERT—Philadelphia blacksmith; captured in 1756 and held as a prisoner of war in Canada

FIEDMONT, LOUIS-THOMAS JACAU DE—captain, Compagnie des Cannonier Bombardiers (colonial artillery); commanded Quebec's artillery

FOLIGNÉ, JÉROME DE—French naval officer; commanded a battery on Quebec's ramparts

FONTBONNE, LOUIS RESTOINEAU DE—lieutenant colonel, Guyenne Regiment; deployed his regiment on the Buttes-à-Neveu during the initial stages of the Battle of the Plains of Abraham

FRASER, MALCOLM—lieutenant, Seventy-Eighth Regiment; author of *Extract from a Manuscript Journal, Relating to the Siege of Quebec*

FRASER, SIMON—captain, Seventy-Eighth Regiment; persuaded a French sentry that Wolfe's landing craft were a French provision convoy

FRASER, SIMON—lieutenant colonel, Seventy-Eighth Regiment; master of Lovat and chief of Clan Fraser

FRONTENAC ET DE PALLUAU, LOUIS DE—governor-general of New France; defended Quebec against besieging New Englanders in 1690

GALLET, FRANÇOIS—militia gunner; wounded at the Battle of the Plains of Abraham

GERE, AMABLE DE—Canadian fur trader and clerk; fought alongside Native American warriors at the Battle of the Plains of Abraham

GIBSON, JAMES—chaplain, HMS *Vanguard*

GLODE—Menominee warrior; fought at the Battle of the Plains of Abraham

GOREHAM, JOSEPH—American ranger; commanded part of a force of rangers, light infantry, and sailors that burned hundreds of Canadian farms

GRACE, HENRY—British prisoner of war; author of *The History of the Life and Sufferings of Henry Grace*

GREENER, WILLIAM—British gunsmith and ballistics expert; author of *The Gun; or, A Treatise on the Various Descriptions of Small Fire-Arms*

GRIGNON, AUGUSTIN—grandson of Charles-Michel Mouet de Langlade; author of *Seventy-Two Years' Recollections of Wisconsin*

HALE, JOHN—lieutenant colonel, Forty-Seventh Regiment

HENDERSON, JAMES—volunteer, Louisbourg Grenadiers; helped to carry a dying James Wolfe off the battlefield

HERBIN, LOUIS-FRÉDÉRIC—captain, *troupes de la marine;* commanded the Canadian militia and Native American warriors on the south side of the battlefield; claimed that one of his militiamen killed James Wolfe

HOLLAND, SAMUEL—lieutenant, Sixtieth Regiment; engineer and surveyor; came to report to James Wolfe during the battle, only to find his general dying

HOLMES, CHARLES—rear admiral, Royal Navy; second-in-command of the British fleet at Quebec; commanded British naval forces above the city

HOWE, JEMIMA—settler from Hinsdale, New Hampshire; captured in 1755 and held as a prisoner of war in Canada

HOWE, WILLIAM—lieutenant colonel, British Army; commanded a light infantry battalion at Quebec

HUMPHREYS, RICHARD—private, light infantry; author of "Rich Humphreys, His Journal, Commencing Cork May 1757 with Its Continuation"

HUNTER, WILLIAM—midshipman, master's mate, and acting lieutenant, Royal Navy; author of "Biographical Memoir of Lieutenant William Hunter"

JACK—African American teamster with the British expedition to Quebec

JEREMY—African American teamster with the British expedition to Quebec

JOANNÈS, ARMAND DE—captain, Languedoc Regiment; negotiated Quebec's surrender to the British

JOB, ELEANOR—British nurse; treated casualties on the Plains of Abraham

JOHNSON, JAMES—settler from Charlestown, New Hampshire; captured in 1754 and held as a prisoner of war in Quebec; author of "Narrative of James Johnson"

JOHNSON, JOHN—quartermaster sergeant, Fifty-Eighth Regiment; author of "Memoirs of the Siege of Quebec and Total Reduction of Canada in 1759 and 1760"

JOHNSTONE, JAMES—lieutenant, *troupes de la marine;* aide-de-camp to Louis-Joseph de Montcalm; author of "Memoirs of a French Officer"

JOSEPH—valet to Louis-Joseph de Montcalm

KACHAKAWASHEKA—Menominee warrior; fought at the Battle of the Plains of Abraham

KALM, PEHR—Swedish botanist; toured New France and British America in 1749 and 1750; author of *Peter Kalm's Travels in North America*

KING, TITUS—settler from Northampton, Massachusetts, and soldier in the Massachusetts militia; captured in 1755 and held as a prisoner of war in Canada

KISENSIK—a chief of the Nipissings of Lac des Deux Montagnes; thanked Great Lakes warriors for helping the Nipissings defend their homes against the British

KNOX, JOHN—captain, Forty-Third Regiment, author of *An Historical Journal of the Campaigns in North America for the Years 1757, 1758, 1759, and 1760*

LA CHEVROTIÈRE, FRANÇOIS DE—ensign, *troupes de la marine;* author of "Mon épitaphe, si je meurs de mes blessures" (My epitaph, if I die from my wounds)

LA CORNE, CHARLOTTE DE—Canadian noble

LA FEUILLE—son of Madame Bernier; born after George Scott's troops burned his home and forced his mother to flee into the forest

LAFONTAINE—commander of the French outpost at the Anse des Mères

LA NAUDIÈRE, CHARLES-FRANÇOIS TARIEU DE—captain, *troupes de la marine;* lost his tent while observing the British fleet sailing up the St. Lawrence toward Quebec

LANGLADE, CHARLES-MICHEL MOUET DE—ensign, *troupes de la marine;* fought alongside Native American warriors at the Battle of the Plains of Abraham

LAPAUSE DE MARGON, JEAN-GUILLAUME PLANTAVIT DE—captain, Guyenne Regiment; author of "Mémoire et observations sur mon voyage en Canada"

LA RIVIÈRE—sergeant, Artillerie Royale (Royal Artillery); took charge of the guns at the north end of the French line when his officer was wounded

LA VISITATION, SOEUR DE (MARIE-JOSEPH LEGARDEUR DE REPENTIGNY)—nun of the Hôpital Général; author of *Relation de ce qui s'est passé au siège de Québec, et de la prise du Canada* (Relation of what happened at the siege of Quebec, and of the capture of Canada)

LAWSON, ELIZABETH—object of James Wolfe's unsuccessful affections

LEGRIS—officer, Canadian militia; sent downriver to meet French supply ships in the spring of 1760

LE MERCIER, FRANÇOIS-MARC-ANTOINE—captain, Compagnie des Cannonier Bombardiers (colonial artillery)

LENOIR DE ROUVRAY, LAURENT FRANÇOIS—captain, La Sarre Regiment; wounded and captured while attacking British forces advancing onto the Plains of Abraham

LESLIE, MATTHEW—captain, British Army; Wolfe's assistant quartermaster general; owned the schooner that Wolfe used to reconnoiter the Anse au Foulon just before the Battle of the Plains of Abraham

LETO—African American teamster with the British expedition to Quebec

LEVASSEUR, NOËL—Canadian sculptor; carved the French royal arms that hung over city gates and the entrances of public buildings in Canada

LE VASSEUR, RENÉ NICOLAS—clerk, ministry of marine; served as a firefighter during the bombardment of Quebec

LÉVIS, FRANÇOIS-GASTON DE—*maréchal de camp* (major general), French army; second-in-command of the French army in Canada under Louis-Joseph de Montcalm

LIGNERY, FRANÇOIS-MARIE LE MARCHAND DE—captain, *troupes de la marine*

LOGAN, JAMES—Philadelphia administrator and merchant; author of "Of the State of the British Plantations in America, a Memorial"

LOWTHER, KATHERINE—James Wolfe's fiancée

MACDONALD, DONALD—captain, Seventy-Eighth Regiment; convinced French sentries at the Anse au Foulon that he had come to reinforce the garrison

MACKELLAR, PATRICK—major, Royal Engineers; James Wolfe's chief engineer

MACLEOD, DONALD—sergeant, Seventy-Eighth Regiment; wounded at the Battle of the Plains of Abraham

MACLEOD, WILLIAM—captain, Royal Artillery

MACPHERSON, ROBERT—chaplain, Seventy-Eighth Regiment; wrote a letter to his brother that provides a detailed narrative of the Battle of the Plains of Abraham

MAGNAN, JEAN-BAPTISTE-PASCHAL—Quebec merchant and adjutant of

the Quebec militia; chose the initial French position at the western
edge of the Buttes-à-Neveu

MALARTIC, ANNE-JOSEPH-HIPPOLYTE MAURÈS DE—captain, Béarn
Regiment; shocked by Montcalm's silence and distressed appearance
just before the Battle of the Plains of Abraham

MARCEL, PIERRE—captain, French army, aide-de-camp to Louis-Joseph de
Montcalm; arranged for the disposal of Montcalm's effects

MARTIN, ABRAHAM, DIT L'ÉCOSSAIS—Canadian sailor, pilot, and farmer
for whom the Plains of Abraham were named

MEMY, JOHN—sailor, HMS *Lowestoft;* killed by gunfire from the French
battery at Sillery as British warships headed downstream toward the
Anse au Foulon

MILLER, JAMES—private, Fifteenth Regiment; author of "Memoirs of an
Invalid"

MILLER, MARIE-JOSEPH—resident of Montreal; married to Mathieu
Valentin Jacques Miller

MILLER, MATHIEU VALENTIN JACQUES—soldier, *troupes de la marine;*
wrote a letter to his wife describing conditions at Quebec in 1759

MISTAHIMASKWA (BIG BEAR)—Cree chief; advocated using peaceful means
to deal with the Canadian government in 1879

MONCKTON, ROBERT—brigadier, British army; Wolfe's second-in-
command

MONTBEILLARD, FIACRE-FRANÇOIS POTOT DE—captain, Corps Royal
d'Artillerie et de Génie (Royal Corps of Artillery and Engineering);
commander of the French artillery during the Battle of the Plains of
Abraham and aide-de-camp to Louis-Joseph de Montcalm

MONTCALM, LOUIS-JOSEPH DE—*lieutenant général des armées* (lieutenant
general), *troupes de terre;* commander of the *troupes de terre* in
Canada and the French army at the Battle of the Plains of Abraham

MONTRESOR, JOHN—lieutenant, Royal Engineers

MONTREUIL, PIERRE-ANDRÉ GOHIN DE—lieutenant colonel, French army;
Montcalm's adjutant general

MULLER, JOHN—author of *The Attac[k] and Defence of Fortified Places*

MURRAY, ALEXANDER—lieutenant colonel, Louisbourg Grenadiers

MURRAY, JAMES—brigadier, British Army; Wolfe's fourth in command

"NAVAL VOLUNTEER"—served aboard HMS *Stirling Castle;* author of a
series of informative letters that describe sailors on the Plains of
Abraham and his own experience as a looter after the battle

OSAUWISHKENO—Menominee warrior; fought at the Battle of the Plains of Abraham

OUIHARALIHTE (PETIT ÉTIENNE)—Huron teenager; his reminiscences provide a Native American account of the Battle of the Plains of Abraham

PALLISER, HUGH—captain of HMS *Shrewsbury;* led the detachment of sailors that occupied Quebec's Lower Town after the French surrender

PANET, JEAN-CLAUDE—Quebec notary; soldier in the Canadian militia; author of *Journal du siège de Québec (Journal of the Siege of Quebec)*

PEARSON, JEREMIAH—American ranger, author of "Jeremiah Pearson His Book"

PERCEVAL, PHILIP—officer, Royal Navy; captain of the *Rodney* cutter, which carried Wolfe's last dispatches to the British government

PERRY, DAVID—American ranger; author of *Recollections of an Old Soldier*

PONTBRIAND, HENRI-MARIE DUBREIL DE—bishop of Quebec

POTE, WILLIAM—resident of Falmouth in what is now Maine and captain of the *Montague* schooner; American prisoner of war; captured at sea in 1745 and held as a prisoner of war in Canada

PRIMAULT, JOACHIM—tanner living near the Hôpital Général

RAMEZAY, JEAN-BAPTISTE-NICOLAS-ROCH DE—captain, *troupes de la marine;* commander of the Quebec garrison

RÉCHER, JEAN-FÉLIX—parish priest of Notre-Dame-des-Victoires; author of *Journal du siège de Québec en 1759* (Journal of the siege of Quebec in 1759)

RIGAUD DE VAUDREUIL, FRANÇOIS-PIERRE DE—captain, *troupes de la marine;* governor of Montreal; brother of Pierre de Rigaud de Vaudreuil

ROBINS, BENJAMIN—British ballistics expert, author of *New Principles of Gunnery*

ROCHEBEAUCOURT—captain, French army; commander of the militia cavalry

ROSS, THOMAS—captain, Seventy-Eighth Regiment; killed in the Saint-Charles valley during the last phase of the Battle of the Plains of Abraham

SAINTE-ELIZABETH, SOEUR DE (MARIE-THÉRÈSE ADHÉMAR DE LANTAGNAC)—nun of the Hôpital Général; operated a mobile aid station during Williamson's bombardment of Quebec

SAUNDERS, CHARLES—vice admiral, Royal Navy; commander of the
British fleet at the siege of Quebec, 1759

SAXE, MAURICE DE—marshal, French army; author of *Mes rêveries:
Ouvrage posthume de Maurice comte de Saxe (My Reveries: Posthumus
work of Maurice, Count of Saxony)*

SCHUYLER, PETER—colonel, New Jersey Regiment; captured following the
surrender of Oswego in 1756 and held as a prisoner of war in
Canada

SCOTT, GEORGE—captain, Fortieth Regiment; commanded a force of
rangers, light infantry, and sailors that burned hundreds of Canadian
farms

SHINGAS—Delaware chief

SKELLY, GORDON—lieutenant, Royal Navy; author of a journal of the siege
of Quebec that describes the British landing at the Anse au Foulon

"STAFF OFFICER"—British officer serving on Wolfe's staff; author of
"Account of Quebec Campaign, June–September 1759"

"SUPPLY CLERK"—clerk at Quebec's Magasin du Roy (Royal Storehouse);
author of the *Journal du siège de Québec du 10 mai au 18 septembre
1759 (Journal of the Siege of Quebec from May 10 to 18 September 1759)*

THET, GILBERT DU—French sailor; fired the first cannon shot against a
British force attacking New France in 1613

THOMPSON, JAMES—sergeant, Seventy-Eighth Regiment; his
reminiscences provide an intimate look at the Seventy-Eighth in the
Battle of the Plains of Abraham

TOWNSHEND, GEORGE—brigadier, British Army; Wolfe's third in
command and one of North America's first cartoonists

TRAHAN, JOSEPH—teenage Acadian refugee serving in the militia; left
a very vivid, very personal account of the Battle of the Plains of
Abraham

TSAWAWANHI—leader of the Huron contingent at the Battle of the Plains
of Abraham; grandfather of Ouiharalihte

VAUDREUIL, PHILIPPE DE RIGAUD DE—governor-general of New France;
warned of the dangers of British westward expansion in 1716

VAUDREUIL, PIERRE DE RIGAUD DE—governor-general of New France and
commander in chief of the French armed forces in North America

VERGOR, LOUIS DU PONT DUCHAMBON DE—captain, *troupes de la marine;*
commander of the French outpost at the Anse au Foulon

VIENNE, FRANÇOIS-JOSEPH DE—Quebec's *garde-magasin* (chief storekeeper)

VILLIERS, LOUIS COULON DE—captain, *troupes de la marine*

VOYER, PIERRE-GERVAIS—Quebec baker, employed by Joseph-Michel Cadet; killed and decapitated during the Battle of the Plains of Abraham

WALSH, HUNT—lieutenant colonel, Twenty-Eighth Regiment

WASHINGTON, GEORGE—colonel, Virginia Regiment

WILLIAMSON, ADAM—captain lieutenant, Royal Artillery

WILLIAMSON, GEORGE—lieutenant colonel, Royal Artillery; commander of Wolfe's artillery at Quebec

WILLIAMSON, PETER—soldier, Fiftieth Regiment; captured following the surrender of Oswego in 1756 and held as a prisoner of war in Canada

WOLFE, EDWARD—lieutenant general, British Army; father of James Wolfe

WOLFE, JAMES—major general, British Army; commander of the British army in the Quebec campaign and at the Battle of the Plains of Abraham

YORKE, JOHN—captain lieutenant, Royal Artillery; commanded a battery of six-pounders at the Battle of the Plains of Abraham

Preface

Best known as a clash between French and British armies, the Plains of Abraham was also an American battle. One in every three soldiers in the British army at Quebec had been recruited in the American colonies. Hundreds more Americans served aboard British warships and the transports from Boston, New York, and Philadelphia that carried part of that army up the St. Lawrence River. During the campaign, the northern colonies played a role similar to that of Britain at the time of the Allied invasion of Europe in 1944 by providing a nearby land base for a great amphibious offensive.

Rangers and Royal Americans apart, colonial soldiers and sailors are almost invisible in accounts of the beachheads and battlefields of the Quebec campaign. Yet they were there for every landing and every battle, and their actions shaped the course of American history.

Long before the emergence of anything resembling a serious independence movement, most of Britain's North American colonies were nascent independent states. Governed by local elites, they were self-financing, economically and demographically robust, and capable when necessary of raising their own fleets and armies.

As early as 1690, colonial America demonstrated its ability to project power into the heart of New France when a New England fleet and army besieged Quebec, a feat Britain would not be able to duplicate for another sixty-nine years. In 1710 and 1744, American armies carried in American ships and supported by Royal Navy and New England warships conquered Acadia, which became the British province of Nova Scotia, and captured the strategic French port of Louisbourg.

In the opinion of observers like James Murray, a senior British officer during the Seven Years' War, the latent power of the American colonies posed a standing threat to the integrity of Britain's North American empire. "New England," he told a French officer, "needs a bridle to keep it under control." For Murray, this bridle was Canada.

Although possessed of a much smaller population and infinitely weaker economy than British America, Canada was organized for war with extensive fortifications, a garrison of professional soldiers, a strong militia system, powerful Native American allies, and an authoritarian, centralized colonial government, all subsidized by the French Crown.

At the apex of this structure stood a governor-general who could mobilize Canada's military resources within days and take advantage of Canada's interior lines of communication to send troops to reinforce Acadia or build a fort in the Ohio valley without any need to consult or bargain with an elected assembly.

So if American colonials had won their victories over New France along the Atlantic coast, where colonial and British sea power gave them a decided advantage, in the interior it was another story. Were Americans ever to consider seeking independence, Canada would have to be neutralized. And neutralizing Canada would mean taking Quebec.

In 1759, Britain, after many false starts dating back to a failed expedition in 1711, decided to do just that. A powerful fleet and army commanded by Charles Saunders and James Wolfe assembled at Halifax and sailed for Quebec.

When the expedition departed, it carried with it not just the prospect of a northeastern North America dominated by Britain from the St. Lawrence valley to the Carolinas but the possibility of an independent America.

Northern Armageddon divides the story of the Battle of the Plains of Abraham into six parts.

Part 1 covers British operations at Quebec from May to September 1759. It follows these operations as far as possible through the eyes of Ashley Bowen, a Massachusetts sailor serving as acting midshipman aboard

HMS *Pembroke,* and master's mate (senior midshipman) William Hunter of HMS *Princess Amelia.*

Part 2 looks at the same time period from a French perspective as the British bombard Quebec and four residents—a priest, a clerk, a nun, and a notary—experience something like the London Blitz of 1940 while the Canadian entrepreneur Joseph-Michel Cadet works to rush provisions to the French army before Canada's defenders are forced to abandon the city.

Part 3 deals with the Battle of the Plains of Abraham itself, arguing that the outcome turned on a collapse of morale among French regulars provoked by battlefield stress. As before, the text alternates between French and British perspectives of the same events.

Part 4 follows the British, as they prepare to blast their way through the walls, and the French, as a mutiny in the Quebec garrison leads to the surrender of the city.

Part 5 takes the story up to the fall of Canada in 1760. Along the way, it looks at the British garrison of Quebec barely surviving the Canadian winter, the emergence of a Canadian resistance movement in British-occupied territory, the French victory at the Battle of Sainte-Foy as the same armies meet on the same battlefield for a second time, and the French siege of Quebec.

Part 6 places the Battle of the Plains of Abraham in a global context as a crucial event in the European occupation of the Americas and the shattering of a hemispheric Native American civilization, then traces its impact up to the twenty-first century on Canada, the United States, Native Americans, and the world. Readers interested in picking up a bit of background on French-British rivalry in North America and the Seven Years' War prior to the Quebec campaign might like to glance through this section first.

This book is based for the most part on the letters and journals of participants and allows them, as far as possible, to speak for themselves. Many of these sources, while solid and reliable, are frustratingly cryptic concerning matters historians would most like to know about. Writing for their own reasons, their authors preferred to write general narratives of the entire battle rather than detailed accounts of events they themselves saw and experienced. Other writers had the annoying habit of using the third person, which makes quotations sound a bit odd at times.

Four of the best sources for the campaign are anonymous. To avoid confusion, each writer has a short descriptive label.

"Cadet's critic," author of the "Memoir of Canada," had a great deal to say about logistics and a low opinion of Joseph-Michel Cadet, who was responsible for supplying the French army with provisions.

The "naval volunteer" served in the Royal Navy during the campaign and wrote a series of informative letters to his uncle, including a reference to his own experience as a looter at the Battle of the Plains of Abraham.

Working in the main government storehouse at Quebec gave the "supply clerk" a unique perspective on the campaign. His *Journal du siège de Québec du 10 mai au 18 septembre 1759 (Journal of the Siege of Quebec from May 10 to September 18, 1759)* combines private rants with shrewd observations on military affairs.

The "staff officer" worked in Wolfe's headquarters and produced the "Account of Quebec Campaign, June–September 1759." Even more inclined to outrage than the supply clerk, his comments on the campaign faithfully reflect James Wolfe's irritation with the Royal Navy and his own senior subordinates.

The spelling in English quotations has been modernized, except where this would distort the meaning or reduce the charm of the original expressions. All quotations from French documents were translated by the author.

Participants in the Seven Years' War in North America spoke of a conflict between the French and the English. The realities behind these labels were a little more complicated and best expressed by a wider range of terms.

In this book, "the British" (who might also have regional identities as Scots, Englishmen, Virginians, Pennsylvanians, or New Englanders) are either residents of Great Britain (also called Britons) or subjects of the British Crown wherever they came from. "Americans" are British subjects from Britain's North American colonies.

"French" similarly refers either to all French subjects, whether North American or European, or to French subjects from metropolitan France. "Canadians" are permanent French residents of Canada. Reflecting contemporary practice, "Canadians" are Canadian with regard to the French and "French" with regard to the British.

All this is actually less confusing than it sounds.

So is the geography of French North America. "New France" is the French Empire in North America, consisting of Canada, Louisiana, Louisbourg, and French-controlled parts of Acadia in what are now New Brunswick and Prince Edward Island. "Nova Scotia" is the British colony occupying the mainland of what is now the province of the same name. "Canada" refers to French settlements in the St. Lawrence valley.

European maps often showed a giant triangle of territory, between Louisbourg, Louisiana, and the prairies, as a French possession. While claimed by France, most of this territory was owned and controlled by Native Americans.

During the Seven Years' War, two types of French regular troops served in Canada. The *troupes de terre* were the regular army of France, placed under the authority of the minister of war. The *troupes de la marine* formed a second French army, controlled by the Ministry of Marine and Colonies. Organized in independent companies, they were also known as the Compagnies Franches de la Marine and are sometimes referred to in English as "colonial regulars." In 1760, the French formed these independent companies into two battalions.

White flags played two seemingly contradictory roles in the 1759 campaign. White was the color of the Bourbon monarchy of France; a plain white flag served as the national flag. Quebec's defenders waved white flags in the air to celebrate their victory at the Battle of Montmorency. Canadians who left for France after the conquest spoke of their desire to remain under the white flag. Yet at the same time, the governor-general of New France ordered the commandant of Quebec to signal his desire to surrender by raising a white flag over the city.

I have no idea how the British worked out what the French were trying to say when a white flag went up, but they seemed to understand. Context, after all, is everything.

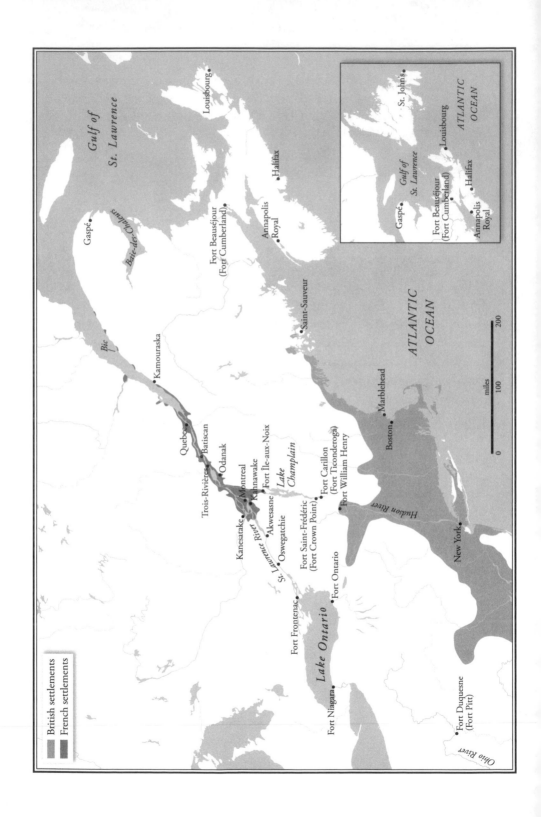

British settlements
French settlements

Gulf of St. Lawrence

Louisbourg

Halifax

Annapolis Royal

Fort Beauséjour (Fort Cumberland)

Gaspé

Baie-des-Chaleurs

Bic

Kamouraska

Saint-Sauveur

ATLANTIC OCEAN

Marblehead

Boston

Quebec

Batiscan

Odanak

Trois-Rivières

Montreal

Kahnawake

Fort Île-aux-Noix

Lake Champlain

Fort Carillon (Fort Ticonderoga)

Fort William Henry

Hudson River

Kanesatake

Akwesasne

St. Lawrence River

Oswegatchie

Fort Saint-Frédéric (Fort Crown Point)

Fort Ontario

New York

Fort Frontenac

Lake Ontario

Fort Niagara

Fort Duquesne (Fort Pitt)

Ohio River

miles

0   100   200

St. John's

ATLANTIC OCEAN

Gulf of St. Lawrence

Louisbourg

Fort Beauséjour (Fort Cumberland)

Halifax

Gaspé

Annapolis Royal

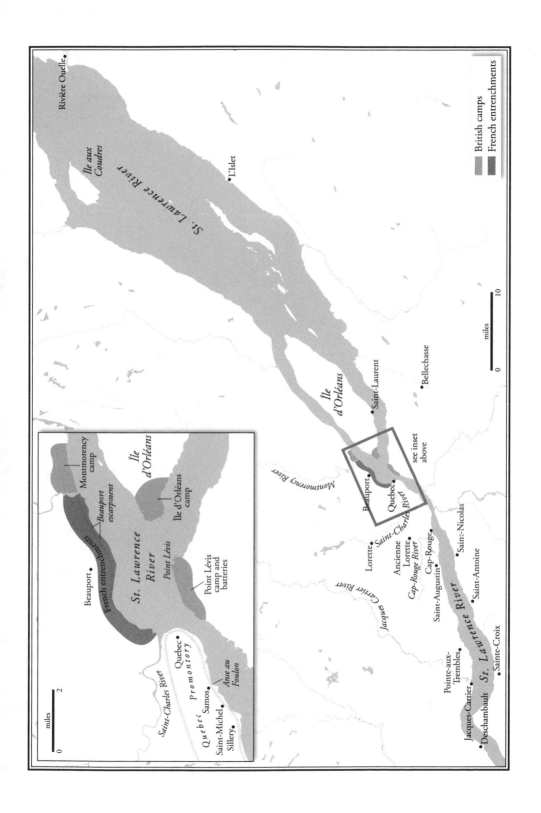

Rivière Ouelle

Île aux Coudres

St. Lawrence River

L'Islet

Île
d'Orléans

Saint-Laurent

Bellechasse

Montmorency River

Beauport

Quebec

see inset
above

Saint-Charles River

Lorette

Ancienne
Lorette

Cap-Rouge River

Cap-Rouge

Saint-Augustin

Saint-Nicolas

Saint-Antoine

Jacques-Cartier River

Pointe-aux-
Trembles

Jacques-Cartier

Deschambault

St. Lawrence River

Sainte-Croix

miles
0   10

British camps
French entrenchments

Inset:

miles
0   2

Montmorency camp

Beauport
escarpment

Île
d'Orléans

Île d'Orléans camp

French entrenchments

Beauport

St. Lawrence River

Point Lévis

Point Lévis
camp and batteries

Saint-Charles River

Quebec

Quebec Promontory

Samos

Saint-Michel

Sillery

Anse au
Foulon

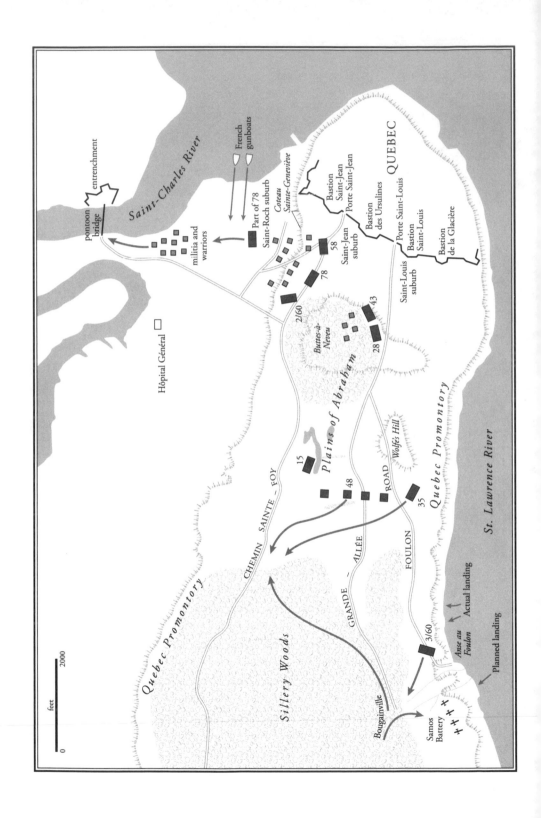

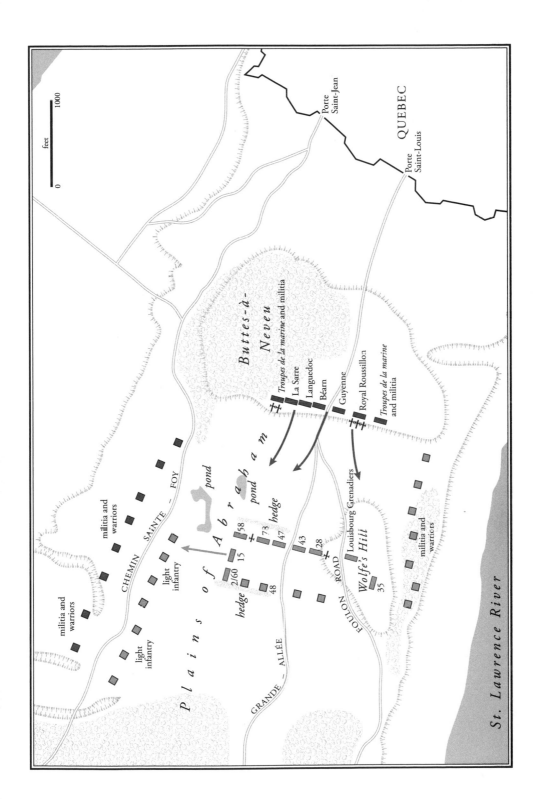

feet

1000

0

Porte
Saint-Jean

QUEBEC

Porte
Saint-Louis

*Buttes-à-
Neveu*

Troupes de la marine and militia

La Sarre

Languedoc

Béarn

Guyenne

Royal Roussillon

Troupes de la marine
and militia

militia and
warriors

militia and
warriors

light
infantry

CHEMIN

SAINTE - FOY

pond

P l a i n s   o f   A b r a h a m

pond   hedge

58

73

47

15

2/60

48

hedge

light
infantry

hedge

43

28

Louisbourg Grenadiers

Wolfe's Hill

FOULON

ROAD

35

militia and
warriors

GRANDE - ALLÉE

St. Lawrence River

I

ATTACKERS

CHAPTER I

500,000 Years of History

HUMANS MAKE WAR; GEOGRAPHY SHAPES THE BATTLEFIELD

The history of the Battle of the Plains of Abraham began with a gentle rain of sediment floating down to the floor of the proto–Atlantic Ocean during the late Precambrian era. Time passed; minute grains of sand and clay settled, accumulated, and hardened into gigantic blocks of sedimentary rock. When tectonic shifts slammed them together, closing the proto-Atlantic and creating the Appalachian Mountains, some of these blocks shifted westward. One massive chunk of folded and faulted limestone, sandstone,

Viewed from Point Lévis, Quebec's geographic strength and its vulnerability to bombardment from across the St. Lawrence River are both starkly apparent.

and shale, six miles long, half a mile wide, and known to geologists as the Quebec Promontory, came to rest against the future Canadian Shield.

Half a billion years later, the fate of Canada, the future United States, and the French and British Empires in North America turned on possession of this block of sedimentary rock.

By September 1759, the Seven Years' War, the titanic struggle for empire between France and Britain that Winston Churchill called "the first world war," had been under way for just over five years. During those five years, British goals in North America had changed from the occupation of the Ohio valley to the conquest of Canada.

Yet although the British enjoyed comfortable margins of naval and military superiority in the region, they had spent most of those years reeling from defeat after defeat at the hands of Pierre de Rigaud de Vaudreuil, governor-general of New France and commander in chief of the French armed forces in North America. Year after year, the British in North America contemplated or attempted the conquest of part or all of New France. Vaudreuil responded by sending Louis-Joseph de Montcalm, his senior field commander, to capture British outposts and smash British offensives before they could threaten Canada.

Sheer force of numbers, however, allowed the British to bounce back from defeat, rebuild their forts and armies, and take to the field once more. As British strength increased, French objectives shifted from blocking British expansion in the Ohio valley to fighting for survival amid the farms and cities of New France.

The crucial campaign of the war began when a British fleet and army commanded by Vice Admiral Charles Saunders and Major General James Wolfe reached Quebec in 1759. Whoever controlled Quebec controlled Canada. If Quebec fell, Canada would fall with it.

As Canada's Atlantic port, Quebec was the sole point of contact between Canada and France. A minor colony with a population of just seventy thousand, Canada lacked the human and material resources to fight a major war on its own. In the words of an anonymous British strategist, "Receiving supplies of men, stores, and provisions by sea . . . [is] absolutely necessary for supporting & maintaining that body of troops which they [the French] employ, Canadian or European, & that number of posts which they possess in America."

Breaking this link would suffocate the French Empire in North America. In theory, the supply lines between France and New France could also be severed by blockade. But despite manifest French naval weakness, the British never managed to isolate Canada. "The doing of this by *cruising* [patrolling] merely," confessed the anonymous strategist, "has already been tried in a certain degree ineffectually, & is perhaps to an absolute degree impossible . . . as the . . . St. Lawrence River must still in a certain degree be open against the most vigilant cruise." Even in 1759, when a British squadron sailed from Halifax to blockade Quebec, more than twenty French supply ships arrived safely by slipping through the same ice fields that prevented the Royal Navy from entering the Gulf of St. Lawrence before it was too late.

The only sure way to isolate Canada from France was to take Quebec. "By going to Quebec," wrote the British commander in chief in North America in January 1757, "success makes us master of every thing."

Success, however, proved elusive.

Perched atop the eastern tip of the Quebec Promontory, Canada's capital towered from sixty-five to one hundred yards above the St. Lawrence River. Attacking Quebec from the river would leave an assault force stranded in Lower Town, clinging to the base of the cliff, trapped and vulnerable. Attacking from the landward side meant finding a way up the promontory. In 1759, the French reinforced these natural defenses by constructing a line of fortifications on the high ground along the Beauport shore between Quebec and the Montmorency River and a chain of outposts extending from Quebec to Cap-Rouge guarding ravines and roadways leading up the cliffs.

When Saunders and Wolfe came to Quebec, they slammed into the Quebec Promontory and the Beauport entrenchments. For three months, Saunders's navy and Wolfe's army tried and failed to take Quebec. Throughout that time, Vaudreuil and Montcalm remained safely inside a strong defensive perimeter, high above the St. Lawrence, protected by 264 cannon and mortars on the city walls and 39 at Beauport.

While Saunders's ships whisked troops up and down the St. Lawrence River, Wolfe's soldiers accomplished nothing beyond losing the Battle of Montmorency on July 31 and adding a new level of brutality to the Seven Years' War as they shelled Quebec into ruins and burned more than a thousand farms in hope of forcing the French to come out and fight. By September, Saunders and Wolfe were teetering on the verge of a humiliating defeat.

Bad news for Saunders and Wolfe. Bad news for the British Empire. But very good news for Ashley Bowen of Marblehead, Massachusetts.

CHAPTER 2

Sailing to Armageddon

ASHLEY BOWEN

For the people of Canada, the British attack on Quebec was an unfolding tragedy. For Ashley Bowen, it represented an opportunity to advance his nautical career by acquiring experience as a ship's officer. One among thousands of British and American mariners on the scene, Bowen is remembered for his autobiography, the first ever written by an American sailor.

Even before he arrived in Canada, Ashley Bowen had led an active life. Born in Marblehead, Massachusetts, fifteen miles northeast of Boston, in January 1728, Bowen began his seafaring career at age eleven. Signing aboard as a ship's boy in 1739, he sailed in the snow (a small, two-masted sailing vessel) *Diligence,* carrying a cargo of tar from Cape Fear, North Carolina, to Bristol, England.

Four months after his return home, disaster struck. His mother died, an event he described as "the greatest part of my ruining as may be seen the following year," and his father promptly remarried "a fine rich widow." Unwanted at home ("To obtain his wish [of marriage to the widow, his father] would separate his own family"), Bowen returned to sea apprenticed for seven years to a merchant captain. A training program like this was meant to qualify a teenager to become a ship's officer and perhaps one day a captain. Instead, the apprenticeship turned into an ugly round of beatings and abuse. In 1744, on a voyage to Gibraltar, wrote Bowen, the master would take his cat . . . and give me a dozen strokes on my back . . . then take his quadrant and look for the sun; then took a tiff of toddy, and so regularly he would do that office, one after another, till the Mate interfered for me and said if I should die on the passage out he would be a witness against him.

Denied instruction in commerce and navigation, Bowen became a competent seaman but not a potential officer. In 1745, he deserted in the West Indies and signed aboard a British privateer. This marked the beginning of a new phase of a career that would take him all around the North Atlantic world and give him enough knowledge and experience to serve occasionally as a ship's officer but mostly as a sailor.

Finally, on March 29, 1759, opportunity knocked. While Bowen was ashore at Marblehead, Robert Hooper, a leading citizen, approached him with an invitation to join the British attack on Quebec, not as a sailor, but as a midshipman—an apprentice officer in the Royal Navy. Bowen accepted the next day. He thereby became one "of the five thousand men [from Massachusetts] which were to be raised to go by sea on board His Majesty's ships at Halifax under Rear Admiral Durell."

British-American maritime power at New York harbor during the Seven Years' War. The captured French ships in the foreground, flying white French flags under British colors, speak to British command of the sea.

THE QUEBEC EXPEDITION

The expedition that Bowen had agreed to join was a massive land and sea offensive, aimed at nothing less than the total elimination of French power in northeastern North America. In the western interior, British and American soldiers lunged at Fort Duquesne in the Ohio valley and Fort Niagara on Lake Ontario. In the east, two more armies headed for Quebec. One would advance down Lake Champlain, capture Montreal, then travel down the St. Lawrence to Quebec. The other would sail straight up the St. Lawrence.

A British-American as well as a Royal Navy–British Army venture, the Quebec expedition involved people and ships from all across Britain's transatlantic empire. On land, about one-third of Wolfe's nine thousand soldiers had been recruited in the American colonies. This surprisingly high percentage reflects both the years that many British units had spent in the colonies during the war and the rising population of British America.

The naval component of the British amphibious force included a quarter of the Royal Navy—forty-nine warships, crewed by 13,500 sailors and 2,100 marines. One hundred and nineteen transports crewed by a further 4,500 sailors carried troops and supplies. Vice Admiral Saunders described seventy-four of these transports as "American," forty-five as "English."

With the fleet "in great want of seamen," Saunders asked for colonial sailors. In response to this request, an unknown but significant number of Americans volunteered to serve with the Royal Navy during the siege of Quebec. Like American provincial troops, they took part in the campaign, then demobilized and returned to their homes in the fall. Two hundred and forty sailors from Boston caught up with the fleet in Halifax before the expedition began. More arrived from New England over the summer. Senior naval officers treated the Americans as a distinct group known as "New England volunteers," a group that included Ashley Bowen.

Prior to the opening of the campaign, Saunders had written to the governors of New York and Massachusetts. After informing them that "the fleet and part of the army in North America will proceed early up the River St. Lawrence to Quebec, and consequently stand in need of frequent supplies of all kinds of refreshments," he asked that they encourage American merchants to send shipments of provisions to the British forces at Quebec. The merchant community seized this opportunity. Throughout the siege, American shipping sailed up the St. Lawrence carrying supplies to the British forces at Quebec.

At least three African American teamsters, "Jack," "Leto," and "Jeremy," accompanied the expedition. They formed part of a body of civilian contractors who cared for eighty oxen and forty-two draft horses that were embarked with Wolfe's army to haul supplies and artillery. A floating herd of 591 cattle from Boston came along to provide fresh meat for the army and the fleet.

BOWEN JOINS HMS *PEMBROKE*

Now a midshipman, Bowen recruited thirty-two sailors and departed with them aboard the schooner *Apollo* on April 12. Bowen and his followers were not the only American passengers aboard *Apollo* who were heading for Quebec. "We have," he wrote, "Captain [Joseph] Goreham with a company of Rangers on board."

On April 16, the *Apollo* entered Halifax harbor. On the seventeenth, Bowen joined HMS *Pembroke,* along with fifteen other New Englanders and fifty-eight soldiers of the Royal American Regiment.

When Bowen came aboard, John Simcoe, captain of HMS *Pembroke,* took some time to get to know his new American midshipman. Bowen recorded their conversation:

> He said to me, "What country are you of?"
>   I said I was born in Marblehead.
>   "Did you serve your time to the sea?"
>   I said, "Yes, Sir."
>   "What trade did you use?"
>   I said, up the Mediterranean.
>   "What part?"
>   I said, "From Gibraltar to Port Mahon and to Cagliari on the Island Sardinia for salt and back to Mahon and home to Boston again."

A day later, Bowen described his accommodations:

The last night I lodged on board His Majesty's Ship *Pembroke*. This morning at eight I turned out and got breakfast. Note: I mess with Mr. Buckels and Mr. Crisp [two other midshipmen]. I mess on the starboard side just abaft the pump well in the orlop [the lowest deck of the ship], and lodge in the best bower tier [where anchor cables were stored] on the same side.

Aboard HMS *Pembroke*, Bowen came under the command of Rear Admiral Philip Durell.

Educated by his aunt, Durell went to sea for the first time aboard his uncle's ship at the age of fourteen in 1721, then spent the next five years learning his trade while serving off the Newfoundland, Nova Scotia, and New England coasts. Promoted to lieutenant in 1731 and captain in 1743, he took part in the first siege of Louisbourg in 1745. In the course of that siege, he assisted in the capture of a French warship and two merchant ships and charted Louisbourg harbor. Ten years later, Durell briefly returned to North America to reinforce a British squadron operating off Louisbourg and Newfoundland. In 1758, he played a key role in the British landing at Louisbourg.

As the British admiral with the most experience in North American waters, Durell could expect to be in the forefront of future campaigns in the region. When most of the army and the fleet that captured Louisbourg sailed for Britain, New York, or New England, Durell and his squadron remained at Halifax, ready to take the lead in the next operation.

FROM HALIFAX TO THE ST. LAWRENCE

As troops and ships assembled in Britain and British America, Durell received orders to blockade the St. Lawrence River as soon as the spring breakup of ice in the Gulf of St. Lawrence allowed him to sail from Halifax.

Following the siege of Louisbourg in 1758, the British had confirmed Canada's vulnerability to a spring blockade when one of Wolfe's officers questioned the crew of a captured fishing boat off Gaspé. "These prisoners," wrote Wolfe, "assured us that there was great scarcity of provisions and great distress at Quebec" and "that the colony must be ruined, unless very early & very powerful assistance" arrived from France in 1759. In an undated note, Wolfe suggested that "a fleet at the Isle of Bic [in the lower St. Lawrence River] early in the year will probably complete the destruction of Canada."

Durell's mission was to do just that. Toward the end of March 1759, he began sending out small vessels to survey ice conditions on the first leg of the sea route from Halifax to Quebec. On April 8, his ships were ready for sea. Owing, however, to unfavorable winds and reports of "such quantities of ice that . . . it is not as yet practicable for ships to pass to the eastward, without running great danger," the squadron did not leave Halifax harbor until May 5.

As Durell's ships approached Anticosti Island in the Gulf of St. Lawrence, the captain of HMS *Pembroke* died on May 15. Ashley Bowen recorded the event in his journal:

> At 12 this night departed this life Captain John Simcoe, who formerly commanded this ship.
>
> [May 17] At 6 . . . read the funeral service over the corpse of Captain John Simcoe and threw him out the Gun Room port, where he sank immediately. We hoisted our ensign and pendent half-staff as did the Admiral [flagship] and the rest of our fleet, and we fired 20 half-minute guns.

A day later, one of Durell's ships captured a French merchant ship, the *Hardie,* sailing from Haiti to Quebec with a cargo of rum, molasses, sugar, and coffee. Questioning its captain seemed to confirm the wisdom of waiting for the ice to clear. "The Master of her," wrote Durell, "reports he has been upon the coast this month past, and has not been able before to get into the Gulf, there being such quantities of ice floating about."

The squadron entered the St. Lawrence River in late May. James Miller, a private in the Fifteenth Regiment, provides a lyrical description of the lower St. Lawrence as seen from the deck of a British ship:

> We had therefore, an opportunity, of viewing, with wonder, this vast river, which resembles the Ocean, for in the middle, no land is to be seen! As you advance higher up, every object appears grand, and sublime! Nature here displays such luxury, and majesty, as

commands, veneration! Rivers like seas! Mountains, reaching thru
the clouds, covered with lofty trees, such variety, of fish . . . sea
cows, seals, and porpoises.

Sublime nature notwithstanding, Durell received shattering news just
a few days after he entered the St. Lawrence River. On May 27, his lookouts sighted a French schooner at anchor near Kamouraska. Captured by
boats from *Princess Amelia,* it proved to be a fishing vessel from Quebec,
carrying letters to French settlements downstream. These letters, wrote
Durell, "give an account that 3 frigates . . . with fourteen transports were
arrived at Quebec, laden with provisions & stores for the King's Commis-
sary there."

This represented a major blow for the expedition and Durell. Had he
arrived in time to intercept the transports, the loss of the supplies they carried would have crippled the defense of Canada. Instead, both Durell and
the blockade had failed, leaving the British facing a long, grim campaign.

FIRST ASHORE

On May 28, *Princess Amelia,* Durell's flagship, anchored off the Île aux
Coudres, less than sixty miles from Quebec. At 6:00 p.m. on that same
day, master's mate (a senior midshipman with greater responsibilities) William Hunter, serving aboard that vessel, became one of the first members
of the expedition to step onto a Canadian beach.

Twenty-eight years old, the Edinburgh-born Hunter first went
to sea with his father at the age of twelve, beginning a career as a merchant sailor. He caught his first glimpse of combined operations in 1745,
when the Crown pressed his ship into service as a troop transport during the Jacobite uprising. Over the next decade, Hunter battled pirates in
the Mediterranean, survived a shipwreck in India, and dodged sharks in
the Caribbean. One anonymous servant of an empire built on trade, he
served on ships carrying tea and porcelain from China, sugar and rum
from the West Indies, rice and corn from British America, and fruit from
the Mediterranean.

Following the outbreak of the Seven Years' War, he abandoned the merchant service and joined the Royal Navy. This represented an immensely
rational decision for an ambitious young man with talent and energy but

very little money. As a merchant sailor, Hunter could never hope to rise higher than second-in-command of a cargo ship. (Most merchant captains were part-owners of their vessels.)

The wartime navy, on the other hand, offered steady employment, reliable wages, and the chance of prize money. (Eighteenth-century navies allowed their sailors to sell captured enemy vessels—"prizes"—and divide up the money among themselves, with the largest shares going to captains and officers.) Moreover, after two years service as a midshipman, Hunter would become eligible for promotion to lieutenant. If he managed to become a commissioned officer, Hunter would gain the social status of a gentleman, a higher salary and larger share of prize money, and the economic security of a half-pay pension at the end of his active service. Viewed through Hunter's eyes, the story of the Quebec campaign becomes the story of his personal quest for a lieutenant's commission in the Royal Navy. Service at the siege of Louisbourg in 1758 won him Durell's patronage and a modest promotion to master's mate. It remained to be seen if service at Quebec would catapult him all the way to a commission as lieutenant.

When lookouts spotted several canoes and a launch on the shore of Île aux Coudres, Durell sent Hunter with three boats rowed by armed sailors to destroy them. Hunter duly smashed the offending craft, but an ebbing tide stranded his own boats above the waterline. "Our situation became now extremely perilous," he wrote, "and as we could only launch one boat at a time, and were much exposed to an attack from the woods by the Indians, I every moment expected a retaliation from the Natives."

Thoroughly alarmed, Hunter and his sailors dragged the boats down to the river and made their escape. Back aboard *Princess Amelia,* the master's mate turned to hydrography.

CHARTING THE RIVER

In the absence of a strong French naval presence in Canadian waters, Canada's first line of defense against attack from the sea was the intricate, dangerous navigation of the lower St. Lawrence River. The first American expedition to Canada had sailed all the way up to Quebec in 1690, but a subsequent British invasion had come to grief on August 23, 1711, when seven troop transports and a storeship ran ashore near Île aux Oeufs. Seven hundred and forty soldiers and about 150 sailors drowned in the wrecks.

British ships sail past Île Percé en route to Quebec. Naval power allowed the British to strike at the heart of New France.

Following this disaster, the senior naval officers resolved that it was too dangerous to proceed farther on account of the lack of competent pilots and "the uncertainty & rapidity of the currents as by fatal experience we have found."

This time, the British weren't taking any chances. The Royal Navy secured the unwilling assistance of a number of Canadian pilots; Durell organized a major survey of the river to plot a safe course for Saunders's warships and transports.

Two British officers, one a soldier, the other a sailor, had become Saunders's experts on the St. Lawrence River. Samuel Johannes Holland, originally from Nijmegen in the Netherlands, had served in the Dutch artillery before becoming a soldier of fortune and joining the British Army. Commissioned as a lieutenant in the Sixtieth (Royal American) Regiment, he had served as assistant engineer during the siege of Louisbourg. James Cook, master (navigator) of HMS *Pembroke,* is best known as Captain Cook, the celebrated Pacific explorer.

Using captured French maps, Holland and Cook spent the winter of 1758–59 producing a chart of the Gulf of St. Lawrence and lower St. Lawrence River. Now they employed the data gathered by Cook himself, other ship's masters, and junior officers like Hunter and Bowen to verify and refine their work. Cook subsequently published the results as *A New Chart of the River St. Lawrence,* which became the standard nautical chart for ships heading for Quebec.

This chart proved to be the single deadliest weapon deployed by the British-American forces in the course of the campaign. Together with sailing directions compiled by Cook and Holland and the enforced assistance of Canadian pilots, it allowed the invasion fleet to breach Canada's outer defenses and ascend the St. Lawrence without delay and without loss.

With the main body of the fleet coming up fast, on June 8 Durell sent the *Boscawen,* a small auxiliary vessel mounting sixteen guns, to sail downstream to deliver this information to Vice Admiral Saunders.

CHARLES SAUNDERS

One of the most remarkable yet unheralded figures of the Seven Years' War, Charles Saunders was competent, professional, and lucky. In the 1740s, the first two qualities allowed him to survive a voyage around the world, leaving as a lieutenant and returning as a captain. The third made him rich, when he gained forty thousand pounds in prize money from the capture of a Spanish treasure ship. George Anson, Saunders's commander on his global cruise, served as First Lord of the Admiralty during the Seven Years' War.

High professional standing and Anson's patronage won Saunders the command of the naval component of the Quebec expedition in 1759. Eclipsed for two centuries by the celebrity of James Wolfe, Saunders played an equally important role in the Quebec campaign and deserves equal standing as a historical actor.

ON TO QUEBEC

Boscawen met Saunders at the Île du Bic, whereupon the admiral ordered it farther downstream to carry copies of the chart and sailing directions to HMS *Diana,* escorting a flotilla of transports.

Upriver, Durell sent part of his squadron past the Île aux Coudres, sounding as they went. By June 9, the leading elements of the fleet had reached the Traverse, a notoriously dangerous channel that ran diagonally across the river from the north shore to the northwest tip of the Île d'Orléans, then between the island and the south shore. Undaunted, the British and American sailors, including Ashley Bowen, pressed ahead, sounding and marking the channel: "At 4 A.M.," wrote Bowen,

> sent pinnace and cutter well armed to sound to the SW of us. The Commodore and the other ships did likewise. I went with our Sailing Master [James Cook] in our cutter a-sounding for the channel through the Traverse.

Looking back in later life, Bowen reveled in detailing his association with the famous navigator:

> Mr. Cook would have me go with him wherever he went a-sounding or discovering . . . and he did not forget me on Banian Days [days when meat was not included in the ship's rations] to dine with him.

By June 14, the survey was complete and the channel marked:

> We sent a boat from our ship and one from the Devonshire and another one on the easternmost rocks of the Traverse and the other on the westernmost, one with a white flag and the other with a red, and, having a leading wind, we all came to sail and run through the Traverse.

Looking ashore at the Île d'Orléans from HMS *Neptune*, Lieutenant Edward Coats later admired "this island which for its fertility, is justly called the Garden of Quebec."

On the twenty-sixth, Saunders himself took station off the island, located just below Quebec. The first soldiers went ashore the next day. For the first time since 1690, a foreign fleet had reached Quebec, and a foreign army had landed on Canadian soil.

At this pivotal moment in North American history, Captain John Knox of the Forty-Third Regiment took time out from the serious business of invasion and conquest to enjoy the local sights and critique the work of Canadian artists: "As we halted for some time on the beach, after we came on shore, I went with some other officers to take a view of the church, which is a neat building with a steeple and spire: all the ornaments of the altar were removed, a few indifferent paintings only remaining."

The safe arrival of the British-American fleet and army represented a triumph for Saunders and a potential catastrophe for New France. Saun-

Charles Saunders. Overshadowed by James Wolfe, Saunders played an equally important role in the Quebec campaign.

ders's most celebrated passenger, James Wolfe, had come to Quebec determined to take the city or destroy it. While crossing the Atlantic to take up
his command, the British major general had declared,

> If, by accident in the River, by the Enemy's resistance, by sickness,
> or slaughter in the Army, or, from any other cause, we find, that
> Quebec is not likely to fall into our hands (persevering however
> to the last moment) I propose to set the Town on fire with Shells,
> to destroy the Harvest, Houses, & Cattle, both above & below, to
> send off as many Canadians as possible to Europe, & to leave fam-
> ine and desolation behind me.

CHAPTER 3

James Wolfe in Love and War

The year 1759 started out very well for James Wolfe. Not only had he received his first independent command, but after years of heartbreak over a failed romance his social life was finally looking up. A year before the outbreak of the Seven Years' War, Wolfe had confessed, "Though I suppose myself recovered in a great measure from my disorder that my extravagant love for Miss Lawson threw me into, yet I never hear her name mentioned without a twitch, or hardly ever think of her with indifference."

Following his triumphant return to Britain after the siege of Louisbourg, Wolfe finally forgot Elizabeth Lawson when he renewed a previous acquaintance with Katherine Lowther, the daughter of a former governor of Barbados. They fell in love and agreed to marry. Before Wolfe's departure, Lowther gave him a book of fashionably depressing verse, the ninth edition of Thomas Gray's *Elegy Written in a Country Churchyard*. He carried this token of future happiness aboard HMS *Neptune,* along with her miniature portrait and a fixed intention to conquer Canada or leave the colony a smoking ruin.

James Wolfe was an eighteenth-century army brat and second-generation amphibious warrior. His father, Lieutenant General Edward Wolfe, took part in a disastrous seaborne attack on Cartagena de Indias (in what is now Colombia) in 1741. Wolfe, who had just received a commission in his father's battalion, the First Marines, did not accompany the expedition.

William DeLaune sketched this portrait inside a copy of Humphrey Bland's *Treatise of Military Discipline,* which he had received as a gift from Wolfe some years before.

He soon transferred into another regiment and embarked for service in Germany.

The young lieutenant quickly displayed a talent for war. Able, ambitious, and enjoying the patronage of his father's network of friends, Wolfe rose rapidly through the ranks. As an adjutant at sixteen and battalion commander at twenty-one, he earned a reputation as a superb administrator and innovative trainer and tactician. Service in Germany and Scotland gave him an opportunity to display both skill and courage on the battlefield. The Seven Years' War ended the land-based phase of Wolfe's career and introduced him to amphibious warfare and siegecraft.

Wolfe's Seven Years' War began in 1757 with an appointment as quartermaster general of a force bound for an amphibious assault on Rochefort, on the western coast of France. The expedition failed, but Wolfe emerged with an enhanced reputation, promotion to colonel, and strong opinions on the conduct of amphibious assaults.

When more senior officers first delayed, then canceled the landing rather than run the risk of bad weather stranding troops onshore, Wolfe ignored naval realities and produced an astringent analysis of their apparent timidity. "Pushing on smartly is the road to success," he wrote. "An Admiral should endeavour to run into an enemy's port immediately after he appears before it, that he should anchor the transport ships, & frigates as close as can be to the land, that he should reconnoitre & observe it as quick as possible, & lose no time in getting the troops on shore."

At Rochefort, he told his father, the British failed because they hesitated and consulted instead of striking fast and hard: "We lost the lucky moment in war, and are not able to recover it."

In 1758, the Louisbourg campaign gave Wolfe his first experience of siege warfare and made him a popular hero. Serving under Jeffery Amherst, Wolfe led the troops that seized a beachhead east of the city and commanded the artillery that demolished a major French battery, destroyed three French warships, and blew a breach in the curtain wall.

It also gave him an opportunity to advocate the export to North America of the brutal tactics employed by the British in Scotland after the defeat of the Jacobite revolt in 1745. "I can't help wishing," he wrote before the siege, "that Louisbourg should be totally demolished, and all the inhabitants of those islands sent to Europe."

Wolfe got his wish. When the French capitulated, the British deported every resident of Louisbourg, soldiers and civilians alike, across the Atlantic to France. Only an empty shell remained, garrisoned by British troops until they demolished the fortifications and abandoned the remaining buildings, which gradually fell into ruin.

CHAPTER 4

River Control, Fireships, Landing Craft, Bombardment

DURELL'S SQUADRON

While Saunders and Wolfe directed the attack on Quebec, Durell, *Princess Amelia,* and the largest warships in the British fleet spent the summer scattered between the downstream end of the Île d'Orléans and the mouth of the St. Lawrence River. Remote from the main action of the campaign, Durell's squadron engaged in what might be called river control, performing an essential supporting role, guiding transports carrying supplies from British America past the navigational hazards of the lower St. Lawrence, supporting minor operations below Quebec, and guarding against intervention by French warships.

Intelligence gathered by Durell suggested that a powerful French fleet might indeed be on its way to Canada. The letters on the captured schooner which (correctly) reported that fourteen French supply ships had reached Quebec added that a senior French admiral "was expected with 20 sail of the line from Brest." But unless and until a French fleet hove into sight, Durell and his ships could expect to confine themselves to exacting but routine activities as they maintained the link between the Quebec expedition and the outside world.

Unable to control four hundred nautical miles of river from any one site, Durell posted ships at four key points along the St. Lawrence— Anticosti Island, the Île du Bic, the Île aux Coudres, and between the Île d'Orléans and the Île Madame. The ships at each location changed in the course of the campaign. Those named here were on station in the first week of September.

While writing to encourage American merchants to send provisions and sailors to Quebec, Saunders had assured colonial governors that "some frigates will always be cruizing at the mouth of the river, from whom they [ships from New England and New York] will receive all the protection and intelligence that may be needful for them." To provide these services, Durell had the frigate *Lizard* on patrol between Anticosti Island and the Gaspé Peninsula.

Up to the Île du Bic, charts and sailing directions prepared by James Cook and Samuel Holland provided sufficient information to allow ships' captains to travel up and down the river in reasonable safety. Above that island, the river became much more dangerous, and ships needed pilots. Durell accordingly kept two vessels, the frigate *Hind* and the transport *Ethan*, at the Île du Bic.

Hind passed on orders to new arrivals and served as a depot for river pilots. Ships and convoys heading upstream picked up pilots at Bic; those going downstream dropped them off. *Ethan* resupplied any passing vessel that was short of provisions.

From the end of May until mid-July, Durell himself remained at the Île aux Coudres. This gave him a central location from which to direct operations as the British fleet sailed upstream and kept a powerful naval force in an area where ships in the channel were threatened with "insult from the Indians and Canadians on the opposite shore."

To help contain the Canadians, Durell garrisoned the island. In May, he landed a detachment of soldiers who remained in place until June 24. When the troops moved upriver, Durell replaced them with armed sailors and fifty marines from *Princess Amelia, Vanguard, Captain,* and *Stirling Castle.* The sailors occupied the eastern end of the island. The marines took post at the west end, where they built redoubts "to hinder any of the enemy from landing."

Once the bulk of the fleet and transports had arrived safely at Quebec, Saunders ordered Durell upstream in mid-July. Durell set sail with most of his squadron, leaving two ships of the line, *Prince Frederick* and *Bedford,* and a few smaller vessels at the Île aux Coudres to assist ships in distress and guard the channel.

On July 20, Durell reached his final station on the St. Lawrence: "At 1/2 past noon I made the signal and anchored with the best bower in

9 fathom water, sand and small stones between the islands of Orleans and Madame and made the signal to moor."

Thus secured, the lower St. Lawrence River became a busy British-American nautical highway. On Thursday, July 12, the master of HMS *Scarborough,* escorting a convoy of eight transports and one schooner from Boston to Quebec, counted a total of twenty-nine vessels in sight.

FLAT-BOTTOMED BOATS

As his squadron took control of the maritime approaches to Quebec, Durell detached Hunter upriver to serve with Saunders. There, Hunter took part in almost every major event of the summer's campaign. From Montmorency Falls to Deschambault he transported troops, supplies, and casualties from ship to shore and back again, often under fire.

Hunter's weapon in this intensively amphibious campaign was one of the dedicated landing craft known as the flat-bottomed boat. Previous experience had taught the Royal Navy that a major landing required more carrying capacity than ships' boats could provide. British amphibious experts blamed the failure of the Rochefort expedition on "the want of proper boats to land a sufficient number of troops at once" and "the sluggishness, awkwardness, and different sizes of the transport boats." Because victory in amphibious operations could depend upon getting as many troops as possible safely ashore in the shortest possible time, resolving this problem became a priority for the Royal Navy.

Within months, the solution appeared in the form of the flat-bottomed boat. Developed and built in 1758, the new landing craft came in two sizes, thirty or thirty-six feet long. Rowed by sixteen or eighteen sailors, they could float in two feet of water and deliver forty to sixty soldiers onto a beach. The sailors lined the outer sides of the boat, working the oars and incidentally providing human shields for their passengers. The officer or petty officer in command sat in the stern, next to the tiller. The soldiers, all from the same company so that they could land ready to fight as a unit, sat facing inboard on two benches running the length of each boat. Army officers and sergeants sat in the bow and stern, where they could watch their troops and (at the stern) consult with the boat's commander. The boats came equipped with a mast, a sail, and a forty-pound anchor.

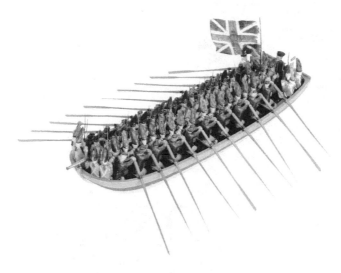

Flat-bottomed boats served as landing craft for British amphibious expeditions in the Seven Years' War.

FIRESHIPS

The Royal Navy arrived at Quebec with 134 flat-bottomed boats and entrusted one of them to Hunter. Now in command of a landing craft—a post that guaranteed him a place at the center of the action—Hunter joined a campaign that was already in trouble.

Saunders's voyage up the river had been a remarkable feat of seamanship. Landing troops on the Île d'Orléans had been more like a well-conducted exercise than an amphibious assault. Apart from a few scouts, the French had evacuated the island, allowing the British to disembark unopposed on June 27. The fleet weathered a major storm and subsequent attacks by French fireships and fire rafts on June 28 and July 28.

The fireship attacks represented nothing less than two attempts by the French to cripple Saunders's fleet. Packed with flammable material and handled by skeleton crews, fireships were aimed at enemy vessels and set alight as they approached. If all went well, their crews took to the boats, and the fireships rammed their opponents. Flames leaped from vessel to vessel and the attackers exchanged small, expendable craft for valuable

French fireships. "The night was serene and calm, there was no light but what the stars produced, and this was eclipsed by the blaze of the floating fires, issuing from all parts and running almost as quick as thought up the masts and rigging."

warships. On June 28, a fascinated Knox watched the fireships from the shore of the Île d'Orléans:

> Nothing could be more formidable than these infernal engines were on their first appearance, with the discharge of their guns, which was followed by the bursting of grenados, also placed on board in order to convey terror to our army . . . some of these dreadful messengers ran on shore, and the rest were towed away clear of our fleet by the seamen . . . They were certainly the grandest fire-works (if I may be allowed to call them so) that can possibly be conceived, every circumstance having contributed to their awful, yet beautiful appearance; the night was serene and calm, there was no light but what the stars produced, and this was eclipsed by the blaze of the floating fires, issuing from all parts and running almost as quick as thought up the masts and rigging.

While Knox observed from the shore, Ashley Bowen, aboard HMS *Pembroke,* was in the thick of the action:

> This night at 12 o'clock I saw a falsefire [signal light] above. I went down and acquainted Mr. Norman . . . that the fire ships were a-coming down and when I came up again there was seven ships on fire from their . . . mastheads . . . and out at the yard arms. Oh what a dismal sight! We had 40 boats alongside and were all ordered to assist them in towing them ashore, and they towed them all safe on shore—3 on our starboard side and 2 on our larboard and two sunk above us so none of them did us any damage.

Thus far the Royal Navy had overcome every obstacle that geography and the French had flung in the way. The land forces, however, were not doing nearly so well. Wolfe's descent on the Île d'Orléans was meant to be the first step in a swift advance on the walls of Quebec. If everything had gone according to plan, Wolfe would have established a base on the island, then shifted the fleet to the north channel to cover a second landing on the Beauport shore between the Saint-Charles and the Montmorency Rivers.

As soon as Wolfe's army disembarked, the troops would march on Quebec and fight the great battle for Canada on the way. "I reckon," Wolfe predicted on May 19, that "we shall have a smart action at the passage of the river St. Charles." Presumably victorious, the army would cross the Saint-Charles, establish entrenchments and siege batteries on the Plains of Abraham, then hammer the walls of Quebec until the garrison surrendered or British and American soldiers stormed the city and overwhelmed the defenders.

LOSING THE INITIATIVE

So as his soldiers secured the Île d'Orléans beachhead, Wolfe set out to select a site for a second landing at Beauport. Accompanied by his aide-de-camp, Thomas Bell, he marched through woods and fields to the western tip of the island. Once there, Wolfe looked across the St. Lawrence and became the first member of the expedition to gaze upon the Quebec

Promontory, the city of Quebec, and the Beauport shore. Wolfe never recorded his reaction to this vista, but the Beauport shore must have been a shock. Expecting an open, inviting shoreline, Wolfe had discovered a coastal fortress. According to Bell, "We saw the town, 4 batteries along Beauport, entrenchments here & there, with 5 encampments, saw their fire stages, two ships moored in the mouth of the river St. Charles, [and] 4 ships before Quebeck."

An anonymous naval volunteer, serving aboard Saunders's flagship in hopes of receiving an appointment as midshipman, described the Beauport heights as "a steep sandy precipice, picketted along, and defended on the top with 8 or 10,000 men, covered with a deep breastwork, incapable of being hurt by our musketry—these lines and breastworks they have continued from the falls quite to Quebec, being a tract of defensive works more than eight miles long."

Vaudreuil and Montcalm had anticipated Wolfe's intentions and seized the initiative. Instead of remaining passively within the walls of Quebec as Wolfe seems to have expected, they had fortified the very place where the British planned to land. Geography, in the form of the heights along the Beauport shore and the shoals that lined the north bank of the St. Lawrence, presented a formidable barrier to the invaders. The intelligent exploitation of terrain by the French made it worse. No one was going to be making an unopposed landing on the Beauport shore and advancing to Quebec anytime soon.

Repeatedly disappointed and increasingly desperate, Saunders and Wolfe spent the next three months reacting to the fortification of Beauport, seeking another way to bring the French army to battle and the British army to the walls of Quebec.

They began by landing troops at Point Lévis, across the river from Quebec, and at the mouth of the Montmorency River, just west of the French entrenchments. Along with their base on the Île d'Orléans, this gave the British three fortified enclaves scattered about the Quebec area but brought them no closer to actually ascending the Quebec Promontory and besieging Quebec.

Ashley Bowen was present for both operations. On June 30, while HMS *Pembroke* lay at anchor within sight of Point Lévis, he described in his journal how at 1 P.M. we saw our troops to march up along the South Shore on the main. At 4 saw our troops and the enemy engage very briskly at St. Joseph's Church upon Point Levy. At 5 sent our barge, pinnace, and longboat to assist landing troops at Point Levy. At 2 A.M. saw the enemy fire very hot in platoons on the North Shore. At 4 sent our longboat and pinnace to land artillery on Point Levy . . . The Sutherland and Richmond engaged the enemy's floating batteries at Quebec who was firing on our soldiers on Point Levy. At 10 all firing ceased.

On July 15, a week after the landing at Montmorency Falls, Bowen recorded that

our longboat and pinnace was sent to land artillery, and I was sent to assist the longboat in the pinnace, and when we arrived at the place below the Falls of Montmorency we were obliged to ground the longboat for the soldiers to get their cannon out.

Their task completed, Bowen and the boat crews were taken aboard the sloop *Porcupine,* where Bowen received a demonstration of the ubiquity of Americans in the Royal Navy that summer:

Our Masters Mate, Mr. Napier, having the command of the longboat, said to me, "Mr. Bowen, I am acquainted with the carpenter of this ship. He is a Boston man. His name is Bently, and we will be well entertained by him." So we dined on board the Porcupine on beef steaks and fine green peas.

After this dinner, Bowen, who had been aboard ship for close to three months, took advantage of the opportunity to make an excursion ashore:

When I came into the camp it seemed to me like Rag Fair, for it had rained the day before, and some appeared overhauling their clothes, some going about as careless as at home.

While he was in the camp, Bowen, who had already served alongside James Cook, had a second celebrity encounter when he caught sight of James Wolfe:

I advanced towards him and the General hailed me. "Who are you?"

I answered him "A friend!"

"What department are you of."

I said of the Marine Department.

"What ship?"

I answered, "His Majesty's Ship Pembroke."

"What are you on board the Pembroke?"

My answer was "Acting Midshipman."

"Where is your uniform?"

I said, "I have none. I come from New England with a company of volunteers to serve His Majesty in the reduction of Canada."

THE POINT LÉVIS BATTERIES

Yet if Quebec's geography and its defenders were proving more challenging than expected, the French were not without their vulnerabilities. Since the beginning of the Seven Years' War, British strategists had been advocating the total destruction of the city through shot, shell, and fire. The author of a particularly aggressive memorandum, unfamiliar with the stone buildings of Canada's capital, asserted in 1756 that "their town is mostly built of wood, and probably must be burnt about their ears." Burning Quebec, wrote another in 1757, would "be greatly assistant to the military force" that conducted the siege. In that same year, a British officer who had been held prisoner in Quebec observed that "the lower town . . . is a fair object for cannon, and the buildings are so much crowded, that a shell can scarce fail to do execution."

Wolfe had already pledged to "set the Town on fire with Shells" if he couldn't take it. And James Wolfe had never been known for false bravado or idle threats. Once it became apparent that the French had forestalled a British landing at Beauport, he ordered his artillery commander, Lieutenant Colonel George Williamson, to bombard Quebec.

Before the invasion, Quebec had been a picturesque provincial capital. The naval volunteer described "this hostile city, the . . . contested prize which is to decide the fate of a western world," with respect and admiration:

> This city, the metropolis of the French dominions in America, may vie with many in Europe, it is the see of a bishop, and contains within its walls seven parish churches, besides a magnificent cathedral. The governor's and bishop's palaces, though not very regular, are fine structures. The college of Jesuits is a noble large building, with spacious gardens; and all the buildings, both public and private, seem to me composed of free-stone, and erected in the European taste; entertaining . . . the beholder with a beautiful and noble prospect.

Wolfe and Williamson changed all that. Beginning in July, Williamson established batteries at Pointe-aux-Pères, just west of Point Lévis. (Although the batteries were actually located at Pointe-aux-Pères, both the French and the British referred to the site as Point Lévis.)

A typical battery of the time consisted of a massive parapet of gabions (wicker baskets filled with earth), platforms for the artillery, and an appropriate number of expense magazines.

Parapets, twenty feet thick and eight feet high and topped by fascines (bundles of sticks), protected the artillery and gunners from counter-battery fire. Inside the battery, cannon and mortars were spaced about eighteen feet apart. This would have made Williamson's first battery, holding five mortars and six cannon, about two hundred feet long. Embrasures (narrow gaps) cut through the parapet allowed cannon to fire at the city. Mortars fired at such a high angle that embrasures were unnecessary.

Cannon rested on fan-shaped platforms, fifteen feet wide at the rear, nine feet at the front, and eighteen feet long; mortars on platforms six feet square. These platforms, made of three-inch planks nailed to heavy beams, prevented cannon and mortars from embedding themselves in the ground.

Twenty to thirty yards to the rear, expense magazines, buried three feet underground and lined with boards, held gunpowder for immediate use. Each expense magazine could service about four artillery pieces.

Williamson's weapons were massive, brutal thirty-two- and twenty-four-pounder cannon and ten- and thirteen-inch mortars that could obliterate a ship, an army, or a city. The cannon, as their names imply, fired solid iron shot weighing thirty-two or twenty-four pounds. The mortars fired hollow iron spheres, packed with gunpowder, and firebombs known as carcasses. Packed with a highly flammable mixture of pitch, corned gunpowder, sulfur, and saltpeter that would burn for about ten minutes, carcasses sprayed jets of flame through holes in the side of the shell.

Cannonballs inflicted damage through sheer kinetic energy; mortar shells (also known as bombs) exploded, smashing buildings and flinging lethal chunks of iron in all directions; carcasses started fires. Each deadly in its own right, they were devastating in combination. Solid shot and exploding shells shattered roofs and broke buildings apart, exposing flammable material. Carcasses set this material alight, starting fires that could rage across a city, destroying everything in their path.

THE BOMBARDMENT BEGINS

"The 6th of July," wrote Williamson, "I began to erect a battery of 5 thirteen inch mortars (one of them iron) & 6 thirty-two pounders, & the 12th began to fire cross the river St. Lawrence (1100 yards from shore to shore) at the town from 1200 yards to a mile range." Ashley Bowen watched the first shots of the bombardment soar across the river:

> At 9 General Wolfe hove a sky rocket in the air on the North Shore to open the batteries on Point Levy against Quebec. Ditto, they began to bombard and cannonade. Likewise the Racehorse, Baltimore, and Pelican began to bombard at the same time, and the enemy returned it.

Their first results were disappointing. Williamson's son, Captain Adam Williamson, noted that "our shells at first fell short . . . fuzes very bad many broke in the air." Fast work by the British gunners quickly resolved these problems. Virtually unhindered by French counterbattery fire, the bombardment of Quebec had begun.

By late August, Williamson had constructed four batteries holding twenty cannon and thirteen mortars. A small army of 474 gunners and 1,095 marines worked the guns and guarded the batteries. On September 2, Williamson reported that they had fired a total of "2498 thirteen inch shells; 1920 ten inch shells; 283 thirteen inch carcases [firebombs]; 93 ten inch carcases; & 11500 twenty four pound shot," as well as, 1,589 thirty-two-pound shot.

On August 9, Ashley Bowen observed,

> At 1 A.M. the shells and carcasses from our batteries on Priest Point [Point des Pères, west of Point Lévis] set the town on fire in two places, which burnt with great violence all day and consumed [a] great part of the lower town.

Week after week, these shot and shells pounded Quebec, reducing Canada's capital to a postapocalyptic urban wasteland. The naval volunteer witnessed this ugly transformation:

> I have seen Quebec three several times involved in a total blaze, the effect of bombs and carcasses, not to mention numerous fires of less distinction. The lower town is one entire scene of destruction, and the upper scarcely brags a better situation—the dismal consequence of war, which spares nothing, however sacred, having laid a cathedral in ashes, which would have been an ornament to the proudest city in Europe.

Edward Coats had admired the cathedral as well and joined the naval volunteer in mourning its destruction. "The Cathedral of Quebec, the largest & most magnificent of all the buildings of the kind in this part of the world, was set on fire by our carcasses, and consumed, together with a great number of houses in the upper town."

Less sensitive members of the expedition reveled in the destruction of a city. "Hot Stuff," a song written by the grenadier sergeant Ned Botwood of the Forty-Seventh Regiment, includes this couplet:

> With Monckton and Townshend, those brave Brigadiers,
> I think we shall soon knock the town 'bout their ears.

The lyrics continue with a reference to the weapons that inflicted the damage and a hearty, campfire-song invocation of the joy of rape:

> And when we have done with the mortars and guns,
> If you please, Madame Abbess,—a word with your nuns:

Each soldier shall enter the convent in buff,
And then, never fear, we shall give them Hot Stuff.

George Williamson, more restrained and more professional, calmly wrote reports as he watched blazing fires across the river in Quebec: "About 300 of their houses are burn'd down (the Basseville [Lower Town] is still burning) amongst which is almost all of the eastern part of the lower town which makes a wretched appearance. Ricochets from the 32 & 24 pounders have done infinite damage to the houses remaining, many of which are in a tottering condition & more which cannot be repair'd."

By September, Williamson was running out of targets: "The place is so much burned & battered it is scarce worth any more ammunition, but now would not be proper to cease fire."

THE CHAPLAIN'S POINT OF VIEW

Yet all the destruction and all the terror inflicted by the bombardment had no effect whatsoever on the strength of the French position atop the promontory and along the Beauport shore. The naval chaplain James Gibson observed in August, "We frequently set their town on fire, have burnt down the large Church, with many other buildings: but I can't learn that we hurt their batteries and therefore individuals suffer rather than the common cause."

Gibson was William Hunter's direct opposite in the navy. Hunter, an aspiring career officer, joined in the attack on Quebec as an ambitious enthusiast. Gibson, a misplaced civilian, watched from the sidelines as a frequently appalled spectator. Educated at Oxford, the thirty-eight-year-old curate of the tiny village of Upham had signed on as the chaplain of HMS *Vanguard* in 1758. Flung from the quiet of the English countryside into the clamor and violence of a great amphibious campaign, Gibson described "my present situation . . . [as] exceeding contrary to my former way of life and education" and himself as "heartily sick of the Employ."

He reserved his enthusiasm for Canada's birds and looked forward to the day when he could present his observations and stuffed specimens to friends in England. For Gibson, the great moment of the campaign came on July 7. That was the day that he sighted a woodcock, then a mysterious bird that British naturalists did not believe even existed in North America—"no small Discovery!"

WEST OF QUEBEC

Wolfe didn't care about birds. He had more important things to think about. Even before he discovered the French fortifications at Beauport, Wolfe had considered the possibility that the British might "steal a detachment up the river St. Lawrence, and land them three, four, five miles, or more, above the town, and get time to entrench so strongly that they won't care to attack."

On the night of July 18–19, Saunders put this plan into action when he sent five warships, including the frigate *Squirrel*, upstream past the city. Carried by a rising tide, shielded by darkness, and covered by a furious bombardment of Quebec's batteries by Williamson's guns, they sailed past the city without incident. Saunders now had an aggressive naval force above Quebec, ready to support a landing. Wolfe ordered four battalions upriver and planned an attack on Saint-Michel, just west of the Anse au Foulon.

Units that had been tasked for the operation began to assemble at Point Lévis, but before they could march, the crew of HMS *Squirrel* had an unpleasant shock. When their frigate came too close to the north shore on July 20, they discovered that the French had erected a battery at Samos, overlooking the Anse au Foulon and just downstream from Saint-Michel.

"The French," wrote the master of the *Squirrel*, "began firing from a gun and bomb battery . . . & holed us and stranded our main stay & wounded our main mast." *Squirrel* backed off; Wolfe had second thoughts about landing at Saint-Michel. "Perceiving that the enemy were jealous of the design, were preparing against it, & had actually brought artillery and a mortar . . . to play upon the shipping . . . it seemed so hazardous that I thought best to desist," he wrote.

Once again, the French had got there first. As soon as Saunders's ships slipped upstream, they extended their defenses westward to cover the pathways and ravines leading up the promontory. For the second time, Canadian geography and French efficiency had neutralized a British assault before it began.

A day later, Wolfe's interest in the Quebec Promontory nearly killed him. Sailing upriver in a landing craft, he passed opposite the Samos battery. The French opened fire; one shot struck home. But instead of smashing Wolfe's boat to kindling, the cannonball shattered the mast and forced the sailors to row the rest of the way.

If Williamson was well on his way to destroying Quebec, Saunders and Wolfe were no closer to taking it. But the British hadn't given up. Wolfe had another plan, and William Hunter and his landing craft were ready to take part in the first battle of the campaign.

CHAPTER 5

Defeat at Montmorency

AMPHIBIOUS ASSAULT

However strongly fortified it might be, the Beauport shore remained the only open shoreline in the Quebec area. A month after his first reconnaissance, Wolfe resolved to launch an amphibious assault on the east end of the French entrenchments.

This was the moment the army had been expecting since the fleet reached Quebec. Wolfe had it all planned to the last detail, including the French response.

Carried and supported by two armed transports, thirteen companies of grenadiers would seize a French outpost in advance of the main line of entrenchments. They would carry entrenching tools and use them to expand and strengthen the captured strongpoint. The French would come out from behind their fortifications to fight the British. Two infantry battalions would follow the grenadiers ashore; six more would cross the Montmorency River at low tide from the camp at Montmorency. A decisive battle would end in a British victory and a triumphant advance to the Saint-Charles River and Quebec.

And it might work, if Wolfe's assessment of the geography was correct, if the tides and currents cooperated, and, most of all, if the French did exactly what they were supposed to. If, however, the French simply remained in place on the high ground and let the British and Americans come to them, the operation might turn out to be, at best, a blow in the air.

From Hunter's perspective, all began well: "Two light armed transports had been prepared by the Admiral [Saunders] to be lain on shore, as a defence against the batteries. One of them was not of the least use after she was aground; but the other was conducted and placed with the utmost judgement by . . . Mr. James Cook."

Then everything went wrong.

The strongpoint turned out to be much closer to the main French lines than the British had suspected. Wolfe, looking up from one of the transports, "observed that the redoubt was too much commanded to be kept without very great loss." Yet he also thought that he saw the French milling about without apparent purpose and decided to launch a general assault. Hunter described the scene: "The boats of the Fleet were filled with Grenadiers. Two Brigades under Lord Townshend, and General Murray, were in readiness to pass the Ford; and to facilitate the passage, the *Centurion* . . . had been placed by the Admiral in the Channel."

But as the landing craft carrying the grenadiers headed for the shore, a French mortar battery off to the left went into action. "Many of the Boats grounded on a ledge, and were some time in getting off," Hunter wrote. "We at length, however, landed under a most tremendous fire."

While Hunter guided his landing craft toward the shore, the naval volunteer watched from HMS *Centurion* as the French "from a large mortar two miles to the westward threw numbers of shells at the ships, and in the midst of our flat-bottomed boats, but without doing much damage." Edward Coats, aboard one of the landing craft, was less detached as "a shell falling so near Mr. Saunders boat that it broke several of the oars . . . filled her half full of water."

Once ashore, the grenadiers charged uphill into disaster. The French, safe in their entrenchments, unleashed a devastating hail of musket balls that tore the attackers' ranks to shreds, inflicting hundreds of casualties. These casualties included the grenadier-songwriter Ned Botwood, killed in action, and the two Williamsons, both wounded. "My son," wrote Williamson, "had his left leg wounded with a musket ball, on the main bone which broke it 3 or 4 inches above the ankle in front. The doctor says he will do well but that it will be a cure of time. I hope he will not go lame.

He is very cheerful, poor fellow, considering. General Wolfe has a particular regard for him which he mentions frequently in conversation . . . I did not escape but had my shin broke with the splinter of a shell at mid leg."

Hunter watched the massacre from his landing craft: "Our men were dreadfully exposed; and not able to make the least impression on the enemy, who had a breast work even with their chins. Fortunately a tremendous clap of thunder, succeeded by a heavy shower of rain, occasioned a cessation in their firing, and gave our men time to retreat."

The rainstorm enforced an involuntary cease-fire by soaking gunpowder before it could ignite, preventing either side from firing, and making the hillside slick, slippery, and very difficult to climb. Unable to fire or advance, the grenadiers gave up and skidded and stumbled their way

The heights of Beauport pose a formidable obstacle as Wolfe's grenadiers charge the French entrenchments, supported by gunfire from the Royal Navy. William Hunter is in one of the landing craft approaching the beach. Jean-Claude Panet is in Quebec (just to the right of a cloud of smoke from the waterfront batteries), watching the battle and listening to Canadians shouting, *"Vive le roy!"*

back down to the shore. The battalions retreated across the mouth of the Montmorency River; landing craft picked up the surviving grenadiers, not without difficulty. "The night had now set in," wrote Hunter, "with a severe storm, and the tide had risen very much . . . After landing such of the wounded as we could secure at the Hospital in the Isle of Orleans, I returned to the *Shrewsbury,* 74 guns."

Boats from HMS *Pembroke* took part in the last phase of the operation. "Sent the longboat," wrote Bowen, "with the stream anchor and cable on board the Centurion to assist in warping up from the falls and 2 flatt bottom boats to transport troops to Point Levy and Orleans."

On the heights of Beauport, the French celebrated their victory by raising the plain white flag of France. "The enemy," wrote Knox, "appear much elated at our miscarriage on the 31st,—and have these two days hoisted several white flags on their entrenchments, they are now very assiduously employed, endeavouring to render their works still more inaccessible."

"I HAVE LAID WASTE THE COUNTRY"

Hunter had only a few days in his temporary berth aboard HMS *Shrewsbury* before he set off on a new operation. Wolfe, who had already kept his promise to shell Quebec into rubble if the campaign didn't go well, now implemented his second pledge, "to destroy the Harvest, Houses, & Cattle."

In the first weeks of the campaign, the pastoral beauty of the Canadian countryside had charmed the more sentimental invaders. John Knox was particularly enthusiastic: "Here, we are entertained with a most agreeable prospect of a delightful country on every side; windmills, water-mills, churches, chapels and compact farm-houses, all built with stone and covered, some with wood and others with straw. The lands appear to be everywhere well cultivated, and, with the help of my glass, I can discern that they are sowed with flax, wheat, barley, peas etc."

After Montmorency, Wolfe unleashed a relentless campaign of calculated terror on this countryside. Carried in Saunders's ships and boats, British and American troops swarmed the shores of the St. Lawrence, burning everything in their path.

Gibson, the reluctant naval chaplain, watched the horizon-to-horizon destruction with dismay: "I am apprehensive the campaign will end in the utter ruin of their country, which we've already begun in burning all their corn [wheat] & houses for 30 miles on each side of the river, which is all the land inhabited as far up as Quebec."

Lieutenant Colonel Alexander Murray, commander of the Louisbourg Grenadiers, took part in these operations. Grenadiers were the toughest, strongest soldiers in the army, but burning civilian homes appalled Murray: "I have been here for ten days past . . . with my battalion covering a body of Highlanders, light infantry, and Rangers, who are employed in destroying a country that is the finest, most fruitful and best inhabited of anything I have seen in America and few places in England even better."

Wolfe did not share these concerns. "I have," he wrote, "laid waste the country, partly to engage the marquis de Montcalm to try the event of a battle to prevent the ravage, and partly in return for many insults offered to our people by the Canadians, as well as the frequent inhumanity's exercised upon our own frontiers."

CHARLES HOLMES'S SQUADRON

When Saunders assigned Hunter to an upriver expedition, the young master's mate became implicated in one small part of this destruction. Ordered upstream as part of a convoy of fourteen flat-bottomed boats, Hunter slipped past Quebec under cover of darkness on the night of August 5, "our oars being all muffled; during which the batteries on Point Levi kept up an heavy fire." On August 6, the landing craft picked up a detachment of regular infantry, light infantry, and marines on the south shore and carried them out to the ships of the upriver squadron, commanded by Rear Admiral Charles Holmes.

A veteran of service in Canadian waters between 1755 and 1757, Holmes was the only senior naval officer who came to Quebec with previous experience of waging war along a major river. The Seven Years' War was both a French-British global war for empire and a European conflict pitting France, Austria, and Russia against Britain and Prussia. When a French-Austrian force captured the Prussian port of Emden in 1758, the Royal Navy sent Holmes to take it back.

The French-Austrian garrison depended upon supply lines running along the Ems River. When the ice cleared in the spring, Holmes took a small squadron up the Ems, blockaded the city, and forced the French and the Austrians to evacuate.

In 1759, perhaps partly as a result of his experience at Emden, Holmes became Saunders's amphibious expert during the attack on Quebec. Placed in command of the upriver squadron, he quickly acquired a wide experience of the St. Lawrence and its navigational hazards.

ATTACKING POINTE-AUX-TREMBLES; BURNING SAINT-ANTOINE

On August 8, Holmes took his squadron upriver to attack Pointe-aux-Trembles. Hunter's account of the operation was short and to the point: "We . . . endeavoured to land at a village named Point au Tremble, but the French were too strong."

After waiting two hours for gunfire from the warships to silence three floating batteries, the landing craft headed for shore at 6:00 a.m. The first two boats ran aground on a rocky shoal. Heavy fire from French forces concealed behind trees trapped those troops that reached the shore on the beach. A rising tide left them standing in water three feet deep. Holmes called off the landing.

When the boat crews moved to obey this order, the mishaps and misunderstandings that make combined operations so hazardous came into play. As sailors maneuvered against strong currents and underwater obstacles, some of the soldiers, under fire from the French and floundering in water up to their waists, thought that they were being abandoned. Enraged and afraid, they threatened to open fire on their naval comrades.

Ignoring their comrades' threats and French gunfire, the sailors pressed on and recovered the landing party. A few soldiers had to swim for the boats; eight were left behind and taken prisoner by the French.

Once the flat-bottomed boats had transferred their casualties to a sloop, Holmes ordered a second attack. As the landing craft approached the shore, a strong force of French regulars and Canadian militiamen opened fire. So heavy was this fire, wrote one Highlander, "that our landing was impracticable . . . nor could our sailors stand by the oars for some minutes."

Recalled by Holmes, the landing craft backed off and returned their passengers to the squadron. "About eight at night," recorded Richard Humphreys, a light infantry private, "we got aboard in a most forlorn condition, all this night and the best part of the next day our surgeon was employed in dressing the wounded."

"We then," wrote Hunter, "attempted the other side, St. Antoine, where we met with little opposition; raised a redoubt on high ground, and left in it a party of Marines."

At 7:30 in the morning of August 10, the landing craft swept shoreward at Saint-Antoine. Led by the light infantry and covered by cannon fire from HMS *Squirrel,* the troops stormed the beach and dispersed about two hundred Canadian and Native American defenders. Over the next two days, teams of sailors hauled the flat-bottomed boats and the sloop *Porcupine* up on the shore. Ship's carpenters set to work repairing battle damage to the landing craft and leaks in the sloop.

On August 13, the burning began. When Canadian skirmishers (who, as soldiers in the militia, had not just the right but the duty to resist an invader) fired on a detachment of four hundred light infantry, the British retaliated by burning every house in the parish of Sainte-Croix. The resistance continued the next day. The British lost seven marines in a skirmish and burned Saint-Nicolas.

THE RAID ON DESCHAMBAULT

On the eighteenth, Hunter and the flat-bottomed boats were on the move again. "We then advanced still higher up the River," he wrote, "and landed at Dechambo, where we destroyed some magazines."

Ninety minutes after dawn the next morning, the flat-bottomed boats touched ground at Portneuf and discharged their troops without opposition. The landing force marched overland to Deschambault. There, they burned a government storehouse containing weapons, munitions, and the personal effects of the French regular officers serving at Quebec. At some point during the day, the troops rounded up several sheep and about one hundred cattle. They shot the cattle and left the bodies on the beach, then waited for the boats.

Following the landing, Hunter and the flat-bottomed boats let the rising tide carry them upriver to Deschambault. Around 3:30 p.m., they took the soldiers aboard along with their sheep. Canadian militia cavalry pursued the raiders right into the river until blasts of grapeshot and cannonballs from Holmes's ships forced them to pull back.

On August 26, the landing craft carried the troops down to Point Lévis, then rejoined the fleet. Hunter returned to HMS *Shrewsbury*.

LESSONS LEARNED

For eighteen days, under the command of Rear Admiral Holmes, Hunter had roved above Quebec, ferrying troops from place to place and taking part in four amphibious assaults. These operations, particularly the reverses at Pointe-aux-Trembles, had taught the British a great deal about the challenges of amphibious operations above Quebec. Fast tides and strong currents were a constant danger, unforeseen obstacles could appear at any time, and any operation ran the risk of a rapid, aggressive response from the French.

Wolfe himself summed up some of the hard lessons the British had learned of the perils of upriver operations: "We have seven hours, and sometimes,—above the town after rain,—near eight hours of the most violent ebb tide that can be imagined, which loses us an infinite deal of time in every operation on the water; and the stream is so strong, particularly here [off Cap-Rouge], that the ships often drag their anchors by the mere force of the current. The bottom is a bed of rock, so that a ship, unless it hooks a ragged rock, holds by the weight only of the anchor."

The landing at Portneuf and the attack on Deschambault, in contrast, delivered a more positive message. Fast movement under cover of darkness, deception, and landing in an unexpected location could pay off handsomely.

BACK TO BRITAIN

On September 5, William Hunter's Quebec campaign came to an end. Summoned aboard the flagship, he received orders from Admiral Saunders to sail for Britain aboard the cutter *Rodney*. The cutter, commanded by

Philip Perceval, would carry both Saunders's and Wolfe's official dispatches and private letters from the soldiers and sailors of the expedition.

More important, as far as Hunter's ambitions were concerned, "the Admiral also added, that he had recommended me to Lord Anson [the First Lord of the Admiralty] for promotion." After four years in the navy, Hunter was about to become a lieutenant at last. Rear Admiral Durell ordered the captain of *Princess Amelia* "to send Wm. Hunter, Mate, and two men to the Rodney Cutter . . . to assist in navigating her." Pleased with his young protégé's conduct during the campaign, he gave Hunter "a very flattering certificate" to present to the Admiralty.

At 10:00 a.m. on Friday, September 7, *Rodney* set sail for Britain. Hunter embarked with mixed feelings. For four months, ever since *Princess Amelia* cleared Halifax harbor on May 5, the Quebec expedition had been his life. Sailing home to reap his reward, Hunter found that "though my mind was buoyed up with the thoughts of promotion, I left the busy scene I had so long witnessed with regret."

His voyage home was uneventful, at least until *Rodney* was caught in a North Atlantic storm: "I observed a most tremendous sea coming, which threatened to break on board us . . . it struck us with such violence as made me think it would turn the cutter end-over-end. It shifted the casks in her hold and, knocking me down, washed the man away from the helm, and nearly overboard . . . Myself and the helmsman were the only persons on deck; and we could not open the scuttle to let our shipmates out, as it was entirely under water."

After a long struggle, Hunter, Perceval, and the ship's thirteen sailors brought the cutter under control and safely into Portsmouth. There, Perceval left for London with the dispatches, while Hunter settled in to wait to hear from Lord Anson.

Days passed, weeks passed, without so much as a word from the Admiralty, let alone a lieutenant's commission. The port admiral paid off the *Rodney*, depriving Hunter of both his residence and his income. He became discouraged: "I began to think that Admiral Saunders had *hummed* me about my promotion."

But the aspiring lieutenant didn't give up. He was a naval veteran now and knew how to work the system. The officer corps of the Royal Navy brought together sailors from a wide variety of backgrounds. In this case, Hunter, a sailor's son, and Perceval, the son of an earl, had become friends during their Atlantic crossing. Rather than wait for the Admiralty to remember him, Hunter visited Perceval, met his influential father, and explained the situation. The earl contacted the Admiralty. Six weeks later, Hunter became a lieutenant, an officer, and a gentleman.

For William Hunter, the first months of the Quebec campaign had been a resounding success. After beginning his nautical career as a merchant seaman—a skilled laborer—he had risen to the financial security, professional standing, and social status of a commissioned sea officer.

In London, however, the dispatches that Perceval and Hunter had carried across the Atlantic cannot have made for pleasant reading. The British had sent their first team to Quebec—a distinguished admiral and a promising young general, a grand armada and a veteran army. The previous year had produced the first significant British victories of the North American war—the capture of Louisbourg in Acadia, the occupation of the site of Fort Duquesne in the Ohio valley, and the destruction of Fort Frontenac on Lake Ontario. So the British government and the British public had every reason to expect news of the conquest of Canada in 1759.

Instead, when they opened their public dispatches and private letters, they learned that Saunders and Wolfe had indeed taken the war to the very heart of French North America. Yet every blow, every attack, every stratagem, had shattered on the brute strength of Canada's geography. All Saunders's ships and all Wolfe's battalions had thus far failed to overcome a half-billion-year-old chunk of sedimentary rock. Britannia had failed; geography had triumphed.

CHAPTER 6

The Triumph of Geography

REPORTING FAILURE

When Perceval and Hunter docked in Portsmouth, they carried a cargo of intense frustration. Much of this cargo came straight from the prolific pen of Major General James Wolfe.

Until he came to Canada, Wolfe's military career had been one long triumph. He had known frustration but never failure. Now, for the first time, he faced the possibility of defeat and disgrace.

Very understandably, given that he was simultaneously undertaking his first independent command and operating in unfamiliar territory, Wolfe was out of his depth for much of the 1759 campaign. None of his previous experience seemed to matter very much at Quebec. He never managed to put his amphibious philosophy into practice. Instead of seizing "the lucky moment of confusion and consternation among our enemies," he was caught off balance when he discovered French troops in possession of his intended landing site on the Beauport shore.

Nor was Wolfe able to exploit the expertise in siege warfare he had acquired at Louisbourg, because he never came close enough to the city to apply it. Only his ruthlessness found expression at Quebec as his troops converted the city into rubble and farms into cinders.

For the first time, instead of standing back and assessing the performance of his superiors, Wolfe had to explain his own actions and report his own lack of success. To his credit, he did just that. His official dispatch began with a stark, honest assessment of the state of the campaign and the strength of Canada's geography:

> I wish I could upon this occasion have the honour of transmitting to you a more favourable account of the progress of His Majesty's Arms; But the obstacles we have met with in the operations of the campaign were much greater than we had reason to expect or could foresee, Not so much from the number of the Enemy (though superior to us) as from the natural strength of the country, which the Marquis de Montcalm seemed wisely to depend upon.

WOLFE'S MISGIVINGS

For James Wolfe, the Quebec expedition had been a high-risk gamble from the very beginning. As soon as he received word of his appointment in December 1758, Wolfe wrote to Jeffery Amherst, commander in chief in North America and commander of the army that would advance on Quebec by way of Lake Champlain. In this letter, Wolfe spoke not of the possibility of victory but of the probability of defeat.

Acknowledging that "the very going up the river with so large a fleet is an undertaking of the most dangerous kind," he played up the concept of the double invasion as a single operation. According to Wolfe's interpretation of British strategy, the two generals shared responsibility for taking Quebec, and the amphibious expedition was more of a diversion to support the main attack than an operation that would succeed or fail on its own: "I can't promise you, that we shall take Quebec, because I neither know the place nor the people appointed to defend it—but . . . let the fleet carry us up, and we will find employment for a good part of the force of Canada, and make your progress towards Montreal less difficult and dangerous."

In writing this letter and others like it, Wolfe might have been papering the files to spread the blame in the event of failure, seeking to ingratiate himself with a superior by playing down the importance of his operation relative to Amherst's, or articulating his own fears of responsibility for his first independent command. But he was also right.

An amphibious invasion of Canada would be a tough, chancy operation; attacking Quebec would be a leap into the unknown. And when the campaign began, reality turned out to be more daunting than Wolfe's darkest predictions.

When Saunders and Wolfe reached Halifax, they found Durell, who was supposed to be blockading the St. Lawrence but had been held back by contrary winds and heavy ice. French supply ships, more fortunate or more enterprising, had already slipped past the ice and into Quebec.

Quebec's defenders proved to be both more numerous and more resolute than expected. Neither shelling Quebec and burning the countryside nor attacking the Beauport lines had pulled the French out from behind their fortifications. Operations above Quebec encountered navigational hazards and strong resistance. Saunders's ships could take Wolfe wherever he wanted to go, but everywhere he went, he found the French there first, solidly entrenched and ready to fight.

MICROBES AT WAR

Moreover, Wolfe's army was a wasting asset, fading fast. Promised twelve thousand troops, he sailed for Canada with only nine thousand. Once there, they came under constant attack from both humans and microbes. "We have continued skirmishes," wrote Wolfe on September 9, "old people seventy years of age, and boys of fifteen fire on our detachments, and kill or wound our men from the edges of the woods." This harassment inflicted a steady drain of casualties and compelled the British and American soldiers to live in fortified camps.

Inside these camps, they became easy prey for microbial adversaries. With thousands of troops living so close together for so long, human waste worked its way into their water supply and spread by touch into their provisions as well. Over the summer, the food and water in Wolfe's camps had become a paradise for a variety of unpleasant bacteria. Leaping to human hosts, they caused dysentery, a vicious and potentially fatal intestinal infection. Symptoms included intense, bloody diarrhea, savage stomach or rectal pain, fever, and dehydration.

"We are greatly hurt with a severe flux [dysentery]," wrote James Gibson on August 23. "I've had my share of it, it has . . . weakened men, but

I thank God, I've got the better of it. A few winters more, in this horrid climate, would un-hinge my Constitution."

Other microscopic predators infected the ticks, fleas, and lice living on the rats that flourished in the British camps. When an ailing tick, louse, or flea bit into a soldier to feed itself on human blood, it was also feeding the bacteria that were excreted in its feces. A soldier who scratched an itching bite rubbed the feces into the open wound and frequently became infected himself.

Running wild inside a human body, the bacteria produced any one of a number of diseases known as typhus, camp fever, or just fever. Victims of typhus endured high fevers, chills, crippling headaches, backaches, muscle pains, dry, hacking coughs, exhaustion, and delirium. Infected soldiers frequently died; survivors were henceforth immune to the disease.

"The troops on this side," observed Knox on August 2, "begin to grow sickly . . . the disorders prevailing among the men are fluxes and fevers, such as troops are usually subject to in the field." The marines who had been posted at Point Lévis to guard Williamson's batteries proved particularly susceptible. Racked by both dysentery and typhus, they moved to a new and larger camp, in hope that they would "have room enough to render their camp more open and airy," making them less susceptible to infection.

By the end of August, disease, wounds, and death had left Wolfe with seventy-five hundred troops, of whom just six thousand remained on their feet and fit to fight.

"THE STRONGEST COUNTRY PERHAPS IN THE WORLD"

But none of this threatened the British campaign as much as Canada's formidable, towering geography. "If," lamented Wolfe in a private letter, "the Marquis de Montcalm had shut himself up in the town of Quebec, it would have been long since in our possession, because the defences are inconsiderable, and our artillery very formidable; but he has a numerous body of armed men (I cannot call them an army) and the strongest country perhaps in the world to rest the defence of the town and colony upon."

Under these conditions, all Wolfe could offer Britain was the hope that maintaining pressure on Quebec might pin down French troops that would otherwise have been redeployed against Amherst. He would, he declared at the end of his report, be "happy, if our efforts here can contribute to the success of His Majesty's Arms in any other parts of America."

AMHERST'S CAMPAIGN

While Wolfe's regiments melted away, Amherst's army never came near Quebec. Instead of taking Montreal and marching down the St. Lawrence to link up with Saunders and Wolfe, Amherst spent the better part of the summer advancing about forty-five miles northward down Lake Champlain. Faced with a French army that blew up their forts and fell back, Amherst came to a dead stop at the site of Fort Saint-Frédéric and embarked on an ambitious construction program directed at defending New York rather than invading Canada. "No time shall be lost," he assured the lieutenant governor of New York, "in building such a fort as from its situation & strength will most effectually cover the whole country, & ensure the peaceable and quiet possession of it on this side."

The massive new Fort Crown Point might have comforted New Yorkers, but it contributed nothing toward the capture of Quebec. Saunders and Wolfe would be on their own for the rest of the campaign.

SAUNDERS'S REPORT

When Saunders wrote his own report, he had less to say than Wolfe, but then he had much less to explain. Bad weather and heavy ice had prevented Durell from blockading the St. Lawrence, but after that the Royal Navy had gone from success to success. Overcoming the hazards of a notoriously dangerous river, the navy had taken Wolfe's army wherever it needed to go. From the Île aux Coudres to Pointe-aux-Trembles, Saunders's sailors had charted the river, carried troops and supplies, conducted amphibious assaults, and provided close support for the army.

Yet at the beginning of September, Saunders's conclusions were as pessimistic as Wolfe's. "We shall remain here," he promised, "as long as the season of the year will permit, to prevent their detaching troops from hence against General Amherst." He added that when the fleet and the army departed, "I shall leave cruizers at the mouth of the River to cut off any supplies that may be sent them."

GENERAL PESSIMISM

Wolfe and Saunders were not alone in their pessimism. When Private Richard Humphreys, who had taken part in the unsuccessful assault on Pointe-aux-Trembles, learned of Amherst's victories on Lake Champlain, he lamented that "this intelligence, otherwise pleasing, brought us no prospect of the approach of any assistance from that quarter." John Knox described the Beauport heights as "high and strong by nature" and called the French position "impenetrable." Major Patrick Mackellar, Wolfe's chief engineer, recorded on August 13 that in the opinion of the army, taking Quebec "now became doubtful, as there was little or no appearance of making good a landing upon a coast naturally strong, and so thoroughly fortified and defended by such superior numbers."

George Williamson suggested to the Board of Ordnance, which oversaw the Royal Artillery, that the campaign had at least weakened the French position in North America and laid the groundwork for a future invasion: "It is the general opinion that destroying both Town & Country as much as we can will render the enemy unable to make resistance next year."

Two days after Hunter's departure, Wolfe produced an even blunter assessment of British prospects at Quebec. On September 7, he sent a second set of dispatches to Amherst by sea. When an Acadian privateer captured their ship in the Gulf of St. Lawrence, Wolfe's couriers threw the dispatches overboard. Released, they continued on to Crown Point with a verbal report. One of the couriers, noted Amherst, "says Gen Wolfe had got almost his whole army above the town & he thinks he will not take it."

II

DEFENDERS

CHAPTER 7

The Man Who Saved Canada

JOSEPH-MICHEL CADET

Geography made Quebec strong. Logistics made it vulnerable.

If soldiers are going to fight, they need to eat, and in the spring of 1759 Canada could not feed its defenders. The 1758 harvest had failed, food stocks were minimal, and the French navy had given up escorting supply convoys across the Atlantic. "We could," wrote Montcalm, "perish from lack of food, without firing a shot."

In the spring of 1759, one person stood between Canada and defeat, the Quebec entrepreneur Joseph-Michel Cadet.

Joseph-Michel Cadet was a Canadian success story. A self-made millionaire, Cadet began life as a Quebec butcher's son who lost his father when he was an infant and his mother when she remarried and returned to France. Decades later, Cadet recalled "his mother's hasty departure" with considerable bitterness. She had, he claimed, spent her way through his inheritance, after which "she went with . . . her husband to Rochefort, abandoning the respondent at Quebec without any means of support . . . when he was twelve years old."

In 1732 the twelve-year-old Cadet signed aboard a Canadian merchant ship sailing from Quebec to Île Saint-Jean (now Prince Edward Island). Returning home, he went to work for his uncle Augustin Cadet, also a butcher, who taught him the trade and "sent him into the countryside to buy livestock for his butcher shop."

Four years later, Cadet went into business with another Quebec butcher, Romain Dolbec, Augustin's godfather. By 1742, when Dolbec won the contract to supply meat to the Crown at Quebec, Cadet was an equal partner in the enterprise. In 1746, during the War of the Austrian Succession (1740–48), he took over the contract himself and began to provide wheat, flour, peas, and biscuit as well.

Cadet later declared that the profits from his first contract "although small in the beginning were the seed of the fortune he has since made." Others credited Cadet himself. An anonymous critic who accused Cadet of belonging to a corrupt cartel that had "worked secretly for several years to entirely control all the commerce of the colony" nonetheless spoke of him with reluctant admiration: "Cadet was of . . . lowly birth . . . without the least education . . . but . . . you never saw a more industrious, more active, and more competent man in the markets. He was himself the sole instrument of his fortune . . . [Y]ou saw only crudeness in his manner; but he was at the same time generous and extraordinary to a fault."

Upon this profitable financial base, Cadet built a small but flourishing commercial empire. He rented or bought farms, flour mills, and fishing stations, which produced provisions he could sell to the public or the Crown. He purchased ships to carry his cargoes and began to export surplus provisions to the French West Indies and import provisions and brandy from France. His butcher business flourished, with two stalls in Quebec's Upper Town and two more in Lower Town.

By the early 1750s, Cadet was halfway to becoming a millionaire, and his career was just beginning. The outbreak of the Seven Years' War would present him with the greatest risks and the greatest opportunities of his life.

CADET'S ARMY

During most of the Seven Years' War, the French in Canada were winning on the battlefield and losing on the home front. Behind the clashes of fleets and armies, they waged a quiet, desperate struggle for survival on the farms and in the warehouses of Canada and along lines of communications extending down the St. Lawrence and across the Atlantic to France.

In a good year in peacetime, Canadian farmers produced enough wheat, beef, pork, and vegetables to feed themselves and Canada's towns, with a modest surplus left over for export to Louisbourg and the French West Indies. During the Seven Years' War, everything came apart. In Governor-General Vaudreuil's considered opinion, "Of all our enemies, famine is the most fearsome."

While French–Native American armies won victory after victory, heavy rains and cool temperatures produced poor harvests in 1754, 1756, 1757, and 1758. Compulsory military service pulled farmers away from their farms, further decreasing agricultural production.

Peter Williamson, of the Fiftieth Regiment, a regular battalion that had been raised in New England for service in North America, fell into French hands following the capture of Oswego in 1756. Although confined at Quebec, he quickly became familiar with conditions on Canadian farms:

> During . . . our captivity, many of our men, rather than lie in a prison, went to work, and assist the French in getting in their harvest; they having then scarce any people left in that country but old men, women, and children, so that the corn [wheat] was continually falling into the stubble, for want of hands to reap it.

Williamson added that even in the countryside food was very scarce, with prisoners working on farms

> having nothing . . . to live on but dry bread, whereas we in the prison were each of us allowed two pounds of bread, and half a pound of meat a day, and otherwise treated with a good deal of humanity.

Imports provided an alternative source of provisions, but throughout the war the Royal Navy dominated the coasts of Europe, resulting in higher freight rates and problematic arrival for supply ships from France. Moreover, as agricultural production fell and importing food became more difficult, the presence in Canada of thousands of French regulars, Native American allies, and prisoners of war sent consumption soaring.

This combination of decreased supply, escalating demand, and hazardous transportation created an ongoing logistics nightmare and an unprecedented commercial opportunity. With a major war under way, wrote Cadet's critic, "supplying provisions is an immense enterprise, the most serious and most profitable" in the colony.

Joseph-Michel Cadet stepped up to the challenge. On October 26, 1756, with the colony suffering the second crop failure of the war, he signed a nine-year contract as *munitionnaire général* (purveyor general) for Canada. This gave him the exclusive right, and the onerous obligation, to supply provisions to the colonial government.

As soon as he received the contract, Cadet began to assemble a massive, formidably efficient organization. At a time when Canada's population was about seventy thousand, the new *munitionnaire* employed four thousand people, mostly on one-year contracts. These included clerks, sailors, laborers, woodcutters, coopers, cartwrights, harness makers, blacksmiths, carters, voyageurs, bateaux crews, butchers, and bakers.

Cadet had large warehouses in Quebec (300 workers), Montreal (250 workers), and Terrebonne (50 workers), and smaller magazines at nine forts in the Ohio valley, in the Great Lakes region, and on Lake Champlain. By 1759, he employed 150 clerks. "This huge number of clerks," wrote Cadet's critic, "astonished everyone, because there were many more than the king had ever employed."

As *munitionnaire,* Cadet displayed a talent for organization and a willingness to take staggering risks as he built up a transatlantic network of shippers and suppliers and imported food to Canada in the teeth of the Royal Navy.

All his efforts could not, however, prevent the suffering and hardship produced by wartime shortages. A letter written in October 1757 by Colonel Peter Schuyler of the New Jersey Regiment, then a prisoner of war in Quebec, reveals just how far conditions had deteriorated over the previous year: "Provisions of all kinds are very scarce; the prisoners and inhabitants being at an allowance of four ounces of bread per day, and a little salt fish; the soldiers at 9 ounces of bread per day and meat only two days in the week."

Eight months later, in the spring of 1758, a Quebec resident confessed, "I lack the words to describe our misfortunes. We are running out of livestock. Butchers can no longer supply a quarter of the beef needed to feed the people of this town . . . Without poultry, without vegetables, without sheep, without calves, we are on the verge of dying of hunger . . . The workers, artisans, [and] day laborers, weakened with hunger, can no longer work. They are so frail that they can hardly stand up."

Yet if soldiers and civilians suffered, no one starved. And thanks to Cadet's efficiency, the French in Canada were never forced to abandon a military operation for want of provisions.

Every year, Cadet sent his agents into the Canadian countryside to buy wheat, peas, cattle, and pigs. His associates in France sent 130 cargoes of provisions to Canada. Controlled and recorded by his clerks, these raw materials were processed by Cadet's butchers and bakers, stored in barrels made by his coopers, then shipped to forts and armies by his carts, canoes, bateaux (large rowboats, which were often equipped with sails), and small sailing ships.

Cadet contracted to provide combatants with a daily ration of two pounds of bread, a half pound of pork, and five ounces of peas. Officers received fine bread and a shot of brandy; soldiers, militiamen, and warriors a whole wheat loaf. Civilians had to be content with a half pound of bread. Ouiharalihte, a Huron teenager who took part in the Quebec campaign, described Cadet's rations as "very good flour and beef, the beef perhaps was sometimes horse flesh; but I don't know anything about that."

As the war in North America became a battle for survival, Cadet demonstrated that he would pay any price and run any risk to keep Canada's defenders fed and able to fight. In the late summer and the fall of 1758, with Cadet anticipating "an English squadron coming the next spring to besiege Quebec," he came up against a new adversary—the French government.

"THE EXCESSIVE RISKS OF THE SEA"

In previous years, the Crown had seconded Cadet's efforts and provided warships to convoy supply ships to Canada. In 1759, Cadet was on his own. After due consideration, the French government had abandoned Canada to its fate. Instead of sending adequate quantities of supplies to Quebec, it planned to wage economic warfare by landing troops on the British coast in hopes of undermining confidence in British finances.

"His Majesty," wrote the French minister of marine and colonies, "would be equally willing to send the same assistance to the colony [as in 1758], but the continuation of the war in Europe, the excessive risks of the sea, and the need to unite His Majesty's naval forces, do not permit us to divide them at this time and risk a part of them to send you supplies that might not arrive and which will be more usefully employed by the state and [for] the relief of Canada in expeditions that are quicker and more decisive."

With French merchants unwilling to supply Canada and the French navy unwilling to escort convoys, Cadet did it all himself. To ensure, he wrote, that "Canada would not run short of provisions, [he] . . . asked his correspondents in France to buy him five or six well-armed ships, and enough large merchant ships to carry the supplies he needed in the spring of 1759."

Two of his senior associates, appalled at the risks he took, abandoned Cadet "in fear of losing what they had already gained." Cadet pushed on regardless. "Expecting that this number of frigates and merchant ships was not enough to bring him all the provisions that he needed, he wrote again to his correspondents asking them to charter all the ships needed to carry all the provisions that he had ordered from them."

He hired captains and sailors, most of whom were Canadian, and organized his own convoy that in the spring of 1759 crossed an Atlantic dominated by the Royal Navy.

Between May 10 and May 20, fifteen transports reached Quebec, laden with provisions and escorted by two rented frigates. (The French navy sent two additional frigates and a supply ship to the colony.) "You should not doubt," wrote the Quebec notary Jean-Claude Panet, who numbered Cadet among his clients, "how happy this news made us."

In all, Cadet's provision fleet carried enough food for twenty thousand rations for three months. With thirty thousand soldiers, sailors, warriors, and civilians to feed at Quebec, Lake Champlain, Lake Ontario, and elsewhere, this was just enough to last the colony through June and July. In August, the Montreal wheat crop would mature, and Cadet's organization would turn to purchasing the harvest and shipping wheat and flour to Canada's frontiers.

Canada had been saved from ignominious surrender in the spring of 1759, not by a great land battle or fleet action, but by the safe arrival of fifteen cargoes of beef, pork, flour, and peas. And Canada was going to need every grain of wheat and sliver of beef that Cadet could provide. Along with provisions, the ships carried a more ominous cargo. Louis-Antoine de Bougainville, Montcalm's senior aide-de-camp, arrived with solid intelligence of British intentions from the minister of marine: "General Wolfe is going to besiege Quebec . . . with 8,000 men."

CHAPTER 8

Soldiers and Shoe Brushes

A CLERK AT WAR

From the perspective of one supply clerk at Quebec's Magasin du Roy (Royal Storehouse), nothing summed up the state of Canada's defenses like shoe brushes. Thanks to Cadet, Canada had just enough food to feed its defenders. But everything else was in critically short supply. Everything except for military shoe brushes, specially designed to scrape mud off a soldier's shoes. With Canadian security dependent upon factors considerably more pressing than clean footwear, this situation became a source of considerable frustration to the supply clerk. Characteristically, he responded with sarcasm: "Our warehouses are empty of all merchandise; nonetheless, we still have any number of shoe brushes . . . but unfortunately no one seems to want them."

Administrators like the supply clerk play an important role in any military campaign. But he would have been forgotten had he not, like many others living through great events, taken up his pen to record his thoughts and observations for posterity. Frustratingly, the journal is unsigned, the author anonymous.

But something of his life and personality leaps from the pages. Married with five children, he lived in Quebec and spent part of his leisure time cultivating a backyard garden. Honest, forthright, and skeptical, he was a keen observer, acerbic writer, amateur strategist, and devoted husband and father. He cared for his city, his neighbors, and the fate of Canada, believed that the British could be beaten, and worried that the French high command might lose the colony through inactivity, incompetence, or negligence.

CANADA'S DEFENDERS

The spring of 1759 was a busy time for the supply clerk and his colleagues. As the colony braced for invasion, regulars, militiamen, and warriors—many of whom needed new clothing, equipment, or weapons—flooded into Quebec. There is no precise list of the French and Native American forces at Quebec, but on June 9 Cadet received instructions to provision 13,574 combatants and four to five thousand civilians.

Quebec's defenders included five battalions from the *troupes de terre,* the regular soldiers of the French army. The soldiers of La Sarre, Languedoc, Béarn, Guyenne, and Royal Roussillon, wearing gray-white coats and red or blue vests, breeches, and cuffs, had been ordered to Canada after the outbreak of the Seven Years' War. (Three additional units, La Reine and two battalions of Berry, spent the summer of 1759 on the Lake Champlain frontier.) The remaining regular infantry at Quebec were *troupes de la marine,* colonial regulars from the Canadian garrison. Recruited in France, led by Canadian officers, and employed by the Ministry of Marine, they were organized in independent companies and wore gray-white coats with blue vests, breeches, and cuffs.

In June, Mathieu Valentin Jacques Miller, a soldier in the *troupes de la marine,* wrote a letter to his wife, Marie-Joseph. In it, he described both conditions at Beauport as the French awaited the arrival of the British and the feelings of a husband and father separated from his family by war:

> Here is the sixth [letter] I've written to you without receiving a single one of yours, which causes me much pain. I hope that your health is as good as mine, because I am feeling very well; all we lack is enough food. We have been reduced to five *quarterons* [one pound three ounces] of bread and a half pound of salt pork. We have already moved [camp] three times, and in all the confusion I lost my pack.
>
> We are camped up to our knees in thick, sticky mud . . . where we will remain until the enemy appears . . . Our major . . .

has told me that fourteen ships have made the crossing [of a channel in the St. Lawrence at the northern tip of the Île d'Orléans].
We have taken twenty-eight prisoners . . . they have told us that
they came with thirty thousand men. I can assure you that we're
not afraid of them at all, if that pleases God . . .

Farewell my dear one. I kiss you with all my heart and every
day ask God to bless you and my dear children, whom you will
kiss for me. I remain until I have the pleasure of seeing you again
your faithful husband, Miller.

As professional soldiers, the regulars of the *troupes de terre* and the
troupes de la marine went where they were ordered and did what they were
told. The militiamen were more enthusiastic and less disciplined. When
Vaudreuil mobilized the militia, he blithely expected that all those obliged
to serve, youths and men between sixteen and sixty, would answer the call.
Instead, in the words of one Canadian officer, "such a competitive spirit
prevailed among the people that you could see old men of 80 and children
of 12 or 13 coming to the camp, refusing to take advantage of the exemp-
tion granted to people their age."

So many militiamen reported for duty that officials, who had planned
to transport them in bateaux, found that there weren't enough boats in
Canada to carry all of the colony's civilian soldiers. Some had to travel to
Quebec in canoes, furnished by the Crown. Instead of uniforms, they wore
their everyday clothing. "I can perceive in the enemy's camp," observed
John Knox, "at least five coloured coats for one French uniform, whence it
is manifest their army consists chiefly of the militia of the country."

MARTIAL MUSIC, PUBLIC OPINION

Officers and officials recorded Canadians' enthusiasm and willingness to
serve at Quebec, but the opinions of the Canadians themselves left few
traces in the historical record. Canadians, however, lacked neither strong
views on the war nor the means to express them. Like many conflicts, the
Seven Years' War inspired the composition of popular songs, which were
written out by the original composers or literate listeners. More notable for
vitality than polish, the lyrics provide a priceless glimpse into the thoughts
and feelings of a people at war.

In their songs, Canadians portrayed themselves as triumphant, successful soldiers, supremely confident in themselves and their leaders, fighting for a good cause against an aggressive, if not very competent, adversary:

> The English search for laurels,
> just like our fighters.
> That's the resemblance.
> The French gather them in heaps,
> the English can't harvest them at all.
> That's the difference.

Even when Canadians missed the Battle of Carillon in 1758, they still sang about what they *would* have done under the leadership of François-Pierre de Rigaud de Vaudreuil, the governor-general's younger brother:

> If Rigaud's troops
> Had been there,
> You would have seen the Canadian,
> Leap into action at the ringing
> Of the carillon of New France.

Canadian songs made military leaders into popular heroes. Of the seven individuals who appear frequently in the lyrics, six were colonial officers and officials. Only one, Montcalm, came from metropolitan France. The colonials included Vaudreuil, Rigaud, Daniel-Hyacinthe-Marie Liénard de Beaujeu, Jean-Daniel Dumas, François-Marie Le Marchand de Lignery, and Louis Coulon de Villiers.

Following his death in action at the Battle of the Monongahela in the Ohio valley in 1755, Beaujeu became the subject of this musical obituary:

> Beaujeu with his military bearing,
> Richly deserves his pedestal . . .
> He is dead but he lives,
> In the hearts of our brave men.

Less seriously, another song makes the names of officer-heroes into ingredients in a comic prescription for a British soldier:

> If you want to make a wonder,
> And heal yourself as you must,
> Take a bottle,
> Of Rigaud powder,
> Thirty Montcalm pills,
> Twenty-one grains of Villiers,
> A pinch of de Lignery,
> And you will certainly get well.

As for their enemies, Canadian songs characterized the British as "crooked and treacherous," driven by "their malice," and poised to invade. "The English are on our frontiers, carrying their banners." The songs gleefully compared this malevolent enemy with the virtuous French:

> The French like the English,
> Claim to fight for their rights,
> There's the resemblance.
> The French seek fairness,
> The English use deceit,
> There's the difference.

When the British tried to take on the French, the results, at least in Canadian songs, could be more amusing than dangerous. After describing the retreat of "terrified" British soldiers who "promptly ran away," one set of lyrics added,

> They left their cannon,
> And lots of muskets and powder,
> So we will wait for them to return,
> [Armed] with their own weapons.
> We thank them most of all,
> For their carts and horses.
> If they ever come back here again,
> We'll lend them some wagons.

One song concluded with a verbal portrait of a Canadian combatant:

> The singer of this song,
> Is a grenadier, a good fellow,

Who would willingly give his life,
For the good of his country.

Mid-eighteenth-century Canada was much more a colony of farmers than fighters. In wartime, many of the militiamen served in noncombatant roles, moving supplies from place to place along the waterways of Canada and the interior. Nonetheless, when the time came to defend their colony against invasion, Canadians more than lived up to the image of themselves that appears in their songs.

All this enthusiasm just meant more work for the supply clerk. Many of the militiamen arrived without working weapons. They turned in their broken muskets at the Magasin du Roy and received new weapons in exchange. With the *salle d'armes* (weapons room) emptying quickly, very soon there would not be a single working musket in store in Quebec. Crown gunsmiths worked to repair the broken muskets but quickly fell behind.

NATIVE AMERICANS

French regulars and Canadian militiamen were not the only ones defending Quebec in 1759. Formidable Native American contingents made Montcalm's army a multinational force.

From the St. Lawrence valley came warriors of the Seven Nations of Canada, composed of the Mohawks of Kahnawake and Akwesasne, the Mohawks, Algonquins, and Nipissings of Kanesatake, the Onondagas of Oswegatchie, the Abenakis of Odanak and Bécancour, and the Hurons of Lorette.

Their presence at Quebec reflected the multicultural nature of New France. The region that Saunders and Wolfe had come to conquer was less a monolithic French colony than a patchwork of French and Native American communities, all with their own governments, laws, armed forces, and external relations. The Seven Nations might reside within the boundaries of New France, but they remained independent powers, each a force to be reckoned with in North American geopolitics.

Other contingents had come from Acadia and the Great Lakes to join in the defense of Canada. The Great Lakes nations had effectively placed Canada under quarantine in 1758, when they refused to venture into the region to avoid infection from a smallpox epidemic. They now returned in force, ready to join the French and the Seven Nations.

Long before the British invasion, Native Americans had been serving alongside the French. They did so not because they shared the geopolitical goals of the French but to maintain a mutually beneficial alliance. This alliance linked them to a power that, among other things, provided them with access to European technology, mediated disputes among nations before they could escalate into war, and threatened neither their home-lands nor their national interests.

When asked at a meeting in New York to remain neutral during the French-British conflict in 1755, Kahnawake representatives politely refused. Employing the metaphor of linked arms, a powerful symbol of alliance and reciprocity, they declared, "The French & we are one Blood & where they are to dye we must dye also. We are linked together in each others Arms & where the French go we must go also."

With British forces threatening Canada, the Seven Nations and their Native American allies fought to defend their homes in the St. Lawrence valley. In 1757, Kisensik, a chief of the Nipissings of Lac des Deux Mon-tagnes, thanked warriors from the Great Lakes for "coming in order to help us defend our lands against the English who want to usurp them." In 1759, western warriors on the Lake Champlain frontier spoke of coming to Canada "to defend the lands of their brothers the [Canadian] Iroquois" against the British.

These warriors made frequent appearances in Canadian popular songs as valued and respected allies. One song about the Battle of the Monon-gahela mentioned three nations that served at Quebec in 1759, along with the practice of scalping and the triumph of the alliance:

> Two thousand Englishmen,
> placed themselves in position.
> But our Hurons and French . . .
> stole their hair . . .

> Five hundred [Englishmen] on the pathway,
> waiting for their funerals,

the Odawas and Algonquins . . .
gave them haircuts.

Terrified, the others . . .
promptly ran away.

Overall, between 1,000 and 1,200 warriors took part in the Quebec campaign. These included 300 Odawas, 400 Kanesatakes, Khanawakes, Oswegatchies, and Abenakis, 200 to 300 Foxes and Potawatomis, 60 to 70 Hurons, and 162 Crees. There were also Atikamekws, Iowas, Malecites, Menominees, Mi'kmaqs, Nipissings, Ojibwas, Sauks, Sioux, and Winnebagos.

Many chose Quebec over other theaters of war. When asked to help defend Fort Carillon on Lake Champlain, one body of Great Lakes warriors refused outright. Their leaders explained that "they did not want to go to Carillon saying that their father Onontio [the governor-general] was on the shore of the great lake, and that they wanted to join him to make the great war."

Only a very few of these warriors are known by name. Carron, Glode, Osauwishkeno, and Kachakawasheka were with the Menominees. Tsawawanhi led a Huron force that included his grandson, Ouiharalihte, or Petit Étienne.

Ouiharalihte, the teenager who praised Cadet's rations, would one day tell the story of the Hurons in the campaign. Describing the allied position at Quebec, he recalled that "the French and Canadian Army stretched from the Falls of Montmorency to the River St. Charles. I accompanied my Grand Father Tsa-wa-wan-hi the head chief of the Hurons, when he joined the army at Beauport with 60 or 70 of our full grown warriors, besides some young men."

HENRY GRACE ALMOST ESCAPES

One reluctant eyewitness left a description of Native Americans traveling to Quebec in 1759. Henry Grace, a British prisoner of war, had been captured in Nova Scotia in the early 1750s. A French officer ransomed Grace for a cash payment of four hundred livres (pounds) and a cask of rum. He then informed Grace that "I was to serve him four years and a half, and then to have my liberty."

When this time was up, he wrote, "my master gave me an honorable discharge, and leave to go to work for my own advantage in any part of Canada." Working as a voyageur took Grace to Detroit and earned him two hundred livres. When he returned to Montreal, "the French told me that the English were coming to take Quebec, and that they were in the river."

Hoping to regain his freedom, Grace spent sixty livres on a dugout canoe, bought some bread, then set out for Quebec. He'd made it as far as Saint-Augustin, on the north shore of the St. Lawrence, about twelve miles from the city. At this point, with success almost within his grasp, "the tide came in so fast I was obliged to go ashore." There, he waited for the next ebb tide to carry him downstream to Saunders's fleet and Wolfe's army.

Before this could happen, Grace's luck ran out when the rising tide forced another group of canoe-borne travelers to seek refuge on the beach. "In the mean time twenty-two canoes loaded with Indians put ashore at the same place I did, they were going down to Quebec to join the French army which was then waiting for the English. I was obliged to run away and leave my canoe to save my life; and they not finding any wood, cut up my canoe and burnt it."

Caught on the wrong side of the river with the entire French army between him and the British, Grace returned to Montreal, presumably by land, and sat out the rest of the campaign as a farm laborer.

THE BEAUPORT LINES

As regulars and militiamen arrived at Quebec, they set to work improving the defenses of the city and constructing a line of fortifications running for six miles along the Beauport shore. James Wolfe had planned to surprise the French with a quick landing at Beauport. In fact, Beauport was the place to be for a landing near Quebec, and just about everyone knew it, including Montcalm.

Even before he came to Canada, Montcalm prepared for his new assignment by doing a little research. "I am reading with great pleasure," he wrote to his mother in 1756, "the History of New France by Father

Charlevoix. He provides an agreeable description of Quebec." Practical as well as agreeable, Charlevoix included a description of the British landing at Beauport in 1690 and their defeat at the hands of the Canadian militia and *troupes de la marine:*

> The next day an English vessel filled with soldiers approached the St. Charles River to see if you could make a landing between Beauport and that river . . . At noon on the eighteenth, we saw almost all of their boats, loaded with soldiers, turn toward the same place . . . As soon as the troops had landed M. de Frontenac sent a detachment of Montreal and Trois-Rivères militia to harass them; some Beauport habitants joined it . . . The fighting lasted for about an hour; the Canadians leaped from rock to rock, all around the English . . . M. de Frontenac . . . ordered a battalion of regulars to guarantee their [the British] retreat, which they sounded as soon as the day drew to a close.

(That Montcalm embarked upon his campaign for Canada armed with a book was typical of the general. In private life, Montcalm was something of a gentleman reference librarian. He owned an extensive library at his home in Candiac and served as a source of advice and lender of books to local historians.)

In September 1757, Montcalm had examined the Beauport shore and made plans to fortify the area, which he called "the only place where the enemy can, and must, make their landing." In 1759, Montcalm's troops constructed a network of entrenchments and batteries between the Montmorency and the Saint-Charles Rivers. They established new batteries inside Quebec, moved the navigation buoys on the St. Lawrence to confuse British sailors, and deployed gunboats and moored floating batteries to defend key points along the shore.

The supply clerk approved: "Work continues every day to extend the lines from one redoubt to another . . . I think that these works will intimidate our enemies, and they will never land in that area, or at least if they are crazy enough [to try], they will be massacred."

Less usefully, some enterprising individuals rushed into business selling brandy to the troops in the Beauport camp. Their activities came to official attention on June 13 when a drunken grenadier from La Sarre insulted Thomas-Ignace Trottier Desaulniers, a merchant and militia captain from Montreal. Desaulniers lashed out with his sword; the grenadier died in the hospital four hours later. After this, the private canteens were officially proscribed. "It is generally the custom in Canada," wrote the supply clerk, "not to anticipate events but to suppress them after an unfortunate accident has occurred."

UNDER ARREST

Along with closing canteens, the French cracked down on security. At least one individual, Lieutenant Michel-Guillaume-Saint-Jean de Crèvecoeur of the La Sarre Regiment, came under suspicion of spying for the British.

Crèvecoeur, whose guilt or innocence remains undetermined, had come with his regiment to Canada in 1755. As soon as he arrived, the education in mathematics, surveying, and cartography that he had received at Normandy's Collège Royal de Bourbon made him a priceless asset to an army that was seriously short of competent engineers. He spent the war mapping French and British forts, taking part in sieges, and building fortifications.

Crèvecoeur's maps won him national recognition on March 8, 1759, when the following notice appeared in *La gazette de France:* "The Sieur de Bougainville, the Marquis de Montcalm's senior aide-de-camp . . . has had the honor to present to His Majesty the plans of the forts and the maps of the places that are the theater of war in that country. These plans were made by the Sieur de Crèvecoeur, an officer of La Sarre employed as an engineer, who has won a great reputation for courage and talent."

A few months later, his military career imploded. Posted to Quebec, Crèvecoeur worked on the Beauport entrenchments until Montcalm ordered his arrest. Crèvecoeur had British relatives and had been living with them in England until shortly before the war. Montcalm, perhaps suspecting that Crèvecoeur might defect to the British with a map of Quebec's defenses, flung the young cartographer into prison and seized his maps and papers.

ENEMY IN SIGHT

While work at Quebec proceeded apace and Crèvecoeur languished in jail, Vaudreuil sent Jean Barré to carry news of the safe arrival of Cadet's supply ships to France. Barré, a sixty-six-year-old militia officer and merchant-ship captain from Gaspé, sailed downstream until he encountered the leading elements of Durell's squadron. Returning to Quebec, Barré informed Vaudreuil of this development, then set sail for France once again. "As much by courage as by skill," according to a note in his personnel file, "he passed through the enemy fleet, and arrived safely at Bordeaux." Barré left his wife, Anne, and two of their children behind at Quebec. They had been forced to flee from Gaspé in 1758 when a force commanded by James Wolfe had landed and destroyed "25 boats, all of his furniture, a schooner, and generally everything he owned."

Barré was not the only one keeping track of the Royal Navy. As Durell ascended the river, Canadian scouts tracked the British squadron and sent back reports of its progress. Even so minor a figure as William Hunter did not escape their attention. When he landed on Île aux Coudres on May 28, Charles-François Tarieu de La Naudière and a party of militiamen were watching. They reported that the British "found 2 bark canoes that they broke, as well as the remains of the rafts."

On June 12, three midshipmen, captured on Île aux Coudres and brought to Quebec, told the French that the British force consisted of twenty-five ships of the line, twelve frigates, and two hundred transports carrying twenty thousand troops. They added "that they regarded the capture of Quebec as a certainty, thinking that all of our regulars . . . were at Carillon, where they will have been beaten by three thousand men who will afterward link up with the fleet, and that they regard that operation as already completed."

In the Magasin du Roy, the supply clerk (who frequently comes across as a classic quartermaster, convinced that equipment should be preserved in storage, not handed out to the undeserving) continued to issue stores and snarl at waste and dishonesty: "At the warehouse, we equip everyone, priests, monks, grooms, and so on. It is truly surprising that at a time as critical as this, we are so generous with the king's property."

On June 12 at 5:00 p.m., he replaced a tent and tarpaulin belonging to La Naudière, who had precipitously abandoned his belongings and returned to Quebec well before the British posed any threat to his scouts. The supply clerk responded to this display of martial prudence with restrained irony: "I have always heard that foresight is the mother of safety."

When thirty-five students from the Quebec Seminary formed a militia unit, known informally as the Royal Syntaxe, they came to the Magasin du Roy. The supply clerk fitted them out with clothing "from head to toe," along with arms and munitions. Muskets and ammunition, he was glad to provide. "But all the rest seem to me to be rather unseemly," he wrote, "all the more because most of these young people belong to good bourgeois families with the means to clothe them; nonetheless, no one is scandalized by a gracious offer; on the contrary, everyone willingly accepts not so much I think out of greed, as because it comes from the king our good master."

Whatever the justice of these requests for arms and clothing, equipping Quebec's defenders kept the staff of the Magasin du Roy fully occupied: "There is so much work at the warehouse that it is impossible to leave for a moment."

TAKING PRECAUTIONS

With Durell's squadron known to be closing on Quebec, noncombatants began to flee. Wealthier residents of Upper Town sent their goods out into the countryside and abandoned their homes. Many moved to Trois-Rivières or Montreal. Less affluent residents of Lower Town left their homes and moved into abandoned buildings in Upper Town. Those in between sought sanctuary in neighboring parishes.

Father Jean-Félix Récher took his own precautions. Récher, who had been born in Normandy in 1724, came to Canada in 1744 to work at the Quebec Seminary. In 1749, he became the parish priest of Notre-Dame-des-Victoires, a post he would hold until his death in 1768. Faced with the possible destruction of his church, Récher transferred the sacred vessels and other valuables to a safer location. The items he removed included four tabernacles, statues of Mary and Saint Louis, the main altar, two small paintings, four reliquaries, four crystal crosses, and all of the ornaments, silver, and linen.

For the supply clerk, these measures were all "proof that they [Quebec residents] do not feel safe in their homes." Sharing the concerns of his fellow citizens, he was already making plans to protect his own family during the siege.

SAUNDERS ARRIVES

Around noon on June 26, word spread in Quebec that four or five British ships had anchored off Saint-Laurent, on the south shore of the Île d'Orléans. The invaders had advanced to within two miles of the city.

An hour later, the supply clerk sent part of his family's effects—their private store of flour and salt pork—and "two of my little children" to a refuge in Ancienne Lorette, safely distant from potential danger. He expected that the British fleet would appear within sight of Quebec at first light the next morning.

He was right. Around 6:30 a.m., Quebec residents saw three British warships advance past the southern tip of the Île d'Orléans and anchor in the Quebec basin. At 3:30 p.m., the rest of his family departed: "My wife left for Ancienne Lorette with three of our children, she suffered on the way from very bad weather caused by an appalling storm." The supply clerk remained behind, one anonymous member of a beleaguered garrison.

CLOSING THE GATE

On June 30, the gates of Quebec closed for the first time during the siege; on July 1, British troops made a second landing at Point Lévis, directly opposite the city. So many soldiers swarmed across the point that the supply clerk thought they might be heading upstream to cross the St. Lawrence, to "try to land near Anse des Mères or elsewhere above [Quebec]," then ascend the promontory to the Plains of Abraham. The French high command, he observed, had a different opinion: "People take everything [that happens] in that area for a feint and constantly expect them [the

British] at Beauport, as if they couldn't land elsewhere; our generals are experienced. Please God that they are not deceived, but I am afraid [that they are]."

The next day, Odawa scouts reported that the British were landing artillery at Point Lévis, just across the river from Quebec. On July 5 at 7:00 p.m., the supply clerk went for a walk along the ramparts. He saw four to five hundred British soldiers building entrenchments, supervised by officers in red and blue.

Royal Artillery officers wore blue coats, so the clerk might have been watching Lieutenant Colonel George Williamson and Captain Adam Williamson going about their business. He was certainly right about what they were doing: "It looked to me as if they were examining a place where they could erect batteries."

The waiting was over. British ships were in the St. Lawrence, British soldiers were ashore on the Île d'Orléans and Point Lévis, and British gunners were preparing to bombard the city.

CHAPTER 9

City at War

MONTCALM'S STRATEGY

For Louis-Joseph de Montcalm, the siege of Quebec was a strategy game between opposing generals: "It's a chess match, we would like a checkmate, and it seems that Wolfe would like a stalemate. He is better at moving pawns than we are. His pawns seem to be worth more; you could say that they're queens, and that he cleverly supports them with his rooks. We don't get as much use out of our bishops as we would like; our knights do not move about very much. Our king marches slowly and seriously."

During the summer of 1759, Montcalm played a cautious, defensive game. While Wolfe's troops raged up and down the St. Lawrence spreading death and destruction, Montcalm took up a strong position, made it stronger with entrenchments, and waited for the British to come to him. Wolfe hoped that burning and shelling civilian targets would lure Montcalm out from behind his entrenchments to face the British in battle. Montcalm refused to budge: "I suspect that the enemy has no other goal than to wear us down and make us abandon our position."

For the supply clerk, the campaign was a rather more intimate experience. For him, the pawns had names, homes, and families: "At 10:00 a.m., the Sieur Colet, merchant, and Colas Gauvreau were struck by a cannonball at the Royal Battery; they both died a few hours later . . . The Sieurs Dufour and Brassard were lightly wounded by another [shell] that landed between them as they stood on a doorstep . . . At 11:00 a.m., a firebomb fell upon Chevalier's home . . . it immediately burst into flames, which spread to [the homes] of Teyvoux, the widow Chenevert, the elder Girard, Madame Boishébert, Sieur Cordeneau, and finally that of Sieur Dacier."

The French enclave strategy, which provided the strongest possible protection against assault for Quebec while leaving it exposed to British bombardment, left the supply clerk frustrated and uneasy. Sounding like any civilian in any war who just wants the military to get on with it, he wrote, "It is maddening to watch every day as this poor city is crushed, without anyone doing anything at all to retaliate."

He continued in the same vein three days later: "The conduct of our generals and the inaction of our troops and militia make me truly despair for the safety of this poor colony; the enemy has landed first at the Île d'Orléans, then at Point Lévis, the [Montmorency] Falls, at Pointe-aux-Trembles, and at Deschambault without anyone doing anything to oppose them."

THE PEOPLE SPEAK

While the supply clerk wrote scalding entries in this journal, other Quebecers took more direct action to express their displeasure with the authorities. New France was in no sense of the word a democracy. But Canadians with grievances were accustomed to protesting to senior officials. These officials, in turn, treated protests as legitimate requests for government action.

In this case, the Canadian militiamen of the garrison felt that they were being treated unfairly with regard to their provisions. At the beginning of July, troops serving in relative safety in the Beauport camp received a full military ration of bread, pork, and peas. Militiamen serving inside the city received only a civilian ration of bread. On July 5, they protested this discrepancy by refusing to mount guard, effectively going on strike.

Montcalm, who strongly disapproved of this "mutiny," threatened to hang one Canadian to encourage the others. Yet when the civilian soldiers made their case, he granted their request, on the grounds that one could not "call militiamen who are about to be bombarded and cannoned an ordinary garrison."

A week later, Quebec residents once again sought to exert a measure of control over events by taking their concerns to the authorities. "The enemy," wrote a Canadian officer, "seems to be working very hard to extend their works at Point Lévis; increasing uneasiness in the town has caused some murmuring among the citizens, because, they say, the enemy has been allowed to peacefully establish the mortar and cannon batteries from which they expect to be crushed."

Alarmed by the passivity of the regular army, Canadians successfully demanded action. On July 12, Jean-Daniel Dumas of the *troupes de la marine* and François-Prosper de Douglas of the Languedoc Regiment took command of an expedition composed of regulars from the *troupes de terre* and the *troupes de la marine,* Quebec militiamen, and Native American warriors. That night, they crossed the river, ready to attack and destroy Williamson's batteries. "Much is expected from this detachment," wrote the supply clerk. "Please God that it succeeds, we badly need it."

DESCENT INTO HELL

Around 9:00 that night, the British fired a signal rocket over Point Lévis, immediately followed by two mortar shells. "Equipped with all the artillery invented in hell for the destruction of humanity," wrote Marie de la Visitation, the British had fired the first shots of a devastating bombardment that would continue for two months.

Marie-Joseph Legardeur de Repentigny, Soeur de la Visitation, belonged to one of Canada's first families. Descended from minor Norman nobles, the Legardeurs had come to Canada in the seventeenth century and played prominent roles in the colony ever since. Born in 1693 and deeply committed to a religious vocation, Marie de la Visitation decided when still a child to join the Augustinian nuns who managed Quebec's Hôpital Général. Thwarted by a royal edict limiting the Augustinians to twelve postulants, she served at Quebec's Hôtel-Dieu until family influence and the intervention of the bishop and the governor-general secured her admission to her chosen order in 1718.

When Williamson opened fire, Récher, who had left the city to watch the detachment depart, had a front-row seat, safely out of the line of fire: "I did not return to the city gates until 9:00 p.m.; finding them closed, I arranged to spend the night in a house opposite Saint-Roch, from where

I saw all the shells and firebombs." From this privileged vantage point, he watched as

> the English began to bombard and cannonade the city with 5 mortars and 4 large cannon that they fired every 25 minutes . . . until the thirteenth at noon without interruption, which filled the city with terror, and seriously damaged many homes and churches, especially the cathedral, the Jesuits' church, and their residence. Two 32-pound cannonballs smashed through our residence . . . The English bombardment . . . kept the whole city in terror, particularly women with their children, many of whom were near the citadel. Tears, laments, and prayers were continual among them; they went by platoons to say their rosaries, and so on.

Inside Quebec, residents waited for the Point Lévis expedition to attack the batteries and end the bombardment; cannonballs, shells, and carcasses continued to fly across the river. The next day, Dumas, Douglas, and their troops returned and reported that one Canadian had been killed and two wounded by friendly fire when the advance guard and main body collided in the dark. The expedition collapsed in confusion; the British gunners remained undisturbed in their batteries.

The supply clerk was not impressed: "There, in a few words, are the achievements of a detachment for which so much was hoped and which really should have performed marvels."

THE HÔPITAL GÉNÉRAL

As the bombardment transformed Quebec from a vibrant colonial metropolis into an urban wilderness of shattered buildings and empty streets, Marie de la Visitation's Hôpital Général became one of the city's last functioning institutions. Located on the south bank of the Saint-Charles River, northwest of Quebec, the hospital was just out of range of the Point Lévis batteries yet close enough to continue to serve civilian refugees, the field army, and the Quebec garrison.

In peacetime, the Hôpital Général had been a place where women of the Canadian noblesse sought challenging careers in congenial surroundings, operating a major health-care facility. Pehr Kalm, a professor of natural history from Åbo Akademi in Sweden, visited the hospital in 1749: "This cloister, which is built very magnificently of stone, lies in a pleasant spot surrounded with grain fields, meadows, and woods, and from which Quebec and the St. Lawrence may be seen. A hospital for poor old people, cripples, etc. makes up part of the cloister and is divided up into two halls, one for men, the other for women . . . Most of the nuns here are of noble families and one was the daughter of a governor . . . The convent at a distance looks like a palace."

During the Seven Years' War, the hospital staff waged their own grim battles and suffered heavy casualties. To stay in the fight, Canada needed reinforcements as well as provisions from France. Crossing the Atlantic on a French troopship, however, left many soldiers sick and debilitated. Some had contracted epidemic diseases like smallpox and typhus. In no condition to fight, they were as lost to the French army as if they had died on the voyage.

Quebec's Hôtel-Dieu, which normally cared for incapacitated travelers, had been partially destroyed by fire in 1755. (The nuns of the Hôtel-Dieu nonetheless admitted 659 sailors during the war.) Responsibility for nursing thousands of disembarked soldiers back to health thus fell upon the Hôpital Général.

Between 1755 and 1758, the hospital treated and released from four to seven hundred patients per year. Some of these were sailors or civilians; most were soldiers. At full strength, a battalion of the *troupes de terre* numbered 577. So thanks to the Hôpital Général, every campaign during these years saw the French army strengthened by roughly the equivalent of a full battalion of regulars.

This immense contribution carried a price. People who cared for victims of epidemics risked becoming infected themselves. In 1757 alone, twenty-two nuns, more than half of the community, fell seriously ill. Seven died in 1757; three more in other years. The situation became so serious that some potential patients preferred to avoid the Hôpital Général. When Titus King, of Northampton, Massachusetts, came down with smallpox while a prisoner in Quebec, he "was tended by a widow woman did not go to the hospital as the disease raged there and was very mortal."

In the summer of 1759, the Hôpital Général assumed an additional role as a refugee center for victims of the bombardment. Wealthy Quebecers, who often had relatives among the nuns, came to the hospital to be near wounded husbands, brothers, and sons. Poorer residents who lacked the money or contacts to seek safety in the countryside or Montreal arrived at the hospital seeking shelter.

The nuns of the Hôtel-Dieu and the Ursulines, who had been forced to abandon their Upper Town convents, joined these refugees. The Ursulines, recorded Marie de la Visitation, had remained inside the city until they were "gripped by fear of the shells and cannonballs that had pierced their walls in several places." Refugee nuns provided valuable reinforcements at a time when the hospital's resources were stretched to the limit. To accommodate the newcomers, "we gave them our rooms to put them more at ease, and we went to [live in] the dormitories."

Along with refugees, the Hôpital Général took in wounded French, British, and Native American combatants until the convent and its outbuildings were filled to capacity. Yet the staff, refugees, and patients could not escape the terror and destruction of the bombardment. Marie de la Visitation described life under fire:

> The firebombs and red-hot shot terrorized everyone who saw them. They suffered the pain of watching the homes of our citizens reduced to ashes; many of our relatives lost their houses; in one night, fifty of the best homes in Lower Town [were lost]. The cellars where people stored their merchandise and their most precious belongings were not safe from fire. Against that terrible fire, we could only oppose our groans and our tears which we scattered at the foot of the altars in the moments that our poor wounded left us.

CHAPTER 10

Bombardment and Fire

BOMB WATCHING

After the initial alarm subsided and most of the population had evacuated the city, life in Quebec settled into a grim routine of bombardment and fire that would have been familiar to Londoners during the Blitz in 1940.

The supply clerk, the most prolific diarist of the siege, began to talk about the bombardment the way other people talked about the weather. He counted missiles as they fell—150 shells and 700 to 800 shot on August 3; 100 shells and 800 to 900 hundred shot on the fourth.

He noted whether the bombardment was mild or heavy: "At 10:00 a.m. the enemy decreased their fire a little, but at 5:00 p.m. they vigorously resumed bombarding us; I think that the night will not be quiet." And he faithfully observed where the missiles were landing—along the Lower Town waterfront, in an Upper Town neighborhood, or in one of Quebec's suburbs. "Since noon the shells have been falling around the Hôtel-Dieu."

From time to time, he added a touch of acid humor: "Throughout the night the enemy has been sending us lots of bombs well-seasoned with cannonballs." "Most of the bombs fell in the Saint-Roch suburb, destroying several houses; nonetheless, they have begun to share their favors around all the neighborhoods of the city; they don't want to make anyone jealous."

CITIZENS ON THE RUN

As the bombardment intensified, everyone who could leave Quebec did. Those whose duties compelled them to remain carried on as best they could.

On July 16, the supply clerk and his colleagues abandoned the Magasin du Roy, "the place being no longer habitable," and camped together in the Saint-Charles valley. They remained there until the twenty-third, when "the cannonballs and shells began to annoy us" and compelled them to move farther inland to a site below the Quebec Promontory, just north of the Plains of Abraham.

Part of Cadet's staff joined the displaced bureaucrats from the Magasin du Roy in this refuge. The newcomers included the baker Pierre-Gervais Voyer, who tore down a house for bricks to build a bakery, a butcher who set to work on the spot, and the couriers who carried messages between

Quebec after Williamson's bombardment. "There remained only the bare outside shells of stately stone-built houses . . . [which] were either made skeletons, or their sides perforated by the shot and pieces of shells, so that they might be seen through."

the Beauport camp and the French provision depot at Batiscan. Even here, however, the staff of the Magasin du Roy and Cadet's people remained at risk. At midnight on August 12, wrote the supply clerk, "five shells and a firebomb landed in our camp . . . It's surprising that they went so far, although in fact they were only 9-inchers."

None of this prevented the supply clerk and his colleagues from continuing to fulfill their responsibilities, including a very delicate operation on July 8: "A bomb fell and razed the *salle d'armes*. We have at least 300,000 cartridges there in an un-vaulted room; nonetheless, we have to remove them tomorrow, provided that they don't blow up today."

The supply clerk commented on this operation in terms that suggest he might have been an uncomfortable, not to say annoying, subordinate for François-Joseph de Vienne. Vienne, Quebec's *garde-magasin* (chief storekeeper), ran the Magasin du Roy and occasionally suffered the slings and arrows of the supply clerk's acerbic prose: "I truly cannot understand why someone was so negligent as to fail to remove such precious and dangerous items to a safe place."

SISTER SAINTE-ELIZABETH AND FATHER RÉCHER

While the supply clerk labored to support the war effort, others strove to help the people of Quebec.

With the facilities of the Hôpital Général already overtaxed, the nuns established an outreach service. Although only twenty-two years old, Sister Sainte-Elizabeth (Marie-Thérèse Adhémar de Lantagnac) took charge of a mobile aid station that roved among Quebec's refugees treating the sick and the injured. Her work was not without its hazards, which came from both British shot and shells and the breakdown of law and order in the Quebec area.

Sainte-Elizabeth was passing out rations to her patients one day when a French regular held a sword to her throat and tore the food out of her hands. Her refusal to allow incidents like these to prevent her from caring for victims of the siege became an edifying story of devotion to duty in the face of danger for future Canadian nuns.

Until July 15, Jean-Félix Récher continued to live in his residence next to his church of Notre-Dame-des-Victoires. He conducted daily services and passed out food to the poor and the victims of the bombardment every evening. On the fifteenth, however, one mortar shell shattered his residence; another smashed the ceiling of the Chapelle de la Sainte-Famille in his church.

The next day, Récher moved his operations to the Quebec Seminary, where he presumably hoped that the solid construction of the building would provide some protection. He prepared provisions for distribution, but no one came "because of the excessive danger posed by the fire of our enemies, who only aim their cannonballs and shells at the [temporary] parish [church] and its vicinity."

Seeking a safer location, Récher moved again. This time, he established a makeshift chapel in a house in the Saint-Jean suburb, just outside the walls. His new chapel lasted until the night of July 20, when the Saint-Jean and Palace districts came under fire for the first time. The bombardment "surprised and alarmed many people who had sought refuge in these places, and obliged them to pass the night standing upright, and then to leave."

Following a sleepless night, Récher relocated to a room in the home of Joachim Primault, a tanner, near the Hôpital Général. Without space to establish another temporary church, he conducted services at the hospital chapel and buried fallen parishioners in the hospital cemetery.

Yet even here Récher remained within range of the cannon and mortars at Point Lévis. At 1:00 a.m. on Sunday, August 12, the same mortar shells and firebombs that fell into the supply clerk's camp landed near Récher's refuge, "which completely surprised us, and made us get up to go to spend the rest of the night at the Hôpital Général."

Only Récher and the supply clerk left an exact account of their movements, but hundreds of other Quebecers must have shared their experience of being chased across the city and down into the Saint-Charles valley by the bombardment while continuing to serve their colony and their king under the most difficult and dangerous conditions.

LAWS AGAINST FIRE

Throughout the bombardment, Quebec's garrison fought to save the fabric of the city from the devastating blazes unleashed by British firebombs.

Most cannonballs or mortar shells affected only a single building. Carcasses, spraying jets of flame in all directions, could touch off conflagrations that destroyed entire neighborhoods. Récher, the supply clerk, and the notary Jean-Claude Panet all formed a part of the army of volunteers fighting fires amid seas of raging flames.

At a time when firefighting technology was rudimentary, burn treatment uncertain, and fire insurance nonexistent, every fire was a potential catastrophe. Urban planning in colonial Quebec had two principal goals, creating a suitably dignified capital and keeping it from burning down. The imposing public buildings that so impressed Wolfe's officers fulfilled the first objective. Regarding the second, successive colonial governments issued a series of regulations that attempted to control the behavior of Canadians and the construction of buildings to prevent fires from starting and spreading.

An ordinance dating back to 1664 required Quebec residents to keep the streets in front of their houses clear of straw and other flammable material that might allow sparks to grow into fires. Subsequent regulations ordered smokers to refrain from flinging the burning wood shavings that they used to light their pipes onto the street, coopers and carpenters to sweep out their shops every two days, and all residents to have their chimneys cleaned every two months to prevent the buildup of flammable deposits.

Whenever two stone buildings shared a common wall, regulations required that the wall continue upward for a yard past the roof in order to prevent fires from leaping from one building to the next. Chimneys had to extend four feet above the roof, which allowed flying sparks to burn out before they could land on cedar shingles and start a fire. Their flues had to be four feet by ten inches to allow space for chimney sweeps to work.

When fire destroyed wooden buildings, they were to be rebuilt in stone. In 1727, the intendant (the colony's senior civil administrator) went so far as to forbid the construction of wooden buildings and the use of cedar shingles altogether. Whether as a result of official intervention or increasing prosperity, by 1740, 75 percent of Quebec buildings were made of stone.

These precautions, intended to limit the effects of accidents and arson, proved reasonably effective in peacetime. They could not, however, shield the city from prolonged bombardment by a mix of solid shot, mortar shells, and firebombs.

CITY IN FLAMES

Williamson's gunners ignited three great fires during the Quebec campaign. At noon on July 16, a falling carcass incinerated one house; the fire quickly spread to eight more. As the fires raged, the shelling continued. The British, observed Récher, "seeing the fire break out fired many bombs and cannonballs into the flames, to prevent our men from working to put it out."

A second major fire broke out on the night of July 22–23. Once again, it began with a carcass striking a single house. Racing across Lower Town, the fires consumed eighteen homes and the church of Notre-Dame-des-Victoires.

Father Récher was there, watching his church burn: "Some spark, some cinder, blown by the wind onto the platforms that had been built above the clock tower, to use for signaling during the siege . . . everything . . . perished, including . . . the Chapter House; and the houses of the residence."

Once again, the bombardment continued after the city was ablaze. "During that fire," wrote Récher, "which was terrible, the English never ceased to fling bombs and cannonballs into the flames to prevent our people from putting it out."

The third and most devastating fire occurred on the night of August 8–9. Three firebombs slammed into Lower Town, starting three fires that merged into one catastrophic firestorm. One bomb landed on a house on the Place du Marché, one on a house on the Rue Champlain, and the third on the home of Jean-Claude Panet.

Panet, the son of a clerk at the Ministry of Marine, had been born in Paris in 1719. Well educated and ambitious but without influential connections, he decided to make his fortune in the colonies. He secured a Crown subsidy for this enterprise by enlisting as a private soldier in the *troupes de marine,* which assigned him to the Canadian garrison in 1740.

Eighteenth-century soldiers had considerable amounts of free time. Like most of his comrades, Panet used this time to seek civilian employment to supplement his income. Unlike most of his comrades, he began to practice law and became so successful that he soon attracted the attention of the governor-general and the intendant. In 1743, his father paid 150 livres to secure Panet's discharge from the *troupes de la marine.* A year later, Panet received an appointment as a royal notary and was on his way to becoming one of Quebec's leading citizens.

In August 1759, Panet described the scene as his home burned to the ground: "That same day proved fatal for myself and many others . . . In vain, people tried to cut off the fire and save my home; a light northeast wind was blowing, and soon the entire Lower Town was nothing but a fireplace . . . The flames consumed everything. Imagine our consternation. There were 167 houses burned."

For the supply clerk, the relentless destruction of his city was an intensely personal tragedy: "It is indeed heartrending to see the damage in that poor place." The fires, however, destroyed more than homes. Quebec was a major commercial center, and some merchants hadn't managed to move their inventories to safety. One Berthou-Dûbreüil, who described himself as an "unfortunate Canadian merchant," lamented that "the general conflagration . . . cost me all of my goods and merchandise . . . amounting to a sum of more than 30,000 livres [which] . . . ruined me forever."

FIREFIGHTERS

Quebec's defenders, however, were not entirely helpless. Damage from cannonballs and mortar shells had to be endured, not resisted. Fires, on the other hand, could be fought.

The colonial government prepared for fires by establishing emergency water supplies, building cisterns, and stockpiling firefighting equipment. Stone-lined cisterns stored water for emergencies wherever wells, fountains, or rivers were too far away. The Château Saint-Louis, the Intendant's Palace, the Jesuit church, and designated private homes held wood and leather buckets, axes, shovels, iron hooks, battering rams, and ladders, ready to be snatched up and carried to the scene of a fire.

When a fire broke out, clanging church bells sounded the alarm. Government regulations prescribed that every citizen race to the fire with a bucket or kettle. Most did so. Officials constantly complained about the rest, who preferred to treat comfortably distant fires as someone else's problem.

At the scene of the fire, carpenters and masons demolished adjacent buildings to isolate the blaze. Other citizens tore off burning roofs, to try to save the rest of the structure, and formed bucket brigades to carry water to the fire. Parish priests, frequently bearing an ostensorium, a sun-shaped vessel displaying the consecrated host in the center, offered up prayers for success. Their efforts provided spiritual support for the firefighters and a welcome boost to morale.

On April 28, 1747, during the War of the Austrian Succession (also known as King George's War) American prisoner William Pote recorded his impression of the first few moments of a major fire in Quebec:

> It was first discovered on the . . . ridge of the roof which was of shingles, they being very dry and the wind blowing fresh it soon spread it self over the whole roof and put those who where in the upper rooms, in great danger of their lives. Some of them stayed too long in the garrets to save their bedding that the fire broke in upon them before they left their room . . . [soon afterward] the house was all on flames.

Pote then described the public response to the blaze: "The drums beating and the alarm bell soon raised the town and all the militia ran together in swarms."

During the summer of 1759, Canadians applied their peacetime firefighting skills to the defense of Quebec. René Nicolas Le Vasseur left a brief account of his service as a firefighter. A clerk from the Ministry of Marine, he found himself pressed into service as first the lieutenant, then the captain, of a company of workers attached to the artillery. Leading this company, he wrote, "I had orders to go to places where firebombs caused frequent fires that successively burned down all of the neighborhoods of the city."

An example of successful firefighting occurred on August 16. Around 9:00 p.m., a firebomb slammed into a house built against the walls of the Récollet residence. The supply clerk watched as the house "caught fire immediately and burned to cinders."

Quick action by two Récollets and two carpenters contained the blaze. The four of them, wrote Panet, "kept the fire from spreading, by climbing onto a neighboring roof . . . and tearing it off in spite of the bombs and cannonballs aimed at the fire."

Inside the Récollet Church. A Récollet friar prays while British soldiers and sailors examine what remains of his church. Although heavily damaged, it is in much better shape than many Quebec buildings.

No one was injured, but Panet had three narrow escapes that evening, which testify eloquently to the hazards of life in Quebec during the bombardment: "Two cannonballs passed right by us, and a cannonball knocked a plank off the roof of the Récollets' church that landed right between Brother Noël and me."

LOOTERS

Not all of Quebec's wounds came from the British. Some were self-inflicted. While shells flew and fires raged, looters prowled the ruins. With the civil population evacuated and most buildings unoccupied, the city was filled with potential targets for thieves from the ranks of the sailors, soldiers, and militiamen that defended Quebec. The supply clerk, unmoved by their enterprising response to adversity, complained vigorously of "the robbery that occurs day and night in the city."

By the last week of July, looting had become too serious to ignore. The colonial government created a special tribunal with powers of summary execution. Jean-Claude Panet served as clerk of the court.

The tribunal hanged its first thief—a sailor—on July 29. Undeterred by this example, two soldiers of the *troupes de la marine* broke into a cellar that night and stole a barrel of brandy. They took it to the home of one Charland, in Saint-Roch, where all three were arrested around 6:30 the next morning.

Récher described the soldiers' fate: "Their trial began at 10:00 a.m., and they were hanged at 4:00 p.m. the same day." The court found Charland mentally unfit and committed him to the care of the Hôpital Général.

More executions followed. And more thefts. A month later, Récher observed that "burglars continued to rob the houses in the city; they smashed in the doors of vaults and even broke through entrances to vaults that had been bricked up."

WATCHING THE ENEMY

To add to Quebecers' distress, their vantage point in the city gave them a perfect view of the devastation of the countryside. Panet, who could on occasion be as sarcastic as the supply clerk, watched on August 21 as "the English, following their praiseworthy custom, set fire to Saint-Joachim and burned the two farms." Two days later, he added, "The fires in the countryside continued, and we watched them all night."

Yet not every view of the countryside was depressing. On July 31, as the British withdrew in disorder from their failed attack on the Beauport lines at Montmorency, Panet heard "in the Saint-Roch suburb a loud cry as women and children shouted 'Vive le roy!'" He ran to the side of the Quebec Promontory and looked downriver: "I saw the first frigate all on fire; a little later, black smoke billowed from the second, which exploded, and then caught fire. It was the English who set the fires for fear that we might profit from the occasion." After the French victory at Montmorency, Marie de la Visitation declared that the British "never dared attempt a second landing; the shame of remaining inactive made them start to burn our countryside."

More than two months of continuous bombardment had shattered just about everything in the city, everything except for the morale of its garrison and the strength of its defenses. Homes, schools, churches, stores, hospitals, and warehouses had been smashed to fragments or burned to cinders. Yet the curtain walls on the west side, facing the Plains of Abraham, remained immune to British bombardment; the batteries guarding the waterfront suffered only minor damage. Referring to preparations to defeat a seaborne assault on Lower Town, the supply clerk remained unshaken by the British threat: "People truly fear that the enemy will attempt to take [Quebec] by assault; I nonetheless think it would be a bad bargain for them, for as long as our batteries remain intact."

CHAPTER II

The Governor, the General, and Just a Hint of Scandal

THE GOVERNOR

Responsibility for dealing with a British assault, if it ever came, lay with Pierre de Rigaud de Vaudreuil and Louis-Joseph de Montcalm. The two commanders worked together remarkably well, considering that they didn't get along and one did not want to be in Canada at all.

It was Canada's good fortune to be governed in a time of desperate emergency by a vastly experienced, thoroughly competent professional. A Canadian-born French noble and the son of a former governor-general, Vaudreuil had devoted his entire working life to New France. Service as a young officer in the *troupes de la marine* took him into the North American interior and gave him experience of both Native American diplomacy and the network of waterways that became military lines of communication in wartime.

Family influence, demonstrated proficiency, and his own aspirations propelled Vaudreuil into a career as a colonial governor. In 1733, he became governor of Trois-Rivières, where he gained a reputation for quiet competence. Nine years later, promotion to governor of Louisiana marked the beginning of almost two decades of responsibility for protecting French interests throughout most of the Mississippi valley. Although governors of

Louisiana were nominally subordinate to the governor-general in Quebec, slow communications made it expedient for them to work on their own and deal directly with the Ministry of Marine in Paris.

Based in New Orleans, Vaudreuil managed wars against the British and the Chickasaws, used a mix of diplomacy and assassination to preserve the French alliance with the Choctaws, helped to place the Louisiana economy on a sound footing, and coped with difficult subordinates and shortages of money and supplies. A second promotion to governor-general of New France in 1755 brought him back to Canada just in time to take command of the defense of that colony during most of the Seven Years' War.

Among his first actions as governor-general was to intervene to protect an American prisoner of war from a sexually aggressive father and son. After ransoming Jemima Howe of Hinsdale, New Hampshire, from her Native American captors, the two Canadians took advantage of her presence in their home to press their attentions upon her. Alerted by another prisoner, Vaudreuil sent the son, an officer in the *troupes de la marine,* away on active service and ordered the father to treat Howe with the greatest respect. A grateful Howe described Vaudreuil as a "humane and generous gentleman."

In his capacity of commander-in-chief of the French armed forces in North America, Vaudreuil pursued a strategically defensive, tactically offensive strategy. Heavily outnumbered, he took advantage of Canada's interior lines of communications along lakes and rivers to shift his forces from place to place. This mobility allowed him to launch preemptive strikes against British outposts before they could be used as staging points for attacks on Canada.

Robert Eastburn of Philadelphia, then a prisoner in Montreal, watched Canadians celebrate the success of the first of these strikes. Following the capture of Fort Oswego and two entire regiments of American regulars in August 1756, he wrote, "I saw the English standards [the colors of the Fiftieth and Fifty-First Regiments] . . . and the French rejoicing at our downfall, and mocking us poor prisoners . . . great joy appeared in all their faces, which they expressed by loud shouts, firing of canon, and returning thanks in their churches; but our faces were covered with shame, and our hearts filled with grief."

Vaudreuil's efforts on behalf of Canada won him enormous popularity among Canadians. One song spoke of

Pierre de Rigaud de Vaudreuil. Vaudreuil's position as governor-general of New France made him commander in chief of the French armed forces in North America, but he could not compel Montcalm and other senior officers of the *troupes de terre* to follow his orders on September 13.

> Vaudreuil under whose command,
> the Canadian lives, breathes,
> [and] runs . . . to fight . . .
> for the good of his country.

Another declared,

> We celebrate the great Vaudreuil,
> his wisdom and his glory.
> All of England mourns,
> at the news of his victory.

Louis-Joseph de Montcalm. The Battle of
the Plains of Abraham was Montcalm's first
experience of battle without direction from
a superior or support from strong, capable
subordinates.

By 1759, however, Great Britain had committed so many regular
troops and so many warships to the North American war that Vaudreuil
was forced back onto the defensive. Sixty years old in 1759, he found himself defending the city in which he had been born against the British and
doing his best to work in harmony with Louis-Joseph de Montcalm.

THE GENERAL

Fourteen years younger than Vaudreuil, Montcalm, like Wolfe, came to
Canada as a veteran soldier and novice general. During seventeen years
of active service in Europe, he had taken part in eleven campaigns, been
wounded five times, and consistently displayed great courage under fire.

Yet through no fault of his own, Montcalm had spent most of his
career taking part in a long series of French defeats and retreats. Prior to

his arrival in Canada, he had never commanded any formation larger than a regiment and never held a significant independent command. He had no experience of amphibious warfare along inland waterways, making war in the vast, and to a European, empty spaces of North America, or cooperating with allies from another civilization.

In 1756, when the French army needed a commander for its battalions in Canada and more senior officers refused the assignment, the minister of war chose Montcalm. Promoted to *maréchal de camp* (major general), he read Charlevoix's *Histoire et description générale de la Nouvelle France,* crossed the Atlantic to Canada, and joined in the struggle for North America.

There, like Dumas, Beaujeu, Lignery, Villiers, Rigaud, and Vaudreuil, he found admirers among Canadians. One contemporary Canadian song suggested that listeners

> From a laurel tree cut a palm,
> to crown the great Montcalm.

Another compared him to classical heroes of Greece and Rome:

> Like Alexander he is small,
> but filled with spirit.
> He has all the courage,
> and swiftness of Caesar.

Admiring songs aside, Montcalm's experiences in Canada were, for the most part, disagreeable. He missed his family, and he missed his home. Before he came to Canada, Montcalm had spent seven years living the quiet life of a provincial noble on his estate in Candiac in southern France. Torn from this idyll by the outbreak of war, he filled his private correspondence with expressions of love for his family and laments for his transatlantic exile. "Farewell, my heart," he wrote to his wife in 1757, "I adore and love you. I kiss my daughters." In 1758, he sadly asked himself, "When will I see my Candiac again?"

That notwithstanding, like many soldiers in many wars, far from home for years at a time, Montcalm responded to isolation and loneliness by seeking a temporary liaison. Yet as he ruefully confessed to François-Charles de Bourlamaque, third in command of the *troupes de terre,* this hadn't worked out very well. After referring to a tricky diplomatic situation, Montcalm lamented, "I am no further advanced in this than with Madame M . . . She is a little like all Canadian women, more willing to be pleasant than to go all the way."

Like most soldiers serving overseas, Montcalm had to cope with knowing that life at home had continued in his absence. Births, deaths, marriages, triumphs, and tragedies occurred in France; Montcalm was an ocean away in Canada. The spring of 1759 was a sad time for Montcalm. When Bougainville arrived from France, he carried heartbreaking news: "Bougainville told me that one of my daughters has died. I am distressed, because I have four of them; I think it is poor Mirète, who resembled me and whom I loved very much."

MONTCALM'S ENEMY WITHIN

As if the pain of prolonged separation from his family were not enough, Montcalm magnified his unhappiness by provoking a series of quarrels with Vaudreuil. Almost as soon as he disembarked at Quebec in 1756, Montcalm perceived himself to be under attack by two enemies, each of whom sought to destroy the regular battalions of the *troupes de terre*. The first was the British army, the second, his own commander in chief. And of the two, Vaudreuil was the more dangerous. Montcalm frequently expressed this opinion to junior officers, whose writings reflect their general's views.

In 1756, prior to Montcalm's capture of Fort Oswego, one of his officers, Jean-Guillaume Plantavit de Lapause de Margon, declared that "the governor-general's desire to capture that fort made him conceal from M. de Montcalm the strength of that post." After Vaudreuil's intelligence proved correct and the expedition produced a quick, decisive victory, Montcalm, wrote Lapause, "thought that the government [Vaudreuil] wanted to sacrifice him."

Two years later, Montcalm's opinion of Vaudreuil hadn't changed. When Montcalm and the *troupes de terre* won a spectacular victory against an invading British army at Carillon, Vaudreuil responded by heaping praise on his general. His official report drew attention to Montcalm's courage in placing himself at the heart of the battle: "M. le Marquis de Montcalm reserved for himself the defense of the center of the entrenchment." He reminded the minister of marine that "we owe this victory, my lord, to the wise dispositions of M. le Marquis de Montcalm," and he commended the officers of the *troupes de terre:* "The officers in general displayed incredible valor, and their example gave amazing courage and daring to the soldiers."

Montcalm, in contrast, followed up his victory by accusing Vaudreuil of plotting to exterminate the *troupes de terre.* As governor-general, Vaudreuil decided how many troops to commit to each operation. Montcalm, unhappy with the size of his force, informed a junior officer that the soldiers and officers of the *troupes de terre* at Carillon "say loudly that M. de Vaudreuil wanted to have us slaughtered by giving me so few men to face a real danger, while he uselessly retained a corps of two to three thousand men sent to accomplish something in the country of the Five Nations where five hundred men would be sufficient."

This was a little too much for Vaudreuil. He informed the minister of marine that if he tried to work with Montcalm on the general's terms, "I will completely compromise the authority that the king has confided to me." After Carillon, he continued, Montcalm had "acclaimed his victory so indiscreetly that he inspired his army to produce the most indecent statements against the government and especially against anything coming from the Ministry of Marine."

Vaudreuil further accused Montcalm of being excessively harsh with both the Canadian militia and Canada's Native American allies. "The Canadians," he wrote, "have suffered greatly from the tantrums and fury of M. de Montcalm." When a delegation of Native American leaders approached Montcalm to congratulate him for his victory, the general had replied with a hysterical tirade: "You have come at a time when I have no more need of you. Have you only come to see dead bodies? Go behind the fort and you will find them. I do not need you to defeat the English."

Vaudreuil concluded by supporting Montcalm's request to return to France, on the grounds of ill health and rising debts. "I consider, my lord, that he deserves promotion to lieutenant general [*lieutenant général des armées*]," he wrote. "He can serve very usefully in Europe. No one respects his excellent qualities more than I, but he lacks those which are necessary for making war in this country."

After due consideration, the Crown gave Vaudreuil half of what he asked for, the wrong half. Montcalm received his promotion but not his recall. This promotion shifted the balance of power in the French high command. Prior to 1759, Vaudreuil and Montcalm had been superior and subordinate. Now they were colleagues.

Promotion to lieutenant general made Montcalm the highest-ranking French officer in Canada. As such, he assumed both command of all French forces in Canada and a share of the responsibility for their deployment. When Cadet's supply ships arrived in May, they carried orders for Vaudreuil to consult with Montcalm "in order to prepare with him the defense plan that you consider to be most appropriate."

This left Vaudreuil disconcerted yet still in overall command and Montcalm thoroughly displeased and suspecting another plot by the governor-general. Like the supply clerk, Montcalm vented his spleen by recording angry outbursts in his journal: "The Marquis de Vaudreuil commands this army, and in the case of a misfortune he will with great care lay all the blame on the Marquis de Montcalm."

The new lieutenant general's invective continued to flow throughout the campaign. "The indecision of the field marshal" and "council of war, to reduce the confusion of M. de Vaudreuil," were about the kindest things Montcalm had to say about the governor-general. More typical was his journal entry of June 12, when Vaudreuil inspected the Beauport fortifications: "The Marquis de Vaudreuil, governor-general and in that capacity general of the army, has made his first tour [of the fortifications]; youth has to learn. Because he had never seen either a camp or a fortification, everything seemed as new to him as it was amusing. He asked the most remarkable questions. You would think that a blind man had been given sight."

He even faulted Vaudreuil for remaining calm in the face of the British invasion: "The Marquis de Vaudreuil [was] as relaxed as if the enemy were not at all of our doors."

But if Vaudreuil retained the supreme command, Montcalm now had a voice in planning the campaign and the power to make his opinions count. He first exercised this authority regarding the logistical arrangements for the defense of Quebec.

CHAPTER 12

Wheat and War

COMMAND DECISIONS AND LOGISTIC REALITIES

In May, Cadet had brought enough food to Canada to keep Vaudreuil's armies in the field until August. Toward the end of July, however, the *munitionnaire général* came face-to-face with two harsh realities.

First, Quebec's provisions depot was nowhere near the city. It was sixty miles upstream at Batiscan, close to Trois-Rivières. Second, the provisions he had imported from France were running out.

Before the campaign began, the minister of marine had instructed Vaudreuil to "determine with the Marquis de Montcalm if it would be appropriate to take the precaution of establishing in advance a store of munitions and provisions at Trois-Rivières or elsewhere." These orders, combined with Montcalm's habitual pessimism and newfound authority, combined to create a challenge for Cadet and a potential catastrophe for Canada.

Vaudreuil believed that the British could be defeated and Canada preserved at Quebec. "The Marquis de Vaudreuil told us at dinner," wrote Montcalm on May 28, "that with the Canadians on the right, the natives on the left, and the French in the center, the English would certainly be beaten. *Amen.*"

François-Gaston de Lévis, generally known as the Chevalier de Lévis, Montcalm's second-in-command, agreed with the governor-general: "Our enemies will not overcome us in a single campaign . . . We can count on the valor of our troops, the goodwill of the Canadians, and the good intentions of the natives."

Montcalm had his own opinion. He thought that Canada was doomed. "Here is Canada," he wrote in the fall of 1758, "surrounded on all sides . . . Only peace can save the colony now."

Anticipating defeat, Montcalm planned a bizarre retreat from Canada to Louisiana by canoe. This would have involved accumulating 250 canoes and seventy days of rations for twenty-five hundred troops, then leaving Vaudreuil behind to surrender after the inevitable British victory while the *troupes de terre* headed for New Orleans. The most intelligent part of this plan, which was rejected out of hand in Paris, was Montcalm's request to "preserve in France and Canada the deepest secrecy regarding this project."

Frustrated in his attempt to reenact the march of a Greek mercenary army across western Asia to the Black Sea in 401–399 B.C. ("the retreat of the ten thousand [that] immortalized the Greeks"), Montcalm turned to preparing for defeat at Quebec and a retreat toward Montreal in 1759.

To provision that retreat, he began the campaign demanding that the French limit their stores at Quebec to two weeks of rations. Everything beyond that could be stored upstream, to supply the French forces after they abandoned the city.

Although Montcalm eventually discarded this plan, Cadet's supply ships nonetheless anchored at Batiscan, where they became a floating supply depot for the French army at Quebec. In his journal, Montcalm claimed credit for taking "every possible measure to make the best of our situation and neglect nothing to assure the supply of provisions for our little army, in case it is forced to retreat."

This decision created a potentially fatal weakness in Quebec's defenses. With the bulk of the garrison's provisions stored upstream, Quebec became vulnerable to British forces operating west of the city. Should Saunders's ships land Wolfe's army between Quebec and Batiscan, the British could force the French to march out and give battle at a time and place of their choosing.

In June and July, Quebec's defenders lived on provisions stored in the area and whatever they could find in the countryside. Toward the end of July, food began to run short. From that point forward, Quebec was on life support, dependent upon regular transfusions of supplies from Batiscan.

CONVOYS ON THE CHEMIN DU ROY

On July 24, Cadet traveled to Batiscan to organize a convoy to carry seven hundred barrels of flour and salt pork from the ships to Quebec. He first considered sending these provisions downriver by bateaux. But with Holmes on the St. Lawrence between Quebec and Batiscan, Cadet decided that this was too dangerous.

Instead, he assembled 271 horse-drawn carts. To conduct the carts to Quebec at a time when most of the adult male population was serving with the militia, Cadet turned to women, children, and elderly men. The carts arrived safely on August 1 and gave Quebec the wherewithal to hold out for two more weeks.

On August 10, as the supplies from the first shipment began to run

A Canadian road. During the Quebec campaign, convoys of hundreds of carts (like the one next to the tallest tree) carried provisions to Quebec along the easternmost section of the Chemin du Roy. When heavy rains turned the surface into a quagmire, Joseph-Michel Cadet resorted to the more dangerous alternative of sending convoys of bateaux down the St. Lawrence. Typical Canadian farm buildings stand beside the road. George Scott, Joseph Goreham, Jeremiah Pearson, and David Perry burned hundreds of buildings like these during their expedition downriver.

out, Cadet organized a second overland convoy of flour. It reached Quebec on August 18, just in time to avert disaster. The army had been down to five days of rations.

These provisions saved Quebec, but moving provisions by land had proved to be difficult and inefficient. The heavily laden carts that made up the convoys traveled along the Chemin du Roy (King's Highway), which ran all the way from Quebec to Montreal. Built in the 1730s, the road was twenty feet wide and flanked by drainage ditches. Its surface was plain dirt; the ditches did not prevent heavy rain from turning the roadway into a long, thin quagmire.

In late July and August 1759, the rains were very, very heavy. Movement along the Chemin du Roy was consequently slow and painful. The carts were coming apart; the teamsters and horses were exhausted. Under these conditions, Cadet decided that sending provisions by land was no longer viable. In the future, he would dare the wrath of the Royal Navy by sending convoys of bateaux down the St. Lawrence River.

CONVOYS ON THE ST. LAWRENCE

Carried downriver by falling tides and followed on land by militia cavalry and Native American warriors, Cadet's first waterborne convoy proceeded without incident until the night of August 17. On or around that date, the bateaux crews chose to ignore the danger posed by nearby British warships. They started talking and shouting among themselves and using flint and steel to light their pipes at night.

The result was a volley of cannonballs out of the darkness. The Canadians pulled for shore. Some bateaux made it to the beach; others ran aground. Despite this contretemps, by August 19 the convoy had reached Pointe-aux-Trembles and pushed on to Cap-Rouge. There, they picked up an additional escort of fifty militiamen. The Canadians marched along the edge of the Quebec Promontory as the bateaux floated down the river, ready to provide covering fire in the event of a British attack.

For the final leg of the voyage, between Cap-Rouge and Quebec, the convoy split in two. On August 23, twelve bateaux reached Quebec. On the twenty-fourth, fourteen more arrived safely. As soon as the boats were unloaded, their crews allowed the next rising tide to carry them back upstream. Quebec now had enough food to last until mid-September.

But that was all. The last of Cadet's supplies had been shipped downriver. At Batiscan, the cupboard was bare. Any further supplies would have to come from the farms of the government of Montreal. (The French divided Canada into three administrative districts, known as the governments of Quebec, Trois-Rivières, and Montreal.)

QUEBEC'S SECOND FRONT

With the exhaustion of Cadet's supplies at Batiscan, the defense of Quebec became a two-front war. One front was military, the other logistic. Each centered on a prominent geographic feature. In the northeast, geography gave Canada strong natural defenses in the form of the Quebec Promontory. To the southwest, it provided a potential breadbasket in the farmland of the Montreal Plain.

On the Quebec front, the allied army of French regulars, Canadian militiamen, and Native American warriors defended Canada against invasion. On the Montreal front, Canadian noncombatants struggled to secure the provisions that would keep this army in the field. Defeat in either battle would doom Quebec to capture and Canada to conquest.

In Canada as in France, whole wheat bread was the staple foodstuff. Eating well meant growing wheat, and the best place in Canada to grow wheat was the Montreal Plain. The Montreal government, with its 150 frost-free days, seventy degrees Fahrenheit mean July temperature, and humus-rich clay and silt loam soil, contained the finest farmland in the colony and produced the richest, most reliable harvests.

If the weather cooperated, the farms of the Montreal Plain could produce a substantial surplus. In 1759, after three years of crop failures throughout the colony, the climate finally handed Canada what it had needed ever since the war began, one good harvest.

The successful wheat crop was as important to Canada in the late summer as the arrival of Cadet's ships had been in the spring. If the Montreal harvest had failed, the defense of Quebec would have collapsed. All Canada would have suffered severe hardship, perhaps even starvation. The colony's best hope might have been a quick surrender on condition that the British supply Canada with wheat from their North American colonies.

Instead, Montreal provided enough wheat to sustain Quebec's defenders in the remaining months of 1759 and, if necessary, to allow the colony to hold out for another year without further supplies from France. Transporting the harvest to Batiscan would be easy. Canada possessed an extensive fleet of small sailing vessels that carried cargo and passengers between Quebec and Montreal. Traveling from Odanak (near Trois-Rivières) to Montreal earlier in the war, the American prisoner of war James Johnson "saw about twenty vessels in Quebeck River at one time which were a kind of brigantines [two-masted merchant ships]."

There was just one catch. All of this wheat still stood in the fields surrounding Montreal, while Montreal's farmers were serving with the militia on the Quebec, Lake Champlain, and Lake Ontario frontiers. Quebec had farmers but no food. Montreal had food but no farmers.

As Montreal's grain matured, this labor shortage became critical. "I see nothing in my government," lamented François-Pierre de Rigaud de Vaudreuil, governor of Montreal, "but women, children, and elderly men who are unable to do the slightest thing." A Canadian observer agreed: "There were moreover no more than women and children, with four or five men, of whom the youngest was seventy or eighty, sick and infirm, and as a result unable to be useful to the colony."

Yet Canada's need was absolute and Vaudreuil's orders peremptory, even desperate. On August 26, he wrote, "It is absolutely necessary that we receive new flour by the tenth of next month [September] to provision the army. It is also very important that we do not lose a single grain of wheat, because the harvest of the government of Montreal is almost our only resource to allow the colony to survive during the winter."

THE OTHER VAUDREUIL

Solving this problem initially fell upon Rigaud, Vaudreuil's younger brother.

A career soldier in the *troupes de la marine* and former governor of Trois-Rivières, Rigaud became a popular Canadian hero in 1756 during the siege of Fort Oswego (Chouaguen). In the course of that siege, he led a colonial detachment that crossed the Oswego River and attacked the British from behind. A contemporary Canadian folk song celebrated Rigaud's leadership:

Already we see our heroes,
A valiant troop,
Advancing across the waters,
of a perilous rapid.
Filled with enthusiasm, sword in hand,
Rigaud marches at their head.
Our enemies tremble and Chouaguen,
becomes our conquest.

But Rigaud's greatest service to Canada came in 1759, when he took charge of securing the Montreal harvest. He approached a difficult situation with firm resolve, subtle propaganda, and skillful management of limited resources.

THE BATTLE OF MONTREAL

Rigaud began his campaign with a letter to the curés of his government.

In New France, the church functioned as an extension of the state, providing social services, particularly education, hospitals, and welfare. Parish priests frequently served as spokespeople for the Crown. This network of priests who could read official announcements to their parishioners gave officials like Rigaud and Vaudreuil a mass medium that could deliver a message to the entire population within days.

They could also exercise influence in their own right. In his letter to the curés, reported Rigaud, "I have asked them to encourage all of the elders, women, and children of their parishes to work together unceasingly and cooperatively everyone for each other."

He divided his government into districts, and assigned inspectors to each district to oversee the harvest. The inspectors were local notables, "the most just and the most knowledgeable regarding that area." They were to "take, in cooperation with the priests, the most effective measures to bring in all the harvest; they must divide all of the women, girls, and children so that they all work alongside one another, while the men bind up the sheaves and cart them away; the harvests of the poor must be brought in just like those of the rich, without any preference whatsoever."

Furthermore, Rigaud broke up a camp of six hundred Montreal militiamen. Elderly but still fit enough to serve, they had been stationed at La

Prairie, ready to reinforce the Lake Champlain frontier. In August, Rigaud distributed them among parishes where the need for personnel was most desperate.

Rigaud encouraged his harvesters with skillful propaganda, spread among the population by local priests. Cadet's critic summarized the information campaign. Rigaud, he declared, "wrote to all of the priests to ask them to explain to their parishioners how desperate the situation in which their fathers, husbands, and children will find themselves will be, if they do not make one last effort to produce provisions for them; [and] that they must cut back on their own [consumption], and give whatever seemed right to them."

When Vaudreuil and Montcalm sent Lévis to take command of Canada's defenses on the Lake Champlain and Lake Ontario frontiers, he became the senior officer in the government of Montreal. Rigaud, proud and capable, resented this usurpation of his authority. Cadet, then present in Montreal, helped to smooth things over. He reminded Rigaud that the governor-general had the right to appoint a general officer to command a region; Rigaud and Lévis settled down to work together.

Lévis detached three hundred militiamen and one hundred regulars of the *troupes de terre* from his force, with orders to remain harvesting until word arrived of the British on the move toward the upper St. Lawrence. Moreover, while Rigaud had mobilized the remaining population of the countryside, Lévis mobilized the citizens of Montreal. Writing on August 14, Lévis noted that he had "encouraged the women, the nuns, the priests and generally everyone in the town, to directly or indirectly help in this work upon which the survival of the country depended."

Once harvested, the wheat was threshed and milled. Normally, millers sifted their flour, but on August 18 Vaudreuil ordered Rigaud to skip this step to speed up production and avoid losing flour in processing. After that, Cadet's workers poured the processed flour into barrels, which were loaded aboard schooners that carried them downriver to the provision depot at Batiscan. From Batiscan, all that remained was to run the flour past Holmes's squadron to Quebec.

There, the Montreal flour played a crucial role in the defense of Canada. Following the French victory in the harvesting campaign, Rigaud proclaimed to the people of the Montreal area that "the battles waged against the English since their arrival before Quebec, where they have experienced the valor and courage of the troops and Canadians, made them lose hope of taking this colony by force. They have no hope except regarding provisions, which they imagine we lack entirely."

But thanks, he continued, to the Montreal harvest, "at the very moment when we were about to run out, we have found . . . a resource to sustain us, as well as allowing us to thwart the designs of our enemies."

So dramatic was the change in French fortunes that a Canadian notary credited divine intervention: "God, who seems not to want to abandon us, has demonstrated his omnipotence in granting us the most abundant harvest."

The Battle of Montreal remains one of the quiet epics of North American military history. Strategically speaking, Canada in August and September 1759 was shaped like a barbell, with the Quebec Promontory at one end and the Montreal Plain at the other, linked by the supply line running down the St. Lawrence River.

With Canada's adolescent and adult male population tied down on the frontiers, Canada's women, elders, and children served in the government of Montreal and along the lines of communications. All of Canada had become a besieged fortress, with virtually every Canadian who was old enough, young enough, or fit enough to help taking part in the defense of Quebec.

Everyone sacrificed; everyone contributed. The soldiers and militiamen who faced Saunders and Wolfe at Quebec were only the tip of the spear, the point of the arrow. And, like a spearhead or arrow point, they were less than useless without the shaft composed of Canada's noncombatants.

CHAPTER 13

Alarms in the Night

PANET ON GUARD

At 10:00 a.m. on September 2, the alarm sounded in Quebec. The British were on the move. The city garrison, including Jean-Claude Panet, stood to arms. When the call to duty came, Panet was ready to serve, although perhaps not very happy about it. "This movement alerted the city," he wrote. "I went, after drinking two shots of brandy, to Magnan's house at the Saint-Jean gate, where we drank a third shot while on the alert. We went to the Saint-Louis gate where the commandant, after observing this maneuver, sent me . . . to go to the Saint-Louis battery."

(Magnan was Jean-Baptiste-Paschal Magnan, adjutant of the Quebec militia, a thirty-three-year-old merchant who had fit out the schooner *Angélique* to cruise as a privateer in 1758.)

Forty boats traveling between three British ships and the Île d'Orléans and Point Lévis had caused the alarm. From his post at the Saint-Louis battery, Panet watched as the boats returned to the point and island, ending the alert.

FALSE ALARMS

This alert was only the latest in a series of nerve-jangling alarms that shook up the city garrison and sent troops from Beauport, summoned by a signal from Quebec, marching to the rescue. Rare in July, increasingly frequent in August, by September they had become an almost daily occurrence.

The first of these alerts had occurred at 4:00 a.m. on July 1 when firing in the Beauport camp caused an alarm in the city. The garrison stood to arms. "We in the city," wrote the supply clerk, "were very worried until at last someone noticed that it was nothing." Rumor suggested that the generals had been testing the readiness of the Canadians.

The next alert produced actual casualties. Vast flocks of migrating pigeons had been flying over Quebec for weeks. On July 24, six hundred Quebec militiamen abandoned their posts and swarmed across the countryside beyond the Plains of Abraham. In the largest engagement of the campaign up to that point, they blazed away in all directions, firing into the flock. Before the shooting stopped, one Canadian had been killed and another wounded. At Beauport, the intense, continuous gunfire convinced Montcalm's army that the militia were fighting off a British assault. Two thousand troops marched for the Anse des Mères, just west of the city walls.

Afterward, a thoroughly unamused colonial administration prohibited firing at pigeons within three miles of the city. The Canadians, demonstrating a fine lack of appreciation of both military discipline and the power of the absolutist state, resolutely ignored the prohibition. Displaying his usual cynicism, the supply clerk observed that "in practice [following the publication] of that regulation everyone fired everywhere; here is how all regulations are obeyed in Canada."

More seriously, at eight o'clock the next morning, word came that the British were landing at Saint-Michel, just above the Anse au Foulon. When a messenger hurried to the Beauport camp, accompanied by the sound of gunfire from upstream, Montcalm sent 250 troops, including three companies of grenadiers. Upon arrival, they discovered that the British had attacked six French gunboats anchored in the cove. Two had been captured, three escaped to Cap-Rouge, and one ran aground.

Twelve days later, at 2:00 a.m. on August 6, a scout canoe sighted British boats off Quebec. The alarm sounded; the garrison stood to arms; French batteries fired into the darkness, hoping for a hit; five companies of regulars reinforced the detachment guarding the Anse des Mères.

On August 12, a soldier reported firing at the Anse des Mères. It turned out to have come from the south shore of the St. Lawrence, where the Royal Navy, including William Hunter, was landing troops at Saint-Antoine after the failed attacks on Pointe-aux-Trembles.

Another report of British landing craft off the Anse des Mères arrived on the night of August 27. The Beauport camp sent 250 reinforcements to Quebec. Lieutenant Colonel Félicien de Bernetz, the acting commandant of the garrison, divided them between Lower Town, the Anse des Mères, the Anse au Foulon, and Sillery.

All of these false alarms turned out to be the result of miscommunication or misinterpretation of British actions. Yet as far as combatants like Panet and Magnan were concerned, any one of them might have heralded a desperate battle for Canada.

DANGER IN THE WEST

Most of the alerts came from immediately west of Quebec. This area was of great concern to the supply clerk, who worried constantly that the French had committed too many resources east of the city and too few to the west. "Beauport," he complained, "is constantly guarded as if it were impossible for the enemy to go anywhere else." A healthy respect for British amphibious mobility heightened his concerns. "I don't know just now where they intend to go," he had written on July 21, "but truthfully I think that they will go anywhere they want."

The supply clerk's worries were not misplaced and demonstrated a real appreciation of terrain and tactics. Approaching from the east would force the British to fight their way through the defenses of the Beauport shore, across the Saint-Charles River, and up the side of the Quebec Promontory.

A western approach would be much more straightforward. Sixty-yard cliffs defended the French perimeter, but these cliffs were merely formidable, not invulnerable. "This place is naturally fortified," he wrote, "but I can't keep myself from worrying about the area." In some areas, the slopes were gentle enough to allow potential attackers to climb up the promontory. Alternatively, the British might land at the Anse des Mères or Anse au Foulon, small coves at the base of roads and ravines leading up from the river.

Of the two coves, the Anse des Mères caused the supply clerk the greatest concern. The ravine that led down to it began on the southern edge of the Buttes-à-Neveu (a fifty-foot hill that dominated both the city walls and the Plains of Abraham). A roadway from Lower Town ran along the shoreline, up the ravine, and across the hill. Attackers landing at the

Anse des Mères could advance quickly up the roadway and occupy the Buttes-à-Neveu, launch simultaneous attacks on Upper and Lower Towns, or even seize the Porte Saint-Louis in a coup de main. British artillery at Point Lévis could cover the noise of the landing and disrupt attempts by the city garrison to intervene. Landing at the Anse au Foulon would allow the British to advance across the Plains of Abraham to seize the buttes.

In July and August, the French army at Beauport had repeatedly demonstrated its ability to quickly reinforce the detachments guarding the cliffs west of Quebec. Bougainville now commanded a chain of outposts west of Quebec and a powerful mobile column above Cap-Rouge. Yet the supply clerk continued to worry. Bougainville, he wrote, "has a lot of ground to guard; I'm always afraid of surprises."

CHAPTER 14

The Last Convoy to Quebec

IN SIGHT OF VICTORY; ON THE VERGE OF DEFEAT

By the first week of September, many French soldiers and civilians at Quebec began to think that the worst was over. After a long, hard summer, victory was in sight. "Monday morning," wrote Récher on September 3, "the English burned their entrenchment at the Falls [of Montmorency], after evacuating [their troops] and carrying off their effects over the previous days." Morale soared. Cadet's critic wrote that "General Wolfe seems to have lost any hope of taking Quebec . . . His preparations and maneuvers herald an imminent departure . . . Everyone in Quebec is filled with joy, and the highest hopes have replaced hardship and despair."

Equally encouraging reports arrived from Montreal. According to a British engineer and six soldiers captured on Lake Champlain, the British would halt their advance toward Montreal at Fort Saint-Frédéric, partway up the western shore of the lake. "This news," declared Récher, "which seems to be true, made us rejoice, all the more because it assures us that the country will not be taken, at least this year, and moreover that the English will not burn the harvest of the government of Montreal, which is so abundant that people think it will amount to sixteen hundred thousand *minots* [2.4 million bushels] of wheat."

With the campaign apparently drawing to a close, French generals and administrators began to prepare for life after the siege. Montcalm allocated winter quarters for the French regulars and winter garrisons for French outposts. Quebec, he decided, would house a token force of just two hundred regulars. With the government of Quebec devastated by the British, the regiments that had been billeted there in previous years would winter in the Montreal area. The colonial administration advised Quebec's more affluent residents to secure their own supplies of flour, because the Crown would cease to provide them with rations after the departure of the British.

Yet even as more and more of Quebec's defenders caught sight of the proverbial light at the end of the tunnel, a logistics catastrophe loomed. Once again, the army and the garrison were running out of food. Within days, the French would be forced to abandon Quebec and march toward their provisions at Batiscan and Montreal.

Frequent, heavy rains had prevented local wheat crops from maturing and made road transport almost impossible. The army at Quebec had completely exhausted local supplies of food. In the course of the summer, foraging soldiers had stripped the French-controlled parts of the countryside of anything edible. They had carried off oxen, cattle, pigs, poultry, peas, and other vegetables to the point that the intendant, François Bigot, lamented that "all the countryside for two leagues around has been ravaged."

So severe were these depredations that French soldiers were causing more damage than the British. When the French reoccupied Montmorency, Panet noted that "the habitants found their wheat standing and less damaged than that which had been near our soldiers."

On August 28, Montcalm reduced the rations. The daily allowance of bread for soldiers, militiamen, and warriors fell by a quarter; the civilian bread ration was cut in half. In place of the missing bread, fighters received a shot of brandy. These cutbacks were just enough to allow the food that arrived on August 23 to last for another five days.

The garrison of Quebec remained on guard; the Beauport army was ready to fight. But logistically, Montcalm's army was hanging by a steadily fraying thread. Canada's survival depended upon the arrival of wheat from Montreal that would have to reach the army by September 15.

THE CONVOY

Help was on the way.

On August 28, Cadet was forty miles west of Quebec, awaiting the arrival of a snow laden with wheat and flour from Montreal. When it arrived on the twenty-ninth, he had the cargo transferred to bateaux, which proceeded downriver.

Two days later, the Royal Navy pounced. As the bateaux approached Pointe-aux-Trembles, about twenty miles from Quebec, a British warship opened fire. The crews pulled for shore, beached the bateaux, and landed the provisions. They had saved their cargo and boats, but the convoy suffered a delay at a time when every hour counted. Worse, Holmes's squadron hovered offshore, trapping the bateaux at Pointe-aux-Trembles. Cadet's workers stored some of the provisions in the local church and loaded the rest into carts.

Then came salvation. In the first days of September, Holmes's vessels abandoned their station off Pointe-aux-Trembles and drifted downstream on the ebb tide. Vaudreuil immediately decided that the convoy should take advantage of this narrow window of opportunity. "Would it not be possible," he wrote to Bougainville, "to profit from this moment to bring the rest of the *munitionnaire*'s provision convoy by water? If so, the people who conduct it must keep on their guard, all the more because we are not in a position to take risks where our provisions are concerned."

The British redeployment gave Cadet's convoy a clear run to Cap-Rouge and eased French fears that the British might land west of Quebec and sever communications with Batiscan and Montreal. Inside Quebec, however, the supply clerk still worried about a landing at the Plains of Abraham. On September 1, he noted that "Beauport is constantly guarded, everyone apparently thinks that it is impossible for them to land elsewhere; I hope so but I'm afraid that they're wrong."

The discovery on September 2 that the British had laid six buoys off the shore at Beauport inflamed suspicions that the invaders were about to make a second attack on the entrenchments. The next day, the sight of boats moving between British warships anchored between the Île d'Orléans and Point Lévis caused the alert in the city that had Jean-Claude Panet gulping down shots of brandy and scrambling to his post. At Beauport, the army lined the entrenchments.

As tension rose, a friendly fire incident occurred in the suburb of Saint-Roch. A sergeant of the Languedoc Regiment failed to hear a sentry's challenge and continued to advance without speaking. The sentry fired, killing him instantly.

On the fourth, a schooner from Montreal arrived at Cap-Rouge with a cargo of flour from Montreal. Around four o'clock in the afternoon the next day, a British frigate opened fire on the schooner, which received three roundshot in the hull. This touched off a gun battle between the frigate and two French gunboats that fired about fifty rounds before the British backed off.

The firing caused another alert. At noon, a British deserter reported that there would be a diversionary attack at Cap-Rouge and a real attack on Lower Town. Cannon fire from upstream (from the engagement between the British frigate and the French gunboats) seemed to confirm this intelligence. The French stood to arms and remained on guard throughout the night of September 5–6.

On the sixth, Panet joined his militia unit at the Porte Saint-Louis when a message from Bougainville reporting British troops marching along the south shore caused another general alert. Five detachments of regulars and a company of grenadiers reinforced the city garrison.

Both Panet and the supply clerk were now increasingly perturbed by British movements west of Quebec. Panet wrote, "They have made marches along the south [shore] that worry us." As for the supply clerk, he noted that "the enemy continues to cannonade and bombard us as usual, with even more intensity; they have made several movements with their ships from Cap-Rouge to Pointe-aux-Trembles, without making any landing, although their troops are in landing craft and ship's boats most of the time."

On the seventh, Cadet's bateaux reached Cap-Rouge, six miles from Quebec. That night, French scouts on the river off Beauport reported hearing the sounds of British boats. Lookouts on the shore spotted the boats. The battalions at Beauport stood to arms as the British serenaded them with a cheer—"houra" (hurrah). The troops remained on alert until dawn, but the British never came.

Still anxious about the weakness of the detachment guarding pathways up the Quebec Promontory, the supply clerk wrote on September 8 that "M. Devergor [Louis Du Pont Duchambon de Vergor] remains constantly with 150 men in the Foulon area, and the son of M. Lafontaine is at Anse des Mères with 15 or 20, these are all the people we have in a place that it seems to me is very exposed."

On the ninth, more bateaux reached Cap-Rouge, carrying thirty-three tons of flour and 525 bushels of wheat, all from Montreal.

Cadet now had two weeks of supplies for the army at Cap-Rouge, but the resupply effort had stalled. Some of the bateaux proved to be too unseaworthy to continue to Quebec, perhaps as a result of being hastily run ashore at Pointe-aux-Trembles. On the morning of September 10, Cadet sent a team of four caulkers to Cap-Rouge to repair the bateaux.

Also on September 10, French lookouts at Sillery noticed three British boats landing on the south shore. Aboard the boats, reported their commander, they caught sight of "several officers, wearing many colors, there was one wearing a blue overcoat with lots of lace, the said overcoat has gold buttonholes."

Under the eyes of the French, the British officers climbed up the riverbank. While a screen of soldiers stood guard, they walked about for a while then returned to their boats and ascended the river with the rising tide. The French commander thought that they were laying out a new camp.

In the early morning of the eleventh, the Royal Navy placed more buoys off the Beauport shore. Although the French noticed the floats bobbing in the river after sunrise and promptly removed them, their presence alarmed Montcalm: "These buoys have caused some concern; people fear for the floating battery and that the place [Quebec] might be captured."

Above Quebec, French lookouts observed that most of Holmes's squadron had floated down to Sillery. Many of Quebec's defenders believed that they would continue downstream past the city as part of a general evacuation of the British forces from Canada. Not the supply clerk. He hoped that this was the case, "but I always fear some surprises."

On September 12, Montcalm and Captain Fiacre-François Potot de Montbeillard, the senior artillery officer at Quebec, inspected the Beauport lines. Montbeillard was feeling very confident that day. "I calculated that our troops, thus entrenched, were invincible."

He might have been even more confident had he known that six miles upstream at Cap-Rouge, Cadet's convoy was ready to make the final run to Quebec past Holmes's squadron. The bateaux had been repaired; tidal conditions would be ideal. Around 2:00 a.m., the falling tide would accelerate the current, carrying the bateaux swiftly and silently downriver. If all went well, they would arrive at Quebec well before first light at 5:30 a.m.

Vaudreuil had already instructed Bougainville to improve communications between convoys and outposts: "As it is important to be prepared for any obstacle, I ask you to please in future have a signal or password and warn the outpost commanders." Now he ordered that Bougainville's troops remain as silent as possible while convoys passed by. As Vaudreuil later explained to the minister of marine, "The necessity of having our provisions carried by water at night was the reason our outposts were warned to make less noise."

Cadet, now at Sillery, warned Bougainville, who was at Cap-Rouge, that the convoy would leave that night. Otherwise, he added, "I will have to send carts tomorrow to collect that food which I absolutely need; but if it comes by water, it will save us a great deal of effort."

Bougainville in turn ordered outpost commanders between Cap-Rouge and Quebec to expect the convoy and take appropriate action. In particular, he warned, the bateaux "must be challenged in a way that does not alert the enemy."

At the outposts, the garrisons stood to arms; lookouts lined the cliffs. Vergor, in command of the detachment at the Anse au Foulon, left a record of his precautions that night. Writing in the third person, he declared, "On the twelfth, he received orders to allow a convoy of bateaux carrying provisions for Quebec to pass on the night of the twelfth and thirteenth. He consequently gave his orders and warned his sentries to allow the boats in question to pass, but only after challenging them."

Within the city, the supply clerk recorded another day under fire: "The ships had not moved since yesterday, the winds were nonetheless from the southwest, very brisk, the weather was very good; they cannonaded and bombarded us as heavily as usual from Point Lévis."

At the Beauport camp, morale was high. "The twelfth of September," wrote Benoît-François Bernier, a French staff officer, "everyone considered the campaign to have finished, and finished gloriously for us; the enemy until then had done nothing but make useless attacks."

BEAUPORT NIGHTS

Around 1:00 a.m. in the early morning of September 13, lookouts along the Beauport shore heard the sounds of oars creaking in rowlocks and boats moving through the water. Montcalm ordered the army to stand to, then

sent an aide to warn Vaudreuil. Montbeillard rode along the French fortifications, making sure that his batteries were ready to engage the enemy.

With his troops deployed and ready for action, Montcalm spent the
night pacing the shoreline, thinking about Cadet's bateaux. His Scottish
aide-de-camp, Lieutenant James Johnstone of the *troupes de la marine,*
paced beside him. In a fictionalized dialogue between Montcalm and
Wolfe that Johnstone wrote after the campaign, he had Montcalm recall,
"I repeated often to Johnstone that 'I trembled lest they [the bateaux]
should be taken, as that loss would ruin us . . . having only provisions for
two days subsistence to our army.'"

Around 3:00 a.m., a guard canoe returned to report sighting British boats off Beauport. A detachment of militia took up position on the
beach where the French expected the British to land. A field gun arrived to
support the militia. Another canoe set out to reconnoiter. As it returned,
wrote Montbeillard, "the city then made the appropriate signal to indicate
that something had happened."

This had occurred many times before, and every time an alert had
produced a powerful, immediate response. Whatever the hour, whatever
the circumstances, reinforcements from Beauport raced westward to inves-
tigate and, if necessary, repel a British attack. On September 13, for the first
time, the French at Beauport chose to ignore a warning. Already on the
alert, they may have believed that it referred to the apprehended British
assault on their position.

Toward sunrise, Montcalm's troops at Beauport heard firing from
upstream. At first, Montcalm feared the worst: the Royal Navy had inter-
cepted Cadet's bateaux. So did Montbeillard: "We did not doubt that the
provision convoy which we were expecting had been attacked and perhaps
captured."

But as the sky brightened and no word came from the west, Montcalm
relaxed. In another passage from the dialogue, Johnstone has him say, "I
began to have more quietness of mind, upon reflecting that if anything
extraordinary had happened I would have certainly been informed of it."

On the river, all was calm. The rising sun revealed the British boats,
beached on the eastern tip of the Île d'Orléans. With the sun up and no
threat in sight, Montcalm dismissed his troops back to their tents.

While the army stood down, a frantic Canadian pounded across the
pontoon bridge at the Saint-Charles River and gasped out his story. He
claimed to have come from the Anse au Foulon, where he had served in

Vergor's detachment guarding a roadway running up the side of the promontory. "This Canadian," wrote Montbeillard, "told us with all the most unmistakable signs of fear that the enemy was on the heights and that he alone had escaped."

Montbeillard was not concerned. In August and September, any number of frantic messengers had run to Beauport to report British attacks that never happened. Besides, the French officers were much too knowledgeable to accept the Canadian's story at face value: "We knew all too well the difficulty of penetrating by that point [the Anse au Foulon], however weak the defense, and did not believe a word of this story from a man who seemed to us to be crazy with fear. I went back to my house for a rest."

Above Quebec, the firing continued. At Beauport, Montcalm and Johnstone returned to Montcalm's headquarters. There, in defiance of all stereotypes, the French general and the Scottish lieutenant sat down to enjoy a soothing cup of tea.

Near the Saint-Charles bridge, Pierre-André Gohin, Comte de Montreuil, Montcalm's adjutant general, encountered another fugitive from the Foulon. Less skeptical and more dynamic than Montbeillard, Montreuil reacted instantly. The Guyenne Regiment had camped near the Saint-Charles; Montreuil sent two detachments, then the entire battalion, into action with orders "to march to the vicinity of Anse des Mères, a landing place between the city and the Anse au Foulon where the enemy has landed, and to attack them, weak or strong."

Each battalion of the Beauport army kept a detachment on standby to be on hand to respond to any emergency. Montreuil ordered these troops over the bridge as well, then rode off to warn Montcalm.

Between 6:00 and 7:00 a.m., Montcalm and Johnstone finished their tea and made their way to Vaudreuil's headquarters to ask about the continuing cannon and musket fire from upstream. There, they learned that a British army had landed at the Anse au Foulon and marched to the Plains of Abraham. Literally and figuratively, the enemy was at the gates.

III

BATTLE

CHAPTER 15

The Anse au Foulon

WOLFE MAKES A PLAN

When Panet, Récher, Marie de la Visitation, and the supply clerk fought fires, dodged shells, cared for the wounded, and migrated across the city seeking a safe place to sleep, it probably never occurred to them that their tormentors at Point Lévis had a disturbing problem of their own. General Wolfe had disappeared.

Throughout the campaign, Wolfe had used the Royal Navy to commute from his headquarters at Montmorency to British outposts along the St. Lawrence River. Around the middle of August, the soldiers, sailors, marines, and gunners at Point Lévis realized that no one had seen Wolfe for days. They began to worry that their general might be seriously ill.

Their fears were confirmed on August 22. Wolfe had collapsed. "The extreme heat of the weather in August," he wrote, "and a good deal of fatigue, threw me into a fever."

The details of this illness are obscure, but it was enough to knock him off his feet, thoroughly alarm his troops, and reduce him to despairing inactivity for weeks. Confined to his headquarters, confined to bed, Wolfe brooded over the campaign, his health, and his suddenly faltering career. He confessed to Saunders, "I am sensible of my own errors in the course of the campaign" and called himself "a man that must necessarily be ruined." He told his mother about "my plan of quitting the service, which I am determined to do at the first opportunity." He began to talk about dying, telling his doctor, "I know perfectly well you cannot cure my complaint; but pray make me up so that I may be without pain for a few days, and able to do my duty; that is all I want." He no longer expected to take Quebec and wrote to Saunders to arrange transportation for his soldiers to winter quarters in the British colonies, "supposing (as I have very little hope of) they do not quarter here."

Too sick to lead his troops into battle, too feeble to meet his officers to deliver routine orders, unable to see a way out of his predicament, Wolfe ceased to exercise command of his army. "I found myself so ill & am still so weak," he wrote, "that I begged the general officers to consult together for the public utility."

Asking his brigadiers for a new plan to take Quebec represented a radical departure for Wolfe. Other generals might hold councils of war; Wolfe expected obedience, not advice, from even his most senior subordinates. Earlier in the campaign, the chaplain James Gibson, passing on what he'd heard in the wardroom of HMS *Vanguard*, wrote of Wolfe, "Every step he takes is wholly his own; I'm told he asks no one's opinion, and wants no advice." On July 7, an outraged Wolfe noted that one of three brigadiers attached to his army actually "threatened [him] with [a] parliamentary inquiry into his conduct for not consulting an inferior officer & seeming to disregard his sentiments!"

By August, Wolfe was barely on speaking terms with the brigadiers. This extract from the private journal of an anonymous officer on Wolfe's staff faithfully reflects his general's opinions. Speaking of the brigadiers Robert Monckton, George Townshend, and James Murray, he wrote, "The first, in action, timid, and of a poor capacity. The second, turbulent and inexpert in military affairs. The third, the very bellows of sedition; envious [and] ambitious."

The brigadiers gave as good as they got. In a celebrated letter, Townshend told his wife that "General Wolfe's health is but very bad. His generalship . . . is not a bit better." An equally acerbic James Murray bluntly asserted that Wolfe's "orders throughout the campaign shew little ability, stratagem, or fixt intention." Yet Murray also harbored wistful regrets regarding the divisions among the British high command: "I wish his [Wolfe's] friends had not been so much our enemys."

Wolfe's illness forced the general and his brigadiers to observe a temporary truce. The brigadiers, after meeting with Vice Admiral Saunders, suggested an attack above Quebec in the vicinity of Saint-Augustin: "When we establish ourselves on the north shore, the French general must fight us on our own terms; We shall be betwixt him and his provisions, and betwixt him and their army opposing General Amherst. If he gives us battle and we defeat him, Quebec and probably all Canada will be ours."

Here, finally, was the plan that had eluded Wolfe all summer. The brigadiers' proposal pitted British strength, the amphibious mobility that allowed them to concentrate a force anywhere on the river, against French weakness, their dependence on supplies from Batiscan and Montreal. For the first time since Montcalm and Vaudreuil had fortified the Beauport shore, the British would be in a position to force the French to react to them.

The plan was not perfect. No plan is. The low shoreline at Saint-Augustin was ideal for a major landing. The French, however, had posted a strong mobile column in the area. This column could not defeat Wolfe's army all by itself. But it could delay the British and buy time for the main body of the French army to respond. With the British twelve miles away from Quebec and posing no immediate threat, Montcalm would have had plenty of time to muster his forces and strike back.

Moreover, there was always the chance that dropping an army across the French supply line would *not* force Montcalm to give battle on British terms. Marching to meet the British at Saint-Augustin would bring the French that much closer to their supplies. Local knowledge might give them a way to bring provisions to their troops or troops to their provisions. No matter how far inland the British might push, there was always the chance that the French might be able to go just a little bit farther. (There was, in fact, a road two miles inland running parallel to the river that would have taken French provision convoys right past a British beachhead.) Nonetheless, the brigadiers' plan represented a solid chance for the British to turn the campaign around.

By August 31, Wolfe was strong enough to appear outside his Montmorency headquarters for the first time in weeks. Still unwell, he passively accepted the Saint-Augustin operation. When he wrote to the British government on September 2, Wolfe expressed no confidence in the brigadiers' plan, saying only, "I have acquiesced in their proposal." Writing to Saunders, he declared, "The generals seem to think alike as to the operations; I, therefore, join with them, and perhaps we may find some opportunity to strike a blow."

· · ·

This lack of enthusiasm might have affected Wolfe's redeployment of his forces for a landing at Saint-Augustin. Instead of concentrating his army to fight a major battle, he divided his army into two components heading off in opposite directions.

One component went downstream. Wolfe placed sixteen hundred rangers and light infantry (about a quarter of all the troops available for operations) under the command of Major George Scott "to burn all the country from Camarasca to the Point of Lévis." Scott's troops, wrote Wolfe, were to remain in the field until "that country . . . is totally destroyed."

To support the infantry, Rear Admiral Durell sent two lieutenants and about two hundred sailors from his squadron aboard the five warships that would escort the schooners carrying Scott's soldiers. They had orders "to act in conjuncture with Major Scott . . . in destroying the buildings and harvest of the enemy on the south shore."

Major George Scott, who had served in Nova Scotia since 1750, struck his first blow against the French as a spymaster who persuaded a French official at Fort Beauséjour to become a British agent. When the British captured the fort in 1755, assisted by the information provided by this agent, Scott commanded a battalion of Massachusetts provincials. During the expulsion of the Acadians that followed the siege, he led his troops on a sweep through formerly French-controlled territory, burning villages that might harbor Acadians who escaped the deportation.

Placed at the head of a battalion of light infantry, Scott served under Wolfe during the siege of Louisbourg and played a dramatic role in the British landing at Gabarus Bay. When Louisbourg surrendered, he took a detachment of light infantry and American rangers to the St. John River in what is now New Brunswick. Under the command of Robert Monckton, Wolfe's future brigadier, Scott hunted down Acadian refugees and led an expedition up the Petitcodiac River burning houses, killing livestock, and destroying stores of grain.

Scott and his principal subordinate, Captain Joseph Goreham, had served together in the Nova Scotia garrison. Born in Barnstable, Massachusetts, Goreham began his military career in 1744 at age nineteen when he joined a ranger company serving at Annapolis Royal. Promoted to captain in 1752, he led his rangers in a long series of skirmishes with Mi'kmaq warriors defending their homeland against a steadily escalating invasion by British soldiers and settlers. In 1758, he took part in the siege of Louisbourg; in 1759, he followed Wolfe to Quebec, where in September he joined Scott's force of rangers, light infantry, and sailors.

Rangers, the Special Forces of their day, were Americans from the frontier, usually employed for scouting and raids that were beyond the capacity of the average British regular. The light infantry were elite regulars, "chosen men" picked for their agility and marksmanship and used for skirmishing and special operations. Rangers at Quebec wore black, sleeved vests, short black sleeveless jackets with blue facings, and blue Scots bonnets. The light infantry wore similar jackets and vests, colored red, and cut-down tricornes that resembled jockey caps. Their jackets had a leather pocket on either side of the chest to hold musket cartridges.

In the Royal Navy, only officers wore uniforms—blue coats, white vests and breeches, and tricorne hats. Sailors dressed for comfort and safety in short jackets (usually blue), vests, checked shirts, neckerchiefs, and loose white trousers. For action ashore or in small boats, they carried "a firelock, cutlass, and cartridge box full of ammunition."

On September 1, 1759, Scott and his troops embarked aboard schooners at Point Lévis and headed downstream for a rendezvous with Durell's squadron and the sailors and ships of the expedition.

As the operation began, Scott split his force in half. One column under his direct command would burn every farm between Kamouraska and Saint-Ignace. Goreham and a second column would ravage the countryside between the Rivière du Sud (near Saint-Ignace) and Point Lévis.

Scott's flotilla, accompanied by the frigates *Echo, Eurus,* and *Trent* and the bomb (mortar) vessel *Baltimore,* sailed on the seventh for Kamouraska, the northeastern limit of Canadian settlement. One day later, Goreham's troops, escorted by HM Sloop *Zephyr,* set out for the Rivière du Sud, just below the Île d'Orléans.

The soldiers and sailors were in high spirits. As Scott's detachment departed, noted the master of HMS *Trent,* they "saluted Admiral Durell with 3 cheers."

The ranger David Perry described their voyage and goals from the perspective of a private soldier: "The country this side [of] the river was settled to the distance of about one hundred and sixty miles below. All the rangers, and one company of Light-Infantry of the British, were ordered to go aboard vessels, and to sail down the river as far as it was settled, then to land and march back towards the City, burning and destroying, in our course, all their buildings, killing all their cattle, sheep and horses, and laying waste the country far and near."

The forty-four hundred regulars that made up the remaining three-quarters of Wolfe's deployable force remained on guard at Point Lévis and the Île d'Orléans or moved upstream to land at Saint-Augustin.

Between September 1 and September 3, the British evacuated the Montmorency camp. Ashley Bowen was there:

> At 2 am our First Lieutenant with pinnace and cutter and longboat went to Montmorency to embark General Wolfe from thence. I went in the cutter and rendezvoused on board the Porcupine till 9 at which time the soldiers set fire to all the houses and marched down to the landing and embarked.

On September 4, a flotilla of empty landing craft passed Point Lévis heading upriver. Bowen continued to ferry troops below Quebec:

> At noon we all set off from about two miles below the west end of Orleans with all General Wolfe's troops, and they began to cannonade us as we passed very briskly, but we all came through safely. At 3 p.m. landed on Point Levy . . . Boats all returned to their respective ships.

On the fifth and sixth, the troops set off upriver on foot to rendez-vous with the flat-bottomed boats, marching up the west bank of the St. Lawrence.

Above Quebec, Wolfe's regulars boarded the ships of Holmes's squadron and prepared for a landing at Saint-Augustin. There, if all went according to plan, they would fight the battle that would decide the fate of Canada and the French and British Empires in North America.

Then nature intervened. Between September 6 and September 9, "fresh gales with hard rain" lashed the Quebec region. Wolfe postponed

Cap-Rouge. The Quebec Promontory (right) ended at Cap-Rouge. Cadet's bateau convoys assembled here before making their final run to Quebec. Wolfe's landing craft began their voyage to the Anse au Foulon at Cap-Rouge; Bougainville and his fifteen hundred elite troops remained here until 8:00 a.m. on September 13 and did not reach the Plains of Abraham until after the battle.

the Saint-Augustin landing. Half the troops disembarked at Saint-Nicolas, on the south shore, to reduce overcrowding aboard the ships and did not come back aboard until the twelfth.

Wolfe's mood matched the weather. He wrote on September 9, "I am so far recovered as to do business, but my constitution is absolutely ruined, without the consolation of having done any considerable service to the State, or without any prospect of it."

Unhappy with the Saint-Augustin plan and compelled to wait for the weather to clear, Wolfe sought another option. He left his floating headquarters on HMS *Sutherland* and traveled downstream. According to his staff officer, "During this interval the General went in Captain [Matthew] Leslie's schooner and reconnoitred close by the shore from Cap Rouge down to the Town of Quebec . . . The General having observed the Foulon, thought it practicable and fixed on it for the descent."

. . .

As Wolfe surveyed the Foulon, Scott and Goreham went into action. At Kamouraska, an entry in the master's log for HMS *Eurus* combined shipboard routine and military operations: "Opened a cask of pork No 130 . . . 282 pieces short 1 piece, at noon boats employed landing the troops from the transports."

"The people," wrote Perry, "fled at our approach, and we caught plenty of pigs, geese, and fowls; and while part of our men were busied in carrying the squalling and squealing booty to the vessels, there came a Frenchmen out of the woods, and ran into the house. We followed after and took him, and carried him a-board the vessels."

The Canadians did more than flee. After burning fifty-six houses, Scott's troops had just settled down to prepare a stolen dinner of pickled salmon when they heard three or four shots. Searching the area, they discovered that local farmers had killed and scalped a ranger. Perry's company, commanded by Captain Moses Hazen, set off in pursuit:

> We marched a little distance and came to a large opening. Here we surrounded and took a Frenchman, from whom we endeavored to learn what had become of those who fired the guns, but he would not tell: and the Captain told him he would kill him if he did not, at the same time directing us to draw our knives, upon our doing which he fell to saying his prayers upon his knees, firmly refusing to tell. Finding him thus resolute and faithful to his friends, the Captain sent him a prisoner to the shipping, and we went to our cooking again.

At the Rivière du Sud, lashed by the same rain that had thwarted Wolfe's assault on Saint-Augustin, Goreham's soldiers piled into ship's boats and headed for shore. Covered by *Zephyr*'s guns, the troops disembarked without meeting any resistance. Strong currents, however, caused some difficulties. "At the landing of the troops," wrote the master of the *Zephyr*, "the boat was stove [and] lost oars belonging to her."

Upstream, Wolfe continued his preparations for a landing above the city. The reconnaissance on September 9 had not been his first look at the Anse au Foulon. Back in July, when Holmes's ships first passed above Quebec, Wolfe had contemplated an amphibious attack west of the city. For all its daunting height, the Quebec Promontory appeared to be much more vulnerable than the heavily fortified Beauport shore. Townshend noted on July 18, "They [the French] seem to have neglected above the town entirely."

On the nineteenth, Samuel Holland accompanied Wolfe on an excursion west of Quebec. Wolfe, who had served with Holland at Louisbourg, had great confidence in his abilities and courage. The engineer, he wrote in 1758, "has been with me the whole siege, & a brave active fellow he is, as ever I met with; he should have been killed a hundred times, his escape is a miracle . . . when there is any business to be done . . . [you] will find him the most useful man in it."

Now Wolfe sought to use Holland's talents in his search for a crack in the geographic barriers that protected Quebec. Together, wrote Holland, they "went towards Etchemin River, nearly opposite the Cove of Foulon, now Wolfe's Cove." At the Etchemin, he continued, Wolfe "halted & in the French language asked me if ever I had observed whether the Indians & Canadians hutted on the brow of the hill came often to the water side. I offered him my spy glass, & he accepted, & could see them now playing in their canoes, & then bathing in the river."

Wolfe continued upstream to the Chaudière River, then turned back to the Etchemin, where he ordered Holland to keep an eye on the French at the Anse au Foulon, noting the number of people who came down to the beach, the time they came down, and how long they stayed. (Holland speaks only of himself, but Wolfe may have posted observers to monitor other potential landing sites.)

Holland took up his telescope and began to watch "the movements made by the people opposite, who I found came down to the beach merely for the purposes of washing, beating their clothes, linen etc. Their stay was but short, as they soon disappeared in the bush, & were afterwards seen at the top of the hill spreading & drying their clothes. Some Indians & Canadians likewise were seen, but not in any number, or in any shape on their guard."

Wolfe abandoned his plan to strike above Quebec but did not forget the Anse au Foulon. Back at Point Lévis, speaking in French, he confided his intentions to Holland: "That [the Foulon], my dear Holland, that will be my last resort."

Holland afterward maintained, not very convincingly, that Wolfe had planned to land at the Foulon all along and the attacks at Montmorency and elsewhere had been diversions. Wolfe's actions suggest that he meant exactly what he said, that landing under the cliffs at the Anse au Foulon was a last resort that might be worth a second look at some moment in the future, if all else failed. On September 9, that moment came.

The next day Wolfe took a party of key officers downstream to the Etchemin River "in order," wrote his staff officer, "to show them the places he thought most accessible." This group, which was sighted by a French officer at Sillery, included Holmes, Monckton, Townshend, Murray, Lieutenant Colonel William Howe of the light infantry, Commander James Chads, the "regulating captain" responsible for the landing craft flotilla, and the engineer Patrick Mackellar.

Writing in his journal, Mackellar summed up British knowledge of the Anse au Foulon as of that afternoon: "The place is called Toulon [sic] . . . The bank which runs along the shore is very steep and woody, and was thought so impracticable by the French that they had then only a single picket to defend it. This picket, which we supposed might be about 100 men, was encamped upon a bank near the top of a narrow path which runs up from the shore; this path was broke by the enemy themselves, and barricaded with an abatis [a barrier of felled trees, with the branches sharpened and pointing toward the enemy]."

Elsewhere on September 10, Scott's detachment was still burning houses in the vicinity of Kamouraska. "[We] marched off," wrote Perry, "three or four miles to a back village and got there before it was light. We were divided into small parties, as usual, in order to take what prisoners we could. I was stationed in a barn with the Lieutenant's party, and while we lay there, a Frenchman came along smoking his pipe, and one of our men, an outlandish sort of fellow, put his gun out of a crack in the barn, and before we had time to prevent it, fired upon the man; the shot carried away his pipe, but did him no other injury and he ran off. But when the Captain heard of it, he flogged the soldier severely."

Farther upriver, the Royal Navy went into action alongside Goreham's detachment when HM Sloop *Zephyr* "landed the seamen to destroy the corn [and] sent on board 2 prisoners."

. . .

Why the Anse au Foulon instead of Saint-Augustin? Wolfe gave his answer in a general order on September 12: "The troops will land where the enemy seems least to expect it." Wolfe's knowledge of French expectations came from a French soldier who had deserted to the British the day before. The deserter had informed Wolfe "that the French Generals suspect we are going higher up, to lay waste the country, and destroy such ships and craft as they have got above; and that Monsieur Montcalm will not be prevailed on to quit his situation, insisting that the flower of our army are still below the town."

Surprise aside, a landing at the Foulon had much to recommend it.

Three obstacles stood between Wolfe and Quebec—the geography of the Quebec Promontory, the city wall stretching across the east end of the promontory, and Montcalm's army. For Wolfe, a landing at the Anse au Foulon offered an opportunity to overcome all three obstacles with minimal risk to the British.

Wolfe respected Quebec's geography, "the strongest country perhaps in the world to rest the defence of the town and colony upon." Landing at the Foulon made this geography work for him. So formidable were the cliffs that the French garrisoned the edge of the Quebec Promontory with tiny outposts that could be overwhelmed by a surprise attack. The result was a long stretch of lightly defended shoreline between the French troop concentrations east and west of Quebec. An attack at the Anse au Foulon would fail or succeed in a matter of minutes. This would give the amphibious British time to either reinforce their beachhead or return to their boats and let the tide carry them downriver to safety before French reinforcements arrived.

Wolfe was less impressed with Quebec's landward fortifications. Everything he knew about these fortifications came from a report prepared by Patrick Mackellar, who had been a prisoner in the city for a few months in 1756. As a prisoner, Mackellar had never been allowed near the walls, but he supplemented his observations with material from Charlevoix's *Histoire et description générale de la Nouvelle France*. According to Mackellar, Quebec's principal defense on the land side was "a wall of masonry three or four feet thick, [that] . . . seems to have [been] designed only against small arms." He predicted that this wall "could hold out but a few days, against a sufficient force properly appointed."

Wolfe accepted Mackellar's assessment: "The defences are inconsiderable, and our artillery very formidable." He further believed that the French shared this belief: "Their plan of defence seems to rest more upon the strong nature of the country, than the walls & fortifications of the town." Securing a beachhead at the Anse au Foulon would place Wolfe's troops a twenty-minute walk from Quebec.

Should Montcalm march out to meet them, Wolfe had no doubt of the outcome. Faced, in his opinion, by nothing more formidable than "a numerous body of armed men (I cannot call it an army)," his troops would smash Quebec's defenders and begin a short, victorious siege.

Whatever his reasons, as soon as Wolfe made his decision, he found himself at war with both his brigadiers and the Royal Navy. These adversaries quickly discovered that the ailing, diffident Wolfe who allowed subordinates to plan his operations had vanished forever.

On the morning of the twelfth, Robert Monckton, second-in-command of the British army, stormed aboard HMS *Sutherland* to confront Wolfe, then stormed away after an acrimonious meeting. He was presumably the "officer of note" who Holland reported to have "ridiculed the thought [of landing at the Foulon] as impracticable."

The staff officer recorded Wolfe's comments following this exchange: "After he [Monckton] was gone Mr. Wolfe said to his own family [staff] that the Brigadiers had brought him up the River and now flinched: He did not hesitate to say that two of them were cowards and one a villain."

Later that day, the regulating captain James Chads boarded the *Sutherland* to meet with Wolfe. Chads, an amphibious expert, had shared a boat with Wolfe at Montmorency. But what might have been a bonding experience counted for nothing on September 12. Chads, said the staff officer, "made many frivolous objections such as that the heat of the tide would hurry the boats beyond the object, &c, &c."

Rather than addressing Chads's concerns, Wolfe brusquely informed the commander that he "should have made his objections earlier, that should the disembarkation miscarry, that he [Wolfe] would shelter him from any blame, that all that could be done was to do his utmost. That if Captain Chads would write any thing to testify that the miscarriage was G. Wolfe's and not Captain Chads that he would sign it. Chads still persisting in this absurdity, the General told him he could do no more than lay his head to the block to save Chads, then left the cabin."

Holmes later made a more detailed exposition of naval reservations. He called the landing "the most hazardous & difficult task I was ever engaged in—for the distance of the landing place; the impetuosity of the tide; the darkness of the night; & the great chance of exactly hitting the very spot intended, made the whole extremely difficult."

He further objected to a unilateral decision that ignored the Royal Navy's technical skills and knowledge of the river above Quebec. "This alteration of the plan of operations was not, I believe approved of by many, beside himself [Wolfe] . . . it was highly improbable that he should succeed."

That evening, Monckton, Townshend, and Murray sent a joint letter to Wolfe, demanding to know "the place or places we are to attack." At 8:30 p.m., half an hour before the advance guard was due to board the landing craft, Wolfe sent back a very stiff reply: "My reason for desiring the honour of your company with me . . . yesterday was to show you . . . the situation of the enemy & the place where I meant they should be attacked."

The brigadiers objected. The navy objected. Wolfe didn't care.

With a new plan in hand, Wolfe became fully himself, brisk, energetic, and confident, sweeping obstacles aside and ignoring contrary advice. There would be no more talk of failure or limited goals. After weeks of sickness, passivity, and despair, James Wolfe was back in the game and playing to win.

CHAPTER 16

Standing on Guard

THE ROAD UP THE PROMONTORY

Jean-Guillaume Plantavit de Lapause de Margon, the officer to whom Montcalm addressed his misgivings about the Oswego campaign, inspected the Anse au Foulon during the summer of 1759. "This cove," he wrote, "is very suitable for a landing, there is a good road [up the cliff]."

Now the Côte Gilmour and part of Avenue George VI, the road ran diagonally up the face of the Quebec Promontory and across the Plains of Abraham until it joined the Grande-Allée. Although steep, the road was suitable for marching troops and hauling heavy artillery, providing amphibious attackers with easy access to the capital of New France.

For six weeks after the arrival of the British, the Anse au Foulon remained unthreatened and undefended. With the British fleet safely downriver from Quebec, there was no possibility that Wolfe might attempt a landing there. But on the night of July 18–19, Saunders sent five warships upstream past the city, shielded by darkness and covered by a furious bombardment from Williamson's batteries at Point Lévis.

As soon as French lookouts sighted the ships, the Quebec garrison stood to arms. Forty soldiers rushed across the Plains of Abraham to the Anse au Foulon. There, they joined a body of Native American warriors encamped nearby and prepared to defend the Foulon against a British attack.

The following morning, nine hundred militiamen and regulars marched west from Quebec. Quickly reinforced by three hundred infantry and two hundred cavalry, they placed detachments at pathways and ravines where the British might ascend the promontory.

A few hours later, Captain François-Marc-Antoine Le Mercier, Canada's senior artillery officer, arrived on the scene with two cannon and a mortar. He used this artillery to establish a battery at Samos, on the west side of the Foulon. The battery went into action almost immediately and shot up both HMS *Squirrel* and Wolfe's flat-bottomed boat.

LOUIS-ANTOINE DE BOUGAINVILLE

On August 7, the defense of the Anse au Foulon and the north shore between Quebec and the Jacques Cartier River became the responsibility of a calculus-loving former musketeer, Louis-Antoine de Bougainville.

Louis-Antoine de Bougainville. As much a scholar as a soldier, Bougainville changed the course of history by warning his outposts to expect a French provision convoy, then failing to inform them that its departure had been postponed.

Twenty-nine years old in 1759, the son of a prominent Paris lawyer, Bougainville had been involved in the Seven Years' War from almost the very beginning.

Following the outbreak of fighting in the Ohio valley in 1754, the French sent a special ambassador to London to seek a diplomatic solution. Bougainville, fluently bilingual, came along as the ambassador's secretary. Also in 1754, he published the first volume of his *Traité du calcul intégral* (Treatise on integral calculus). This brilliant work quickly won him an international reputation, membership in Britain's Royal Society, and the patronage of the French minister of war.

Returning to France, Bougainville resumed the military career that began in 1751 when he joined the Mousquetaires Noirs. In 1756, the minister of war promoted him to captain and assigned him to serve in Canada as Montcalm's aide-de-camp. When he briefly returned to France carrying Montcalm's dispatches in the fall of 1758, Bougainville received a promotion to colonel and the Croix de Saint-Louis.

On August 9, Montcalm sent the fledgling colonel to take command of the French forces above Quebec. Describing his new assignment and authority, Bougainville wrote, "I was then detached . . . to defend the lines of communication between the army . . . and the ships that held our provisions and Montreal. There were five hundred men scattered along that line . . . under my orders."

When the British evacuated their camp at Montmorency and Wolfe sent more troops above the city, Montcalm reinforced Bougainville with a body of militiamen and regulars, giving him a powerful force of twenty-two hundred.

Two hundred and eighty of these troops guarded outposts along the cliffs from the Anse des Mères to the Cap-Rouge River. A further 820 served in detachments above the promontory between Cap-Rouge and the Jacques Cartier River. Most of them were good, average regulars and militiamen.

The elite of Bougainville's force, and of the army as a whole, formed a mobile column twelve hundred strong, ready to reinforce threatened positions and fight off British attacks. These included the grenadiers and volunteers from the regular battalions. Grenadiers were the tallest, strongest soldiers in the army; volunteers the French equivalent of British light infantry. The Canadians attached to this column were among the finest in the militia and included a cavalry detachment.

OUTPOSTS

Two of Bougainville's outposts guarded the Anse au Foulon. To the west, by September the Samos battery mounted three twenty-four-pounder cannon and one thirteen-inch mortar. Thirty soldiers from the Languedoc Regiment served the guns.

François-Prosper de Douglas, a Franco-Scottish captain of that regiment, was in command. Born in France, Douglas had served in Canada since 1755. Fortunate in both love and war, he had married the Canadian noble Charlotte de La Corne in 1757 and received the Croix de Saint-Louis after the Battle of Carillon in 1758. Earlier in the Quebec campaign, he had been co-commander of the unsuccessful attack on the British batteries at Point Lévis.

On the east side of the Foulon, separated from the Samos battery by two ravines carved out of the side of the cliff by the Saint-Denis Brook and a second creek, another detachment guarded the road leading up the promontory from the beach. About one hundred militiamen and *troupes de la marine* occupied a tented camp sixty yards above the river. Some of these troops provided a chain of sentries along the edge of the cliff. The remainder stood ready to defend the trench and abatis that blocked the roadway fifteen yards down the road to the cove.

Captain Louis Du Pont Duchambon de Vergor of the *troupes de la marine* commanded the road guards. A native of Sérignac, France, Vergor had made his career in Acadia. Wounded twice during the first siege of Louisbourg in 1745, Vergor later received the Croix de Saint-Louis. Returning to Acadia in 1754, he commanded Fort Beauséjour until its capture by the British the following year. Released by a prisoner exchange, he served on the Lake Champlain frontier and at Quebec. On September 2, 1759, Vergor took charge at the Anse au Foulon.

Ten days later, Bougainville informed Douglas and Vergor that a convoy of nineteen bateaux carrying flour from Montreal would pass by that night on the way to Montcalm's army. Vergor placed his detachment on alert and ordered his sentries to allow the bateaux to pass after establishing their identity. Then both Vergor and Douglas joined their lookouts and settled in to await the convoy whose arrival or nonarrival would save or doom Quebec.

CHAPTER 17

Ashore in the Dark

RIDING THE TIDE

The British began their advance to the Plains of Abraham on the evening of September 12 off Cap-Rouge. At 9:00 p.m., the first of Wolfe's soldiers clambered down the sides of Holmes's ships into landing craft and ship's boats.

For most of the evening, the tide had been moving upriver, making downstream travel slow and difficult. But just before ten o'clock, the moon rose above the Île d'Orléans. Its gravitational field first slowed the tidal flow to a standstill, then began to drag the waters of the St. Lawrence ever faster downriver.

As the tide turned, more British troops marched north from Point Lévis. Until that night, the Second Battalion of the Royal Americans and the Forty-Eighth Regiment had been guarding British camps and batteries there and on the Île d'Orléans. Now, led by Lieutenant Colonel Ralph Burton of the Forty-Eighth, they left these installations in the hands of the marines. Beginning at 1:00 a.m., they headed up the south shore toward the Etchemin River.

With them came a Royal Artillery column led by Lieutenant Colonel Williamson in person. Williamson described their march upriver: "The night of the 12th I sent up in boats as many more [guns] as made 22 in all including some royal howitzers & that night I took Captain [William] Macleod (next for duty) & a detachment to complete the whole &

together with Colonel Burton & a large party set out about 1 in the morning for Goreham's post [at the mouth of the Etchemin] opposite to the plains of Abraham & concealed our selves in the hedges."

There, they waited until landing craft could ferry them across the St. Lawrence to join up with the main body.

Knowing the risks of a night landing at the Foulon, Saunders, Holmes, and Wolfe had each planned a diversion to draw French attention elsewhere. Below Quebec, Saunders filled his ship's boats with sailors and marines and sent them across the river to hover off Beauport. They allowed themselves to be seen and heard, to give the impression that "our grand aim was still below Quebec & pointed towards Beauport." Ashley Bowen described his role in this operation: "Admiral made a signal for all boats manned and armed, and we went and made a feint at the River St. Charles, and at 11 I repaired on board our ship Pembroke."

At Cap-Rouge, Holmes let his ships drift upstream with the flood tide in order, wrote Townshend, "to draw the attention of the enemy above."

Finally, Wolfe placed Samuel Holland in command of two gunboats, each mounting a twelve-pounder cannon and crewed by thirty marines and sailors. Once the real attack began at the Anse au Foulon, Holland would open fire on the French outpost at Sillery to "make a false alarm" and confuse the French regarding the precise location of the British assault.

When the ebb tide reached a speed of 2.4 knots, the British began to move. "At 2AM," wrote the master of HMS *Seahorse,* "the flat bottomed boats dropped down the river per signal with troops." "Now was the time," wrote Edward Coats, "to strike a stroke which in all probability would determine the fate of Canada."

Eight landing craft carrying four hundred light infantry were out in front. Led by Lieutenant Colonel William Howe, future commander of the British army in North America during the early years of the American Revolution, the light infantry were to spearhead the British assault.

Disembarking just above the Anse au Foulon, they would cross the Saint-Denis Brook, dash up the roadway, and overwhelm the French defenders. A detachment of twenty-four volunteers, commanded by Captain William DeLaune, would lead the attack.

Behind the light infantry came twenty-two more landing craft and a collection of ship's boats carrying the first wave of the main body. Like all of Wolfe's soldiers that morning, the troops carried nothing but their weapons, seventy rounds of ammunition, two days of rations, and canteens filled with rum and water. Their tents and other equipment remained below Quebec and would not be delivered until after the battle.

Despite his argument with Wolfe and lack of confidence in the operation, James Chads remained in command of the landing craft. Wolfe warned his officers to respect the authority of their naval counterparts, who alone had the expertise to bring the boats to their destination: "No officer must attempt to make the least alteration or interfere with Captain Chads particular province lest (as the Boats move in the Night) there be confusion and disorder amongst them . . . the officers of the navy are not to be interrupted in their part of the duty."

It took half an hour for the landing craft to clear the anchorage. At 2:30 a.m., three armed sloops laden with troops, two six-pounder field guns, and extra ammunition for the landing force followed them downstream. Williamson had detached Captain John Yorke, "as being known to General Wolfe," to command the guns. Wolfe sent Yorke and his gunners "on board the armed sloops to regulate their fire, that in the hurry our own troops may not be hurt by our artillery."

An hour later, HMS *Lowestoft, Seahorse,* and *Squirrel* and the transports *Laurel* and *Adventure* departed, carrying the soldiers of the second wave. *Sutherland* remained off Saint-Nicolas for an hour to "keep an eye on the enemy's motions, their floating batteries, and small craft." Holmes warned every ship's captain to be prepared for any contingency: "Should any accident occasion so much disaster as to oblige our troops to retreat, the Captains of the Lowestoft, Seahorse, Squirrel & Hunter are directed to go each of them in a boat to where the flat bottomed boats are & give all the assistance in their power to prevent confusion in the boats & facilitate the speedy & safe re-embarkation of the troops. And should any accident happen to Captain Chads, Captain [William] Adams [of HMS *Hunter*] is directed to go in & take the command of the boats."

· · ·

Landing at the Anse au Foulon. In this action-filled painting, flat-bottomed boats carry the first wave to the shore, light infantry climb the cliff, the French at the Samos battery and the Anse au Foulon open fire, British troops disembark and form up on the beach, ships carrying the second wave arrive on the scene, and landing craft ferry the third wave across the river. Off in the distance, French and British armies clash on the Plains of Abraham.

Once on their way, the British flotilla traveled close to the north shore, alert for navigational hazards and following the same course used by French provision convoys. The current accelerated as the ebb tide progressed; Chads's landing craft moved faster and faster. The boats reached a maximum speed of 5.7 knots (6.56 miles per hour) at the narrows, now crossed by the Pont de Québec and the Pont Pierre-Laporte, then slowed to 4.3 knots (4.95 miles per hour).

Swept along by the tide, the British made good time. Around 3:00 a.m., the first eight landing craft fell in with the sloop *Hunter* off Sillery. Captain Adams passed on the news that two French deserters, variously described as coming from Guyenne, La Sarre, or Royal Roussillon, had paddled out to the sloop four hours before. Aboard HMS *Hunter,* they revealed that nineteen French boats carrying provisions were expected to come down the St. Lawrence to Quebec that night.

Armed with this information, the British bluffed their way past a series of French outposts. Captain Simon Fraser of Fraser's Highlanders, who had served in the Dutch army and spoke fluent French, responded to challenges by declaring that the flat-bottomed boats were, in fact, the French provision convoy.

AMPHIBIOUS ASSAULT

Around 4:00 a.m., the lead landing craft, commanded by Lieutenant Gordon Skelly, touched ground near the Anse au Foulon. Pehr Kalm had examined the beach and cliffs in 1749: "The shores of the river consisted . . . of a species of slate. They are very steep and nearly perpendicular here, and the slate of which they consist is black, with a brown cast. The slate is divisible into thin shivers, no thicker than the blade of a knife . . . the shore is covered with fine grains of sand which are nothing but particles of such mouldered slate."

Kalm made his observations in daylight. Skelly was looking into preindustrial darkness, illuminated by the quarter moon and the faintest hint of sunlight on the eastern horizon, all filtered through an overcast sky. Under these conditions, the sixty-yard cliff was a vast, dark, towering mass, blotting out the stars. The lieutenant's first thought was that the venture was impossible. His landing craft had beached at the "foot of the eminence, which seemed inaccessible."

The landing proceeded regardless. Seven more flat-bottomed boats grounded along the shore. Four hundred soldiers leaped over the bows. DeLaune pulled out his pocket watch. There was just enough light to make out the time. It was, he wrote two years later, precisely "seven minutes past four o'clock when the advance party landed at Anse de Foulon."

As the light infantry swarmed ashore, Howe and DeLaune pondered what to do next and perhaps spared a moment to reflect on the advisability of listening to the expert opinion of naval officers. Chads had warned that "the heat [speed] of the tide would hurry the boats beyond the objective." Chads had been exactly right. The light infantry had reached the north shore but in the wrong place. Wolfe had planned to land above the Foulon and make a quick advance up the roadway. The tide had carried the British some distance downriver. Their goal lay somewhere to the west, shrouded in darkness.

Instead of losing time looking for the road, Howe led his light infantry straight up the cliff. Either while searching for a reasonably scalable section of the slope or during the climb itself, the assault troops drifted apart in the darkness. They broke up into at least two groups, one led by Howe, another by Simon Fraser.

Some sections of the promontory in this area are steep but easily climbable. Others are practically vertical. Climbing over a fairly broad front, the light infantry encountered both these conditions, seeking the first and trying to avoid the second. Descriptions of their ascent reflect variations in the terrain.

Saunders reported that troops climbing the wooded sections of the cliff "were obliged to pull themselves up by the stumps & boughs of trees that covered the declivity." Edward Coats, who witnessed the assault from a flat-bottomed boat below a patch of exposed limestone, saw the light infantry ascending "with incredible difficulty climbing over the rocks."

The beach at the Anse au Foulon. Wolfe and his army disembarked on this beach in 1759. "Seven minutes past four o'clock . . . the advance party landed at Anse de Foulon . . . In less than a quarter of an hour we had assembled and had climbed the Height."

. . .

Down below, DeLaune and his twenty-four troops ran westward along the beach toward the Foulon road. The first eight flat-bottomed boats remained on the beach, ready to evacuate the light infantry if they were thrown back by the French.

While the light infantry scaled the promontory, the first wave of the main body reached the Anse au Foulon. More accurate or more fortunate in their navigation, their landing craft came much nearer the target than the first eight. Although still on the "wrong" side of the Saint-Denis Brook, they were conveniently close to the foot of the roadway.

As the first wave arrived, the soldiers and sailors in the boats and on the beach heard gunfire and saw muzzle flashes at the top of the cliff. The crackle of musketry might have drowned out the noise of the light infantry scrambling up the promontory, but it was more than a little alarming for the sailors and soldiers waiting on the beach or floating in the cove. "By the time we had run our boats ashore," wrote Skelly, "and the troops began to draw up, the enemy were no longer in doubt, and now began to fire irregularly from above, into us in the boats, which were scarce perceptible, it being extremely dark, but they killed one or two officers of the army, one midshipman, and several men in a little time."

John Knox listed the casualties in a single landing craft: "In the boat where I was, one man was killed; one seaman with four soldiers were lightly wounded, and two mortally wounded." Moments later, the Samos battery opened fire.

The sound of muskets, mortars, and cannon at the Anse au Foulon was Holland's cue to begin his diversion at Sillery. He ordered his gunners to fire; two twelve-pound cannonballs flew shoreward. The gun crews reloaded and fired again; a dark shape loomed out of the twilight. Seconds later, a British vessel slammed into Holland's gunboat. Flung unceremoniously into the St. Lawrence, he lost his musket, a gift from James Wolfe "which I deemed invaluable," and swam for his life amid the wreckage of his first and last nautical command. Bereft of musket, gunboat, and dignity, Holland floundered in the water until an armed sloop carrying ordnance stores appeared and took him in tow.

Back at the Anse au Foulon, Skelly and the landing craft crews waited in suspense: "Whilst our people were attempting to mount the eminence, we kept our boats close to the foot of it in case of a retreat, and we for some time heard nothing but a war whoop or cry made use of to make their numbers seem greater, as they fired upon us from the bushes."

Neither Wolfe nor anyone else in the boats and on the beach knew if the up-the-cliff attack would end in victory and an aggressive advance to the city walls or defeat and a humiliating retreat downriver. In the latter case, the failure of the light infantry assault would lead to the departure of the British army and fleet and the end of the Quebec campaign.

CHAPTER 18

Night Battle

DEFENDING THE ANSE AU FOULON

Just as they had expected, sentinels at the Samos battery sighted several bateaux coming down the river with the ebb tide just before 4:00 a.m. Douglas himself watched them passing within pistol shot of his position. One of his soldiers called out a challenge. The *troupes de la marine* officer Nicolas Renaud d'Avène des Méloizes recorded the ensuing dialogue.

> "Who goes there[?]"
> . . . "France!"
> "What regiment?"
> . . . "Don't make noise! These are the nineteen boats from Cap-Rouge, loaded with flour."

Douglas allowed the boats to pass and sent a runner on ahead to alert sentries to the east.

When a watcher at the head of the Foulon roadway spotted the boats, Vergor ordered him to make a challenge. Once again, a voice from the darkness replied that they were carrying provisions to Quebec.

Vergor, however, noticed that instead of making their way toward the city, the boats were turning in at the Anse au Foulon. He called his troops to arms and ordered them to open fire. As the Canadians fired into the predawn twilight, Vergor wrote out a message to Bernetz, still the acting commandant of Quebec, informing him that British troops were landing at the cove. Across the ravine, alerted by the sound of gunfire at the Foulon, the Samos battery roared into action, flinging shot and shells toward the British landing craft.

At the Foulon, everything appeared to be going according to plan. As far as the French could tell, the attempt to surprise the garrison had failed. The British were still in their boats, and Vergor had a hundred muskets blazing away at them, supported by Douglas's artillery. Before long, a lookout ran up to Vergor and told him that French reinforcements were advancing from the east along the edge of the cliff.

Moments later, muskets fired into the backs of Vergor's soldiers. The defenders heard a British cheer—"Huzza!"

Vergor's first reaction was utter shock that the British had slipped past his lookouts and caught him by surprise from the rear. But he recovered quickly and turned his troops around to face the attack.

In the ensuing engagement, Vergor was wounded twice. One musket ball broke his leg; a second shattered his hand. The British closed in and made prisoners of Vergor and about half his detachment.

The rest of Vergor's troops refused to give up. Commanded by his lieutenant, they fell back toward Quebec and took cover amid the wheat fields on the western edge of the Plains of Abraham. After a brief interval of calm, the British lunged into the wheat. They wounded the lieutenant and captured most of his force. A few Canadians slipped away and continued to resist. "The remainder," observed Patrick Mackellar, "made their escape along the edge of the bank towards the town, and with some small flying parties posted there kept firing upon some of our boats."

Two Canadians ran all the way to the French camp at Beauport, carrying the news of the British landing. The remaining survivors presumably linked up with French forces on the Plains of Abraham later in the morning.

STORMING THE QUEBEC PROMONTORY

When Howe's troops reached the top of the promontory, they turned left and began a cautious advance to the west. A sentry called out a challenge.

Captain Donald MacDonald, another Fraser Highlander, answered in the colloquial military French he'd learned in the French army. Giving a convincing imitation of an irascible French officer, wrote Knox, MacDonald "came up to him [the sentry], told him he was sent there, with a large command, to take post, and desired him to go with all speed to his guard, and to call off all the other men of his party who were ranged along the hill, for that he would take care to give a good account of the B—— Anglois, if they should persist; this *finesse* had the desired effect, and saved us many lives, &c."

With the sentries out of the way, the light infantry advanced to Vergor's post and attacked from behind. Down on the beach, Skelly continued to listen and wait: "Presently we were apprised of our troops having found a way up by hearing their voices as they gave a loud Huzza! and fell amongst the enemy, by which means the musketry ceased, and at daybreak we found that they had got possession of the grounds above."

The road at the Anse au Foulon. "A convenient road . . . wide enough even for carriages." After Samuel Holland cleared away the French fortifications, Wolfe marched his battalions and sailors hauled Yorke's guns up the roadway to the top of the Quebec Promontory.

The French survivors fell back toward the Plains of Abraham; Howe made no attempt to follow. Instead, his troops prepared to defend themselves against an unidentified force advancing from the east. Two light infantrymen stepped up and challenged the newcomers. They proved to be Simon Fraser and his troops, who had lost touch with the main body during the climb up the cliff. Reunited, the light infantry charged after the French and attacked once more.

As fighting raged atop the promontory, DeLaune's detachment of twenty-four volunteers reached the Saint-Denis Brook. They turned right and raced up the roadway. By the time they reached the trench and abatis, Howe had overcome Vergor's detachment. They completed their ascent without incident. DeLaune checked the time again. It was about 4:20 a.m. "In less than a quarter of an hour," he wrote, "we had assembled and had climbed the Height."

The exact timing of Wolfe's arrival remains uncertain. Soon after he reached the landing site, however, he was on his way again. "Some of our boats," wrote Mackellar, "had by mistake dropped down too far that way [downstream], where the general was obliged to follow in his own boat to order them back." Wolfe performed this operation while under fire from survivors of Vergor's detachment who were sniping from the top of the cliff.

When Wolfe returned to the cove, the wounded and prisoners were on their way down to the beach. Wolfe and Major Isaac Barré, his adjutant general, disembarked and ascended the promontory. They almost certainly walked up the road, allowing Wolfe to see for himself if it was suitable for troops and artillery.

As soon as they reached the top, Wolfe sent Barré back down to the beach to order the first wave to remain in their landing craft "until he had an opportunity of knowing the enemy's strength there, & whither & whether they might not be in numbers sufficient to prevent his establishing himself."

But when Barré reached the cove, he found the entire first wave ready to disembark. "Knowing how much General Wolfe was desirous to bring the enemy to an engagement," he wrote, "& thinking from the knowledge he had of Mr. Wolfe's intentions, that the orders he had received were in consequence of his not expecting the troops could be got landed so soon," Barré ordered the troops ashore. When he reported back to Wolfe, the general "was much pleased to find himself established on shore with his army sooner than expected."

After a shaky start, the landing had been a complete success. More inclined to give credit to the army than the navy, Wolfe told the staff officer that he was "highly pleased with the measures Colonel Howe had taken to gain the Heights, wished that Mr. Howe might outlive the day that he might have an opportunity of showing his merits to the government."

In landing at the Anse au Foulon, Wolfe executed a daring plan with caution and circumspection, taking every possible precaution to limit the danger to his troops and himself. Wolfe was brave, not reckless. He planned an assault that would place the minimum number of troops at risk and ordered a pause in the landing to prevent needless loss of life in the event of failure.

Regarding his personal safety, Wolfe dressed inconspicuously in the plain red coat, vest, and breeches that were an unofficial battle dress for British officers. He carried a musket and bayonet instead of wearing a sword. While perfectly willing to risk his own life, Wolfe did so as a prudent professional rather than a gallant adventurer. "You may be assured," he wrote to his uncle in May 1759, "that I shall take all proper care of my own person, unless in case of the last importance, when it becomes a duty to do otherwise. I never put myself unnecessarily in the way of danger."

Wolfe furthermore had every intention of surviving the coming battle, if at all possible. His conversations with Chads and others reveal that win or lose, Wolfe was already making plans about what he would do at the end of the campaign.

With the landing site and road secured, part of the light infantry scattered in an arc about the head of the road to cover the beachhead. The others worked their way along the edge of the cliff toward Quebec, clearing out pockets of resistance.

Holland, by this point, had been "towed on shore by an artillery boat" at the Anse au Foulon. When the hapless engineer crawled onto

From the cove to the battlefield. Wolfe and his army followed this road (referred to as the "Foulon road" in the text), running along the cliff above the river, from the Anse au Foulon to the Plains of Abraham. The Martello tower atop the Buttes-à-Neveu marks the southern end of Montcalm's battle line.

the beach, soaking wet, he fell in with Vergor at the foot of the roadway. The two soldiers, neither of whom had had a very good day, traded stories of their experiences that morning. Vergor, despite his wounds, retained sufficient strength to energetically curse "les Diables d'Anglois" who had overrun his position by attacking from behind, something he'd thought was impossible.

This conversation concluded, Holland headed up the road and took charge of clearing away the French fortifications. Troops working under his supervision tore down the barricade and filled in the trench. With the removal of these obstacles, the British secured the use of "a convenient road . . . wide enough even for carriages."

Down on the beach, the disembarkation of the first wave proceeded smoothly and efficiently. "This grand enterprise," wrote Knox, "was conducted and executed with great good order and discretion; as fast as we landed, the boats put off for reinforcements, and the troops formed with much regularity." When the roadway opened for traffic, battalion after battalion marched up the Quebec Promontory.

At 5:34 a.m., the sun began to rise. Light flooded across the St. Lawrence River, the Quebec Promontory, the city, and Beauport. By 6:00 a.m., *Lowestoft, Seahorse, Squirrel, Laurel,* and *Adventure* were passing Sillery, where *Hunter* joined the flotilla. The French opened fire and killed John Memy, a sailor aboard HMS *Lowestoft*. At 7:00 a.m., the ships anchored off the Anse au Foulon.

To minimize confusion, Holmes had assigned a precise position for each type of vessel in the cove: "The flat bottomed boats will be nearest the enemy's shore. The armed vessels & vessels with ordnance will be without them. The men of war will be without the armed vessels, & the two transports will be without the men of war ready to disembark the troops when the flat bottomed boats come for them."

The Samos battery, reported *Seahorse,* "fired several shot over us . . . but [the ship] received no damage." *Squirrel,* less fortunate, "had several shot fired at us which cut away part of our running rigging, two went through our flying jib and one through our hull abaft the fore chains."

Soon afterward, the Samos battery came under attack. A detachment of Wolfe's grenadiers charged the battery. Most of Douglas's thirty soldiers abandoned the cannon and picked up their muskets. Douglas formed them up between the British and the guns. Behind them, gunners wheeled a cannon around to face the British. The soldiers of Languedoc fired a volley; the twenty-four-pounder fired a single shot. Howe's light infantry arrived and joined the attack. Douglas and his troops remained at Samos long enough to spike the cannon and mortar, then withdrew down the side of the cliff.

With the loss of the Samos battery, the French presence at the Anse au Foulon had been reduced to a single fugitive from Vergor's detachment who slipped into the brush near the Foulon road. "Famishing with cold and hunger," afraid to move, he remained in hiding for two days.

· · ·

Forced to defend themselves against the grenadiers and light infantry, Douglas's troops stopped firing at the vessels in the cove. Down below, landing craft rowed out to meet the ships and began to ferry the troops of the second wave ashore.

Just after 6:00 a.m., the tide reached low water, and the current began to slow down. Boats could now cross the St. Lawrence without fighting tidal flows. Sailors loaded the French and British casualties, including Vergor, into two landing craft that carried them across the river to a field hospital in the church at Point Lévis. Other flat-bottomed boats rowed to the south shore and returned laden with the soldiers and the artillery of the third wave.

MARCHING AND BURNING

Seventy-five miles downriver, Major George Scott and his marauders were beginning another day of marching through Canada. Scott kept a careful account of his achievements. One hundred and sixty-five homes burned on September 9 and 10, 120 on the eleventh, 55 on the twelfth.

While his commander kept score, David Perry described day-to-day life in Scott's detachment:

> The main party marched up the river, burning and destroying everything before them: and our company followed on some distance in the rear, collecting the cattle, sheep and horses, and burning the scattering buildings, &c. In this way we continued our march at the rate of about twelve miles a day. Every six miles we found large stone churches, at one of which we generally halted to dinner, and at the next to supper, and so on. We lived well, but our duty was hard—climbing over hills and fences all day; always starting in the morning before break of day . . . We were very often fired on by the enemy, and many of our men were killed or wounded in these excursions. When there was a bridge to cross . . . they would . . . secrete themselves on the opposite side and fire on us unawares.

The ranger Jeremiah Pearson was more concise when, on September 11, he summed up the entire day in a single sentence: "We marched from the church & burnt as we marched."

Goreham and his force were just as active. On the eleventh, wrote the master of HMS *Zephyr,* "the regulars and seamen [were] burning and destroying all on shore." On the twelfth, *Zephyr* "made the signal for all boats manned & armed & sent them on Crane Island [Île aux Oies] to burn & destroy there, there were several houses & [it] was a plentiful island."

HUMANS AND GEOGRAPHY

The French defeat at the Anse au Foulon, like many battles before or since, was largely the result of humans interacting with geography. The Quebec Promontory gave the French immensely strong natural defenses at the Anse au Foulon in the form of a sixty-yard cliff. Yet that same strength lulled their senior officers into a false sense of security that left the Foulon vulnerable to attack.

In planning the defense of the promontory, the French behaved as if rugged terrain and small outposts could stop a British landing all by themselves and hold out until reinforcements arrived. "I swear to you," Montcalm assured Vaudreuil, with reference to the Anse des Mères, which lay between the Foulon and Quebec, "that 100 men posted there could stop a whole army & give us the time to wait for daylight & march there from . . . [Beauport]."

On another occasion, he acidly reminded the governor-general, "We don't have to believe that the enemy has wings that allow him to cross [the river], disembark, ascend the pathway, and climb over the [city] walls, all the more because they will need ladders for the latter operation."

So confident were the French in the ability of a small garrison to fend off attack that they had neglected the elementary precaution of establishing a system of signals or mounted couriers to allow outpost commanders to quickly send for help in the event of an attack. Not that there was anyone nearby to answer a summons.

Deeply concerned by the possibility that the British might land in force above the Quebec Promontory or at Beauport, the French placed their mobile column of elite troops above the promontory and the main body downriver. There were no reserves stationed near the cliff-top out-posts. When the British attacked, Vergor and Douglas were on their own.

Moreover, the French failed to consider geography when they fortified the Foulon. They deployed their troops and constructed their barricade to defend against exactly the kind of attack that Wolfe planned to make—a rush up the roadway and a frontal assault on the trench and abatis. If British forces landed at the Foulon, lookouts would alert the abatis guard, which would be reinforced by troops from Vergor's camp at the edge of the promontory. This would have been a sound plan if the road was the only way up the cliff. But it wasn't.

When Lapause inspected the Anse au Foulon, he had warned that it wasn't enough to just throw an abatis across the roadway. "The slope near [the road]," he wrote, was "accessible, although rather challenging. To guard this vital post with so few people, we need to build a fortification that crosses the road ten fathoms [sixty feet] down and extends to the right and left according to the terrain."

His advice was ignored. The French constructed a fortification that blocked the road but guarded only a fraction of the vulnerable space.

For the British, on the other hand, the terrain presented as many opportunities as hazards. Formidable from a distance, the cliff near the roadway proved upon closer inspection to be climbable, providing a way up that allowed Howe to take Vergor's detachment by surprise from the rear. Boldness, skill, and a willingness to improvise enabled the light infantry to convert a potential setback—landing below their planned destination—into a brilliant success.

A second aspect of human interaction with geography facilitated this success. It was not a coincidence that the boats carrying Wolfe's first wave appeared off the Foulon at exactly the same time and place as the bateaux the French were expecting. The tides of the St. Lawrence that night were ideal for both a French provision convoy and a British amphibious assault.

Three individuals played key roles regarding the convoy. Bougainville canceled the operation but failed to inform his outposts. This lapse was serious, but the most important actors of the day were the two anonymous French deserters. When they paddled out to HMS *Hunter,* they carried with them the most valuable commodity on the battlefield—timely information. Knowledge of the French provision convoy gave the British the key that unlocked the French defenses at the Samos battery and the Anse au Foulon.

This knowledge, however, would have been less than useless to the British had they lacked a cadre of French-speaking officers. Political and economic instability in Scotland combined with an international market for military talent gave the British at least two officers who could take advantage of this intelligence windfall. Many British officers and soldiers, including James Wolfe, were reasonably bilingual. Donald MacDonald and Simon Fraser, on the other hand, didn't just speak French; they spoke it fluently and easily, "according to the French manner."

Vergor's force at the Anse au Foulon was composed of local militia-men from the parish of Lorette and regulars of the *troupes de la marine*. Their attackers were elite light infantry. Surprised and outnumbered four to one, the French resisted as best they could. Details of the combat are obscure, but Vergor, the only individual from the Foulon detachment whose fate is known, fought until he was badly wounded. His detachment rallied and continued to resist after losing its commander. Casualties from the brief engagement filled two landing craft.

With only thirty soldiers, Douglas had barely enough troops to work his guns, let alone defend the Samos battery. Nonetheless, when the light infantry and grenadiers attacked, he held out long enough to spike the cannon and mortar, thereby preventing the British from using them to defend Wolfe's beachhead.

The assault on the Anse au Foulon was a British success rather than a French failure. Taken by surprise, the French recovered quickly and defended their posts until overwhelmed by sheer numbers. The British, for their part, seized a crucial position quickly and efficiently and opened the road that would take them to the Plains of Abraham.

CHAPTER 19

The Plains of Abraham

WOLFE CHOOSES HIS GROUND

With a beachhead secured and the army coming ashore, Wolfe had a decision to make. Where was he going to fight the French?

A conventional European battle required an open space long enough to give armies room to assemble outside musket range, wide enough to allow them to form in line, and level enough to let them maneuver without breaking formation.

The Foulon road had taken Wolfe's army up the promontory and into a forest that the British called the Sillery Woods. This was no place to fight a battle, which meant that Wolfe needed to find a better venue, and quickly. He sent a messenger to collect Samuel Holland, still clearing away the French fortifications. Holland reported immediately "to Genl. Wolfe, with whom I went to reconnoitre the ground & marched [from] the spot . . . where we had first formed to the field of action, where the Battle was fought."

Striding through the forest, Wolfe, Holland, and their escort likely followed the road that began at the Foulon and ran along the cliff side until the trees fell away and they were standing on the western edge of the Plains of Abraham.

Looking east across the plains, they saw a landscape of pastures and wheat fields, bounded by forest to the west and cliffs to the north and south. Beyond the fields, instead of the walls of Quebec, vulnerable and exposed, Wolfe and Holland saw the Buttes-à-Neveu rising fifty feet above the plains and extending most of the way across the promontory.

Canadians had named the plains after Abraham Martin *dit* l'Écossais (nicknamed "The Scot"), a seventeenth-century settler who actually farmed land a little to the northeast. The surveyor general Joseph Bouchette published an idyllic description of this terrain in 1815. A half century after Wolfe and Holland reached the Plains of Abraham, neither land use nor ownership had changed significantly: "As one walks westward along the Grande-Allée, to the left there are many large properties belonging to the Hôtel Dieu and the Ursuline convent; on the other side, there are rich pastures and well-cultivated fields all the way up to the Sainte-Foy Road."

Pehr Kalm, the Swedish botanist, examined Quebec's pastures in 1749: "Almost all the grass here is of two kinds . . . narrow leaved meadow grass . . . [and] white clover . . . [T]he meadow grass . . . is pretty tall, but has very thin stalks. At the root of the meadow grass the ground is covered with white clover, so that one cannot wish for finer meadows than are found here."

In both wheat fields and pastures (former wheat fields), furrows a foot deep every two or three yards scarred the ground. The standing wheat was dense enough to conceal skirmishers.

Two east-west roads crossed the plains. Both still exist. To the north, the Chemin Sainte-Foy skirted the north side of the Buttes-à-Neveu and led to Quebec's Porte Saint-Jean. To the south, the Grande-Allée ran right over the hills on its way to the Porte Saint-Louis. The road from the Foulon crossed the low elevation on the south side of the plains, which was once known as Wolfe's Hill, and joined the Grande-Allée at the foot of the buttes.

Brush and trees covered other parts of the plains. A clump of trees stood at the base of the buttes, just south of the Grande-Allée, flanked to the south by a dense field of wheat. Two prominent hedges ran in a straight line along field boundaries from the Grande-Allée halfway to the Chemin Sainte-Foy.

Two shallow rainwater ponds lay south of the Chemin Sainte-Foy. A freshwater spring, which still survives, burbled on Wolfe's Hill. Just west of the plains, a Canadian physician had discovered another spring, which Kalm described as "a well of mineral waters which contains a great deal of iron ochre and has a pretty strong taste."

The Buttes-à-Neveu were a natural strongpoint. North of the Grande-

Allée, trees and heavy brush blanketed the hills, providing perfect cover for skirmishers. South of the road, wheat fields and fenced pastures supplied concealment and barriers. The hillside running down to the plains and the ground beyond the slope were a tangled nightmare for soldiers on the move. French officers describing this terrain used phrases like "difficult, obstructed, irregular, and partly covered with brush and fields of wheat" and "covered by shallow ravines and fenced fields."

These hills overlooked both the Plains of Abraham and Quebec's Upper Town. Whoever held the buttes could defy or destroy an army on the plains or cannonade the walls with impunity.

Wolfe, however, chose to ignore the buttes. If he followed the Foulon road, it took him directly to Wolfe's Hill, now occupied by the Pavillon Baillairgé of the Musée National des Beaux-Arts du Québec. Here, Wolfe chose to make his stand. He would deploy his troops in a line running north from Wolfe's Hill to the Chemin Sainte-Foy.

All was quiet. The firing at the Anse au Foulon had stopped. Wolfe, Holland, and their escort stood alone, a tiny patch of scarlet in a sea of green pastures and amber wheat fields. There was no sign of the French army. There was no sign, in fact, that Canada was even at war.

LOST IN THE FOG OF WAR

Inside Quebec, Bernetz struggled to make sense of conflicting reports of British landings, withdrawals, and attacks. He had already made the sig-

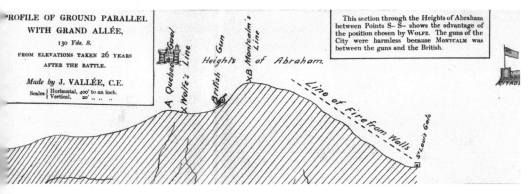

Profile of the Plains of Abraham, Buttes-à-Neveu, and walls of Quebec. The Buttes-à-Neveu dominated both the plains and the city walls.

nal to alert the army at Beauport. At 5:45 a.m., he flung everything into a quick, confusing note to Vaudreuil:

> A messenger from the Foulon just warned me that the enemy has landed at the Foulon, it is essential to send troops there immediately. M. de Vergor's messenger told me that there had been a great deal of firing. I think that the enemy has nonetheless departed, because the sound of muskets has stopped. Lower Town has been attacked by an enemy from the Anse des Mères.

Bernetz's letter highlights the crippling weakness of the French that morning. The British knew exactly what was going on—Wolfe and his army had landed at the Anse au Foulon to fight a decisive battle—and could plan and act accordingly. Engulfed in the fog of war, French officers like Bernetz, Montreuil, Montbeillard, and Montcalm had to make decisions based on stray bits of intelligence that might or might not be accurate. For all they knew, the landing at the Foulon could have been just a minor raid. Or a feint to draw the French army away from Beauport. Or yet another mistake by a nervous sentry with an overactive imagination.

SEIZING THE LOW GROUND

While Wolfe and Holland reconnoitered the plains, British battalions formed up along the road to the Foulon with their backs to the cliff, facing inland. Once Wolfe had reached his decision, he returned, recalled the troops from the Samos battery, and led his infantry to the Plains of Abraham. By 6:00 a.m., he was back on the plains, just as it began to rain. Under leaden skies and pattering raindrops, Wolfe ordered his grenadiers and light infantry forward to secure his chosen battleground.

Moving quickly, they expelled detachments of Canadians from the Quebec garrison from some houses along the Chemin Sainte-Foy and the brush and wheat fields at the foot of the buttes. The Louisbourg Grenadiers occupied Wolfe's Hill. The volunteer James Henderson took part in this operation. "The General did me the honour to detach me with a few grenadiers to take possession of that ground and maintain it to the last extremity which I did," he wrote.

Like William Hunter, Henderson had come to Quebec in search of an officer's commission. When Wolfe passed by Louisbourg en route to Canada, Henderson had just arrived to serve with the Twenty-Second Regiment. Discovering that it would remain behind at Louisbourg, he applied to the governor for permission to attach himself to the regiment's grenadier company, which was to form part of the Louisbourg Grenadiers. The governor, wrote Henderson, both granted permission "and recommended me strongly to General Wolfe."

Wolfe arranged the first three battalions to reach the field in a thin battle line across the Quebec Promontory. He then sent the light infantry to occupy the houses on the Chemin Sainte-Foy and form a screen along the north flank and the rear of his position.

As the morning progressed, more battalions and Yorke's two six-pounders landed at the Foulon and headed for the plains. The third wave crossed the river from the south shore in flat-bottomed boats and reached the field around 8:00 a.m.

Along with the infantry came a contingent from the Royal Artillery consisting of Lieutenant Colonel Williamson, Captain William Macleod, and four six-pounders, two royal howitzers, and their crews. They had, wrote Williamson, remained concealed until "the boats came for us at break of day when we rowed over as fast as the boats could take us." At the Anse au Foulon, Williamson pushed on ahead to join the main body. Macleod took charge of landing the guns.

PLANNING THE BATTLE

When James Wolfe led his army across the plains to Wolfe's Hill, he came with a plan. Bring Montcalm to battle, break the French army, establish batteries, and besiege Quebec. He would fight this battle on the tactical defensive, by taking position and waiting for the French to make a frontal assault. "We prepared" for battle, wrote Williamson, "expecting they would attack us."

The ground Wolfe selected was ideal for the engagement he planned to fight. To reach him, the French would have to cross a long interval of rough, broken terrain that would pose a formidable obstacle to movement while leaving Wolfe's troops a clear field of fire.

Yet in taking up this position, Wolfe had ceded the commanding heights of the Buttes-à-Neveu to the French. Emplaced on the heights,

Wolfe could have forced the French to fight a battle to prevent him from establishing batteries and blowing a breach through the walls of Quebec. If he had sent scouts over the buttes, he would have discovered that the guns on Quebec's ramparts were located on the sides of bastions to cover the approaches to the walls. They could not fire at the hills, which would have prevented them from supporting the French army in a battle for the buttes.

Down on the plains, it was Wolfe who would be vulnerable to bombardment from an opponent that could draw upon the artillery and garrison of Quebec and construct batteries and field fortifications out of the timber and stone from hundreds of shattered buildings. Wolfe, on the other hand, could only threaten the French by advancing up a rugged fifty-foot hillside and forfeiting all the advantages of the tactical defensive. If he remained in place, the only French soldiers he could threaten were those who ventured within musket shot of his position. To fight and win his battle, Wolfe needed complete and wholehearted cooperation from the French.

TAKING THE HIGH GROUND

Nothing happens instantly in war. As soon as word arrived of the British landing, Bernetz gave orders to reinforce the Anse au Foulon and the Anse des Mères. Yet by the time troops had been awakened and dispatched, Vergor and Douglas had been overrun, Wolfe had completed his reconnaissance, and British battalions were approaching the plains.

For the militia captain Jean-Baptiste-Paschal Magnan, who had shared a glass of brandy with Panet during a false alarm in August, the day began when he was "ordered . . . to go with thirty men to the Anse des Mères to oppose the enemy landing."

Magnan's mission was quickly overtaken by events. When he reached the Anse des Mères, there was not a Briton in sight, just twenty Canadians on guard. Heavily outnumbered and entirely unsupported, Magnan took his detachment over the Buttes-à-Neveu. They reached the Plains of Abraham around 6:00 a.m., just in time to see the leading elements of Wolfe's army emerge out of the Sillery Woods. Magnan led his troops forward and attempted to hold back the British advance.

A second detachment from the garrison rushed along the Chemin

Sainte-Foy, occupied the houses on the north side of the road, and opened fire on the British advance guard.

Steady pressure from Wolfe's grenadiers, however, compelled the Canadians to give ground. Magnan reported that his party was "forced by a vigorous resistance to submit to superior numbers and make a fighting retreat." At the houses, wrote the supply clerk, "the Canadians . . . fired vigorously, but as enemy numbers increased from moment to moment . . . there weren't enough of them to hold off the enemy."

Elsewhere, Captain Laurent François Lenoir de Rouvray of La Sarre led a party onto the field. He "traded fire with the enemy for a long time but was wounded many times and taken prisoner."

After a series of firefights, the Canadians conceded the field, but not the battle, to the British. An anonymous French officer recorded that "in spite of all the efforts the Canadians made to prevent them [the British] from assembling, they could neither halt them by their continuous fire nor oppose their march to within a quarter of a league from Quebec, because it proved impossible to send reinforcements from the Beauport camp quickly enough."

Magnan withdrew to the Buttes-à-Neveu, where he fell in with the detachments from the Guyenne Regiment that Montreuil had sent from Beauport. Mixing his pronouns, Magnan later recalled how "he [Magnan] . . . fortunately joined him [the senior Guyenne officer present] in time to prevent him from flinging himself against three nearby enemy columns . . . profiting from his [Magnan's] knowledge of the terrain, he [the Guyenne officer] deployed his troops advantageously and halted the enemy advance."

Following Magnan's advice, the Guyenne detachments occupied the leading edge of the Buttes-à-Neveu, a site the Chevalier de Lévis described as "the strongest position" on the field. A half hour later, Lieutenant Colonel Louis Restoineau de Fontbonne led the rest of the regiment onto the buttes. The standby detachments from Royal Roussillon, La Sarre, Languedoc, and Béarn arrived shortly thereafter, with orders "to support the Guyenne battalion." Troops from the Quebec, Trois-Rivières, and Montreal militias and *troupes de la marine* followed close behind.

As reinforcements arrived, Fontbonne deployed the regulars in line along the edge of the buttes, roughly 550 yards from the British. Today, two Martello towers mark the approximate axis of the French line. Captain Pierre Marcel, Montcalm's other aide-de-camp, noted that "the Canadians from the different governments formed many small squads which were placed in front of the battle line to harass the enemy with their musketry."

Guyenne's arrival stabilized the situation on the plains. With Fontbonne's regulars and militiamen in place, only a major British attack could threaten the French.

MORNING IN BEAUPORT

Montbeillard never managed to lie down for his morning rest. Continued gunfire from the west, a glimpse of the boats that had appeared off Beauport beached on the Île d'Orléans, and the sight of French troops marching toward Quebec were enough to dispel his doubts regarding a British landing above the city.

As the senior French artillery officer at Quebec, Montbeillard was responsible for all munitions, including musket cartridges for the infantry. To prepare for a major battle, he ordered his gunners to round up five wagons and fill them with cartridges from Beauport magazines. Montreuil appeared and stopped to assure him that the situation was under control and "Guyenne alone would contain the enemy." Unconvinced, Montbeillard continued to gather ammunition.

Leaving Montbeillard and his wagons behind, Montreuil rode on until he found Montcalm, Johnstone, and the rest of the general's entourage. Crossing the pontoon bridge over the Saint-Charles, they met up with Captain Charles Deschamps de Boishébert of the *troupes de la marine*.

While other French officers pondered the meaning of distant gunfire, frantic messengers, and British boats bobbing offshore, Boishébert learned about the British landing by looking out a window. Years of hard service as a partisan commander in Acadia followed by a summer on the front lines at Quebec had landed Boishébert in the Hôpital Général. When musket shots at daybreak roused hospital residents, Boishébert glanced up at the promontory and saw British soldiers on the march.

Unwilling to remain in the safety of the hospital while Wolfe threatened Quebec, Boishébert left immediately to rejoin his company of *troupes de la marine* at Beauport. Meeting Montcalm, Boishébert confirmed that the British had landed, adding that he had seen British battalions forming up on the Plains of Abraham. Montcalm sent Boishébert on to Beauport "to speed up the arrival of the rest of the army," then continued on his way.

THE SIMPLE JOY OF ARSON

Boishébert didn't know it yet, but by nightfall he would have lost his country home and most of his income. On the same day that he crawled from his sickbed to lead his company into action, Scott's column paid a visit to Rivière Ouelle, Boishébert's prosperous seigneury.

Boishébert later estimated that Scott's visit "caused him to lose more than 50,000 [livres], without counting lost rents from his seigneury." When the smoke cleared, smoldering wreckage was all that remained of his manor house, flour mill, sawmill, and fishing boats.

Yet Boishébert was one of the lucky ones. His home and fortune lay in ruins, but his family was safe. Another resident of the south shore of the St. Lawrence, Madame Bernier from L'Islet, along with many others, had suffered considerably more. The arrival of Scott's troops forced her to flee into the forest, nine months pregnant. As Bernier fled, she went into labor. The baby, born on a bed of leaves, survived to be nicknamed "La Feuille" (Leaf) and passed on the name to his descendants.

For Scott and Goreham, though, it was just another day. The master of HM Sloop *Zephyr* recorded that "the boats returned [from the Île aux Oies] and had destroyed what they could." Goreham modestly reported that his troops were marching west but that so far "they had only burned Bellechasse."

Scott noted that "Thurs the 13th took one prisoner had one of the Rangers wounded and burnt two hundred and sixteen houses from the upper part of the River Ouelle along the east side of it, also burnt one schooner and six shallops [sloops]."

Pearson too made a routine entry in his journal, almost apologizing for the lack of any item of particular interest: "We marched along up & we burnt all as we went. Capt Starks Company . . . was fired upon and had 1 man mort wounded so that he died. I cant tell you no more nuse today."

MALARTIC AND MONTCALM

Captain Anne-Joseph-Hippolyte de Maurès de Malartic of the Béarn Regiment, riding alongside Montcalm that morning, worried about the lieutenant general. In over three years of service together, he lamented, "I never saw him as bleak as he was that day. He seemed . . . [overwhelmed by] our misfortunes . . . He who normally chatted with me . . . about everything didn't say a word to me from the time we left the camp."

Montcalm's gloomy reserve was hardly surprising. Ahead lay one enemy, Wolfe, who had just outwitted and outmaneuvered him. Behind, he believed, lay another, Vaudreuil, ready to steal the credit if Montcalm won and blame him if he lost. With the decisive moment of the campaign upon him, he led an army he didn't trust to defend a city whose fall he had predicted even before the campaign began.

This reserve, however, carried a price. Surrounded by trusted officers and personal friends, followed by an army of thousands, Louis-Joseph de Montcalm rode toward his destiny alone.

CHAPTER 20

Preparing for Battle

MONTCALM TAKES CHARGE

Unlike Wolfe, Montcalm did not control his army during the early phases of the battle. Bernetz and Montreuil sent the first French troops into action; Magnan chose the initial French position on the buttes; Fontbonne formed the regulars into line.

By the time Montcalm heard about the landing, the equivalent of two battalions of regulars and militiamen were already on the march or engaging the British. When he arrived on the scene, the leading elements of the French army were already deployed. Taking charge, Montcalm approved Fontbonne's arrangements, sent Magnan and Montreuil to Beauport to inform Vaudreuil and bring up the rest of the army, and ordered Bernetz to send five twelve-, six-, and four-pounder cannon from the city to the buttes.

These tasks completed, he sat back and awaited events. Significantly, Montcalm chose not to send a messenger to Bougainville. Instead, he acted as if he assumed that his subordinate would hear the gunfire, know that a major battle was developing, and show up in the right place at the right time.

NATIVE AMERICANS

While Montcalm waited, Native American warriors from many nations joined the French and the Canadians on the road to the Plains of Abraham. Carron, Glode, Osauwishkeno, and Kachakawasheka of the Menominees were there, accompanied by Ensign Charles-Michel Mouet de Langlade of the *troupes de la marine* and Amable de Gere. So were Tsawawanhi and seventy Hurons.

Unlike the French and the Canadians, the warriors hadn't been ordered into action. Each nation had sent its own fighters to Quebec; they decided for themselves when and how they would participate in a given engagement. Among the Hurons, this decision had been quick and unequivocal. Ouiharalihte tells the story of their response to the alarm: "The fire of Musketry was first heard at Cap Rouge [*sic*].—Our warriors rushed across the Saint-Charles, leaving Beauport at full speed to take their share in the engagement. None of the Indian nations surpasses the Huron nation in bravery and knowledge of war."

The other Native American contingents were just as fast off the mark, ready to make a stand alongside their French allies. Fifty-six years before, an Abenaki speaker explained the Native American–French alliance to a New England delegation. He portrayed the allies as equals occupying adjacent territories and leading separate lives according to their own customs and traditions but ready to help each other in time of need: "Know that the Frenchman is my brother . . . we live in the same cabin with two fires; he has one fire and I have the other . . . Am I going to sit quietly on my mat while my brother is attacked in my cabin? No, no, I love my brother too much not to defend him."

This willingness to join the French at war was not, however, unconditional. Throughout the history of their alliance, Native Americans and the French had practiced parallel warfare, with each party pursuing its own goals and making war in its own way in the course of the same operations. The French went into battle to achieve specific objectives like the destruction of an enemy army or the defense or capture of a key location. Native American warriors fought to secure prestige and status within their communities by taking prisoners and scalps. This was the case even

among nations like the Abenakis, who were fighting to defend their homelands against invading New Englanders during the Seven Years' War. The
French were willing to fight in the open, attack fortifications, and sacrifice
the lives of their troops to attain an objective. Native Americans made it
very clear that they were not.

In 1756, prior to the siege of Oswego, a Nipissing chief laid down
the conditions under which warriors were willing to fight alongside the
French. He asked Montcalm "never to expose the natives to the fire of
artillery and musketry from the forts, because their custom was never to
fight against entrenchments or stockades, but in the forest where they
understood war and where they could find trees for cover."

On many occasions, this preference for practicing different styles of
war provoked tensions between Native Americans and the French. At the
Plains of Abraham, however, Wolfe's decision to post his army on a plain
surrounded by trees, brush, broken ground, cliffs, and fields of standing
wheat gave Native Americans (and Canadians) an unmatched opportunity
to play a prominent role in a clash between bodies of European regulars.
Between 6:00 and 10:00 a.m., they kept the British under constant fire
while Montcalm's French battalions marched to the buttes, formed up,
and waited for orders. When they reached the field, the warriors shunned
the battle line and joined the Canadian militia on the flanks.

But not Ouiharalihte. Like the Canadian militia, the Huron contingent included some of the oldest and youngest men from their community. As the Hurons approached the Plains of Abraham, Tsawawanhi's age
began to make itself felt, along with concern for the safety of his grandson.
"My grand father," recalled Ouiharalihte, "was too old to keep up with his
Warriors—he desired me to accompany him, but just as soon as he got in
sight of the Hurons, and was about to join them, he commanded me to go
back,—I obeyed him; but went back only a small distance, and concealed
myself to see what was going on."

GUNS ON THE HEIGHTS

Still not sure exactly where to find the British, Montbeillard formed up
his wagons at Beauport and headed west, "without any path to follow
other than that provided by the whistling of musket balls." Marching to

the sound of the guns took him to the Buttes-à-Neveu. Just as he arrived, Yorke's artillery opened fire.

A British field gun "that fired straight down the Samos [Foulon] Road" posed a threat Montbeillard couldn't ignore. When cannon from the city reached the buttes, Montbeillard placed the first three opposite the British six-pounder and began to fire back. After a brief interval, he took two more guns to the north end of the French line "to attempt to expel the enemy from a fortified house they had occupied."

Montbeillard's gun crews included both regular and militia gunners. Vaudreuil took note of the services of one "canonnier milicien," François Gallet. Gallet, wrote the governor-general, "served [at the Battle of the Plains of Abraham] with great enthusiasm and bravery and had his arm torn off by a cannonball."

Moving along the French line to supervise his guns, Montbeillard encountered Montcalm. The general, he wrote, "ordered me to withdraw the guns on the right [north] back a little out of fear that the Canadians who were fighting there might run away and they [the guns] would be lost. I went there and pulled them back, because they were too close [to the British]."

He remained at the north end of the line until a messenger arrived with a request for ammunition from Royal Roussillon.

A GENERAL IN WAITING

Hours passed; battalions arrived. As his army assembled, Montcalm rode down the line, speaking with the troops. He "asked the soldiers if they were tired." They replied they were ready to fight. "The entire army," wrote Marcel, Montcalm's second aide-de-camp, "seemed to be waiting impatiently for the order to charge the enemy and heatedly demanded it."

Joseph Trahan, an eighteen-year-old Acadian refugee, watched and remembered: "I can well recollect . . . how Montcalm looked before the engagement. He was riding a dark or black horse in front of our lines, bearing his sword high in the air, in the attitude of encouraging the men to do their duty. He wore a uniform with large sleeves, and the one covering the arm he held in the air, had fallen back, disclosing the white linen of his wristband."

FRENCH SKIRMISHERS

Standing in place on the Plains of Abraham, Wolfe's army temporarily became less a threat to Canada than one huge target for the Canadian militia and Native American warriors. Between 6:00 and 10:00 a.m., they kept the British under constant fire while Montcalm's French battalions marched onto the buttes, formed up, and waited for orders.

None of the Native American or Canadian participants left accounts of this skirmishing that entered the written record. Augustin Grignon later recalled that Glode, Osauwishkeno, and Kachakawasheka continued to "speak of the battle" into their old age but did not record the details. He did, however, preserve an anecdote of Langlade in battle that he had heard from Amable de Gere. This might or might not have happened at the Battle of the Plains of Abraham, but it does at least provide an intimate look at one of the participants in action:

> De Gere used to say, that he never saw so perfectly cool and fear-less a man on the field of battle as my grandfather [Langlade]; and that either here [on the Plains of Abraham], at the Monongahela, or at Ticonderoga [Fort Carillon], I have forgotten which, he saw my grandfather, when his gun barrel had got so hot, from repeated and rapid discharges, that he took occasion to stop a little while that it might cool, when he would draw his pipe from his pouch, cut his tobacco, fill his pipe, take a piece of punk-wood, and strike fire with his steel and flint, and light and smoke his pipe, and all with as much *sang froid* as at his own fireside; and having cooled his gun and refreshed himself, would resume his place and play well his part in the battle.

BRITISH SKIRMISHERS

The British spent four hours under constant attack by Canadian and Native American skirmishers on their front and flanks. Just the sort of situation, one might think, where sixteen hundred American rangers and British light infantry might have come in handy. With these troops other-wise engaged, the irregulars forced Wolfe to divert whole battalions away from the battle line to guard his flanks.

"About 6 o'clock," wrote the staff officer, "the enemy's light troops began to swarm in the bushes and behind the hillock, and perpetually thickened and kept a very hot fire on the troops." Knox, with the Forty-Third at the British center, observed that although French artillery had opened fire with round shot and canister, "what galled us most was a body of Indians and other marksmen they had concealed in the corn [wheat] opposite to the front of our right wing, and a coppice that stood opposite to our center, inclining towards our left; but the [Lieutenant] Colonel [John] Hale, by Brigadier Monckton's orders, advanced some platoons, alternately, from the forty-seventh regiment, which, after a few rounds, obliged these skulkers to retire."

These "skulkers" might have withdrawn, but they were soon back in action. Wolfe, wrote Quartermaster Sergeant John Johnson of the Fifty-Eighth, eventually "ordered us all to lie flat on the ground on our arms; which we did, for a considerable time, before we perceived them to make any advance towards us." This meant spending hours lying on damp clover and mud, soaked by the early morning rain, but it kept the troops relatively safe.

To the south, the militia and warriors never seriously threatened the British. A single battalion, the Thirty-Fifth, managed to hold them off.

The north flank was another matter. Here, Canadians and Native Americans pushed so hard that Townshend, who commanded that sector, thought that Montcalm "showed his intention to flank our left."

Wolfe responded by deploying the Fifteenth Regiment on the British north flank at right angles to the battle line. When the Second and Third Battalions of the Sixtieth (Royal Americans) reached the plains, he sent them to reinforce the Fifteenth. (Wolfe later sent the Third Battalion to guard the Anse au Foulon). Samuel Holland found himself drawn into the fighting along the Chemin Sainte-Foy, "where with the grenadier company of the 60th I had been posted near a small barn, to keep a fire on the Canadians who outflanked us."

The desperate struggle continued as both sides fought for possession of the two houses. When Townshend recalled this battle within a battle, he wrote that "the houses into which the light infantry were thrown were well defended being supported by Colonel Howe who taking post with 2 companies behind a small copse & frequently sallying upon the flanks of those who attacked them drove them often into heaps."

Pressure from the Canadians and Native Americans became so intense that Wolfe decided to fortify his north flank. He summoned Holland and ordered him to collect sixty soldiers from the Forty-Eighth Regiment, standing in reserve behind the main battle line, and "erect a redoubt on the left" to shore up the British position.

Under other circumstances, this hours-long clash between three British battalions and nearly a thousand skirmishers on the north flank might have entered history as a military epic. On the morning of September 13, it was just a sideshow, a prelude and accompaniment to the explosion of violence that was about to occur on the plains.

CHAPTER 21

Montcalm's Decision

VAUDREUIL'S LAST ORDER TO MONTCALM

At Beauport, Vaudreuil was both confident that Wolfe had stepped into a trap of his own making and worried that Montcalm might mishandle the battle. Montcalm's initial reaction to news of the landing had left Vaudreuil less than impressed: "This happened slowly with much indecision." Now, unwilling to trust Montcalm's judgment and afraid that a precipitate attack would have "lost the heights that his army occupied . . . and at the same time given the enemy the advantage of terrain," Vaudreuil ordered his general to hold fast on the buttes:

> I wrote to M. de Montcalm [telling him] that the advantage the British had gained by forcing their way past our outposts would inevitably lead to their defeat, but that we should do nothing . . . prematurely, that the British must be attacked simultaneously by our army, reinforced by 1,500 troops that it would be very easy to bring from the city and by Bougainville's corps, by which means they would find themselves surrounded on all sides, and would have no alternative but to retreat, or face certain defeat.

He sent the order to Montcalm and followed in his carriage at the head of two battalions of Montreal militia.

WOLFE'S BATTLE LINE

After the battle, Townshend reported that Wolfe landed at the Anse au Foulon with forty-four hundred troops. Of these, twenty-one hundred waited on the battle line to face the main body of the French army. The remaining twenty-three hundred held the north and south flanks, waited in reserve, or guarded the Anse au Foulon.

When complete, the British formation was roughly rectangular. Six battalions formed the battle line facing Quebec, with the south end anchored on Wolfe's Hill. From north to south, the Fifty-Eighth, Seventy-Eighth (Fraser's Highlanders), Forty-Seventh, Forty-Third, and Twenty-Eighth Regiments and the Louisbourg Grenadiers prepared to engage the regulars of Montcalm's army. Wolfe had placed one of Yorke's six-pounders on his south wing, next to the Louisbourg Grenadiers, and the other on the north wing next to the Frasers.

Wolfe's battalions did not form a continuous line. A forty-yard interval separated each unit from its neighbors. Arrayed in two lines (three, in the case of the Highlanders) with the soldiers spaced a yard apart, they gave the impression of fragile vulnerability. This fragility was more apparent than real. A European battalion was a murderous instrument. However thin and disconnected the line might be, a linear formation allowed a disciplined army to bring every available musket to bear and deliver a series of devastating volleys.

The Second Battalion of the Royal Americans, along with the Fifteenth and light infantry toward the Chemin Sainte-Foy and the Thirty-Fifth on Wolfe's Hill, formed the north and south sides of the rectangle. Deployed at right angles to the main line, they defended Wolfe's position against attacks from the flanks.

The Forty-Eighth, divided into four blocks of troops and waiting in reserve, became the fourth side of the rectangle. Six hundred paces beyond them, more light infantry screened the rear against attacks from the Sillery Woods.

The Third Battalion of the Royal Americans advanced to the Plains of Abraham, spent some time on the north flank, then returned to the head of the road up the promontory to guard the Anse au Foulon.

Wolfe's deployment took maximum advantage of terrain. The Thirty-Fifth, on the south flank, and the Louisbourg Grenadiers and part of the

Twenty-Eighth on the battle line stood atop Wolfe's Hill. The Fifty-Eighth and Fraser's Highlanders were behind a hedge that marked a field boundary from the Grande-Allée north toward the Chemin Sainte-Foy. Part of the Forty-Eighth stood behind the hedge that marked the western border of the same field. The light infantry converted two houses at the north end of the line into miniature forts.

Both the British and the French battle lines were roughly nine hundred to one thousand yards long.

KILTS AND RED COATS

Most of Wolfe's army wore the familiar red coat, vest, and breeches and white leggings of British infantry. Regular infantry wore black tricornes; grenadiers tall, pointed miter hats. One battalion stood out. The uniform of the Seventy-Eighth combined Highland clothing and standard British military dress. Like their comrades, the Frasers wore the red that marked them as British troops. But instead of coats, breeches, and hats, they wore short Highland jackets, tartan kilts, and dark blue bonnets with a black cockade.

Most of Wolfe's soldiers had been recruited from among the marginal populations of Britain and British America. Individuals who found themselves deprived of any other way to earn a wage or living lives so relentlessly grim that any alternative seemed preferable frequently sought refuge in an army that provided a desperate chance for subsistence, escape, and adventure.

James Wolfe referred to the first of these motives in 1756 when, ordered to Gloucestershire to deal with unrest among local weavers, he noted, "I hope it will turn out a good recruiting party, for the people are so oppressed, so poor and so wretched, that they will perhaps hazard a knock on the pate [head] for bread and clothes, and turn soldiers through sheer necessity."

The soldiers of the Seventy-Eighth were a special case. Recruited by Lieutenant Colonel Simon Fraser, master of Lovat and chief of Clan Fraser, they came for the most part from Scottish clans that had rebelled against the Crown in 1745.

In joining this battalion, Highlanders were serving not so much the Crown as their colonel's ambition. A prominent rebel, Lovat's father had been executed for his role in the Jacobite rebellion of 1745–46. Lovat, who played an equivocal role during the uprising, had raised the regiment in hopes of buying his way back into the good graces of the British government with the lives of his fellow Scots. Wounded earlier in the summer, he remained in camp convalescing while his regiment went into battle without him.

MONTCALM'S BATTLE LINE

By about 10:00 a.m., Montcalm had placed the greater part of his army between Wolfe and Quebec. La Sarre, Languedoc, Béarn, Guyenne, and Royal Roussillon formed a line three ranks deep above the western slope of the Buttes-à-Neveu, with detachments of *troupes de la marine* and militiamen at either end and "groups of Canadians out in front, hidden behind some trees." At the north end of this line, a body of Quebec militiamen and *troupes de la marine* "were placed to the right of La Sarre, a little in advance of the battalion, and extending into the bushes, which were everywhere on the extreme right."

On either side of the battlefield, Canadians, colonial regulars, and Native Americans relentlessly harassed the flanks of Wolfe's army. Jean-Daniel Dumas, adjutant general of the *troupes de la marine* in Canada, commanded a force of nine hundred on the north flank. Captain Louis-Frédéric Herbin of the *troupes de la marine* led eight hundred to the south.

The most detailed account of the French army comes from Townshend's report to the British government. He gives a strength of nineteen hundred for Montcalm's battle line and fifteen hundred for the skirmishers, making a total of thirty-four hundred. This matches Lévis's estimate of "three thousand five or six hundred men . . . very few of whom were regulars." Vaudreuil reported that the French had "more than 3,000" combatants in the field, Bigot thirty-five hundred.

The British thus outnumbered the French on the plains by approximately one thousand. Wolfe's deployment of troops to the flanks, the Foulon, and his reserve line, however, left a French battle line of two thousand opposing a British line of about the same strength.

The French troops on the buttes spent the morning in continuous motion. The arrival of successive battalions from Beauport obliged those already formed to contract their frontage to make room for the newcomers. This shuffling from place to place lacked drama but was absolutely essential. Once they engaged the enemy, victory or defeat would turn in part on the regular battalions retaining coherence in attack or defense.

Thanks to Magnan and Fontbonne, Montcalm occupied a very strong position. To attack the French atop the Buttes-à-Neveu, the British would have had to make an uphill charge over rough terrain that would multiply the power of the defenders many times over. Montcalm had inflicted devastating defeats on British armies at Fort Carillon in 1758 and Montmorency in 1759 by occupying a strong position and allowing the British to come to him. Now he had a British army at his mercy once more.

If Wolfe wanted to threaten Quebec, he would sooner or later have to take the buttes. In the meantime, the land route to Cap-Rouge and Batiscan remained open by way of roads passing north of the Quebec Promontory, which were in no way threatened by the British army on the plains.

All this meant that Montcalm was under no pressure to act immediately. Waiting would simply allow the French to grow stronger as more troops and guns arrived on the field and the British to grow weaker as irregulars to the north and south and artillery on the buttes wore them down. In the hours that it took his army to assemble, Montcalm had more than enough time to assess the situation at length and make appropriate plans.

WOLFE'S PLAN FOR VICTORY

With his army in position and the French assembling on the Buttes-à-Neveu, Wolfe strode up and down his battle line, constantly on the move. Everywhere he went, he spoke with his officers to explain his intentions for the coming action.

Briefing junior officers was important for Wolfe. His experience of battle in Germany and Scotland had convinced him that it was best to allow individual officers to decide when to open fire. In his general orders of 1754, he stressed the desirability of "making every platoon receive the word of command, to make ready and fire from the officer who commands it; because in battle the fire of the artillery and infantry may render it difficult to use any general signals by beat of drum."

If he was following his own advice, Wolfe expected his officers on the

Plains of Abraham to pass this information on to their troops: "The officers to inform the soldiers of his platoon, before the action begins, where
they are to direct their fire; and they are to take good aim to destroy their
adversaries."

William DeLaune, serving with the light infantry screening the north
flank, encountered Wolfe on the morning of the thirteenth. Seven years
before, Wolfe had given DeLaune a copy of a popular military textbook,
Humphrey Bland's *Treatise of Military Discipline*. In 1761, DeLaune wrote
out Wolfe's final instructions on the flyleaf: "On the very morning of the
battle before Quebec he spoke in these terms—'Receive,' said he, 'the Enemy's fire first and preserve your own last. Those of the enemy who remain
unhurt will be put to such disorder and confusion by the thought of what
is coming that they will be beaten men when your broadside comes.'"

Sergeant Johnson of the Fifty-Eighth recorded how these instructions
reached the soldiers in the ranks: "Our orders were positively, not to fire
a shot, until they [the French] were within forty yards of the point of our
Bayonets."

The southern edge of the Plains of Abraham. Canadian militiamen and Native American warriors fired at Wolfe's south flank (in the vicinity of the cluster of buildings
facing the Martello tower) from the slope between the plains and the edge of the cliff.

PIPERS, GUNNERS, AND SAILORS

Viewed from a distance, Wolfe's battle line consisted of six neat scarlet blocks stretched across the Quebec Promontory, waiting in awful silence to unleash a torrent of firepower on a word of command. Up close, Wolfe's army, like Montcalm's, was a bustling, jostling collection of individuals, some of whom had their own ideas about what they should be doing that morning.

Wolfe's defensive tactics allowed British soldiers only the most limited scope for individual decision making. His troops were stationary and out in the open under the eyes of their officers and sergeants. Under these conditions, virtually all of Wolfe's soldiers, some of whom might otherwise have elected to break the bonds of discipline and comradeship, chose to remain in the line and fight. Faced with a French army atop the Buttes-à-Neveu, they held their ground and obeyed orders.

Open terrain and close supervision did not, however, prevent the soldiers of Fraser's Highlanders from deciding for themselves who should take part in the impending firefight and who should slip away. Sergeant James Thompson recorded the story: "At the Battle of the Plains of Abraham we had but one piper, and because he was not provided with arms and the usual means of defence like the rest of the men he was made to keep aloof for safety."

For soldiers to absent themselves before an engagement, then discreetly rejoin the ranks, was and remains a very common battlefield phenomenon. More unusual were individuals—in this case a crowd of sailors—who decided to fight, whether the commanding general wanted them or not.

As the first French battalions appeared on the Buttes-à-Neveu, Wolfe had instructed Yorke to bring his guns to the field. Gordon Skelly observed this operation: "Gen. Wolfe . . . sent orders to the cannon which were landed to be brought up immediately to the line. We were ordered to place our seamen to them, who drew them up a small road to the left of the landing place."

This task performed, Wolfe undoubtedly expected the landing craft crews to meekly return to the Foulon and leave the soldiers to their work. Instead, crowds of aggressive sailors, ready for a brawl but lacking the training and weapons to fight on the battle line, tried to force their way into Wolfe's battalions. Sailors on the north wing of the battle line were persuaded to remain behind the line in reserve. The naval volunteer described their reaction: "Such was their impetuosity to engage, and their resentment at being kept out of danger, that, according to their accustomed politeness, they were perpetually d-mm-g their eyes, &c. because they were restrained from pushing into the heat of the fire."

The sailors who dragged a six-pounder to the south end of the line were more successful. The London *Gazetteer* printed a report on their activities in April 1762: "On the return of the sailors to go on board again after drawing up the cannon at the siege of Quebec, they observed the foot soldiers drawn up for [the] engagement, when, instead of continuing their route, they fell into the ranks among the soldiers, some having cutlasses in their hands, others sticks, and some nothing at all."

Confronted with this unwelcome enthusiasm, Wolfe thanked the sailors for hauling the six-pounders to the plains, then tactfully asked them if they would please go away.

"God bless your Honour," replied a sailor, "pray let us stay and see fair play between the English and the French."

Wolfe, who "could not help smiling," again requested that they leave. "Upon this some complied; but others, when the General's back was turned, swore 'that the soldiers should not have all the fighting to themselves, but that they would come in for [a] share some way or other,' and actually remained in the ranks."

NORTHERN ATTACK

Just before 10:00 a.m., Dumas's Native American and Canadian skirmishers advanced on the British north flank. Pushing very hard, they drove in Townshend's outposts and attacked British strongpoints in the houses on the Chemin Sainte-Foy. The British set fire to the houses and withdrew. A column of smoke rose over the battlefield and drifted off toward the northeast.

Montcalm sent a lieutenant of La Sarre and thirty soldiers to push ahead of the north end of the French battle line. They had orders to raise the alarm if the British attempted to outflank Montcalm "while concealing their movement behind smoke from the two burning houses."

MONTCALM'S DECISION

On Thursday, September 13, 1759, Louis-Joseph de Montcalm faced the most important decision of his life. Wolfe was on the plains; Montcalm had to decide what to do about it. He would make this decision alone, neither consulting his subordinates nor obeying his commander in chief.

Montcalm thought that Wolfe's presence on the plains posed a significant and escalating threat to Quebec. From his vantage point on the Buttes-à-Neveu, he had watched the British infantry arrive and take their places in Wolfe's line. He had seen the Royal Artillery bring up field guns and open fire. He thought that the British were throwing up earthworks and that as the morning progressed their position would only get stronger. Montcalm believed, wrote Montreuil, that he would face "certain defeat if he waited any longer," because it would be impossible "to dislodge the enemy once they seized control of the Plains of Abraham, a half-cannon shot from Quebec."

His own army, in his opinion, would never be strong enough to attack a fortified enemy. Montcalm had faith in the regulars but not in the Canadians. Already that morning he had told Montbeillard that he didn't trust the militia to protect the French artillery on the north side of the buttes. Earlier in the campaign, he had described the militia as largely composed of "old men or boys who are not fit to march and have never been on an expedition, or to war."

At some point that morning, Montcalm resolved to attack as soon as all of his regulars had reached the field. He sent orders to the battalions that were still marching from Beauport to speed up and settled in to await their arrival.

Montcalm was still waiting when Montbeillard, heading south to resupply Royal Roussillon, met him once again: "I stopped for a moment with the Marquis de Montcalm who told me, 'We cannot avoid a battle. The enemy is entrenching; he already has two pieces of cannon. If we give him the chance to dig in, we will never be able to attack with the kind of troops that we have.' He added with a sort of shudder, 'Is it possible that Bougainville doesn't hear that [gunfire]!'"

Not everyone agreed that immediate attack was the best possible course of action. But no one was saying no to Montcalm that morning.

Montcalm's officers were simply too intimidated to tell their general that they thought he was about to make a serious mistake and that standing fast and awaiting reinforcements might be the better option. Montbeillard barely managed to hint that there weren't enough French soldiers on the field: "He [Montcalm] left without giving me time to reply, except to say that our army was very small."

Montreuil summoned up his courage and timidly made the same suggestion: "Although I regarded M. le Marquis de Montcalm as too brilliant to dare to give him advice, I nonetheless took the liberty of saying to him . . . that our army was too small to attack the enemy."

Neither one of these officers presented his misgivings forcefully; neither one influenced Montcalm.

In previous campaigns, Montcalm had been accompanied by the brilliant Lévis and/or the very competent brigadier François-Charles de Bourlamaque, whose advice had contributed to his victories in previous engagements. But Montcalm was on his own that morning. Lévis was in Montreal and Bourlamaque at the north end of Lake Champlain. There was no one on the buttes with sufficient stature and self-confidence to advise Montcalm to reconsider.

When the last battalion reached the buttes, the French army was, as far as Montcalm was concerned, as strong as it would ever get. All of the reliable troops at hand were on the Buttes-à-Neveu. There were fifteen hundred Montreal militiamen on the way with Vaudreuil, but they were Canadians. There was no telling when Bougainville might show up.

At 10:00 a.m., the last soldier stepped into place, breathing hard after a six-mile march. Montcalm took his place at the head of Guyenne and Béarn and issued the single most important battlefield command in Canadian history, a command that would shape the futures of Canada, the United States, Native Americans across the continent, the French and British Empires, and the world.

At this moment, the great moment of his life, Montcalm ignored geography and treated a rugged, broken hillside as if it were a flat, unobstructed plain. Rather than instructing his senior officers to make a slow, careful advance to preserve the French formation until they came within musket range, he simply ordered his army into action.

Once again, Johnstone describes Montcalm's actions through a line of invented dialogue based on his eyewitness observations: "I sent all the officers to their posts, and made the drummers beat the charge."

Elsewhere, fifteen hundred Montreal militiamen continued their march from Beauport toward the plains. Inside Quebec, a garrison of twenty-one hundred regulars, militiamen, and sailors guarded the city against an attack that never came. At Cap-Rouge, twelve hundred elite French and Canadian troops stood by to repel a British landing west of the Quebec Promontory; the crews of nineteen bateaux awaited orders to carry their cargoes of provisions to Montcalm's army. Far downriver, eighteen hundred rangers, light infantry, and sailors marched and burned. On the St. Lawrence, Saunders's ships rode at anchor off the Anse au Foulon and the north and south ends of the Île d'Orléans.

Sixty yards above the river, two lines of soldiers, one mostly red, the other mostly gray white, each about two thousand strong, faced off against a background of green trees and meadow grass, yellow wheat fields, and drifting smoke. To the north and south, fifteen hundred warriors and militiamen harassed the flanks of the British army; twenty-three hundred British soldiers skirmished with these irregulars, formed a reserve behind Wolfe's line, or defended the roadway leading down to the Anse au Foulon.

The early morning rain had stopped. The skies were partly cloudy; the sunlight comfortably warm. A light breeze blew across the field from the southwest.

CHAPTER 22

The French Charge

THE FRENCH BEGIN TO MOVE

The French charge began as an expression of the will of a single individual. Montcalm commanded; his army obeyed.

Staccato drumbeats communicated his intentions to every soldier in the army. Orders flowed down the chain of command through brigade, battalion, and company commanders to sergeants, corporals, and privates.

Obedient to their general, Montcalm's army stepped forward. Montbeillard watched from opposite Wolfe's Hill: "I was at the cannon on the left, when I saw our army begin to move, led by the Marquis de Montcalm on horseback."

DOWNHILL TO VICTORY

Montcalm's soldiers began the advance in high spirits, brimming with confidence. Montcalm had never been defeated. His army had overcome British garrisons and armies at Oswego in 1756, Fort William Henry in 1757, and Carillon in 1758. Six weeks before, they had beaten Wolfe's army at Montmorency.

Back in the spring, when Montcalm predicted that "Canada will fall to the English, maybe this campaign, or the next," his officers had been expressing unbounded faith in their general and his army. "The *troupes de terre*," wrote Montreuil, "and those of the colony have great confidence in the Marquis de Montcalm." Another assured the minister of war, "I have never seen such enthusiasm and good will among the troops. The Marquis de Montcalm's long and careful preparations make us expect that we will beat the English everywhere."

As for the soldiers in the ranks, ever since the capture of Oswego in 1756 they had been literally singing Montcalm's praises:

> Fear nothing, my dear friend,
> it's Montcalm who leads the way.
> He's a hero, loved by all,
> who invites you to the ball.

Every officer who commented on the morale of the French troops that morning spoke of their impatience to engage the enemy. Malartic watched as "the troops marched eagerly into battle." Lapause reported that "the troops displayed enormous resolve and enthusiasm."

As the French troops took their first steps toward the invaders, there is no indication that any soldier in Montcalm's army did not believe that the path down the slope of the Buttes-à-Neveu was the path to victory.

WOLFE TAKES HIS PLACE

With the French army advancing, Wolfe moved to Wolfe's Hill. "After the action began," wrote Mackellar, the general "kept on a rising ground where our right stood, from whence he had a view of the whole field." This placed him just to the right of the Louisbourg Grenadiers, many of whom had been recruited in the American colonies. Wolfe, the quintessential English general, thus elected to go into the most important battle of his career surrounded by Americans. Henderson, the volunteer Wolfe had stationed on the hill, was there to meet him when "the General came . . . and took his post by me."

"A DAY THAT I'D LIKE TO FORGET"

French morale might have been a little too high. Malartic also observed that the troops were moving "much too fast."

Instead of advancing methodically, the French began to run, cascading like a waterfall down the western slopes of the Buttes-à-Neveu. Uneven terrain, heavy bush, and tall wheat made cohesive movement difficult and supervision almost impossible. Moving to avoid obstacles squeezed some soldiers together and forced others apart. As they ran down the hillside and onto the plains, soldiers followed ravines, climbed fences, splashed through puddles and ponds, and skidded and slipped on wet grass and mud. "Our troops," wrote a Canadian officer, "fell recklessly upon the enemy, but their poorly formed ranks broke very soon, partly because of their speed, partly because of the rough ground."

If their officers had attempted to keep formations intact, they might just have made things worse. Maurice de Saxe, one of France's great eighteenth-century commanders, once noted that during a charge, when "the majors shout, *close up:* the troops crowd toward the center, impercep-tibly the center breaks; & in that center, the troops are stacked eight deep, & on the wings, four deep, this opens up gaps between battalions."

The charge had hardly begun when the French line broke apart into three clusters of running soldiers. One thousand troops from the militia, *troupes de la marine,* La Sarre, and Languedoc formed the northernmost cluster. Led by Montcalm in person, 400 soldiers from Béarn, Guyenne, and the militia were in the center, straddling the Grande-Allée. The south-ern cluster contained 530 troops from Royal Roussillon, the militia, and the *troupes de la marine.*

The clusters moved at different speeds in different directions. Malar-tic, in the center with Béarn, reported that "we hadn't gone twenty steps before the left was too far behind and the center too far in front." Instead of charging straight toward the British, the north and center clusters veered to the right, heading for the northern end of Wolfe's line. The southern cluster angled left toward the southern extremity of the British position. No one was heading for the British center.

Moments into the attack, Montcalm had lost control of his army. Authority plummeted down the chain of command as individuals and small groups made their own decisions about whether to go right or left, speed up or slow down, stick together or break apart. For Malartic, September 13, 1759, was on its way to becoming "a day that I'd like to forget for the rest of my life."

WATCHING THE FRENCH

The French charged; the British waited. Each army saw the other grow from a distant patch of color into a collection of clearly visible individuals.

Of all those on the battlefield who recorded their memories of Montcalm's charge, Knox had the best view. Standing with the Forty-Third Regiment in the British center, unthreatened by the French advance, Knox could watch quietly and take it all in.

Earlier that morning, he had seen the French take position on the Buttes-à-Neveu: "The enemy had . . . likewise formed the line of battle." Now he watched them charge down the hillside to the plains: "About ten o'clock the enemy began to advance briskly in three columns, with loud shouts and recovered arms [holding their muskets vertically in front of them], two of them inclining to the left of our army, and the third towards our right."

Lieutenant Colonel Alexander Murray, commanding the Louisbourg Grenadiers, provides a quick insight into what his troops were feeling as they watched the French advance. Since the war began, British soldiers had been hearing lurid stories of the torture and mutilation of prisoners by Native Americans. When Montcalm's army charged, wrote Murray, "we advanced very slowly and resolutely to receive them, the men being determined to conquer or die in their ranks rather than be scalped and hacked."

As they watched the French advance, the British troops very likely heard the same cries and shouts that Edward Coats had noticed during the Battle of Montmorency: "We were saluted all the time by the infernal clamour of the Indians and Vive L'Roys of the French."

THE SOLDIERS TAKE COMMAND

As Montcalm's army closed on the British, everything became much, much worse. Charging an enemy battle line over open ground was a terrifying experience. Every step took a soldier closer to thousands of enemy

Part of the Buttes-à-Neveu. The formidable height and steep, broken slopes that made the buttes a natural strongpoint appear very clearly in this nineteenth-century painting. When Montcalm's soldiers charged down the hillside, their formation broke apart. The Martello tower on the right still stands in the Battlefields Park, overlooking the St. Lawrence River and marking the approximate location of the south end of Montcalm's line.

muskets. As troops advanced and tension rose, Montcalm's soldiers experienced an almost irresistible desire to use their weapons.

This kind of behavior was not at all unusual. Humphrey Bland warned in *A Treatise of Military Discipline* that "in advancing towards the enemy, it is with great difficulty that the officers can prevent the men . . . from taking their arms, without orders, off from their shoulders, and firing at too great a distance."

James Wolfe, an admirer of Bland's, had seen this firsthand as a sixteen-year-old ensign fighting his first battle at Dettingen in 1743: "The third and last attack was made by the foot on both sides. We advanced towards one another; our men in high spirits, and very impatient for fighting . . . The Major and I . . . before they came near, were employed in begging and ordering the men not to fire at too great a distance, but to keep it till the enemy should come near us; but to little purpose. The whole fired when they thought they could reach them, which had like to have ruined us. We did very little execution with it."

On September 13, a similar phenomenon affected Montcalm's army. About 130 yards from the British line, the French came to a ragged halt and prepared to open fire.

No one gave an order to shoot. But all across the Quebec Promontory, fingers squeezed triggers, flint struck steel, sparks flew, and powder exploded. In the Béarn Regiment, according to Malartic, "the Canadians of the second rank and the soldiers of the third fired without any order." Propelled by rapidly expanding gases, thousands of .69-caliber musket bills streaked out the muzzles, flew across the Plains of Abraham, and fell harmlessly to the ground.

Often dismissed as inaccurate, muskets were short-range firearms, most effective at distances under forty yards. Beyond that range, muskets were more noisemakers and smoke generators than reliable weapons. Twentieth-century tests by the Styrian Provincial Armory at Graz, Austria, confirm that musket balls lose most of their kinetic energy after traveling thirty-two to fifty-four yards. In 1841, the British gunsmith William Greener conducted a series of experiments with smoothbore muskets. "I have," he wrote, "invariably found that, when fired perfectly horizontal . . . at the height of five feet, the average distance at which the ball came to the ground, was under 130 yards."

BULLETS BOUNCING OFF CHESTS

Mackellar described the first French volley: "Their front began to fire before they got within reach, and immediately followed throughout the whole in a wild scattering manner." Knox observed that the French were "firing obliquely at the two extremities of our line." Casualties were low, explained the anonymous author of *An Accurate and Authentic Journal of the Siege of Quebec,* "owing to the enemy's firing at too great a distance for their balls were almost spent before they reached our men; several of our people having received contusions on parts where the blow must have been mortal, had they reserved their fire a little longer."

As stray musket balls bounced off their chests, Wolfe's soldiers stood patiently, waiting for the order to fire.

TOWNSHEND'S COUNTERATTACK

On the north flank, Canadian militiamen and Native American warriors continued to press forward. Townshend sent detachments from the Fifteenth Regiment to reinforce the light infantry. A vigorous counterattack forced the Native Americans and Canadians to withdraw. As the battle lines clashed, the struggle continued.

Holland's redoubt might have proved very useful at this point, if he'd had time to build it. However, he recalled, "whilst I was preparing to carry his [Wolfe's] orders into effect . . . the French were advancing fast, & . . . the fire on their part was becoming brisk. I found the impossibility of throwing up the intended works." Ignoring the developing battle, Holland set off southward to inform Wolfe that the troops would just have to manage without a redoubt.

MILITIAMEN AND REGULARS

The charge down the hillside broke Montcalm's army into groups of battalions; the first French volley broke the battalions into fragments. These battalions were composite units, each formed from a mix of metropolitan regulars and Canadian militiamen.

European regulars were the product of intense training and iron discipline that turned recruits into instruments of the state, capable of marching, loading, and firing in unison, maneuvering in formation under fire, and standing on a level field and trading volleys with adversaries a short distance away. Training and discipline did not erase soldiers' freedom of choice. It attempted, as far as possible, to ensure that they would make the *right* choices and place their obligations as soldiers over their survival as individuals.

The clothing, lifestyle, occupation, and discipline of European regulars all distinguished them from the general public. The Canadian militiamen, on the other hand, *were* the general public. Even after five years of relentless hostilities, they remained armed civilians, temporarily at war.

During the Seven Years' War, their training consisted of occasional exercises conducted by former sergeants from the *troupes de la marine*. François Domas, sergeant major of Quebec, drilled the militia of the government of Quebec. Vaudreuil once had occasion to describe this aspect of Domas's responsibilities: "Returning from these campaigns, he was sent to drill the militia . . . on Sundays and holidays he went to the northern and southern parishes, taught them the drills and had them perform military maneuvers to prepare them to fight head-to-head with the enemy."

This was all very well, but with forty-five parishes in the government of Quebec, no company received anything close to the level of training it would have needed to perform effectively on the battle line.

Each battalion of Montcalm's army consequently contained two very different kinds of soldiers, with different training, expectations, abilities, and discipline. When the French opened fire, these differences completed the process of tearing that army apart.

Firing a flintlock musket during a charge didn't just involve pulling the trigger on the run. It meant stopping and standing still for as long as it took to reload.

After the first, spontaneous volley, Montcalm's soldiers acted according to their previous experience and personal inclinations. The regulars remained upright, reloaded quickly, then ran on toward the British. Some Canadians ran with them. Many remained behind, still reloading. A few lay down to load, which was very awkward and time-consuming but would have been much safer if the British were firing back. Some remained in place after they reloaded; most followed the regulars toward the enemy but proceeded more slowly.

As individual Canadians and regulars made their own decisions about how they would fight and what risks they would run, the battalions disintegrated. The French army now resembled a trio of comets streaking across the field at the speed of a running soldier. Each consisted of a dense mass of regulars up front, trailing a cloud of militiamen.

With every step, the leading regulars left more of the militiamen farther behind, until Montcalm's soldiers were scattered over a rectangle 1,000 yards across and 130 yards deep. As they ran, the French, unwilling to wait until they came within effective range, continued to fire, reload, and fire again, slowing their advance while inflicting very little damage on the British.

Within a few moments, Montcalm's force had changed from an army on the attack into an impending catastrophe. In the words of the Chevalier de Lévis, "The power of the infantry lies in discipline and order . . . A disorganized army is almost always beaten and often destroyed."

DANGEROUS ENEMIES

Viewed from Wolfe's line, the soldiers of Montcalm's fragmenting battalions remained powerful, dangerous enemies. A British witness described the ragged clusters of French infantry as "three Grand Columns with which they pushed towards our troops." Others interpreted the broken French formation as a powerful "line of battle, which was at least six deep" and "in some places nine deep," and spontaneous musketry by scattered groups and individuals as "firing by platoons, advancing in a very regular manner."

For many of the British, it must have seemed as if a French juggernaut were racing toward a very thin, very frail red line.

CHAPTER 23

Firefight

THE FIREFIGHT BEGINS

Between thirty and forty yards from the British line, the leading edges of the three clusters of French troops came to a halt. For the first time since the charge began, Montcalm's force regained the appearance—if not the reality—of an organized formation, or rather three formations, two in the north, one in the south, with a wide gap between them.

The French had stopped. The British held their ground. Chaplain Robert Macpherson of the Seventy-Eighth described the ensuing confrontation between Fraser's Highlanders and the French. They stood, he wrote, "looking at one another for 2 or 3 minutes, the one desirous that the other would give first fire."

Whichever side fired first would hand the advantage to the other. While quick-firing opponents reloaded, soldiers could take their time and aim carefully, without the pressure of facing a row of leveled muskets.

Time passed. The French watched the British. The British watched the French. Every moment, more French troops joined their comrades facing the redcoats. The southwest breeze blew across the battlefield. Skirmishing continued on the north and south flanks; artillery rumbled in the east as the batteries at Point Lévis bombarded Quebec and batteries in the city shot back.

"At last," wrote Macpherson, "the enemy began & made 2 most furious discharges." Either spontaneously, in response to commands, or a combination of both, enough French soldiers opened fire at more or less the same time to give the appearance of a volley into the battalions posted on the north and south wings of Wolfe's army.

"The oblique fire of the enemy," wrote Knox, aimed as it was at the extremities of the British line, meant that "the forty-third and forty-seventh regiments, in the center," were "little affected" by this or subsequent French volleys. Even where the French attacked head-on, their "most furious discharges" were almost entirely ineffective. "Their first fire," wrote Lieutenant Malcolm Fraser of the Seventy-Eighth, "did little execution."

"A CLOSE AND HEAVY DISCHARGE"

Wolfe's army had been preparing for this moment for months. Before the army sailed for Quebec, his troops had trained hard, not just to fight in formation, but to take careful aim before they pulled the trigger. "The regiment," wrote Knox in April 1759, was "out daily at exercise, and firing at the target."

During the campaign, Wolfe made sure that his battalions maintained their proficiency at fighting in linear formation. In the course of an inspection on July 15, Knox and his regiment demonstrated the tactics that many of Wolfe's soldiers would use in action. "The method we were ordered to observe did not admit of any confusion, though we fired remarkably quick," Knox wrote. "Our firings were from right and left, to the center, by platoons; and afterwards by subdivisions; taking the word of command from their respective officers."

On September 13, the British put this training into practice. All along the line, British officers gave the order to open fire; two thousand soldiers fired the first of the volleys that still reverberate through history.

The form of these volleys varied from place to place along the British line.

On the northern and southern wings of Wolfe's line, the British fired as they had trained. "As they came nearer," wrote one officer, "we fired on them by divisions." The two regiments in the center advanced and gave a general volley, "as remarkable," wrote Knox, "a close and heavy discharge, as I ever saw performed at a private field of exercise."

To the north, wrote Malcolm Fraser, "We . . . continued firing very hot for about six, or (as some say) eight minutes." In that time, wrote Macpherson, the Highlanders fired "4 or 5 General Discharges." At the other end of the line, according to a sergeant major from the Louisbourg Grenadiers, the exchange of fire lasted "about a quarter of an hour."

TRADING VOLLEYS

The French responded in kind, matching the British shot for shot; a savage firefight ensued between soldiers standing upright and shooting at one another across open ground. "Our firing," observed Marcel, "was very heavy from the right to the left; the enemy responded with equal force all along their line."

Killing at this range was an intensely personal act. Soldiers could see their enemies fall and hear them scream as their shots struck home, feel the blood of wounded comrades splatter across their faces, and choke on acrid clouds of black-powder smoke.

These clouds of smoke grew larger as firing continued, billowing across the battlefield, blotting out the sun, and making friends and enemies appear and disappear. Every time they fired, soldiers felt the brutal kick of a recoiling musket slamming into their shoulders hard enough to bruise. Tearing open cartridges while gripping them with their teeth spilled grains of powder into their mouths that sucked out moisture and induced a tormenting thirst.

Yet French and British soldiers continued to pull cartridges apart, pour a pinch of powder into the priming pan and the rest down the barrel, followed by the cartridge paper and bullet, use their ramrods to shove everything into place, present their weapon, aim, fire, and do it all again. On the drill field, this could take twenty seconds. In action on the Plains of Abraham, over a minute was closer to the mark.

LETHAL IMPACTS

Simultaneously aspiring killers and potential victims, soldiers on the plains faced death at every second. At this range, the British Land Pattern musket and the French *fusil d'infanterie* were lethal, accurate weapons.

Benjamin Robins, an eighteenth-century student of ballistics, published this assessment of the performance of a flintlock musket in 1742: "A leaden ball of 3/4 of an inch in diameter, and weighing nearly 1 1/3 oz. avoirdupois, if it be fired from a barrel of 45 inches in length, with half its weight of powder, will issue from that piece with a velocity which, were it uniformly continued, would carry it near 1700 feet in 1" [second]."

Robins's muzzle velocity of 1,700 feet per second may be a bit high. His instruments were primitive; the speed of a bullet depended upon a wide range of variables, from the composition of the powder to the humidity in the air. Tests on an early-eighteenth-century flintlock at the Styrian Provincial Armory in the 1980s produced a muzzle velocity of 1,479 feet per second, falling to 1,283 feet per second at thirty-three yards. But Robins's measurements of the penetrating power of a musket ball remain chillingly precise: "When a leaden bullet, 3/4 of an inch in diameter, was fired against a solid block of elm, with a velocity of about 1700 feet in 1" [second], I found that in a great number of trials it had penetrated from 4 1/2 to 5 1/2 inches deep."

In the 1830s, William Greener performed similar tests by firing a smoothbore musket at an iron plate. The results were just as alarming for anyone who found himself facing the wrong end of a Land Pattern musket or *fusil d'infanterie:* "I have fired at a body of sheet iron, [from] 1/4 of an inch thick up to 3/8 of an inch . . . the musket at from 25 to 30 yards would put the ball through; at 35, scarcely; at 40, not at all."

MULTIPLE GUNSHOT WOUNDS

Only their shirts, vests, and coats, not five inches of elm wood or a half inch of iron plate, protected soldiers that morning. Three soldiers from the *troupes de la marine* recorded their multiple wounds in letters to the minister of marine.

Amable de Boucherville, a younger son of a great Canadian family that had been "established in Canada for five generations," fought in the ranks as a volunteer. "I was hit by two musket balls, the first tore the thumb off my right hand, the second pierced my right thigh."

Ensign Cuisy d'Argenteuil was hit three times. Seeking a pension after the war, he wrote of "his wounds, one in the stomach, another in the knee, a third through the arm."

"Two musket balls" struck Captain Louis-Frédéric Herbin, "one in the thigh, the other in the arm."

At least one Canadian officer chose to immortalize his injury in verse.

Ensign François de La Chevrotière of the *troupes de la marine,* already hit in the jaw during a skirmish in 1758, was wounded again at the Battle of the Plains of Abraham. In an official letter to the minister of marine, he delicately referred to a bullet striking "his left thigh."

He used a slightly different expression just after the battle, while he was recuperating in the Hôpital Général. Felled by a wound serious enough to leave him crippled for life, La Chevrotière retained his sense of humor. Surrounded by concerned friends who were becoming a bit too solicitous, the young ensign composed his own epitaph:

> My Epitaph, if I die from my wounds
> Here lies La Chevrotière,

Charles Huot, *The Battle of the Plains of Abraham.* French troops form on the Buttes-à-Neveu above the Plains of Abraham, facing a British line stretching across the plains. To the right, clouds of gunsmoke drift across the field as Canadian militia and Native American warriors confront the invaders.

Who, for a hundred crowns a year,
Received one shot in the teeth,
And another in the rear.

THE FIREFIGHT CONTINUES

As the minutes passed, the British gradually gained the upper hand. There was simply no comparison between the effectiveness of troops formed in ranks and under discipline and that of troops scattered in handfuls across the field. One was an army; the other was not. British soldiers drew strength from the proximity of comrades and the presence of officers and NCOs; French soldiers lacked both this support and the means to coordinate their efforts. At the south end of the field, the troops on Wolfe's Hill enjoyed the same benefits conferred by holding the high ground that Montcalm had thrown away when he ordered a charge. In the center, the British were not even under direct attack.

While the French scrambled to re-form under fire, the British remained in formation, with every soldier and officer in his place. In many sections of the French clusters, soldiers stood several ranks deep, providing the British with a dense, inviting target and preventing soldiers at the rear from using their muskets. The British (except in those parts of the line where sailors had joined the redcoats) stood a yard apart, presenting a more difficult target and allowing every soldier to bring his musket to bear.

Exact numbers are elusive, but more British regulars were firing at fewer French regulars. Disorganized groups of individual soldiers, however brave, however skilled, could not compete with a disciplined battle line. From one side of the promontory to the other, French troops were falling faster than British troops.

Alongside the infantry, Yorke's six-pounders continued their cannonade. As the French approached, his gunners switched from round shot to grapeshot, converting their cannon into giant shotguns firing deadly swarms of oversized musket balls. In his official reports and private letters, George Williamson, never one to indulge in false modesty, presented the battle as an artillery victory, won by Yorke and his gunners with just a little help from the infantry: "We fired our cannon so briskly, seconded by the regiments, that we fairly beat them [the French] in the open field."

TOO MUCH TO BEAR

Flayed by thousands of potentially lethal projectiles every few moments, the French regulars stood their ground, "delivering and receiving," wrote Armand de Joannès of Languedoc, "three or four volleys" and suffering terrible losses. Malartic noted that in the Béarn Regiment, "most of our soldiers in the front rank who had fired two or three shots were killed or wounded."

Finally, it became too much to bear. "Heavier enemy fire," wrote a French officer, "overpowered our own." The French made their strongest effort against the northern part of Wolfe's position. They hit the British from two sides, as Dumas struck from the north and Montcalm from the east. Yet it was here that French soldiers of Languedoc and La Sarre became the first, consciously or unconsciously, to weigh the chances of survival against the possibility of victory and begin to fall back. Guyenne and Béarn, in the center cluster, broke next. Finally, Royal Roussillon retreated as well. "Our right [north]," wrote Lapause, "gave way and was followed in turn by the entire left, with the greatest disorder."

The result, according to the naval officer Jérome de Foligné, was "a rout, which I dare say was unprecedented, in which our troops became as cowardly as they had been brave at the beginning of the action."

When French officers described the mood of the army, they spoke of terror so great that it became a kind of insanity. Johnstone portrayed the regular infantry as needing "to cure their madness and settle their wits, which had been terribly astray ever since the battle." Marcel referred to "unequalled terror"; Foligné to "a panicked terror."

Some officers attempted to stop the rout. They failed completely. Marcel watched, appalled: "Nothing . . . could stop the fugitives . . . [F]inally, the disorder became so great that it was impossible to rally the troops . . . [T]he pathetic remnants retreated." The French fled so quickly, confessed an officer of the *troupes de terre,* that "we hardly had time to carry off some of our wounded."

BATTLEFIELD PANIC

French regulars were no less resolute and no less disciplined than their British counterparts. They had beaten British armies before. They would do so again. But on September 13, they reached their limit. Fighting with valor and determination, the survivors of Wolfe's fusillade stood their ground until they had nothing more to give.

Wolfe's musket balls had spared their bodies but seared their souls. After perhaps fifteen minutes of gunfire, Montcalm's battalions suffered a complete collapse of morale and will to fight.

Battlefield panic is contagious, leaping from soldier to soldier like a ravenous virus, changing each one from a fighting combatant into a traumatized individual and entire armies into crowds of fugitives. This had happened before in the Seven Years' War in North America, but always to the British, never the French.

After the Battle of the Monongahela in 1755, British officers and soldiers were so demoralized that their acting commander marched them off to winter quarters in July. They did not regain their combat effectiveness until the following year. Three years later, a defeated British army quit the field at Carillon in good order, then shattered into panicked fragments in the face of an imagined French counterattack.

In each case, the British fled after suffering heavy casualties in a battle lasting hours. At the Plains of Abraham, the French endured the same trauma in a matter of minutes, with the same results.

No longer under discipline, no longer an army, they turned away from their enemies and fled for their lives, abandoning not just the battlefield but their best chance of saving Quebec.

CHAPTER 24

Dying Generals

CHARGING INTO THE SMOKE

By the time the French began to give way, so many shots had been fired that in parts of the battlefield both sides were firing blindly into swirling clouds of black-powder smoke. On the north wing of the British line, the Frasers took a few moments to realize that their opponents had fled. With "the fire slackening and the smoke of the powder vanishing," wrote Malcolm Fraser, "we observed the main body of the enemy retreating in great confusion towards the town."

In the center, the Forty-Third and the Forty-Seventh advanced a few steps and fired a general volley. While smoke billowed about the British, the French turned and ran. "By the time the cloud of smoke was vanished," wrote Knox, "our men were again loaded, and, profiting by the advantage we had over them, pursued them almost to the gates of the town."

Other British units made use of the smoke to attempt to charge the French undetected. One officer recorded that the British troops in his vicinity "gave them a full fire, fixed our bayonets, and under cover of the smoak push'd at them."

At the south end of the British line, reported Townshend, James Wolfe placed himself "at the head of Bragg's [the Twenty-Eighth] & the Louisbourg Grenadiers, advancing with their bayonets."

HERBIN'S CANADIANS

Captain Louis-Frédéric Herbin watched them come. As the British ran down the side of Wolfe's Hill through swirling smoke and deafening noise, he might not even have noticed the officer in the plain red coat, carrying a musket instead of a sword, who led the charge. But later when he described his role in the battle and the achievements of his troops, Herbin declared that he "commanded the 800 Canadians on the left of the army who killed the English general."

THE DEATH OF WOLFE

When Wolfe led the bayonet charge down Wolfe's Hill, James Henderson was right beside him. This made Henderson perhaps the best-placed Briton on the field that day. Staying close to Wolfe meant that any displays of "courage and resolution" by Henderson would occur within sight of a patron who could transform him from an unpaid volunteer into a commissioned officer.

Things didn't work out as Henderson might have hoped. Wolfe, he wrote, "was scarce a moment with me till he received his fatal wound. I my self received at the same time two wounds for I was close to him, one in the right shoulder & one in the thigh."

A naval officer's letter provides the most detailed account of Wolfe's injuries: "He first received a musket ball through his right wrist, which tore the fingers cruelly but he wrapped his handkerchief round it, and marched on. The next he received was in his belly, about an inch below the navel, and the third shot just above the right breast. He then went reeling aside, but was soon supported by his officers."

Henderson, Lieutenant Henry Browne of the 28th, and a soldier of the Louisbourg Grenadiers rushed to support their wounded leader. "When the General received the shot I caught hold of him and carried him off the field, he walked about one hundred yards and then begged I would let him sit down, which I did."

Holland, returning from the northern flank to report to Wolfe, "found him mortally wounded and carrying [sic] off the field." Joining Browne, Henderson, and the grenadier, "I assisted in supporting his wounded arm while we brought him down the hill to the right of the 48th regiment."

They lay Wolfe on the ground. Henderson opened Wolfe's vest "and found his shirt full of blood." The surgeon's mate from the Forty-Eighth examined the general's wounds but found him past saving. Holland gives a sparse, bleak account of Wolfe's death: "The dear General with an anxious wishful look continued his eye fixed on the field of battle. On a wounded grenadier coming towards us, & crying out The French Run, he was near his last moments & on my repeating it, he closed his eyes & breathed his last without a groan. From the time I came to him, he never uttered a single syllable . . . His body was conveyed directly to the water side."

At the Anse au Foulon, Gordon Skelly was present as Wolfe's "body was brought down to the landing place, and carried on board the Lowestoft . . . Besides the wound in his breast, which proved mortal, he received another before that in his wrist, both of which we saw upon putting his body into the boat."

By 11:00 a.m., an hour after the French charge began, sailors had rowed Wolfe's body out to HMS *Lowestoft*.

Benjamin West, *The Death of General Wolfe*. The iconic image of the Seven Years' War in North America.

"KILL'D BY MY GRAPESHOT"

As the infantry charged and Wolfe died, British gunners continued to fire. Williamson, in his official report, portrayed this phase of the engagement as another triumph for the artillery. Yorke's cannon, he wrote, "drove them [the French] part into the town the rest ran precipitously over Charles River." He furthermore gave his gunners credit for inflicting the most celebrated French casualty of the battle: "General Montcalm was killed by my grapeshot from a light 6 pounder."

THE DEATH OF MONTCALM

Montbeillard had left his guns behind to follow the charge down the hill. When the French army broke, he rode back to the cannon opposite Wolfe's Hill and brought them down the road to the Porte Saint-Louis. Outside the gate, he paused to survey the wreckage of the French army—soldiers running "as fast as their legs could carry them," the British in hot pursuit, and "eight hundred men from all the battalions," driven by fear, swarming through the gates into the city. "I then saw M. le Marquis de Montcalm arrive on horseback," Montbeillard wrote, "supported by three soldiers."

Montcalm had been riding toward the city when a shot slammed into the small of his back, shattering bones and tearing through muscles and internal organs. The three soldiers had reached him just in time to save their general from falling to the ground. Montbeillard joined Montcalm and rode with him through the gate.

Inside the city, they made their way to the home of the Quebec surgeon André Arnoux, who was serving on the Lake Champlain frontier. Examined by another surgeon, Montcalm asked how long he could expect to live. The doctor replied that he might survive until about three in the morning.

At some time in the afternoon or evening of September 13, Montcalm performed his final official act as the commander of the French army in Canada. Drawing on his last reserves of strength, he dictated and signed a letter to James Wolfe. Disregarding Vaudreuil's authority as governor-general, the escape of most of his army, and the absence of anything resembling an immediate threat to Quebec, Montcalm attempted to hand over the city.

Sir,
Obliged to surrender Quebec to your arms, I have the
honor to ask your Excellency to see to the care of our sick
and wounded and to ask you to fulfill the terms of the treaty
of exchange between His Most Christian Majesty and His
Britannic Majesty.

Montcalm passed the night chatting with Marcel and a few other officers, lived an hour or two past the predicted time, and died around 4:00 or
5:00 a.m. on September 14, 1759.

Foligné described the funeral: "At 8:00 p.m., M. le Marquis de Montcalm . . . after receiving the last sacraments, was buried in a shell hole
under the choir of the Ursulines' church."

THREE OFFICERS IN SEARCH OF A PATRON

Soldiers on both sides mourned the loss of their generals. A few worried
that the shots that killed Wolfe and Montcalm might have killed their
careers as well.

As sailors rowed Wolfe's body out to HMS *Lowestoft*, Henderson
despaired. For him, Wolfe's death represented potential professional disaster: "I thought [that] in him I had lost all my interest." This pessimism
proved premature. "Gen. Monckton . . . upon his first taking the command, inquired for the volunteer that distinguished himself so much on
the 13th Sept with Gen. Wolfe as he thought it a duty incumbent on him
in honour to Gen. Wolfe's memory to provide for that Gentleman. And in
a few days he sent me my commission . . . in the 28th Regiment . . . which
is one of the finest . . . in the service."

Alexander Murray, who had counted Wolfe as a patron as well as a
friend, was less fortunate. After the battle, he lamented to his wife that his
career might have hit a dead end: "I hear no confirmation of the promo-
tions I mentioned to you. I have nobody now to represent my services . . .
since I lost my good friend Wolfe, who would have set my actions off in a
true light had he lived . . . I must own his death has given me more afflic-
tion than anything I have yet met with, for I loved him with a sincere and
friendly affection, and he told me that I was to go home with him & he

would give me everything in his power; and now after this stroke he would have got anything he asked for, but nothing is sure in this world."

Inside Quebec, Marcel grappled with the same problems. Unlike Henderson and Murray, however, he began to search for a new patron even as he saw to the disposition of Montcalm's effects.

Regarding those effects, Marcel kept the general's silver plate, silverware, sword, pistols, and personal seal to return to the Montcalm family. He sent Joseph, Montcalm's valet, to Montreal with the rest of the general's possessions.

More important, Marcel carried out Montcalm's request to ensure that his papers ended up in the right hands. When Joseph left Beauport, he carried a briefcase filled with confidential documents. Marcel wrote to Lévis to warn him to expect Joseph and to let him know that he could find a box containing additional papers in Montcalm's rented house in Montreal or in the Montreal Seminary.

As for his career, Marcel chose to approach both Lévis and Bernetz. "You know my situation," he wrote to Lévis, "without means and without a protector . . . I beg your protection and your goodwill for someone who could not hold you in greater esteem and respect." For the moment, though, he placed himself under Bernetz's command—"I will try to win his friendship and approval"—and prepared to take part in the defense of Quebec.

MONTCALM AND WOLFE

However prominent Montcalm and Wolfe might have been before and after the firefight, surviving participants did not record any positive action whatsoever on the part of the two generals during the battle itself. Between the moment that Montcalm ordered the French army to charge down the Buttes-à-Neveu and the moment that Wolfe led a charge down the side of Wolfe's Hill, the generals remained effectively invisible. They issued no dramatic orders to fire, stand, or retreat and exercised no discernible influence over the course of events.

Eyewitness accounts speak instead of masses of soldiers and officers,

locked in formation or scattered in handfuls, caught up in the coldly brutal dynamics of a black-powder battle. Montcalm and Wolfe led from the
front, running the same risks as any other combatants on the field. But
it was their anonymous soldiers who fought the battle and changed the
course of history.

CHAPTER 25

The British Charge

THE MISSING PIPER AND THE HIGHLAND CHARGE

Of all the British units charging across the Plains of Abraham, Fraser's Highlanders attracted the most attention.

To outsiders, the Highland charge was something out of the past, with wild Scots in primitive costumes shrieking Gaelic and brandishing claymores. Ordered by Brigadier James Murray to pursue the French, the Frasers surged forward. Ouiharalihte, banished from the battlefield by his grandfather, watched admiringly: "I here saw for the first time soldiers dressed in short petticoats like women. They were good warriors and as fleet of foot as we Indians. They seemed to be always in the front."

A sergeant major from the Louisbourg Grenadiers described how the "Highlanders rushed in amongst the thickest of their column with their broad swords, with . . . irresistible fury."

Yard-long basket-hilted broadswords, claymores were terrible weapons that inflicted ghastly wounds. James Thompson saw a French soldier that "had one of his cheeks lying flat down upon his shoulders." The naval volunteer, whose sailors had observed the battle from behind the Highlanders, shuddered at the sight. "The bullet and bayonet are decent deaths, compared with the execution of their swords."

Viewed from within, the Highlanders were a little less feral and much more idiosyncratic. Willing to fight and inflict terrible injuries, many Fras-

ers flinched away from the carnage of the battlefield. At least one chose not
to fight at all.

When the Frasers advised their piper to stay off the firing line,
they'd expected him to return to play if the battalion charged. Then they
would advance to the music of the pipes, a wild, intoxicating howl that
inspired Highlanders and intimidated their enemies. Instead, the piper
remained prudently out of sight. James Thompson witnessed this rather
awkward moment in Scottish-Canadian military history: "When our lines
advanced at the charge, General Townshend [probably James Murray]
observing that the piper was missing, and he knowing well the value of
one on such occasions, he sent in all directions for him, and he was heard
to say aloud 'Where's the highland Piper?' and 'Five pounds for a piper!'
but devil a bit did the piper come forward the sooner. However the charge
by good chance was pretty well effected without him, as all those who
escaped can testify."

Outraged, the Frasers imposed their own sanctions on their missing
musician: "For this business the piper was disgraced by the whole of the
regiment, and the men would not speak to him, neither would they suffer
his rations to be drawn with theirs, but had them served out by the com-
missary separately, and he was obliged to shift for [look after] himself as
well as he could."

Bereft of their musical accompaniment, the Highlanders flung down their
muskets, drew their swords, and charged into a slaughterhouse. Malcolm
Fraser observed, "In advancing, we passed over a great many dead and
wounded, (French regulars mostly) lying in front of our regiment." James
Thompson later described how the French "lay there as thick as a flock of
sheep, and just as they had fallen, for the main body had been completely
routed off the ground and had not an opportunity of carrying away their
dead and wounded men." Crossing this carpet of suffering humanity left
Thompson thoroughly shaken: "It was horrid to see the effect of the blood
and dust on their white coats!"

Wherever they could, the Scots took prisoners. "When the French
gave themselves up quietly," wrote Thompson, "they had no harm done
to them, but . . . if they tried to [out]strip [outrun] a Highlandman, they
stood but a bad chance, for whack went the broadsword."

The Highlanders suffered casualties as well as inflicting them. A rumor after the battle had Ewan Cameron killing nine French soldiers before a cannonball ripped off his sword arm. "He immediately," wrote a British officer, "snatched up a bayonet, and wounded several more; but an unlucky bullet penetrating his throat, leveled him with the ground." A musket ball smashed the arm of Donald MacLeod. The seventy-year-old sergeant from the Isle of Skye kept on going until a second shot fractured his shinbone. Only then did he allow himself to be helped off the field and taken to the Anse au Foulon.

Meeting minimal resistance, the Highlanders swept across the plains, up the hillside of the Buttes-à-Neveu, across the hills, and down the other side until they came within musket shot of the Bastion des Ursulines.

Although they never managed to catch up with the main body of the French, some Highlanders believed that the Seventy-Eighth could have taken Quebec all by themselves, had it not been for the Canadians and the Native Americans. Macpherson declared that "they pursued them to the very sally port of the town and killed several men in their ditch and glacis and might have entered easily were our army large enough to afford them a proper support and to provide against about 5000 Canadians and Indians that had been posted . . . on our flanks and rear in the woods."

Adam Williamson recorded his father's experience: "Colonel Williamson pursued [the French] at the head of the Highlanders & was following the enemy into town, but for an order from Brigadier Murray," to withdraw to confront the skirmishers in the bush. Without this order, in Adam Williamson's opinion, the Frasers would have broken into the city and had "the inhabitants flying out of town as fast as possible."

Murray's command brought the Seventy-Eighth back to the western edge of the buttes, where Montcalm had lined up his battalions earlier that morning. Along the way, they rounded up numerous French soldiers who had been left behind by the charge.

JOSEPH TRAHAN, TEENAGER AT WAR

Joseph Trahan, the teenage Acadian who had watched Montcalm ride along the French line, remembered the Highland charge as a fast-moving, chaotic nightmare, with French regulars and Canadian militiamen fleeing in panic, Canadians and Native Americans shooting down their pursuers, Frasers slashing with their claymores, French fugitives hacking at wounded Scots or mutilating their corpses, and combatants from both sides hopelessly intermingled:

> I can remember the Scotch Highlanders flying wildly after us, with streaming plaids, bonnets and large swords—like so many infuriated demons—over the brow of the hill. In their course, was a wood, in which we had some Indians and sharpshooters, who bowled over the *Sauvages d'Ecosse* in fine style. Their partly naked bodies fell on their face, and their kilts in disorder left exposed a portion of their thighs, at which our fugitives on passing by, would make lunges with their swords, cutting large slices out of the fleshiest portions of their persons.

Faced with this horror, Trahan turned and fled. He ran until a musket ball slammed into the calf of his leg and he fell to the ground, convinced that he was about to die.

TO THE WALLS OF QUEBEC

While the Highlanders charged with their claymores, the rest of Wolfe's battle line charged with bayonets. Much less colorful and not quite as fast as their kilted comrades, they were equally effective.

Most eighteenth-century foot soldiers carried bayonets; very few ever attacked anyone with them. Attaching a bayonet to the muzzle converted a musket into a formidable spear. But it was the threat of impalement rather than the shock of cold steel that broke lines of infantry. Fleeing soldiers ran just as fast as charging soldiers, making bayonet charges more an exercise in sprinting than stabbing.

On the south side of the Plains of Abraham, however, the Louisbourg Grenadiers actually used their bayonets in a bayonet charge. Leaving the dying Wolfe behind, they managed to stab at least a few of their adversaries. "Several of my Grenadiers' bayonets were bent," wrote Alexander Murray, "and their muzzles dipped in gore."

Just north of the Louisbourg Grenadiers, the Twenty-Eighth and the Forty-Third pursued the French to the walls of Quebec. Most of the guns on Quebec's ramparts had been mounted on the sides of the bastions, to fire on attacking infantry. As the British came into range, a single cannon opened fire with grapeshot. The British pulled back out of the cannon's arc of fire and began to look for a less dangerous target.

The Forty-Seventh charged alongside the Frasers but soon fell behind. Lacking writers and raconteurs like Malcolm Fraser, Macpherson, and Thompson, they dropped out of sight for the rest of the battle. The Fifty-Eighth advanced a few moments after the Scots and chased the French into the Saint-Jean suburb. Sergeant Johnson described his battalion in action: "Every man, exerted himself, as if possessed with a spirit of enthusiasm, for the honour of his country; crying out aloud one to another, *Death or Victory;* every one striving to excel his comrade, and to fix a laurel on his own brow."

Somewhere along Quebec's fortifications, British soldiers shifted their fire from fleeing French soldiers to by-standing spectators, either by accident or because they were so stressed and excited that they couldn't stop shooting. An anonymous British officer recorded, "We followed them almost to the gates of the town, which they forgot to shut for almost 2 hours after the action, they were in such confusion, a fair opportunity for us to enter. Our musket shot killed some people who were on the walls to see the affair."

JAMES JOHNSTONE'S GREAT ESCAPE

Separated from Montcalm and caught up in the retreat, James Johnstone fled for his life. Any other officer of Montcalm's staff, or, for that matter, any soldier in Montcalm's army except a few British deserters, could surrender into an honorable captivity. Not Johnstone. As a known rebel against the British Crown and a British subject serving in the French army, Johnstone could reasonably anticipate a quick trial and unceremonious execution if he fell into British hands.

He tried to avoid Quebec, afraid of being trapped inside; fleeing soldiers dragged him irresistibly toward the city: "I was carried off by the flow of the fugitives without being able to stop them or myself until I got to a hollow swampy ground where some cannoneers were endeavouring to save a field piece which stuck there."

When the officer commanding the guns at the northern end of the

French line had been wounded, Sergeant La Rivière of the Artillerie Royale took charge. He ordered the gunners to cease fire and move the cannon back to the city. Everything went well until one of the field guns sank into the mire.

Pausing for just long enough to shout out a few words of encouragement to La Rivière and his gunners, Johnstone turned and rode back up the buttes, where he found himself surrounded by British soldiers (probably from the Fifty-Eighth Regiment). They noticed him too. Like any number of soldiers before and after him, Johnstone felt as if every single musket were firing directly at him: "Taking me for a general on account of my fine black horse they treated me as such by saluting me with thousands of musket shots from half of the front of their army which had formed a crescent."

Galloping for safety, Johnstone rode down the slope on the north side of the Quebec Promontory called the Coteau Sainte-Geneviève. He passed about two hundred Canadians who had rallied near Cadet's bakery and were climbing back up the promontory to rejoin the battle. At the foot of the slope, he rode for a French entrenchment covering the bridge over the Saint-Charles. The story of his dash to safety lost nothing in the telling: "I escaped their terrible fire without any other harm than four balls through my clothes which shattered them, a ball lodged in the pommel of my saddle, and four balls in my horse's body, who lived notwithstanding his wounds until he had carried me to the hornwork [entrenchment]."

ACTION ON THE NORTH FLANK

As the charge continued, Townshend remained on the British north flank with the Fifteenth Regiment and light infantry. Still engaged by Dumas's skirmishers, he sent the Second Battalion of the Sixtieth to hold the space formerly occupied by the Fifty-Eighth and the Seventy-Eighth. Their presence, he hoped, would restrain "the enemies right & a body of their savages which worked still more towards our rear opposite our light infantry posts, waiting of an opportunity to fall upon our rear."

When Canadian resistance on the north flank slackened, Townshend ordered the Royal Americans to advance to the Buttes-à-Neveu. As soon as they arrived, they joined in the second battle of the day, a battle that the British appeared to be losing.

CHAPTER 26

The Canadians Strike Back

THEIR FINEST HOUR

Wolfe's volleys had won the battle but not the war. Montcalm's battalions were on the run, but for as long as they remained intact, Canada could continue to resist. If, on the other hand, the British could run the fugitives to ground, the Seven Years' War in Canada would effectively be over by noon. The remaining French forces—Bougainville's column at Cap-Rouge, Bourlamaque's army on Lake Champlain, and the Quebec and Great Lakes garrisons—lacked the strength to defend the colony on their own.

Yet so far the British had only defeated the French regular infantry. Canadians who began the charge in the battle line but dropped out to fight in their own way had, in avoiding the close-range firefight, also avoided the trauma that broke the regulars. They retained both their ability to fight and their desire to defeat the British. Canadians and Native Americans on the north and south flanks missed the clash of heavy infantry altogether and never stopped fighting. While the professionals fled, the militiamen and the warriors remained in the field and continued the battle.

For the Canadian militiamen, the Battle of the Plains of Abraham became their finest hour. Faced with devastating British firepower followed by a charge with broadswords and bayonets, they ran just as fast as the French regulars but not nearly as far. Not every Canadian was a hero. Some fled with the regulars, some stayed to fight, some compromised by continuing to run while striking out at the British when they could do so without risk to themselves. Others ran right off the battlefield, then stopped, turned around, and rejoined the fighters. In any event, enough stayed and fought to stop the British dead in their tracks.

Captain Étienne Charest, the only militia officer to receive the Croix de Saint-Louis during the Seven Years' War, recalled the battle in terms that speak to the pride of Canadians in their achievements that day: "At the action of September 13 on the heights of Quebec, he withstood at the head of his company the strongest efforts of the enemy and ran the greatest risks."

The first Canadians to turn on the British came from among those who had been attached to the regular battalions. A *troupes de la marine* officer with a classical education compared these Canadians to both Native Americans and the Parthians, mounted archers whose favorite tactic was to feign flight, then whip round and open fire: "Only the regulars collapsed completely. The Canadians, accustomed to withdraw like the natives (and the ancient Parthians), then turn to hit back at the enemy with more confidence than before, rallied in several places and, taking cover in the bush, which was everywhere, forced various [British] units to fall back, but finally had to yield to superior numbers."

More organized resistance began under the walls of Quebec. With Montcalm wounded and the army collapsing, Vaudreuil assumed tactical command on the battlefield.

The governor-general had been on his way to the buttes with two battalions of Montreal militia when the firefight began. Hearing heavy gunfire from the Plains of Abraham, Vaudreuil left the infantry behind and raced ahead in his carriage. When he reached the Saint-Charles bridge, he found the army broken and a mob of regulars milling about alongside the river.

Catching sight of Montreuil, the senior officer present, Vaudreuil sought his assistance in organizing a counterattack. Montreuil, who preferred to dig in at the entrenchment on the far side of the bridge, ignored a direct order from his commander in chief. Vaudreuil exploded in anger; Montreuil refused to yield.

Montbeillard arrived from Quebec in time to witness this confrontation. Listening in silence, he privately ridiculed Vaudreuil, his desire to renew the action, and the Canadians: "What an idea! Lead a few scared Canadians into a new battle, or rather, have someone else lead them."

Confronted with Montreuil's unwillingness to obey orders and running out of time, the governor-general gave up. He crossed the bridge and the Saint-Charles valley, then passed through Quebec and out the Porte Saint-Louis into a crowd of fugitives. The British, he wrote, had "pursued them into the Saint-Louis suburb: it was at this moment that I arrived on the heights of Quebec."

Calling out, he appealed to the regulars and the militiamen, attempting to persuade them to return to the fight. The regulars ignored him. "The Canadians were more attentive to my voice," Vaudreuil wrote. "I assembled 1,000 to 1,200 who returned to the heights where they fired for a long time." Vaudreuil sent them forward "to cover the retreat of the right of our army, commanded by M. Dumas."

This description makes it appear that Vaudreuil rallied the troops all by himself. In fact, he also called upon officers of the *troupes de la marine* to organize detachments of militiamen and colonial regulars and lead them back into action. Vaudreuil gave particular credit to Ensign François-Marie Balthazara d'Albergati-Vezza of the *troupes de la marine*.

Born in Bologna, in northern Italy, Albergati-Vezza had come to Canada in 1750 and been shot through the knee while besieging George Washington's Fort Necessity in 1754. Five years after the Battle of the Plains of Abraham, Albergati-Vezza told his story: "On September 13, 1759, he covered the retreat of the French army at Quebec with a body of troops and militia, that he had . . . assembled, and following the orders of the Marquis de Vaudreuil, and in his presence, successfully confronted the enemy until the army returned [safely to Beauport]."

The French retreat had left Dumas hanging in the air. He accordingly broke off his attack on Wolfe's north flank and slid his force eastward to the Buttes-à-Neveu and Coteau Sainte-Geneviève. There he joined the fight against the Highlanders, and, reported Vaudreuil, his troops "forced the enemy left to fall back three times."

Vaudreuil had planned to reinforce Dumas and Albergati-Vezza with the Montreal battalions: "From moment to moment I expected the militia I'd left behind to arrive, but they had been stopped on the bridge by the adjutant general [Montreuil]."

When an angry Vaudreuil returned and demanded an explanation, Montreuil asserted "that he had seen about forty boats" that might land troops at Beauport. Vaudreuil, who considered the destruction of Wolfe's army to be the first and only priority for the French, dismissed this as a flimsy excuse—"as if we had to worry about that if we could beat the enemy before Quebec."

BRITISH RETREATS

With Canadians and Native Americans continuing to resist in the brush atop the Buttes-à-Neveu and along the north side of the Quebec Promontory, Murray had the Frasers turn north and march through the trees to shove them off the field. Moving toward the Saint-Charles valley, they ignored an ineffective cannonade from the city walls, then ran into a wall of fire from sharpshooters in the brush and the Saint-Louis and Saint-Jean suburbs.

The French collapse and the British charge had shifted the battle from an open field suitable for a face-to-face clash between heavy infantry to rugged terrain ideal for the skirmishing tactics of the Canadians and the Native Americans. On the Plains of Abraham, the Highlanders had enjoyed a significant advantage over militiamen whose lack of bayonets denied them a weapon suitable for close-quarter combat. In the brush atop the Buttes-à-Neveu and along the Coteau Sainte-Geneviève, the situation was reversed. Here, branches and tree trunks became shields that prevented the Highlanders from using their otherwise deadly swords; trees, bushes, and the buildings in Quebec's suburbs provided cover and concealment for Canadian and Native American sharpshooters.

Before long, the Scots were in trouble. In Macpherson's words, "When the Highlanders were gathered together, they were laid on a separate attack against a large body of Canadians on our flank that were posted in a small village and a bush of wood; here, after a wonderful escape all day, we suffered great loss both in officers and men."

Unable to penetrate more than a short distance into the bush, lashed by fire from concealed Canadians and Native Americans, the Highlanders

The Coteau Sainte-Geneviève. Displaying "incredible rage and despair . . . they [Canadians] disputed the ground inch by inch from the top to the bottom of the height." The Canadian militiamen made their stand and Johnstone galloped for safety just beyond this section of the hillside.

withdrew to the Grande-Allée. For the first time since the battle began, the French had compelled a British battalion to give ground and retreat.

After the Highlanders re-formed at the Grande-Allée, Murray ordered them to march along the edge of the brush toward the Coteau Sainte-Geneviève. This time, the Frasers managed to push the Canadians and the Native Americans out of the trees and off the Buttes-à-Neveu. They advanced on the Coteau Sainte-Geneviève; skirmishers along the hillside opened fire. Fifteen minutes of intense, accurate musketry, wrote Malcolm Fraser, "killed and wounded a great many of our men, and killed two officers which obliged us to retire a little and form again."

Forced to retreat for a second time, Murray reorganized his troops and attacked once more. This time, the Frasers had help. Unknown to Murray, the Twenty-Eighth and Forty-Third Regiments, led by Lieutenant Colonel Hunt Walsh of the Twenty-Eighth, were already striking at the Canadians farther south. After grapeshot from Quebec's artillery drove them back from the city walls, Hunt's battalions, wrote Knox, "wheeled . . . to the left, and flanked the coppice [small wooded area] where a body of the enemy made a stand, as if willing to renew the action; but a few platoons from these corps completed our victory."

At the Coteau Sainte-Geneviève, the Fifty-Eighth had come from the Saint-Jean suburb and the Second Battalion of the Royal Americans from the plains to reinforce the Frasers. Unlike the Highlanders, these regiments still had their muskets and were thus able to shoot back at their adversaries.

All three battalions drove northward and managed to force the Canadians off the promontory. Resistance was fierce and British casualties heavy. Malcolm Fraser names some of the dead: "It was at this time and while in the bushes that our regiment suffered most. Lieutenant Roderick, Mr. Neil of Bana, and Alexander McDonell, and John McDonell, and John McPherson volunteer, with many of our men were killed."

"INCREDIBLE RAGE AND DESPAIR"

After about ninety minutes of determined resistance, relentless attacks by larger and larger numbers of British regulars finally forced the Native Americans and the Canadians down the Coteau Sainte-Geneviève. With no hope of overcoming the British and reversing the course of the battle, the defenders continued to fight. Displaying, wrote Johnstone, "incredible rage and despair . . . they disputed the ground inch by inch from the top to the bottom of the height."

REFUGEES IN FLIGHT

The spread of the fighting into the suburbs and down into the Saint-Charles valley forced thousands of refugees who had sought sanctuary from the bombardment to flee once again. Quebec's suburbs and refugee camps emptied as permanent and temporary residents poured out of buildings and tents and scrambled toward the Hôpital Général or into the city.

Fugitives of another kind also made their way across the valley to the hospital. "On that day," noted Benoît-François Bernier, the official responsible for the care of sick and wounded troops, "three to four hundred wounded arrived there." These casualties included Augustin Cadet, the uncle who had taught his abandoned nephew the butcher's trade. He died of his wounds and was buried in the hospital cemetery on September 21, 1759.

A few able-bodied French soldiers tried to follow the wounded. Bernier had posted a guard at the hospital at the beginning of the campaign. After the battle, he wrote, "I used it that day to hold off the fugitives who wanted to flee here to avoid the pursuit of the enemy, who in the heat of action could have destroyed this building by fire and gunfire."

Within the Hôpital Général, the nuns were dismayed by the carnage and afraid of the British invaders. "We saw," wrote Marie de la Visitation, "this slaughter from our windows. It was then that charity made us forget . . . the risks we ran within sight of the enemy. Surrounded by hundreds of the dead and dying . . . many of whom were our close relatives . . . we had to set aside our sorrow and find room for them . . . With the enemy dominating the countryside and two steps from our house, exposed to the fury of the soldier, we had everything to fear."

DEATH OF A BAKER

The British followed the Canadians down the hillside and pushed as far as Cadet's bakery, where they killed the baker Pierre-Gervais Voyer beside his own ovens and a Canadian named Clément in a nearby house.

When they attempted to continue their advance, they came under fire from two ships, each mounting eight guns, that had been deliberately run aground at the mouth of the Saint-Charles River. "Captain Thomas Ross," wrote Malcolm Fraser, "was mortally wounded in the body, by a cannon ball from the hulks [ships] . . . of which he died in great torment, but with great resolution, in about two hours thereafter."

Two or three shots from the ships were enough to persuade Murray's troops to break off their attack and withdraw back up the Coteau Sainte-Geneviève. The British had finally overcome the Canadians and the Native Americans, but it had taken the combined efforts of five battalions to drive them off the field.

• • •

Even before the British forced them down into the valley, the Canadians and the Native Americans had already won their battle. Behind them, the regular battalions had crossed the bridge to Beauport and survived to fight another day. With Quebec still in French hands and reinforcements from Bougainville's column presumably on the way, there was still reason to hope that the Quebec campaign might end in a resounding French victory.

END OF THE ACTION

Around noon, both sides broke off the action. The Canadians and the Native Americans could no longer resist the British; the British could not advance against the fire of the French gunships at the mouth of the Saint-Charles. At about the same time, the last French regulars crossed the bridge to safety in Beauport.

The French suffered a shattering defeat at the Plains of Abraham, but their losses were only slightly higher than those of the British. French casualties in the exchange of volleys were roughly balanced by British losses at the hands of the Canadians and the Native Americans.

French accounts of casualties are vague and uncertain, reflecting the chaos and confusion among the French forces and their abandonment of the battlefield. Vaudreuil estimated that 44 officers and about 600 other ranks had been killed, wounded, or made prisoners. As for the British, Townshend reported the loss of 71 killed, 591 wounded, and 3 missing.

From the first shots fired by Vergor's detachment and Douglas's battery until the last shots fired by the gunships at the mouth of the Saint-Charles, the Battle of the Plains of Abraham lasted about eight hours. The master of HMS *Captain,* riding at anchor below the Île d'Orléans, noted the approximate times of the beginning and end of the fighting at Quebec: "At 4 [a.m.] . . . heard very hot firing of great guns and small arms, which continued until noon."

WHOSE VICTORY?

James Wolfe created the Battle of the Plains of Abraham; thousands of French soldiers and Canadian militiamen determined its course and outcome.

Wolfe took the decisions that brought both armies to the plains. Accompanied by Holland, he chose both the battlefield and the ground where the British would form their line. With his army in place, he waited to fire volley after volley into a French army advancing from the east. By allowing Montcalm to occupy the Buttes-à-Neveu, Wolfe eliminated any other option for the British than awaiting a French attack. He could not cannonade the city walls; attacking the French would mean an uphill charge over rough ground.

Faced with a British army just outside Quebec, Montcalm did exactly what Wolfe expected. He assembled his battalions and charged down the broken hillside of the Buttes-à-Neveu and across the plains, straight into Wolfe's killing zone.

In so doing, Montcalm produced a situation in which he lost control of his army. Without direction from above, individual soldiers and militiamen made their own decisions regarding when and how to advance, halt, fire, and retreat. Montcalm's soldiers displayed considerable bravery that day—the regulars in standing their ground under withering fire for longer than they should have, the militiamen and warriors in resisting the British advance. But the disorganization that characterized the French charge produced a series of ineffective volleys, the loss of the firefight, and with it the loss of the battle.

Montcalm based his decision to charge upon a pessimistic assessment of the capabilities of his battalions: "If we give him [Wolfe] the chance to dig in, we will never be able to attack with the kinds of troops that we have."

The French general did not specify what he meant by "kinds of troops" or why he believed that the battalions that defeated the British at Carillon in 1758 had become so much less formidable a year later. In the course of the 1759 campaign, however, Montcalm had made two significant changes to the *troupes de terre* at Quebec. He inserted Canadian militiamen into the ranks of each battalion and split up his regulars into a small elite force serving west of the Quebec Promontory and a larger body of less proficient soldiers at Beauport.

Like most French regular officers, Montcalm considered Canadians to be brave but undisciplined and thus unsuited for service in a European-style battle. Yet as the campaign opened, he elected to attach five to six hundred Canadians to the *troupes de terre*. Then, having created an army of composite battalions, he questioned their ability to perform on the battlefield.

All of which begs the question, what did Montcalm expect from these Canadians? They bulked out the ranks, but without proper training, advancing across level ground in line, let alone trading volleys with an enemy, would have been too much for them. As a veteran officer, Montcalm knew very well that it took time to produce disciplined heavy infantry. But he acted as if simply shoving Canadians into the battalions were enough to convert farmers, artisans, storekeepers, and clerks into regulars.

Montcalm's army spent three months waiting behind entrenchments before the battle. Those months were hardly idle, but they represented an opportunity for Montcalm to organize an intensive training program for the Canadians. Conventional wisdom held that while it took up to three years to complete a soldier's training, a few weeks was enough to turn out troops who could perform reasonably well on the battlefield. Montcalm had those weeks, along with an army's worth of sergeants to act as instructors. But there is no indication that he chose to take advantage of either of these resources and no indication that he did anything else to forge his composite battalions into an army that he thought was strong enough to hold its own against the British.

To give Bougainville a strike force powerful enough to contain a British landing above the Quebec Promontory, Montcalm sent him all of the best troops in the French army. In so doing, he divided the regular component of his army into two parts that differed considerably in skill and determination. Normally, the elite grenadiers and volunteers and their merely competent comrades worked together on the same battlefield, the one contributing enhanced fighting power, the other mass. Separated, they were each weaker for the absence of the other.

This wouldn't have mattered if Wolfe had done what Montcalm expected and struck above or below the Quebec Promontory. If Wolfe had landed above the promontory, Bougainville's elite force could have held off the British while waiting for the rest of the army to arrive. If he had attacked Beauport, the composite battalions could have remained behind the fortifications until Bougainville's mobile column appeared.

Montcalm apparently never considered that he might find himself in a situation where he would engage the British with only a fraction of his regulars and that the grenadiers and volunteers wouldn't be there when they were most needed. James Johnstone, for one, believed that to face the enemy without the elite regulars would be to invite defeat: "The example of the bravest and most courageous soldiers in a regiment, which are the grenadiers and volunteers, suffices to hearten and animate the most cowardly, who follow the road that they show them but cannot lead the way."

Individually, each of Montcalm's decisions responded to a pressing military necessity—the need to strengthen the regular battalions and establish a strong mobile strike force west of the Quebec Promontory. Together, they created what Montcalm himself considered a flawed instrument. His tactics on September 13 sought to compensate for his army's defects. Instead, they led directly to the collapse of his army into a crowd of individuals that charged down the Buttes-à-Neveu to disintegration and defeat.

CHAPTER 27

After the Battle

TOWNSHEND TAKES COMMAND

Victory left the British as scattered and disorganized as the French. Following the death of Wolfe, leadership of the British force had passed by default to George Townshend, James Murray, Hunt Walsh, and individual battalion commanders. Directed by these officers, battalions and groups of battalions moved about the battlefield, each pursuing a worthwhile objective but without coordination or any regard for broader goals. Everyone was out of touch. No individual had an overall picture of what was going on. No one was implementing any sort of a plan to follow up Wolfe's victory.

As soon as Wolfe died, Holland had run to what had been the center of the British line in search of Brigadier Robert Monckton, Wolfe's second-in-command. The battalions Monckton had led into action were long gone, but Monckton was still there, seriously wounded. "I had myself," wrote Monckton, "the great misfortune of receiving one [wound] in my right breast by a ball that went through part of my lungs, & was cut out under the blade bone of my shoulder—Just as the French were giving way which obliged me to quit the field." Unable to exercise command, Monckton was carried off to the Anse au Foulon, along with a number of other wounded officers. By 10:30 a.m., he was aboard HMS *Lowestoft*.

Next down the chain of command came Brigadier Townshend, still directing operations on the north side of the battlefield. Word, however, had spread across the plains that Townshend, like Wolfe and Monckton, had been struck down at the head of his troops. Further inquiry established that Lieutenant Colonel Guy Carleton, not Townshend, had been "wounded . . . *(very severely)*, and was carried off the field before the main body of the enemy came to the charge."

Finally, a messenger reached Townshend with the news that Wolfe was dead, Monckton was wounded, and he was in command. Townshend moved to the center, where he found "the pursuit had put part of the troops in disorder." The sergeant major from the Louisbourg Grenadiers was a little less tactful when he described Townshend taking over an army that was "pursuing the enemy, in a confused disorderly manner."

Townshend sent officers to recall the battalions, which eventually returned and re-formed on the plains. No sooner had the British army reassembled than a second French army approached from the west. Townshend sent the Thirty-Fifth, the Forty-Eighth, and two field guns to meet the new arrivals. The French and the British exchanged a few shots; the French withdrew.

Townshend made no attempt to engage the French more closely. He explained (or excused) this decision in a letter to the British government: "You will not I flatter myself blame me for not quitting such advantageous ground, & risking the fruit of so decisive a day for his Majesties affairs by seeking a fresh enemy posted perhaps in the very kind of ground he could wish for in the woods & swamps."

BOUGAINVILLE'S ATTACK

Approaching the battlefield from the west, Bougainville had sent two officers and one hundred volunteers to recapture the Samos battery and Anse au Foulon. When the British opened fire, all but the officers and eighteen soldiers abandoned the assault; those who pressed the attack ended up prisoners. The French lost forty soldiers and gained nothing.

Bougainville pushed on toward the western fringe of the Plains of Abraham. However, wrote Lévis, "having learned after having come within a certain distance of the enemy army that our own had been beaten, he retired . . . and sent to M. le Marquis de Vaudreuil for new orders."

September 13 had not been a good day for Bougainville, a bright, amiable young man with very little military ability and a withering contempt for all things Canadian. Rather than taking responsibility for his part in the French defeat, he blamed Vergor and, to a lesser extent, Montcalm: "A man allowed himself to be surprised at Anse des Mères [*sic*]; I was at Cap-Rouge. The enemy landed at midnight, no one told me until 8:00 a.m. M. de Montcalm marched and felt obliged to attack without waiting for me; when I arrived within striking distance, the army was in flight, and all the enemy forces came to [attack] me."

CARING FOR THE WOUNDED

The battle won, the British turned their attention to caring for the survivors. Most wounded soldiers on the Plains of Abraham were hours away from medical care. Redcoats who were still on their feet picked up wounded comrades and French soldiers, then carried them to a casualty clearing station (temporary hospital) on the beach at the Anse au Foulon. From there, landing craft brought officers out to the ships in the cove, where naval surgeons saw to their wounds, and ferried the other ranks and prisoners to the British field hospital at Point Lévis.

James Thompson later told the story of how he took part in evacuating casualties. "Our men had nothing better to carry them [the wounded] on than a kind of hand barrow with canvass laid across it . . . The business going on very slowly, I at last got out of patience looking at them. So I set to work, and took up a wounded man to my own share, and did not let him down at the top of that hill, but landed him safe at the temporary hospital. By the time that we had done with them I was fatigued enough, and after I spoiled my red coat in the bargain! The poor devils would cry out lustily when they were in an uneasy position, but we could not understand a word of what they said."

Only a privileged few, beginning with James Wolfe, received immediate treatment on the spot, either from the surgeon and surgeon's mate of the Forty-Eighth Regiment or from the nurse who was the only woman known to have been present during the engagement.

Eleanor Job, thirty-six years old and married to a Royal Artillery gunner, was one of more than five hundred women who accompanied Wolfe's army to Quebec. Women in eighteenth-century armies played essential roles as laundresses and nurses; Job served as head nurse in the British field hospital. Her skill and her willingness to take risks on the battlefield to bind up the wounds of fallen soldiers won her the nickname Good Mother Job among Wolfe's troops.

When the Royal Artillery advanced to the Plains of Abraham, Job came with them. She treated British wounded throughout the engagement and added to her reputation for coolness under fire. After the battle, she embalmed Wolfe's corpse before it was shipped to London for burial.

LOOTING THE DEAD

While Thompson and Job did their best for the wounded, enterprising Britons and Americans looted the bodies of the slain. Private soldiers sought to supplement their pathetically small incomes; volunteers and officers looked for trophies and souvenirs.

The sight of French corpses slashed and mutilated by Highland broadswords had shaken the naval volunteer, but not enough to keep him from surveying those same corpses in search of anything he could steal: "Happy in escaping unhurt, I traversed the field of battle . . . strewed with bleeding carcasses, and covered with unemployed arms."

A few steps across the killing zone, and he found his reward: "A neat silver-mounted hangar [short sword], fastened to the side of an apparently headless trunk, and which consequently was useless to its original French possessor, attracted my attention." Attempting to secure his prize, he received another lesson in the brutal power of the claymore: "When the body was turned over, in order to unbuckle the belt, my astonishment was indeed great: his head lay underneath his breast, one stroke upon the back of his neck, having cut through the whole, except a small part of the skin of the throat, by which it remained connected with the body."

Alexander Murray, another enthusiastic looter, had a different experience. He found battlefield robbery so much fun that he joked about it in an affectionate letter to his wife: "I had almost forgot to tell you that I am a Knight of the Order of St. Louis myself, for I took a cross and a sword in the action with my own hands from an officer of the Regiment of Guyenne."

JOSEPH TRAHAN, TEENAGER ON THE RUN

Joseph Trahan, who had survived the Acadian deportation, also survived the Battle of the Plains of Abraham. Brought down by a bullet in the leg, he feared death at the hands of the Frasers. Instead, the fighting passed him by, leaving him lying among the dead and the wounded. After remaining where he fell for hours, perhaps unconscious, perhaps paralyzed by fear, he managed to rise to his feet and continue on toward the safety of Beauport.

Crossing a landscape strangely empty of both French and British troops, Trahan made his way down the Coteau Sainte-Geneviève to the Saint-Charles valley. He stopped at Cadet's bakery, where he faced one last horror on a horrifying day.

The baker Pierre-Gervais Voyer had built the bakery to produce bread for Montcalm's army and refugees from Quebec. Looking down, Trahan saw Voyer's body lying on the ground next to the ovens. But only the body. Someone, most likely a claymore-wielding Highlander, had decapitated the baker. Voyer's head had been carefully placed, with the macabre humor of the battlefield, atop a stack of loaves.

Eyeing the fresh bread and the severed head, Trahan found himself torn between hunger and revulsion: "Hunger getting the better of me, I helped myself to a loaf all smeared with gore, and with my pocket-knife removing the crust, I greedily devoured the crumb. This was in the afternoon, and the sun was descending in the west."

IV

SIEGE

CHAPTER 28

Besieging Quebec

THE FRENCH RETREAT

Vaudreuil refused to consider the defeat on the Plains of Abraham as anything more than a temporary setback. From the moment he learned of the repulse of the French battalions, his first and only thought was to reassemble the French army and hit back hard. To prepare for the counterattack, Vaudreuil sent a courier to find Bougainville and deliver an order to bring his mobile column to Quebec.

That afternoon, Vaudreuil assembled a council of war at his headquarters in Beauport to determine how and when to strike. Those attending included Bigot, Montreuil, Dumas, and the commanders of the five battalions of the *troupes de terre*. Vaudreuil began by informing his subordinates that "he thought that they could counterattack the next day at dawn, after assembling all of our forces." ("All of our forces" included Bougainville's elite troops, the city garrison, the survivors from the Plains of Abraham, and the Montreal militia battalions.)

This proposal did not go over very well. With Montreuil leading the attack, the military officers "unanimously rejected" renewing the battle "because of the weakness, the dispersal, and the exhaustion of the troops." They recommended instead that the French retreat to the Jacques Cartier River, about twenty-five miles upriver from Quebec.

In their opinion, faced with "a victorious army, superior in number

and quality," the French could not defend Beauport. Under these conditions, "retreat seemed to be the only viable military option."

Vaudreuil and Bigot argued that abandoning the army's tents and
equipment would cripple any future campaigns. The officers remained
unmoved; Vaudreuil bowed to their judgment: "If I had attacked against
the opinion of all of the senior officers, I might have lost the battle and
the colony."

Opinions at this crucial council of war split between officers who had
taken part in the Battle of the Plains of Abraham and officials who hadn't.
Vaudreuil's opponents, including Dumas, a distinguished colonial officer,
had witnessed the devastating effect of the battle on the French battalions.
They had seen the cataclysmic British volleys, been caught up in the subsequent carnage, and shared the horror and terror with their soldiers.

When they spoke, the officers stressed the capabilities of the army,
obliquely conceding that the regulars were just not going to fight and that
they themselves were incapable of restoring morale. Simply remaining at
Beauport made them feel exposed and vulnerable. They did not believe
that their battalions could effectively resist a British crossing over the
Saint-Charles.

Vaudreuil, on the other hand, had seen only the retreat, not the battle.
He had watched the Canadian militiamen, Native American warriors, and
troupes de la marine fight the British to a standstill. Bigot hadn't been there
at all. The two officials spoke from a wider perspective of the overall needs
of Canada and the French Empire. Losing Quebec would mean the end of
French North America north of Louisiana. Defending Quebec was worth
making every effort, running any risk, incurring any number of casualties.

In the end, Vaudreuil and Bigot advocated what *should* be done; the
metropolitan and colonial officers spoke of what *could* be done with the
army in its present state.

Defeat had left the French regular battalions battered but intact, with
reinforcements close at hand, a water barrier obstructing a further British
advance, an open line of communication to the west, and a vital position to
defend. But defeat can tear the heart out of an army just as surely as gunfire
tears apart the bodies of its soldiers. On the afternoon of September 13, the
professional component of the French army was like a wounded animal,
thinking only of safety and flight. Nothing that Vaudreuil and Bigot could

say was going to change this. At the end of the meeting, Vaudreuil reluctantly ordered the army to retreat to the west and abandon Quebec.

That afternoon, the regulars, militiamen, and warriors returned to their camps behind the Beauport entrenchments. Around 5:00 p.m., the troops drew their rations for the retreat. They received orders to take nothing but food and ammunition and to leave their tents standing.

"FRIGHT, DISORDER, AND CONFUSION"

At 9:00 p.m., the army set out from Beauport. Malartic described the order of march. First came the militiamen of Quebec, Montreal, and Trois-Rivières, then the five regular battalions, and finally a rear guard composed of the garrison of the entrenchment covering the bridge over the Saint-Charles. His description made everything seem neat and organized, more like an exercise than a desperate retreat. Montbeillard, in contrast, was aghast. "The disorder," he snapped, "began at the moment of departure. The divisions and equipment were so tangled up and confused that fifty men could have destroyed the rest of our army."

Montbeillard blamed the Canadians, and particularly those Canadians serving in the regular battalions, for this tangled confusion: "The French soldier had forgotten discipline, and instead of training the Canadians, he had picked up all their bad habits."

Johnstone, whose experience of defeat in the Jacobite rebellion of 1745–46 had made him something of an authority on retreats, was even more scathing: "It was . . . not a retreat, but a most horrid and abominable flight, a thousand times worse than that in the morning upon the Heights of Abraham; with such fright, disorder, and confusion that if the English had known it, three hundred men sent after us would have been sufficient to destroy and cut all our army to pieces."

The Hurons, on the other hand, withdrew quietly and efficiently. Ouiharalihte described the movements of the Huron contingent on the afternoon of September 13: "We hastened to the Village [Lorette, now Wendake]. The French and Canadian army that had fought the battle retreated."

That evening, Ouiharalihte watched as the French army passed through Lorette: "He [Vaudreuil] had marched by the Charlesbourg road,—there were not more than five or six and twenty regular soldiers with him, the rest were Militia.—These were in very great numbers, I should think that there were more than 1000;—it took them half a day to pass by the village."

With their allies heading west, the Hurons held a council and decided to evacuate their community. "By 12 o'clock that night we and our women and children had commenced our march," Ouiharalihte explained. "But before doing so, we concealed all that we had in the woods, in the neighbourhood of the Village, taking nothing with us but the ornaments and sacred vessels of our Church."

GEORGE TOWNSHEND

The British won the Battle of the Plains of Abraham, but the French still held the city of Quebec. On Quebec's landward side, a stone wall, backed by an earthen rampart and linking six bastions mounting fifty-two cannon and mortars, sealed off the eastern tip of the promontory. Although insignificant by the standards of European fortresses, these defenses were strong enough to force the British to undertake a formal siege. Responsibility for directing this siege fell on the shoulders of George Townshend, one of North America's first cartoonists.

Townshend secured this title by producing a series of caricatures, some with text balloons, mocking James Wolfe's appearance, character, and conduct of the campaign. Featuring subjects like Wolfe admiring himself in a mirror, inspecting latrines with a telescope, and smugly addressing kneeling Canadians, these cartoons provoked considerable amusement among some of Wolfe's subordinates. They did not, however, improve relations between Wolfe and his brigadiers.

A graduate of Cambridge University, George Townshend joined the British Army as a volunteer in 1742. Like Wolfe and Monckton, he saw action for the first time at the Battle of Dettingen in 1743. Seven years later, he resigned following a quarrel with (and the sketching of several unflattering caricatures of) the commander in chief of the British Army. In 1758, with a new commander in chief in office, Townshend used his political connections to secure a post as brigadier in Wolfe's expeditionary force.

Prior to 1759, Townshend had never commanded any unit larger than a company, never worked with the Royal Navy, and never taken part in a siege. His previous military career had shown him to be an uneasy subordinate, frequently at odds with senior officers. Now he led an entire army and organized the siege of Quebec, in partnership with Saunders and under Monckton's supervision.

The siege of Quebec was very much a combined operation. Marines served ashore alongside the soldiers; the navy provided the logistical services that made the siege possible. On the afternoon of September 13, Saunders wrote to Townshend pledging his unqualified support: "As I have not heard how you are situated, I have sent all the 24 pounders with the ammunition that I had boats for . . . I heartily wish you farther success, and should be glad to know what I can do to promote it."

Although Townshend directed operations in the field, Monckton remained in overall command of the British army at Quebec. Throughout the siege, Townshend sent regular reports to his commander: "I am doing the best I can to make our situation strong, to secure our communications with the river at all events, and taking all the posts I can, consistent with these intentions . . . adieu dear Bob, no man wishes your health more than your obedient servant."

Townshend's closing phrase is significant. With Wolfe's death, everyone in the British high command started getting along much better than before. There is no evidence whatsoever that James Wolfe's military subordinates and naval colleagues ever called him Jim.

QUEBEC'S DEFENDER

When Vaudreuil left with the field army, responsibility for the defense of Quebec fell on the shoulders of an invalid who had spent the past month in the Hôpital Général.

Captain Jean-Baptiste-Nicolas-Roch de Ramezay, fifty-one years old, belonged to the colony's leading Scottish-Canadian family. Ramezay's Scottish ancestors had settled in Burgundy around 1500 and made a place for themselves in the French nobility. His father, Claude de Ramezay, came to Canada in 1685 to serve as an officer in the *troupes de la marine*. A successful immigrant, he built Montreal's Château de Ramezay and served as governor of Trois-Rivières and Montreal and acting governor-general of New France.

Following his father's example, Ramezay joined the *troupes de la marine* as an ensign in 1720. Distinguished service in Acadia and the Great Lakes region won him promotion to captain and the Croix de Saint-Louis. In 1749, he became town major of Quebec, responsible for military discipline, supply, and general administration. Ramezay described his duties in slightly apologetic terms: "During the nine years that I held this post, which did not lead to a career of dazzling action . . . [I dealt with] immense numbers of [minor] details, especially in wartime."

Vaudreuil rewarded this exacting but unspectacular service in 1758 when he appointed Ramezay king's lieutenant. This made him responsible for the garrison and fortifications of Quebec. He remained in command until August 1759, when, "greatly troubled by a serious cold," he checked himself into the Hôpital Général, leaving the Chevalier de Bernetz as acting commandant. Still in his sickbed when Wolfe landed at the Anse au Foulon, Ramezay left the hospital and resumed his responsibilities.

He returned to a city in peril. Before the day was over, Montcalm had been defeated, and the British were at the gates. To hold Quebec, Ramezay had a garrison of 345 regulars from the *troupes de terre,* 130 *troupes de la marine,* 19 gunners, 740 sailors, and 820 militiamen.

Yet of all his troops, Ramezay trusted only the five hundred regulars: "I did not have . . . any confidence in Quebec's useless militia, all artisans who never went to war, mostly older married men, exhausted by the inadequate rations they had been forced to endure for a long time." As for the sailors, "during the siege most of them spent more time robbing cellars than doing their duty."

Nor did he draw any comfort from the fortifications: "Everyone acquainted with the colony knows that that city is not at all fortified, or at least that its fortifications do not make it defensible."

Nonetheless, with a powerful French army close at hand, Ramezay remained confident that Vaudreuil would defend Quebec by defeating the British Army: "I dared to hope that the council of war would decide to force the enemy, either that very night or at least on the next day, to abandon the strong position he had occupied."

Instead, around 6:00 p.m. he received a letter from the governor-general informing him that the army was retreating and Quebec was on its own. With this news came orders to hold out for as long as he could, but not to the point of risking a storm. As soon as provisions ran out, Ramezay was to negotiate a capitulation following a list of terms that Vaudreuil obligingly provided. Most important, in the context of a war that had already seen the deportation of the Acadians and citizens of Louisbourg and the destruction of hundreds of Canadian farms, Ramezay was to insist that the people of Quebec be left in undisturbed possession of their homes and property.

Along with the departure of the army and the defense of Quebec, Ramezay had to cope with a massive refugee crisis. Returning refugees who had fled to safety during the battle had filled the city with women, children, and elders, many of whom had husbands, fathers, and sons serving in the militia of the garrison. Already hard-pressed to feed Quebec's two thousand defenders, Ramezay had to care for twenty-seven hundred refugees as well.

At this point, Ramezay could have been excused for wishing that he'd stayed in the Hôpital Général. "To be deserted so quickly by our army, which alone could defend the city, was a blow." Vaudreuil and the army, he declared, had "abandoned the city to its own resources, or rather, abandoned it to the enemy . . . No one doubted at all that as soon as the army retired, the city necessarily became prey for the enemy."

Seeking to preserve morale among the garrison, Ramezay refrained from publicly announcing the retreat. The fall of night and the tents left standing by the army facilitated this deception. When the sun rose the next morning, wrote Ramezay, "we saw the tents in the same position as before, which made people in the city think that our army was still at Beauport."

If Ramezay had looked west as well as east, he would have seen clouds of black-powder smoke rising above Quebec's landward fortifications. Until September 13, Quebec's gunners had confined their activities to firing at Williamson's batteries at Point Lévis and passing ships and boats. With a British army on the Plains of Abraham, they turned their attention to the city's landward side.

GUNS ON THE RAMPARTS

Captain Louis-Thomas Jacau de Fiedmont commanded Quebec's artillery. An Acadian from Cape Breton who joined the colonial artillery as a noncommissioned officer in 1743, Fiedmont had risen to the rank of captain by 1757. A veteran of three sieges, he had taken part in the defense of Fort Beauséjour in 1755 and attacks on Forts Oswego and William Henry in 1756 and 1757. Now he employed all his accumulated experience to defend Quebec.

Fiedmont's waterfront artillery spent September 13 firing at targets at Point Lévis and on the river. Jérome de Foligné commanded one of the batteries. "During the battle and throughout the rest of the day," he noted, "the city kept up a heavy fire on the landing craft and longboats that carried munitions and provisions from Point Lévis to the battlefield."

The British occupation of the Buttes-à-Neveu presented Fiedmont with a threat that Quebec's fortifications had not been designed to meet. Most of the cannon had been mounted on the sides of bastions—projections on the city walls that served as artillery platforms—to fire obliquely at attackers approaching the city. If the British stormed the walls, these guns would exact a vicious toll. But in the meantime, they posed no danger whatsoever to any siege batteries the British might erect on the buttes to batter down the walls.

Beginning on September 14, Fiedmont did the best he could with what he had. The British were encamped beyond the buttes on the Plains of Abraham, but that didn't mean Fiedmont couldn't hurt them. Townshend's camp and fieldworks weren't out of range, just out of sight.

Hours of hard labor, which must have involved cutting new embrasures in the wall and shifting artillery pieces around, allowed Fiedmont to bring three cannon and two mortars to bear on the British. Unable to assail the enemy with aimed, direct fire, he used these guns to fling shot and shells over the Buttes-à-Neveu into the west. There was no way to tell if they were having any effect, but Quebec's gunners kept on firing regardless. The bombardment continued all through the night of September 14–15.

THE SIEGE BEGINS

By the early afternoon of September 13, Townshend's soldiers had been on their feet or on the move since they boarded their boats around 9:00 p.m. the night before. They had spent hours seated in landing craft or marching north from Point Lévis, then ascended the promontory and advanced to the Plains of Abraham, been rained on, lain down on wet ground, fought one battle against the French regulars and another against the Canadians and the Native Americans, breathed choking clouds of black-powder smoke, and charged all the way from Wolfe's battle line to the walls of Quebec and the floor of the Saint-Charles valley. Now, for the first time since the landing craft began to drift downstream, they could pause for a moment to rest, eat, and clean their weapons. When they had finished, Townshend put them to work.

While the soldiers ate, the Royal Navy had been busy. Sailors had landed boatloads of entrenching tools—shovels, axes, picks, and saws—at the Anse au Foulon, then carried them by hand to the plains.

Some soldiers took up these tools and cleared away the brush that had screened the Canadians and the Native Americans during the battle. Holland oversaw the construction of a chain of earthwork fortifications to protect Townshend's camp and line of communications to the Foulon. An advanced outpost at the edge of the promontory guarded the Coteau Sainte-Geneviève and the Saint-Charles valley.

Other troops roamed the plains, gathering French and British wounded and carrying them down to the Foulon for transport to Point Lévis. One of the wounded would probably have preferred to be left alone. Too severely injured to flee the field, he was discovered by former comrades who identified him as a deserter from the Royal Americans. In spite of his injuries, wrote Knox, the former British soldier "was immediately tried by a general court martial, and was shot to death, pursuant to his sentence."

Corpses were left where they lay. Except for looters, the British were too concerned with the living to pay much attention to the dead.

By nightfall, the joint efforts of Townshend's soldiers and Saunders's sailors and marines had converted a pleasant stretch of farmland into a formidable fortress. The British were firmly ensconced on the Plains of Abraham and ready to begin the siege of Quebec.

Just one more task remained. Around 10:00 p.m., right at the end of a very, very long day, Townshend left the camp and tramped down into the Saint-Charles valley. John Knox provides a brief narrative: "Brigadier Townshend went, with a detachment of two hundred men, to the French general hospital, situated on the river Charles, and about a mile from town . . . The Brigadier found an officer's guard at the convent, but he immediately took possession of the place, by posting a Captain's command there."

THE FALL OF THE HÔPITAL GÉNÉRAL

Fighting on the battlefield had ended at noon; inside the Hôpital Général, the horror continued into the night. Already crammed to capacity, the hospital was almost overwhelmed by refugees from Quebec's suburbs and casualties from the Plains of Abraham. The flow of casualties tapered off during the afternoon, but the mood among patients, refugees, and caregivers remained tense and apprehensive. Marie de la Visitation shared these concerns: "Although we lacked neither faith nor hope, the approach of night redoubled our fears."

When they were not caring for the wounded, the nuns prayed at the foot of the altar for the mercy of God. Toward 10:00 p.m., they heard the most terrifying sound of a terrifying day: "The silence and fear that prevailed among us allowed us to hear a series of violent and repeated blows on our doors."

Two novices carrying soup to the wounded were passing by just as the doors crashed open, revealing a crowd of British soldiers bursting out of the night. Despite the "pallor and fright that seized them," the young women stood their ground. An instant later, Townshend appeared and ordered his troops to remain outside. The brigadier posted guards and summoned the superiors of the three communities of nuns. "He told them," wrote Marie de la Visitation, "that part of his army was going to surround and take possession of our house, out of fear that our [army] which they knew was nearby, would attack them in their entrenchments."

Townshend's arrival at the Hôpital Général marked a grim moment for Canadians. Up to this point, the British had seized control over large blocks of French territory, but this land held nothing but abandoned farms and empty buildings. Canadians had fought the invaders, fled from them, and been held prisoner in their camps or aboard their ships. But they had never submitted to British rule. Now, for the first time, Canadians were living under foreign military occupation; a major Canadian institution had fallen into the hands of the invaders.

CHAPTER 29

Townshend's Siege

THE SCIENCE OF SIEGECRAFT

The British army and fleet spent September 14–17 making preparations to begin a formal siege of Quebec, thereby initiating a process that was as much a ritual as a military operation. One step followed another until a fortress (or city) surrendered, a relief column lifted the siege, or the besiegers gave up. Convenient handbooks like John Muller's *Attac[k] and Defence of Fortified Places* laid out every phase of the attack and every countermeasure for the defense.

Most sieges centered on the construction of a network of trenches, known as "parallels" and "approaches," that surrounded a fortress and allowed besiegers to get close enough to establish "breaching batteries." In a successful siege, these batteries, mounting the besiegers' heaviest guns, cannonaded the walls until they established a "practicable breach"—an opening large enough for soldiers to march through.

At this point, diplomacy took over. Storming a breach would produce heavy casualties among both attackers and defenders. Fortifications were not meant to be invulnerable, just strong enough to delay an attacker and hold out for a few months until relief arrived. A successful storm would almost invariably lead to a general massacre inside the fortress.

Rather than stand a storm, a fortress commander, per military etiquette, would send out an emissary with a list of terms under which the

View of Quebec from the Buttes-à-Neveu. "There are several knolls or hillocks within 400 yards of the works [walls] very capable of containing bastions of 9 & 10 guns each." Following the Battle of the Plains of Abraham, George Townshend established batteries on the buttes (foreground) and prepared to cannonade the walls of Quebec.

garrison would agree to surrender. Following some give-and-take, both sides would agree to articles of capitulation that protected the lives and safety of the garrison and civilians, along with their personal property.

Just as important, attackers would recognize an honorable defense by granting the garrison the "honors of war." This allowed the garrison to march out carrying their weapons, flying their colors, and hauling one artillery piece. If the defenders had a band, they would play music associated with the attackers to demonstrate that they too could honor a valiant adversary.

At the siege of Quebec, Townshend could forgo the construction of parallels and approaches. With the Buttes-à-Neveu overlooking the city, there was no need for anything more complicated than batteries protected by redoubts along the western edge of the hills. The engineer John Montresor noted that "there are several knolls or hillocks within 400 yards of the works [walls] very capable of containing bastions of 9 & 10 guns each."

Geography had turned against Quebec. In French hands, the Buttes-à-Neveu had been a shield, protecting the capital from an attacker on the plains. Occupied by the British, they became a dagger pointed at the heart of Canada, a massive platform for Townshend's siege artillery.

LANDING ARTILLERY, BURYING THE DEAD

On Friday, September 14, sailors continued to land artillery and haul it to the Plains of Abraham. The log of HMS *Stirling Castle* describes the maritime side of this operation: "At 9 all the longboats in the fleet, loaded with cannon and artillery stores, assembled alongside the *Shrewsbury*. At 10 they put off and went above the town to our army."

One British soldier found the sailors rather amusing. Captain James Calcraft watched as "some hundred sailors were employed in drawing . . . cannon up a road . . . a laborious employment, which the honest tars set about with the greatest alacrity. It was really diverting, to hear the midshipmen cry out, *Starboard, Starboard, my brave boys.*"

Calcraft might smile, but in three days the sailors hauled sixty cannon and fifty-eight mortars and howitzers up the Foulon road and overland to Townshend's artillery park.

On the Plains of Abraham, shot and shells sailing over the Buttes-à-Neveu into the British camp wounded several officers and soldiers. Despite this interference, the British continued to prepare for the siege. Army commissaries established a provision depot at the Anse au Foulon. Fascine and gabion making began. Soldiers buried the dead in unmarked mass graves. Along with corpses, the burial parties found a few wounded soldiers who had spent the night in the open. Tacitly acknowledging that his soldiers were looting the bodies, Townshend ordered them to send all the documents they discovered to his headquarters.

As the day progressed, many soldiers chose to avoid hard work and French shells by slipping past the defended perimeter. For the rest of the day, these enterprising individuals roamed the countryside, housebreaking and looting. Attempting to rein them in, Townshend issued the first in a long series of orders on the subject: "No soldier to presume to stroll beyond the outposts." When this failed to have any effect, he issued a second order at 3:00 p.m.: "General Townshend desires the commanding officers of corps will order the rolls to be called every half hour, as the soldiers have been marauding, notwithstanding this day's orders." The marauding continued regardless.

Townshend ignored Montcalm's attempt to surrender Quebec but quickly drew up orders recalling Scott and Goreham. After months of venting his frustrated disapproval of Wolfe's ruthless tactics in letters to his wife, Townshend must have taken some satisfaction in knowing that Wolfe's terror campaign was about to come to an abrupt end.

Still unaware of events at Quebec, the rangers, light infantry, and sailors continued to carry out Wolfe's commands. On September 14, *Zephyr's* log reported that Goreham's soldiers and sailors were "burning & destroying [to] the westward." Scott and his detachment "marched from the River Ouelle in the forenoon to St. Anne's, and on our way burnt one hundred and fifty one houses . . . In the afternoon . . . burnt Ninety houses, a sloop and a schooner." Jeremiah Pearson had a different experience: "We marcht all day & burnt nothing. Strainge today."

COLLAPSING MORALE

The withdrawal of the French army from Beauport might have been necessary, but it proved to be fatal. Shattered morale among the regulars led to the retreat to Jacques Cartier; the disappearance of the army broke the morale of the militia serving in the city garrison.

Ramezay's silence and the illusory presence of the army at Beauport created a false sense of security that lasted for most of the day on the fourteenth. Even when it became apparent that the camp had been abandoned, the Quebec garrison remained reluctant to accept that the army had forsaken it. "They could hardly believe it," wrote Ramezay. "When they saw nothing move in the camp throughout the day of the fourteenth . . . [T]heir despair was complete and their discouragement universal . . . [T]he complaints and muttering against the army that had abandoned us became a public uproar."

This "public uproar" found formal expression on September 15. On that day, twenty-four leading public officials, merchants, and militia officers of Quebec, including Jean-Claude Panet, assembled in what remained of the home of François Daine, Quebec's senior magistrate.

There, they discussed the military situation and considered their options. Shaken by the precipitate withdrawal of the French army and the prospect of a British assault, they concluded that their city's best interests lay in ending the siege by negotiating a capitulation.

Throughout the summer, the twenty-four notables agreed, the Quebec garrison had endured bombardment, fire, short rations, long watches, and constant alerts. They had lost their homes and property to shot, shells, and firebombs. Yet they never lost confidence in ultimate victory, a confidence "sustained by the army that protected us."

With the army on the run and British troops massed outside Quebec, this certainty had vanished. Like Ramezay, they did not believe that the city could defend itself without an army in the field. Apprehension of the consequences of an assault had replaced confidence in victory. "Is there not therefore," argued the notables, "every reason to fear that at any movement a strong and numerous enemy will force or bluff their way into the heart of the city, sword in hand, and kill everyone they see without regard to social rank, age, or gender?"

This was not an idle fear. Three years before, a party of Canadian militiamen and French regulars had attacked the British outpost of Fort Bull on the New York frontier. When the garrison rejected a summons to surrender, the attackers stormed the fort. Of the fifty-nine men and three women within the walls, only four men and one woman survived.

The "mostly older married men" of the militia refused to risk incurring the same fate for members of their families who had sought refuge in Quebec after the battle. Instead, they shifted their priorities from defending the city to attempting to protect "their wives and their children . . . and save their few [possessions] that survived the fires."

Before the French retreat from Beauport, the citizens of Quebec sought survival through armed resistance. Now they turned to accommodation, hoping to come to terms with the British under conditions that would allow them to continue to lead their lives, as far as possible, on their own terms. Their goal remained the same, only the means had changed.

With defeat seemingly inevitable, they concluded that circumstances had left them "no other choice but to make their yoke [the hardships of life under foreign rule] as light as possible" by negotiating a quick capitulation. They drew up and signed a petition and sent Daine to deliver it to Ramezay. In the last paragraph, they reminded the king's lieutenant that "there is no shame in surrender when victory is impossible."

. . .

Daine's visit represented another devastating blow for Ramezay: "In this request, you could see the mood of the militia officers, and thus the mood of those they commanded . . . [It was] this request that made me realize that I could not count on my militia." With the sailors, in his opinion, more inclined to loot than fight, Ramezay's effective garrison had been reduced to a few hundred regulars and gunners, not nearly enough to defend the city.

Ramezay reacted to this development by summoning fourteen senior officers to a council of war "to discuss the means [available] for the defense of Quebec." He had Vaudreuil's orders of the thirteenth read to the assembled officers, including this crucial passage: "We warn M. de Ramezay that he must not wait until the enemy takes [Quebec] by assault, thus as soon as he runs out of provisions he will raise the white flag and send his most capable and intelligent officer to propose a capitulation."

Cadet's senior clerk in Quebec spoke next, reporting that an exhaustive search had turned up enough food for four days on full rations or eight days on half rations.

Following this exposition, Ramezay asked his officers for their opinions in writing. Thirteen of his fourteen subordinates advised immediate surrender. The response of Philippe-Marie d'Ailleboust de Cerry, captain of the port of Quebec, was typical: "In view of the complete lack of provisions without any hope of resupply, my advice is to give up the place and leave with as much honor as we can." One dissented. Fiedmont bluntly advised Ramezay "to reduce the ration again and hold out until the last extremity."

When every officer had expressed his opinion, Ramezay made his decision: "Considering the instructions I have received from Monsieur le Marquis de Vaudreuil and the shortage of provisions, demonstrated by the reports I have received and the searches I have ordered, I have decided to seek the most honorable possible capitulation from the enemy."

AN ARMY RECOVERS

While Fiedmont's artillery kept the British from getting too comfortable on the Plains of Abraham, the French army completed its retreat. Moving quickly—Johnstone said of the march, "We run [*sic*] along in flight all night"—the troops sidestepped past the British by marching north through Charlesbourg and Lorette, then south to Ancienne Lorette. At Ancienne Lorette, they halted around 6:00 a.m. on the fourteenth and made camp as best they could without their tents, kettles, and other equipment.

After a few hours' rest, they were on the move again. Around 5:00 p.m., the head of the column reached Pointe-aux-Trembles, where the army took shelter for the night in barns. Word arrived that Wolfe had been killed and Monckton wounded, leaving Townshend in command of the British army. One Canadian, who evidently regarded Townshend as a major improvement over Wolfe, described him as an officer "whose manners everyone already praised."

The army set out once more at dawn on the fifteenth, then halted on the east bank of the Jacques Cartier River when a broken bridge forced them to wait until noon for boats to ferry them across. Housed once again in local barns, they settled in to rest and recover from their ordeal. Bougainville's elite troops remained at Pointe-aux-Trembles as an advance guard.

The Hurons of Lorette, bringing up the rear, made more leisurely progress. Ouiharalihte gives this account of their movements:

> We marched the whole night [of September 13–14] and reached Capsa, which is just beyond the limits of Old Lorette, about 7 o'clock on the following morning. We passed the whole of that day and the following night there. The next morning as soon as we had boiled our kettles (breakfasted,) we again commenced our march, and reached the hither side of Jacques Cartier River that night; and we put up our cabins on the high lands at its mouth. We crossed this river the next day in the canoes of some of our hunters and with the assistance of the ferryman who had received orders to that effect.

Upriver in Montreal, a courier from Vaudreuil reached the Chevalier de Lévis on the morning of the fifteenth. Informed of the battle at Quebec and ordered to join the army at Jacques Cartier, Lévis prepared to depart immediately. He passed on the news to Rigaud and Bourlamaque and was on his way within two hours.

. . .

At Jacques Cartier, two days of hard marching and then a day of rest, food, and safety on September 16 went a long way toward restoring the army's will to combat. Vaudreuil planned to take the army back to Quebec to lift the siege as soon as Lévis arrived to assume command.

Cadet began accumulating provisions to support the advance and resupply Quebec. This was easier now that the army was above, rather than below, Holmes's squadron and twenty-five miles farther up the French supply line. His task was presumably facilitated by the provision-laden bateaux from Cap-Rouge that had been expected at Quebec on the night of September 12–13. Once the tide had carried them back upriver, he could issue their contents to soldiers or set them aside for transport to Quebec. By the end of the day, Vaudreuil had sent an officer to Saint-Augustin to assemble carts and ordered Bougainville to stand by to escort the convoy to Quebec. Cadet had reported, "By tomorrow I hope to be able to provide several days provisions for the army."

With these preparations under way, Vaudreuil had Thisbé de Belcourt and a cavalry detachment ride back to Quebec to inform Ramezay "that the army had reassembled and that I planned to attack our enemies . . . to save the city."

Belcourt, a naval lieutenant, had come to Canada on the frigate *Le Machault* in the spring of 1759. On June 20, he took command of a cavalry company. Canada's cavalry, organized at the outset of the campaign to provide scouts and messengers, consisted of militiamen led by regular officers. Knox caught a glimpse of them later in the war: "Their light cavalry, who paraded along shore, seemed to be well appointed, clothed in blue, faced with scarlet; but their officers had white uniforms."

Before long, one of Belcourt's troopers returned carrying a disturbing letter from Captain Armand de Joannès, Ramezay's adjutant. While Vaudreuil prepared his relief expedition, the Quebec garrison was preparing to capitulate: "I will not hide from you, sir, that if we do not receive word from you by 10:00 a.m. tomorrow I think that [surrender] negotiations will begin."

. . .

George Townshend. With Wolfe dead and
Monckton wounded, Townshend directed the
British siege of Quebec.

BUILDING BATTERIES

On Saturday, September 15, a French deserter from the city carried a
rumor to the British camp that Knox found very encouraging: "Monsieur
de Ramesay, who commands in the town, and the principal officers of the
garrison, are settling the preliminaries for a capitulation; and the citizens
and the Canadians in general are much dissatisfied, and impatient to have
the town delivered up to us."

That notwithstanding, French cannonballs and shells continued to
soar over the buttes and land on the British. Lacking his own batteries to
respond in kind, Townshend limited his response to moving the British
camp farther away from the city.

The Royal Navy came under fire as well when a French mortar began
to bombard the Anse au Foulon. Its shells, however, neither inflicted any
damage nor slowed logistics operations. Instead, the tempo picked up as

merchant marine longboats and sailors joined their naval counterparts in carrying stores for the army. The log of HMS *Stirling Castle* recorded the day's activities: "At 7 1 flat bottomed boat with tents, 4 with powder and cartridges, 4 with shot, and 1 with 2 8-inch howitzers, together with several men of war and merchant's longboats, 6 heavy 24-pounders, 6 heavy 12-pounders, 4 light 24-pounders, 2 8-inch howitzers, assembled alongside the Pembroke, 1/2 past 10 they put off and went above the town to our incampment."

While shells flew and the navy worked, a party of Highlanders captured the last French soldier remaining on the field. Moving along the road leading to the Anse au Foulon, they discovered a Canadian from Vergor's detachment in the bushes at the edge of the cliff. Asked why he had remained in hiding for so long, "he said he . . . was afraid to attempt his escape from that place, though famishing with cold and hunger, lest he should not get quarter, if he were taken." The Frasers sent him out to the ships as a prisoner of war.

That night Townshend's troops erected a redoubt opposite the Porte Saint-Louis. This redoubt covered the ground where his engineers planned to establish a battery to cannonade the Bastion Saint-Jean.

The fifteenth of September also marked the beginning of the end of Wolfe's campaign against Canadian farmhouses. At four o'clock that afternoon, the captain of HMS *Eurus* passed on Scott's new orders. In Pearson's words, "We lay still today & news came to Major Scott not to bourn no more houses & that our army has had a battle & lost 80–100 men & they have killed 1500 dead on the spot & General Wolfe is killed."

On the same day, *Zephyr* received instructions "to embark the troops and to proceed to Point Levy with all dispatch, [and] began to embark." Local residents marked the departure of Goreham's detachment with one final act of resistance. A Canadian on "the south shore fired a shot at a long boat which was too nigh the shore at anchor."

GIVING UP HOPE

Inside Quebec, the garrison grew weaker as a steady stream of deserters slipped away, mostly at night, occasionally in broad daylight. Some went to the French army, some to the countryside, some to the British camp.

Among the latter was a sergeant who stole the keys to the gate he was supposed to be guarding and turned them over to the British.

More resolute members of the garrison remained alert and ready for action. On September 15, a party of British sailors, daring enough or drunk enough to try breaking into a few houses below Cape Diamond, found this out the hard way. A French detachment opened fire, then took them all prisoner.

Also on the fifteenth, Fiedmont and his gunners came up with a new trick. They moved a heavy mortar to the southernmost bastion and opened fire on British ships above Quebec. Elsewhere on the city wall, three cannon and two mortars continued to bombard the Plains of Abraham all day and all night.

The next morning, Fiedmont's guns found a more promising—and more ominous—target. Sunrise revealed the first siege works, in the form of a redoubt six hundred yards from the Bastion Saint-Jean. During the day, the besiegers threw up a second redoubt facing the Bastion des Ursulines. The British redoubts were well placed and hard to hit. They had, observed Foligné, been "opened in such rugged ground that they could hardly be seen from our ramparts."

This didn't stop the French from trying. They increased the rate of fire from every cannon and mortar they could bring to bear. Shot and shells flew almost continuously toward the redoubts on the Buttes-à-Neveu, the camp on the Plains of Abraham, the boats on the river, and the batteries at Point Lévis.

The sixteenth was also the day that Quebec regained contact with the outside world. An officer from Quebec on his way to search for provisions in the Beauport camp encountered Belcourt and thirty troopers. Belcourt, who appears to have remained on the Beauport side of the Saint-Charles, told him that the army had reassembled and would soon be on its way back to Quebec with Lévis in command.

Seeking confirmation of this hopeful news, Ramezay summoned Joannès and Magnan. He ordered them to ride out to make contact with Vaudreuil "to find out what was going on and whether I could expect him to counterattack."

Their journey began with an unsettling encounter. "I spoke," wrote

Joannès, "with M. de Belcourt, who did not say precisely the same things to me [as he had told the first officer he met] and was very ambiguous in his replies."

They nonetheless continued on to Lorette, where Magnan discovered that Vaudreuil was at Jacques Cartier. Because Ramezay expected them to return before dark, Joannès wrote a letter to the governor-general, warning him that Ramezay was considering capitulation. He handed the letter to a courier, then headed back to Quebec with Magnan to report. "They told me," wrote Ramezay, "that there was so little discipline and . . . so much disorder in the army that there was no reason whatsoever to hope that it was going to come to expel the enemy from his position outside the city."

A NEW BRITISH BATTERY

The British planned to establish a battery opposite the Bastion des Ursulines on the night of September 16. For once, however, interservice cooperation broke down, probably as a result of excessive drinking among the boat crews. "The tools," wrote Townshend, "that was to be brought from Point Levy for the work, after they were put in the boats the sailors threw them out again."

The rest of the navy was rather more helpful and spent the sixteenth continuing to transport supplies, camping equipment, munitions, and artillery to the Anse au Foulon. On the return journey, they carried prisoners and wounded soldiers back to the British camp and hospital at Point Lévis.

READY TO MARCH

At 10:00 a.m. on the morning of September 17, Lévis rode into Jacques Cartier. "His return," wrote Malartic, "filled everyone with joy." Ordered by Vaudreuil to take command of the army and save Quebec, "he announced an advance the next day, saying that, even if we had lost a battle, there was no need to abandon 10 leagues [twenty-five miles] of the country."

Vaudreuil and Lévis planned to lunge eastward to Cap-Rouge, ascend the Quebec Promontory, then approach the British from the west under cover of the Sillery Woods. "If," wrote Lévis, "we had found their army poorly positioned we could have attacked it, or at least by approaching it prolonged the siege with the help that we sent there, in troops and provisions, had we found ourselves unable to sustain a defense [of Quebec], we could have evacuated or burned it, to ensure that nothing remained to allow our enemies to winter there."

As the main body of the army prepared to march, three separate detachments set out for the embattled city.

Each of these detachments moved in a sort of nightmare slow motion. Three days of the fair weather that facilitated the French retreat had been succeeded by high winds and heavy rain. At a time when every moment counted, events consequently unfolded at the speed of a horse and rider, a marching soldier, or a laden cart traveling over wet, muddy roads.

The operation proceeded regardless. First and fastest came Belcourt and twenty troopers. Captain de la Rochebeaucourt, commander of the militia cavalry, gave Belcourt a message for Ramezay: "I will carry 100 quintals [about 1,000 pounds] of biscuit to him this evening."

Next, not quite so fast, Rochebeaucourt himself rode for Quebec at the head of one hundred troopers, each with a sack of hardtack biscuit strapped to his saddle. Along with this token supply of rations, Rochebeaucourt's detachment carried word "that the army was marching to rescue the place [Quebec] at any cost."

Well behind Rochebeaucourt and moving much more slowly came Bougainville and six hundred elite infantry, escorting a convoy of carts carrying provisions. Once inside Quebec, Bougainville's column would provide a strong reinforcement for the garrison.

Cadet needed one more day to accumulate provisions. On September 18, the French army would march for Quebec.

CHAPTER 30

Ramezay's Surrender

NEGOTIATING SURRENDER

Inside Quebec, tension soared as morale collapsed. Joannès, after encountering militia officers who "threatened to do nothing less than abandon their posts" and have their troops do the same, finally lost his temper: "The unseemly declarations of these officers drove me to the point of falling on two of them with my sword." He presumably struck them with the flat of his blade, making the sword into a metal club that could inflict a painful blow without actually drawing blood.

Spirits remained much higher among Fiedmont's gunners. On September 17, Foligné remarked that "in spite of everything [they] maintained a heavy fire on the workers in the trench." Yet by that day, the French had received an infinitely discouraging piece of intelligence. Fiedmont was hurting the British, but not nearly enough to affect the progress of the siege. "According to the English officers who walked from their camp to the Hôpital Général," wrote Foligné, "our cannonballs and bombs had not inconvenienced them, and within three days at the latest they would have a battery of twenty-six to thirty thirty-six-pounders to batter a breach."

Under other circumstances, this news might have shaken the resolve of the garrison and its commander. But the question of how much or how little Fiedmont might be slowing down the construction of the British siege works no longer mattered to Ramezay. Early that morning, he decided that the time had come to surrender: "I found myself abandoned by all the

militiamen, who were in pitifully reduced circumstances. I could only provide their families with a *quarteron* [four ounces] of heated corn [per day],
which produced some very angry words among all of the people . . . [I
had] the enemy camped on the Buttes-à-Neveu, no battery of any use . . .
[and] a city whose walls could no longer prevent a coup de main in several
places where there are nothing but palisades."

Joannès objected. He withdrew his recommendation for capitulation
at the council of war on the grounds that help was on the way and offered
to make his own search for stores of flour inside the city. Ramezay agreed,
and the question of capitulation was left in abeyance.

During the day, Belcourt arrived with word that provisions and reinforcements were moving toward Quebec. His news had no apparent impact
on events. After Bernetz took him out to the walls to see the British siege
works on the Buttes-à-Neveu, Belcourt left the city. With him, he likely
carried the letters that members of the garrison, including Ramezay and
Bernetz, had written to officers with the field army.

Bernetz's letter to Bougainville was an urgent appeal for speed: "Nothing could be better, Sir, than the promises of food and . . . assistance which
you made to M. de Ramezay and the garrison of Quebec, your arrival
cannot be too prompt . . . M. de Ramezay does not want to sacrifice the
population by allowing [Quebec] to be taken by assault . . . [T]here is not
a moment to lose."

When he left Quebec, Belcourt took his detachment to the entrenchment that had guarded the bridge over the Saint-Charles. Finding cannon
that were unattended but intact, Belcourt turned his troopers into gunners
and opened fire on a British outpost at the Coteau Sainte-Geneviève.

Around six o'clock that afternoon, Quebec's endgame began when
Ramezay received three separate reports of threatening British movements.
First, a messenger told him that British soldiers in landing craft were closing on Lower Town. Next came word that eight ships of the line were
off Point Lévis, apparently intending to attack Quebec. Finally, lookouts
reported a column of infantry heading for the Intendant's Palace in the
Saint-Charles valley, where only a wooden palisade shielded the city.

Reports of an impending amphibious attack on Lower Town and a land assault from the Saint-Charles valley later proved to be false. Foligné, at his battery overlooking the St. Lawrence, was not alarmed by the appearance of Saunders's ships. Their presence opposite the city, he wrote, "made people think that they wanted to moor in the night, which will allow them to keep a good watch over the batteries on the ramparts that defend the anchorage." Ramezay nonetheless had his drummers sound the alarm and ordered all of his troops to their posts.

Faced with a terrible choice between loyalty to their families and loyalty to their king and colony, the Canadians of the garrison chose their families. All across Quebec, the militiamen heard the drumbeats and laid down their arms. Believing that the British were about to storm the city, they returned their weapons to the magazine "so that when the enemy enters, he will find them unarmed and will not put them to the sword." As far as the militiamen were concerned, "from that moment they no longer saw themselves as soldiers, but as townspeople."

Ramezay sent an aide to make sure that his orders had been executed. The officer returned and informed him that the militia refused to fight. A moment later, a delegation of militia officers arrived and told Ramezay that they had no intention of resisting an attack. They explained their decision by informing him that they knew he had been ordered to surrender before the British could mount an assault. The militia officers added that "if the army had not abandoned them, they would have continued to give evidence of the enthusiasm that they had made it their duty to demonstrate throughout the siege." Given the circumstances, they refused to risk their lives for a lost cause: "Not seeing any further means [of defense], they did not feel obligated to allow themselves to be massacred in vain, because the sacrifice they would make of their lives would not have delayed the capture of the city by an hour."

The Quebec militiamen had, not to put too fine a point on it, mutinied. Given lawful orders in the presence of the enemy, they chose to disobey and walk away from the war. Once again, the decisions of senior officers proved less important than those of hundreds of individual soldiers in determining the outcome of a military operation.

Ramezay could have had the militia officers placed under arrest or shot on the spot for mutiny and treason. Joannès, for one, would have been happy to oblige. Ramezay could have attempted to persuade them to return to duty. Instead, the king's lieutenant, who might have felt considerable sympathy for the militiamen, accepted their decision to make a separate peace with the British.

After consulting Bernetz and his other senior officers, Ramezay had flags of truce raised over the curtain wall and in Lower Town. Joannès saw the flags go up. Thinking this must be a mistake, he gave orders to take them down. But at that instant, he received instructions from Ramezay to open negotiations.

For Joannès, this order came as an unpleasant, if not entirely unexpected, shock. He had his own ideas of what needed to be done, which did not involve negotiations or surrender. In what must have been a very tense conversation, Fiedmont and Joannès met with Ramezay and advocated abandoning Lower Town and using its garrison to reinforce Upper Town. Ramezay refused.

A disgusted Joannès felt that Ramezay had no idea of what he was doing: "That officer, who has no experience of war except in a forest, did not know how to defend a post."

Unlike the Quebec militia, Joannès chose to obey an unwelcome order. He traveled out to the British camp to meet with Saunders and Townshend. They quickly reached agreement on all but one point of the draft capitulation.

The garrison would receive the honors of war. Canadians would remain in undisturbed possession of their property, provided they surrendered their weapons. The British would neither compel Canadians to leave the colony nor punish those who had served in the militia. They would allow Canadians to freely practice their religion, and protect the personnel and property of the Catholic Church. The French would turn over Quebec's artillery and munitions, along with a complete inventory. French wounded and those who cared for them would not become prisoners of war.

Following Vaudreuil's instructions, however, Joannès had asked that Quebec's defenders be allowed to rejoin the French army. The British insisted that the regulars and the sailors of the garrison be carried to a French port in British transports. Hoping to delay a final agreement until Vaudreuil's reinforcements arrived, Joannès claimed to need to seek Ramezay's consent regarding this change. Townshend gave him until 11:00 p.m. to meet with Ramezay and return.

Joannès returned to the city at 7:00 p.m. and reported to Ramezay. Ramezay agreed to the change and sent Joannès back at 10:30 with a sergeant, a drummer, and eight soldiers to escort a British hostage back to Quebec. (This symbolic hostage would ensure Joannès's safety while he spent the night in Townshend's camp.)

No sooner had Joannès and his escort left Quebec by the Porte Saint-Louis than Rochebeaucourt and his troopers entered by the Porte du Palais, near the Saint-Charles River. After riding all day through driving wind, lashing rain, and clinging mud, the cavalry had arrived just a few minutes too late.

Ramezay remained unmoved. He dismissed the provisions that Rochebeaucourt had brought to Quebec as "18 to 20 sacks of damp biscuit . . . which did not reach the city until the business of the capitulation had been completed." As for the reinforcements that Rochebeaucourt promised were following behind, Ramezay said of the French field army, "It hadn't dared to face the enemy before they entrenched. Should I have hoped that it would come to attack them in a fortified camp protected by heavy artillery?"

In conversation with Rochebeaucourt, Ramezay showed no inclination to recall Joannès and attempt to save Quebec. "M. de Ramezay," wrote the cavalry commander, "told me that it was too late, that his desperate situation had forced him to capitulate, and that M. Joannès was with the English to complete this business." Rather ingenuously, however, Ramezay hinted that if the British refused to accept one of the terms of capitulation, he would break off the talks provided that four to five hundred reinforcements arrived on the eighteenth.

Before he left the city, Rochebeaucourt wrote to Bougainville:

My Dear Friend,
I arrived in the city just as M. de Joannès signed the articles of capitulation, such hopes as M. de Ramezay gave me made me leave the biscuit but I see very well by the movement of the enemy that everything is finished.

SAUNDERS'S THREAT

Monday, September 17, began with the British still dodging shells and cannonballs from Fiedmont's batteries. "The enemy," wrote Knox, "fire now, almost incessantly, into our advanced works, our camp, and our batteries on the south side of the river; an officer of the twenty-eighth regiment, sitting at the door of his tent, had one of his legs so shattered by a shot from the town, that he was compelled to undergo immediate amputation."

That afternoon, everything changed. "At noon," wrote the master of HMS *Stirling Castle,* "weighed and got under sail, as did all the ships of the line . . . moored midway between Point-Levis and Bowport."

After three days of loyal support for Townshend's siege, Saunders and his sailors had changed the rules. While the army proceeded slowly and methodically, gradually building to the point where it could open fire and blast a breach in the walls, Saunders threw his largest ships of the line into the equation. An eighteenth-century battleship represented a brutal concentration of force; every one was a floating fortress carrying an immensely powerful battery of heavy guns. Saunders, wrote Holmes, "moved seven of the best line of battle ships within random gun shot of the town; which struck them with the apprehension of their coming up along side of the lower town with the night tide, and that they would be stormed by sea and land."

This implicit threat had the desired effect. Between 2:00 and 3:00 p.m., Joannès came out from Quebec carrying a list of proposed articles of capitulation. Townshend sent for Saunders, and negotiations began.

The opening of talks with the garrison did not prevent Townshend from continuing to prosecute the siege and warning his troops that the French outside Quebec "have signified their intention to the Sieur de Ramsay of endeavoring to dispossess us of this ground with all the force of Canada." That night, British engineers marked out the sites for two nine-gun batteries facing the Bastion des Ursulines and the Bastion Saint-Jean.

A difficult shoreline and contrary winds prevented Scott from embarking his troops on September 15 or 16. The major, who was nothing if not thorough, chose to treat this as an opportunity rather than an inconvenience. On the sixteenth, he wrote, his force "marched up to the east part of the

Parish of Cape St. Ignace, and on our way burnt one hundred & forty houses, had 1 ranger wounded in a little skirmish with the enemy and took six women & five children."

On the seventeenth, "the tide preventing the vessels coming up to take us off early in the morning," Scott seized one last chance to pillage and destroy. Waiting for the tide to turn, "we burnt sixty houses more, from within three miles of the church at Cape St. Ignace to the place where we lay at the night before." Finally, the ships arrived at 11:00 a.m. By five in the afternoon, the troops were all aboard, and Scott sailed away from the riverside communities that he had reduced to a wilderness of smoking ruins.

QUEBEC SURRENDERS

Quebec surrendered on the morning of September 18. Joannès returned from the British camp with three copies of the capitulation, signed by

American midshipman Ashley Bowen spent the 1759 campaign aboard HMS *Pembroke,* seen here at Quebec after the surrender.

Saunders and Townshend. Ramezay added his signature, kept one copy, and sent the other two back to the British.

At 3:30 that afternoon, George Williamson took fifty gunners, one field gun, and a Union Jack into Quebec, with orders to raise the flag in the most conspicuous possible location. In his own words, "The enemy surrendered the 18th & I hoisted our Union flag on the walls of Q——c that same day."

Behind the gunners came Alexander Murray and the Louisbourg Grenadiers. The troops marched to the parade ground in front of the Château Saint-Louis, residence of the governor-general. From there, they fanned out to secure the city gates and government buildings.

Quebec's surrender left Lieutenant Colonel Murray feeling righteous and triumphant: "You can not conceive how large and beautiful a town this is, but all in ruins and almost every inhabitant undone; people worth 12 or 14000 £ sterling not worth a groat, their harvest lost and not a morsel of bread for the wretched inhabitants to eat; surely the hand of God has at last reached them for all their barbarities, and made honest Wolfe (who I never can think about without tears) and his little gallant army the instrument of his divine vengeance."

The Royal Navy took control of Lower Town. Captain Hugh Palliser of HMS *Shrewsbury,* wrote Knox, "with a large body of seamen and inferior officers, at the same time took possession of the lower town, and hoisted colours on the summit of the declivity leading from the high to the low town, in view of the bason and the north and south countries below Quebec."

Bowen watched the operation unfold from the deck of HMS *Pembroke:*

At 3 P.M. we had the happiness of seeing Eng[lish] colors marched into the City of Quebec and our troops soon struck their flags of truce. At 6 our barge went with a Master's Mate to take possession of the lower town. Most of the ships sent a boat to the lower town.

Townshend informed the army of the surrender in a general order: "The capital of Canada having this day surrendered to his Britannick Majesty's arms, upon terms honourable to a victorious army, all acts of violence, pillage, & cruelty are strictly forbidden. The garrison are to have the Honours of War, the inhabitants to lay down their arms, and are by the capitulation entitled thereupon to his Majesty's protection."

. . .

The final shots fired in defense of Quebec came from the entrenchment at the Saint-Charles. Belcourt's troopers used its cannon to harass the British until Ramezay sent an officer to order them to cease fire. When Belcourt withdrew, his cavalry detachment became the very last component of the French army to leave Quebec.

MARCHING ON QUEBEC

On September 18, the French army, "all of them," noted Johnstone, "well disposed, impatient, and eager to repair the misfortune of the 13th," marched at dawn. Carrying rations for two days, they crossed the Jacques Cartier River and prepared to camp that night at Pointe-aux-Trembles.

As the head of the column arrived, a courier from Rochebeaucourt rode in from the east with word that Ramezay had opened negotiations for a capitulation. Lévis refused to give up. "Upon this news," he wrote, "I sent orders to M. de Bougainville to leave immediately, to speed up his march, and to do everything possible despite the rain to get his convoy inside Quebec."

Lévis rode on ahead to join Bougainville's convoy on the nineteenth, only to find it falling back toward the main body. Bougainville had been just over a mile from Quebec when he received the news of Ramezay's surrender.

The French nonetheless continued their march toward the city until an officer arrived from Ramezay bearing a letter to Vaudreuil reporting that final negotiations for a capitulation were in progress. The army camped that night at Saint-Augustin and remained for three days, while working parties salvaged what they could from the Beauport camp.

On the twenty-fourth, Lévis and his troops returned to Jacques Cartier, where they built a fort to guard the new frontier between French- and British-controlled territory.

PLANNING A COUNTERSTRIKE

In the first weeks of November, the French army stood down. The militia-men returned to their homes, joined by the regulars, who would be staying with Canadian families over the winter.

Canada's remaining defenders spent the winter of 1759–60 preparing for a spring assault on Quebec. Lévis reorganized the army, pulled the militiamen out of the regular battalions, and prepared to deploy them as expert skirmishers instead of untrained heavy infantry. The troops built scaling ladders and other siege equipment and underwent a rugged train-ing program. Assisted by the public, Cadet scraped together just enough provisions and Bigot just enough munitions to supply a single campaign. The coming offensive would be a grand gamble, a final roll of the dice that would end with the French in possession of Quebec or so bereft of resources that defending Canada would be almost impossible.

Vaudreuil and Lévis remained optimistic. Quebec had fallen once to the British. It could fall again to the French.

A PEOPLE IN MOURNING

Behind Vaudreuil and Lévis's steely resolve to recapture Quebec lay a trau-matized colony. Shock and dismay cut across lines of class, gender, occupa-tion, and region.

On September 23 at Cap Santé, just west of Jacques Cartier, Mont-beillard sat down and began to write. Pondering the abrupt reversal of fortune at the Battle of the Plains of Abraham, he struggled to express his feelings: "I have nothing but misfortunes to write about. Twenty times I have taken up my pen, and twenty times sorrow has made it fall from my hands. How can I recall such a shattering series of events! . . . [W]e were saved; now we are lost!"

Rattled as he was, Montbeillard viewed the campaign from the per-spective of a professional soldier temporarily stationed in Canada. If he lived through the war, he could look forward to continuing his life and career in a France that remained unthreatened by foreign rule. For Cana-dians, the French had lost more than a battle on the Plains of Abraham. British possession of Quebec posed a mortal threat to the very survival of New France.

John Knox commanded the guard at the Hôpital Général between October 11 and October 19. There, he mingled with members of the Canadian elite and noted their reaction to the Battle of the Plains of Abraham and the capitulation of Quebec: "I lived here, at the French King's table, with an agreeable society of officers, directors, and commissaries; some of the gentlemen were married, and their ladies honoured us with their company; they were generally cheerful, except when we discoursed upon the late revolution, and the affairs of the campaign; then they seemingly gave way to grief uttered by profound sighs, and followed by an *O mon Dieu*."

Writing after the end of the war, Marie de la Visitation recalled the sentiments of the staff of the Hôpital Général following the battle and capitulation: "We hoped in vain that the peace would give us back our rights [under the French Crown] and that the Lord would treat us as a Father and only punish us for a time, but his rage has lasted. Our sins must be very great . . . Many of our people lack a spirit of penitence . . . despite their continued desire and hope that we will soon find ourselves back under the authority of our former rulers."

Marie de la Visitation and Knox's agreeable companions all belonged to the upper echelons of colonial society, where social standing, power, careers, and finances were tightly linked to the French Crown. Their sorrow and alarm are not surprising. But what about the people who hewed the wood, drew the water, raised the children, worked the fields, and paddled the canoes? Their lives would go on much as before, regardless of which European power held Quebec or ruled Canada.

Henry Grace, last seen attempting to escape to Wolfe's army, was working on a farm near Montreal when news of the capitulation arrived. He provides a rare glimpse of the reaction of "ordinary" Canadians to the loss of their colonial capital: "One day as I was driving a cart-load of hay, I met the people going to church; and when I came back, saw them all crying. I asked them what was the matter; they told me the English had taken Quebec."

V

AFTERMATH

CHAPTER 31

Occupied Canada

ROBERT MONCKTON AND THE BRITISH OCCUPATION

Once they had occupied Quebec, the British could survey the damage they had inflicted. George Williamson, the first British soldier to enter the city, took the time to count the buildings: "The town is much more battered than I imagined. 535 houses are burned down, besides we have greatly shattered most of the rest."

Knox passed through Quebec on September 20, on his way to catch a boat to Point Lévis in Lower Town. "The havoc is not to be conceived," he wrote. "Such houses as are standing are perforated by our shot, more or less; and the low town is so great a ruin, that its streets are almost impassable."

Regarding the interiors, the naval volunteer gloated over the damage in a triumphal letter home: "I have the pleasure of transmitting this to you, wrote in the midst of ruin—in some merchant's dining room, whose present ornaments are two pier and one chimney glass [mirrors], shivered with their frames upon the floor; a marble slab and a turkey ice-jar, a fretted ceiling and panelled cedar wainscot, in the same shattered condition; manifestly the effect of a bomb, that had fallen through all the upper rooms of the house, into the kitchen on the second floor."

Converting this city of ruins into a viable outpost of the British Empire fell to Brigadier Robert Monckton. On September 19, Monckton, who had been convalescing aboard HMS *Medway*, visited Quebec for the first time to meet with Townshend and Saunders. A week later, Townshend was able to write that "General Monckton . . . is so far recovered as to command us."

Of all the senior British Army officers on the scene, none had more North American experience or was better prepared to administer an occupied city and province. In 1752, Monckton had come to Nova Scotia and taken command of Fort Lawrence. This outpost faced Vergor's Fort Beauséjour across the boundary dividing British- and French-controlled territory in Acadia, placing Monckton at a key flash point between the rival empires.

Following the outbreak of the Seven Years' War, Monckton captured Fort Beauséjour in 1755 and participated in the expulsion of the Acadians. Appointed lieutenant governor of Nova Scotia, he remained in that post for three years. In 1758, Monckton led an expedition more than sixty miles up the St. John River, seeking out and destroying Acadian refugee camps. The following spring, he joined Wolfe and Saunders's expedition to Quebec.

As British commandant of Quebec, Monckton faced two fundamental challenges—establishing order and providing the British garrison with the basic necessities of life.

Monckton's immediate concern was maintaining law and order, not among the Canadians, but among his own troops. After months of pillaging farmhouses, enterprising British soldiers now had an entire city to loot.

Just over a week after the occupation began, Monckton angrily noted that "several houses & cellars belonging to the inhabitants have been broke open & plundered" while beyond the walls troops continued to "molest or interrupt the French inhabitants or people in the country, by taking their canoes or any other property of theirs."

Monckton did his best to keep his army under control. He offered rewards for information leading to the arrest of soldier-criminals and established an elaborate system of patrols and checkpoints. Malefactors were punished severely. A soldier of the Fortieth Regiment who broke into a house and two soldiers of the Thirty-Fifth who stole a quantity of wine received one thousand lashes apiece. When a soldier committed a "notorious robbery on the house of a French inhabitant," he was tried by a court-martial, "found guilty, and adjudged to suffer death." British authorities responded promptly and effectively to complaints from Canadians. When, wrote Knox, "some of the female inhabitants of Point Levi having preferred a complaint against the soldiers incamped in that quarter, of their being robbed, and otherwise much abused by them, the several detachments were ordered out, that the women might pitch upon the particular aggressors."

In the end, however, Monckton's only instrument for enforcing the law was the very army that was committing the crimes. British soldiers patrolling the streets and guarding the gates had to be treated more like prisoners at large than guardians of law and order: "The general desires the officers of the several guards, will take great care to keep their guards sober & together, by frequently taking the rolls, & confining each as neglects their duty."

Monckton's concern about his patrols was not misplaced. On October 21, Knox recorded that "a Serjeant and eleven men, belonging to a guard in the low town, went into an adjoining cellar in search of plunder, where, having lighted a candle, they threw the piece of burning paper they had used for that purpose on the ground, which instantly caught a quantity of powder, placed there accidentally or otherwise, and blew up; by this unhappy disaster four men were killed on the spot, and the rest were miserably scorched and disfigured."

Monckton's troops might have felt themselves to be the victims of a double standard. On September 20, Scott, Goreham, and their troops returned from downriver. Knox observed that they brought with them a "great quantity of black cattle and sheep [and] an immense deal of plunder, such as household-stuff, books, and apparel."

Scott summarized the results of his expedition in a report to Monckton: "Upon the whole, we marched fifty two miles, and in that distance burnt nine hundred and ninety eight good buildings, two sloops, two schooners, ten shallops [sloops], and several batteaus and small craft, took fifteen prisoners (six of them women and five of them children), killed five of the enemy, had one regular wounded, two of the rangers killed and four more of them wounded."

Two days later, the rangers visited Quebec. "Today," wrote Pearson, who might have spent the previous night celebrating the British victory, "we had the pleasure to land in the city and walk through it & I can tell you I am not very well." Perry, in better health, or perhaps just less hungover, took time to observe the sights and applaud the work of Williamson's gunners: "It was truly surprising to see the damage done to the buildings, etc., by the shot and shells that were thrown into the town by our artillery . . . cannon balls stove holes through the buildings in many places, and remained in the walls."

Monckton's next priority was providing the essentials of daily life—food, water, shelter, warmth, and medical care.

Food was not an immediate problem. Throughout the campaign, the British had lived off a massive shipborne supply train, supplemented by whatever they could steal from Canadian farms. It speaks volumes for the scale and efficiency of British logistics and pillaging to note that of the 591 cattle that the British brought from Boston to provide the army with fresh meat, over half remained alive at the end of the campaign. As soon as Quebec surrendered, the Royal Navy began landing provisions for the British garrison.

Some of these provisions came from Saunders's fleet. Following the capitulation of Quebec, Saunders put his sailors on short rations and delivered the surplus to the garrison. In addition to food, every major warship handed over its entire stock of powder and shot, except for a minimal thirty rounds for each caliber of cannon. HMS *Captain* and *Neptune* landed twenty twelve- and twenty-four-pounders to strengthen Quebec's defenses.

Drinking water caused some concern in the first weeks of the occupation. Some British soldiers, Knox included, suspected that the French garrison had poisoned the city's spring wells with the bodies of dead cats and dogs prior to the surrender. Seeking to avoid an epidemic, Monckton announced that because "the water of the town is thought to have occasioned illness, the commanding officers will make their men bring their water from the river which is wholesome."

Shelter was another matter. Williamson had obligingly flattened Quebec for James Wolfe. Now Monckton had to put it back together. Compelled to undertake an impromptu urban renewal program, he combed the ranks of his army for carpenters, bricklayers, smiths, and other skilled workers. While their comrades began to clear away the rubble that made just walking down the streets a challenge, the artisans set to work repairing the private homes and public buildings that would shelter the British army over the winter.

A few officers described their new accommodations. Knox found himself preparing to face the Canadian winter in a "cart-house and a stable . . . [with] no ceiling, save a parcel of boards laid loose." Montresor was in similar straits: "I'm quartered in a house that has no roof, not a single board." Both officers threw themselves into brisk home renovation projects, producing quarters that, if not luxurious, at least spared them the prospect of spending the winter gazing at the stars through holes in the roof.

Despite all the efforts of the British, along with those of Canadian residents of the city, Quebec retained the appearance of a forsaken urban wasteland. A British sailor who visited Quebec in the spring of 1760 described the wreckage: "This once splendid city remained in a ruinous condition . . . [T]here remained only the bare outside shells of stately stone-built houses . . . [which] were either made skeletons, or their sides perforated by the shot and pieces of shells, so that they might be seen through; and large concave places like horse-ponds might be seen on the streets, where shells had fallen and danced about before they burst."

Along with an urban renewal challenge, Monckton faced an impending energy crisis. Keeping his army from freezing to death during the Canadian winter was going to take a mountain of firewood. Monckton began by ordering his battalion commanders to organize working parties to tear down ruined houses to salvage their wood, then organized the first of the woodcutting expeditions that would continue until spring. On September 25, he sent five hundred rangers and regulars to Île Madame to cut wood, for which they would be paid five shillings per cord. Two days later, Monckton reinforced the woodcutters with a further three hundred regulars.

Also on the twenty-seventh, he dispatched an amphibious force to collect a stack of firewood that had been left by the French atop the Quebec Promontory, four miles upriver. Two frigates landed a detachment of rangers and sailors. The rangers ascended the promontory and threw the firewood down to the beach; the sailors bundled the wood into cords. French scouts observed this operation but did not attempt to interfere.

Some of Monckton's troops went looking for firewood on their own. Montresor, for one, could see the bright side of living amid the ruins of a city: "I am providing that article [firewood] in a very ample manner, thanks to our well directed shells which have knocked in several houses that are not tenable and so condemned."

To make his limited supplies of fuel stretch as far as possible, Monckton instituted what might have been Canada's first official energy conservation program: "It is recommended to the officers & men of this garrison, to be very saving of wood, as there will be difficulty in providing a sufficient quantity for which reason the guards are not to keep fires till it is specified in orders."

With hundreds of sick and wounded on his hands, Townshend had already acknowledged the superiority of the Canadian health-care system by transferring French and British casualties to the Hôpital Général. "I hope," he wrote to Bougainville, "that the attention of these ladies will be better for them than those of our sailors." They were. Knox, commanding the British guard at the hospital, observed that the casualties "were indeed rendered inexpressibly happy; every patient has his bed with curtains allotted to him, and a nurse to attend him . . . the beds are ranged in galleries on each side, with a sufficient space, between each, for a person to pass through; these galleries are scraped and swept every morning, and afterwards sprinkled with vinegar, so that a stranger is not sensible of any unsavoury scent whatsoever; in summer, the windows are generally open, and the patients are allowed a kind of fan."

Admitting English-speaking patients to a hospital with a French-speaking staff could have caused communication problems. A certain number of British private soldiers, however, spoke at least some French. Monckton ordered their battalion commanders to send them to the hospital to work as orderlies.

LIVING UNDER OCCUPATION

The first reaction of many individuals from the Quebec population and garrison to the British occupation was immediate flight. Foreign troops guarded Quebec's gates, but every night soldiers, sailors, and Canadians escaped to the French army. From time to time, British gunners responded with a blast of grapeshot. But the exodus continued.

Canadians who stayed behind quickly found themselves obliged to swear allegiance to the British Crown. On September 21, wrote Foligné, "the townspeople and habitants of the government of Quebec living within three leagues [seven miles] of Quebec took an oath of loyalty, in a ceremony that lasted from the morning until 3:00 p.m."

Women, considered to be wards of their husbands and fathers, were not invited. Men assembled in their militia companies, took the oath, and had their names recorded. John Knox described a similar event in 1760: "The men stand in a circle, hold up their right hands, repeat each his own name, and then [repeat the oath]." The official text of the oath read, "I solemnly promise and swear before God that I will be faithful to his Britannic Majesty King George the Second, that I will not take up arms against him, and that I will not give any intelligence to his enemies who might in any way injure him."

Oaths like this were routine, but the condition of the Canadians who came in from the countryside on the day of the ceremony shocked Foligné: "It was on that day that you could see our poor women come out from the depths of the woods, pulling their little children, [who were] eaten by flies, without proper clothing, [and] crying from hunger, which must have stabbed their poor mothers like a dagger . . . [These mothers] didn't know if they still had husbands or where to find them and what help they could give their poor children."

Taking the oath allowed Canadians to return to their homes and live in peace. "But," asked Foligné, "what property did they want our habitants to occupy after the ravages they had made, burning the houses, carrying off the livestock, and stealing the furniture?"

As if oaths of allegiance and a foreign garrison weren't enough to remind Canadians that they were living in occupied territory, the British took care to remove the most prominent remaining symbols of French sovereignty. These were the French royal arms that hung over Quebec's gates and the doors of public buildings. Carved by the Canadian sculptor Noël Levasseur in 1727, the arms featured the royal crown of France above three golden fleur-de-lis on an oval blue shield surrounded by the ornate collars of two orders of knighthood.

Saunders carried one of these coats of arms back to England, where the navy displayed it on a plaque wreathed in carved laurels and surrounded by weapons and flags. An inscription read, in part, "This trophy was taken down from the gates of Quebec when that place was conquered in the 18th of Sept., 1759."

(In 1917, the Royal Navy repatriated the trophy to Canada. The arms now hang above a replica of a French city gate in the Canadian War Museum in Ottawa.)

RUMORS, MURDER, AND LIES

Long after the smoke cleared on the battlefield, the events of September 13 remained a topic of conversation, speculation, and inquiry.

Samuel Holland developed a mild obsession with Wolfe's death. He began to question local Canadians, seeking the identity of the sharpshooter who killed his general. Finally, he found his answer: "From what I could learn, a Canadian boy from Jacques Cartier was the person who fired the fatal shot."

While Holland made his inquiries, a sensational rumor made the rounds among the French. Montcalm hadn't just been killed; he'd been murdered, presumably by an irate Canadian expressing his opinion of Montcalm's generalship. "It was reported in Canada," wrote Johnstone, "that the ball which killed that great, good and honest man was not fired from an English mousquet; but I never gave credit to it."

Rumors of another kind disturbed Louis-Antoine de Bougainville.

"Someone," he complained to Townshend, "told me that Lieutenant Colonel [Alexander] Murray has been saying that the English owe me a great deal." Sensitive to the charge that his actions had facilitated the British landing at the Anse au Foulon, he lied through his teeth, vehemently informing Townshend, "I was not responsible for that area," and asking the brigadier to "correct . . . Colonel Murray."

THE GARRISON DEPARTS

On September 22, the former Quebec garrison embarked aboard four British transports that would carry them to France. Along with Ramezay, there were 615 soldiers and an unspecified number of sailors. Granted the honors of war, Ramezay's troops marched down to the docks with drums beating and carrying their personal weapons. Along with the troops came two cannon, a supply of gunpowder, and twenty-four cannonballs.

At six o'clock that morning, Foligné encountered Ramezay, who assigned him a place on a ship carrying 280 sailors, including 68 who had served under his command. Foligné spent the next three hours collecting his possessions and saying good-bye to friends at the Quebec Seminary, where he had taken his meals during the summer. At 9:00 a.m., he left Quebec for the last time and boarded the transport. The ships raised anchor the next morning around 10:00 but had to wait until the wind changed to west-northwest at noon before they began their voyage.

As they progressed down the St. Lawrence, the French passengers encountered constant reminders of the British naval power that had made the campaign possible. Although the main body of Saunders's fleet remained behind at Quebec, off the northeast end of the Île d'Orléans Foligné counted eleven ships of the line, including two massive three-deckers, accompanied by two frigates or sloops. At the Île aux Coudres, he saw two frigates, a bomb ketch, and five other warships.

Discouraging glimpses of British naval power aside, Foligné was not enjoying his cruise to France:

> It was our miserable fate to find ourselves aboard a wretched ship, piled up one atop another, without any food but spoiled biscuit or porridge made from oatmeal that was half straw, with a bit of butter mixed with fat. That was what they fed us on Monday, Wednesday, and Friday. Sunday, Tuesday, and Thursday they gave us rotten salt beef or reasonably good salt pork. Finally on Saturday they gave us a few green peas, butter, and a little cheese. That was how they treated us, and what we had to endure until we arrived in France.

Fortunately for Foligné, another French naval officer who had brought along a substantial private stock of more palatable provisions was willing to share with his companions in adversity.

The transports lay at anchor off the Île aux Coudres for three weeks, waiting for Durell. Ramezay, who considered this a violation of the British agreement to return the garrison to France as quickly as possible, sent Joannès upriver to protest. Shortly thereafter, Durell appeared on October 19. Informed by Ramezay that the French prisoners were running short of provisions, the British admiral sent additional supplies aboard their transports, along with a hogshead (about sixty-five gallons) of wine for the officers.

At 10:00 a.m. the next day, the fleet weighed anchor and set off for Europe. Foligné and the other French prisoners were hugely relieved to be on their way at last: "Our sailors willingly lent a hand to raise the anchor and make sail."

Their voyage lasted until November 13. On that day, wrote Foligné, "at four o'clock we saw land before us four leagues distant and recognized the Île Dieu" off the coast of France.

French prisoners from the campaign and the Battle of the Plains of Abraham, who were not covered by the terms of the capitulation, remained aboard Saunders's warships, waiting to begin their journey to British prisons. The British gave a few Canadian prisoners two days' rations and released them on the Île d'Orléans. The remaining Canadians joined their French comrades in captivity overseas. They would not return to Canada until after the end of the war.

DEPARTURES

On September 30, the last phase of Ashley Bowen's Quebec campaign began when HMS *Pembroke*'s first lieutenant returned from Durrell's flagship and addressed the New England midshipman: "I have some good news for you, sir. You and all the Marblehead men are to get ready to go on board a transport for Boston." The next day, Bowen boarded the *Thorton*, a New York merchant ship. A week later, when a total of 160 New England

American sailors, including Ashley Bowen, disembark from HMS *Pembroke* for the last time as they prepare to return to New England.

volunteers had come aboard, he wrote, "We sailed with the ship Thorton for Boston from Quebec."

On October 18, Saunders's fleet fired a twenty-one-gun salute, weighed anchor, and sailed for England. Townshend traveled with Saunders aboard the flagship.

Some soldiers wished they were going with them. The capture of Quebec had been a glorious triumph for the Royal Navy and the British Army; Saunders and Townshend could expect to return to a hero's welcome. In comparison, remaining behind to occupy an isolated city in a colony known for its bitter cold, deep snow, and aggressive inhabitants seemed somehow anticlimactic. Many soldiers applied for their discharge and passage home.

On October 19, Monckton responded by informing the army that everyone was there for the duration: "As it has been thought necessary to leave a strong garrison here to secure this valuable conquest gained by his Majesty's Arms the General can not think of discharging any soldier at present, he therefore hopes that they will as cheerfully enlist for another year as they have gone through the fatigues of the campaign, at the expiration of which he promises most strictly to comply with their request."

Two weeks later, Monckton sailed for New York to recuperate from his wound. Of all the senior officers, only James Murray, Wolfe's most junior brigadier, remained behind to command the garrison and enjoy the character-building pleasures of the Canadian winter.

As for Ashley Bowen, on November 10 the *Thorton* reached Boston. The next morning, wrote Bowen, "I came over the ferry and took horse and came to Marblehead safe and sound." He would return to Quebec the following year as master and pilot of the schooner *Swallow,* sailing from Boston with a cargo of twenty-eight cattle.

JAMES MURRAY

The fifth son of an aristocratic Scottish family, the thirty-seven-year-old Murray had, like Simon Fraser, begun his military career in the Scots Brigade of the Dutch army. After four years in garrison at Ypres, a future Canadian battlefield, he joined the British Army in 1740. By 1759, he was the colonel of the Second Battalion of the Royal Americans. Extensive amphibious experience in the Caribbean, where he joined Wolfe's father in attacking Cartagena, Europe, and Louisbourg, where he served under Wolfe, made him an ideal candidate to serve as one of Wolfe's brigadiers. In practice, he became a sharp critic of Wolfe's performance at Quebec. Command of the Quebec garrison gave Murray a chance to demonstrate that he could do better.

"THE LIVING ALMOST ENVIED THE DEAD"

The admirals, generals, soldiers, and sailors who left Quebec in a hurry knew what they were doing. For Murray's garrison, the winter of 1759–60 became a relentlessly savage ordeal. American rangers instructed their comrades in some of the nuances of cold-weather survival but could not prevent cold and disease from inflicting more casualties than the Battle of the Plains of Abraham.

James Miller of the Fifteenth Regiment described the season from the perspective of a private soldier: "A severe winter, now commenced, while we were totally unprepared for such a climate, [with] neither fuel, forage, or indeed anything, to make life tolerable. The troops were crowded inside vacant houses, as well as possible, numbers fell sick, and the scurvy made a dreadful havoc among us."

As temperatures fell below the freezing mark, firewood became for the British what provisions had been for the French, a vital commodity that could only be obtained through considerable effort. For Murray's garrison, deep in French territory and cut off from outside assistance, making it through the winter was less about holding Quebec against attack than securing enough wood to keep themselves reasonably warm. If they failed, they would die, allowing the French to reoccupy the city at their leisure.

"The duty became extremely hard," wrote Miller, "for after being up all night, on guard, the men, were obliged, to go over six miles, through the snow, to cut wood, and then to drag it home on sledges. From the severe frost, the wood was as hard as marble, and Europeans, who had never been accustomed to cut wood, made but small progress, a constant and daily supply was however necessary, and required the greatest perseverance."

Under these conditions, it is not surprising that many soldiers sought comfort in brandy or rum and even less surprising that some of them paid for this indulgence with their lives: "Liquors were extremely scarce, and when the men could possess them, they generally drank to excess, it was no uncommon thing, in the morning, to find several men frozen to death from the above cause."

Even without the assistance of alcohol, the cold alone could kill or cripple. "Many lost the use of their hands and feet during the winter. I was also frost bit, in the right foot, while on guard," Miller wrote, "however by taking it [inside?] in time, lost no bones."

By April 24, 2,312 members of the garrison had been hospitalized, and 682 lay stacked like firewood on the frozen ground, awaiting burial in the spring. In Miller's opinion, their deaths had been as much a release as a misfortune. "The fatigues of the winter was so great that the living almost envied the dead."

CHAPTER 32

Canadian Winter

WINTER AT QUEBEC

Canadian civilians who remained in Quebec also endured a harsh winter. Living in occupied territory, they were compelled to accept foreign troops into their homes, obtain permission from the British to enter or leave the city, and endure searches for weapons and repeated assaults and thefts by British soldiers.

Not all soldiers behaved like thugs. On September 25, Knox was pleased to record that "to-day I saw about twenty of our men assisting those poor people in cutting and binding their sheaves of corn [wheat]." British officers maintained amicable relationships with the staff of the Hôpital Général. But every British soldier had the opportunity to decide if he felt like behaving like a thug on any given day, an option not open to the Canadians.

Moreover, any Canadian could be arrested at any time and treated as guilty until proven innocent. When an elderly priest came under suspicion of "enticing our men to desert," wrote Knox, the British authorities ordered his arrest. "I was accordingly detached for this purpose," Knox explained. "I found him in his house, and arrested him in the name of his Britannic Majesty: the poor old man was greatly terrified, and entreated me earnestly to tell him his crime: but I made no other delay than to post a sentinel, whom I had taken with me, in the apartment with this ancient father." The British released the priest four days later after he had "been strictly examined."

As some Canadians endured arrest and interrogation, others lost what was left of their homes. Henri-Marie Dubreil de Pontbriand, bishop of Quebec, described their fate: "The English . . . have taken over the least damaged houses in the city. Every day they evict some townspeople from homes that they [the townspeople] have used their money to repair . . . or forced them to live in such small spaces as a result of the number of soldiers they have lodged there that almost all of them have been compelled to abandon that unhappy city."

Then he spoke of the hardships endured by those who remained: "The people of the city lack wood for the winter . . . [They are] without bread, without flour, without meat, and living only on the bits of biscuit and pork that English soldiers sell from their rations. Such is the situation to which the wealthiest townspeople are reduced; you can . . . imagine the misery of the ordinary people and the poor."

Very few Canadians actively collaborated. On October 2, a Canadian informed the British that two French sailors had told him that a convoy would shortly be sailing past Quebec en route to France. He received, wrote Knox, "a suitable reward for this instance of attachment to us." Other betrayals followed, but most Canadians confined their interaction with the British to the minimum necessary for survival—trading for food, sharing accommodation, surrendering weapons, or caring for sick and wounded troops in the Hôpital Général.

"The English," wrote Marie de la Visitation, "did not omit to demand the oath of allegiance for their king. But our habitants did not feel obliged to honor that allegiance, which had been imposed by force." A resistance movement quickly developed, involving the vast majority of Canadians in the occupied zone. While attempting to maintain a facade of cooperation and avoiding direct confrontations that might have led to reprisals, Canadians seized every possible opportunity to strike back against the British.

This nonviolent resistance was particularly effective with regard to energy supplies. Desperate for fuel, the British demanded that Canadians supply them with firewood. They did, very slowly and in very small quantities, but with such circumspection that Murray was never able to determine what was going on. "Every measure," he complained, "has been taken to encourage the Canadians to be active in bringing in the wood, yet that affair goes on very slowly—whether from the natural sloth of the people, not much used to work, or from disaffection, cannot well be said."

Canadians once again combined resistance with prudence when Murray demanded that they hand over their snowshoes to equip British patrols and woodcutting expeditions. "This search," he wrote, "produced but a few, the country people alleging they had lost theirs, and had not any opportunity to supply themselves with new."

Some Canadians, including many priests, encouraged members of the garrison to defect. Skilled artisans like blacksmiths and carpenters were particularly sought after. Murray had several Canadians arrested for aiding and abetting deserters, hanged at least one, and expelled a priest from the city. One deserter earned a pardon by turning in the Canadians who had persuaded him to exchange his red coat for a French uniform. Canadians nonetheless continued to assist deserters, every one of whom was as lost to the British as a soldier killed in action.

Marie de la Visitation and her colleagues at the Hôpital Général found another way to strengthen the French army. The Battle of the Plains of Abraham had left the hospital filled with French soldiers. When their patients were well enough to travel, the nuns provided them with clothing and provisions to allow them to escape to French-controlled territory.

Murray, who considered captains of militia to be agents of the British Crown, requested that they provide him with reports on the movements of French scouts and raiders; the militia officers made vague and misleading replies. At the same time, the captains and other Canadians provided Lévis and Vaudreuil with a steady stream of intelligence about British actions and intentions. A few of Vaudreuil's agents fell into British hands. In January, Knox noted that "a Frenchman is taken up for walking round our batteries; and others are apprehended and confined in separate prisons, on suspicion of sending intelligence to, and corresponding with, the enemy." The survivors continued to gather and pass on information.

With the French army short of munitions, Quebec residents did their best to help out. Daring thieves scaled the ramparts under cover of darkness and made off with cannonballs. They were careful, however, to only steal shot that could be fired from French artillery.

Although they themselves had been disarmed, Canadians from the government of Quebec continued to support French agents and French military operations. On January 19, Murray discovered that "the boatmen of Point Levi had passed over French soldiers in disguise." Marie de la Visitation was pleased to record that Canadians "joined our patrols whenever they could." This could prove very dangerous. When Canadians became caught up in the defense of a French outpost, wrote Knox, the British "burned a parish in the neighborhood of Point au Tremble, called St. Joseph; and laid waste that side of the country, on account of the inhabitants having revolted from their oath of fidelity."

Normally, though, British countermeasures were less drastic. Fully aware that Canadians were not cooperating as closely as they could, Murray attempted to persuade them to fulfill what he considered to be their obligations to the British Crown. On November 18, Knox observed that "proclamations are every-where dispersed, and some are fixed up at the public parts of the city, threatening more rigorous measures, if the Canadians do not adhere to their engagements, and pay more respect to the governor's [Murray's] orders and demands, in supplying us with provisions, sleigh carriages, horses, &c. &c. and in case they shall neglect to acquaint his Excellency, when any of the enemy came into their neighbourhood."

Canadians who were tempted to succumb to Murray's threats, or individuals caught between loyalty to France and their need to deal with the British to survive, could find themselves in an exceedingly awkward situation. Knox describes one such incident in the fall of 1759: "An unfortunate Canadian was taking boat a few days ago, at Point Levi, to come over here with a quantity of fresh provisions, he was set upon by ten of the light cavalry, who, not content with plundering him, beat and abused him most inhumanly, by wounding him with their sabres, and scarifying his wrists and arms with their knives; at leaving him they said, 'Now go and tell your fine English governor how we have treated you, and we hope soon to serve him, and his valiant troops, in the same manner.'"

All things considered, it is perhaps not surprising that several British officers confessed to Marie de la Visitation "that they had never seen a people so attached and so faithful to their prince as the Canadians."

CHAPTER 33

The Second Battle of the Plains of Abraham

FRENCH PREPARATIONS

An attacking army appears on the Plains of Abraham. The defenders form a battle line. Their commander orders a charge. Armies clash. The defenders withdraw. The attackers prepare to besiege Quebec.

It all happened on September 13, 1759, then again on April 28, 1760.

History never repeats itself, but in 1760 it came very close when Montcalm's army and Wolfe's army, now commanded by Lévis and Murray, met in battle for a second time on the Plains of Abraham.

FRANÇOIS DE LÉVIS

Poor but well connected, François de Lévis belonged to one of the oldest noble families in France. After he joined the army as a second lieutenant in 1735, his own merits and the patronage of a cousin who became a field marshal (*maréchal de France*) in 1751 allowed him to rise to brevet colonel before his career stalled for lack of funds to purchase command of a regiment. Service in Canada as Montcalm's second-in-command with the rank of brigadier solved his promotion problem. Three campaigns on the Lake Champlain frontier prior to 1759 earned him a reputation as one of the outstanding leaders on either side in the war for North America, along with promotion to major general. Unlike Montcalm, he maintained good relations with the colonial administration throughout his time in Canada. Following his accession to command of the French army, Lévis worked in harmony with Vaudreuil as they made one last effort to save the colony from conquest.

Like the original plan for the British attack on Quebec in 1759, the French campaign of 1760 depended for success upon two armies converging on Quebec from different directions.

To create the first of these armies, Vaudreuil and Lévis had mustered every potential combatant in unoccupied Canada—7,620 regulars, militiamen, and warriors—leaving only minimal garrisons on the Lake Champlain and Lake Ontario frontiers. Only one twenty-four-pounder, eight eighteen-pounders, nine twelve-pounders, and eight six- and eight-pounders were available for the expedition. (Most of Canada's heavy artillery had been on the walls of Quebec and the entrenchments at Beauport.) None of the heavier guns were in very good condition or fit for extended use.

With French resources steadily diminishing, every Canadian household contributed a week's rations for family members serving in the militia and regulars who had stayed with them over the winter. Added to the provisions assembled by Cadet and Bigot, this was just enough to feed the army for one campaign.

Commanded by Lévis, the army was strong enough to besiege Quebec. It could not, however, reasonably hope to recapture the city without the help of a second army, an army that might not arrive in time or might not exist at all.

At the end of the 1759 campaign, Lévis had asked the French government to send an artillery train, munitions, four thousand recruits for the *troupes de terre* and *troupes de la marine,* and an army of six thousand that would help to capture the city, then return to France. Of these requests, the artillery was the most important. Without siege guns to batter a breach in Murray's defenses, Lévis would be unable to seriously threaten the British in Quebec.

To facilitate the arrival of a convoy from France, Vaudreuil arranged for Canada's St. Lawrence River pilots to gather on the Île-aux-Oies, just northeast of the Île d'Orléans. There, they were to guide the ships past the navigational hazards of the river to French-controlled territory. He furthermore sent a militia officer named Legris to establish a chain of lookouts along the lower St. Lawrence, meet the ships, and direct them to the waiting pilots. In his orders relating to this expedition, Vaudreuil confidently referred to the convoy's imminent arrival, writing of "the ships that will enter the river" and "the warships and transports . . . that are presently at the mouth of the river."

When the ice broke on the St. Lawrence, the French were ready. On April 20, the troops that had wintered in and around Montreal set off downstream, gathering reinforcements and supplies along the way. Five days later, Lévis's army landed at Saint-Augustin and headed for Quebec. By the morning of the twenty-eighth, the advance guard was marching out of the Sillery Woods onto the Plains of Abraham.

BRITISH PREPARATIONS

While Lévis marched, Murray made his own preparations. Suborned by one of Murray's officers, half a dozen merchants from France, resident in Quebec, had agreed to become British agents. In exchange for access to their inventories, which had fallen into British hands when the city surrendered, they traveled to Montreal, where they sold their goods for a substantial profit and gathered intelligence for Murray. On March 28, one of these agents reported that the French were on their way.

"My plan of defense," reported Murray, "was to take the earliest opportunity of entrenching myself upon the Heights of Abraham [the Buttes-à-Neveu], which entirely commanded the ramparts of the place at the distance of eight hundred yards, and might have been defended by our numbers against a large army." On "the 23, 24th, and 25th" of April, he continued, "I attempted to execute the projected lines, for which a provision of fascines and of every necessary material had been made, but found it impracticable, as the earth was still covered with snow in many places, and every where impregnably bound up by frost."

Murray nonetheless managed to bring the French army to a temporary halt on April 27 by deploying troops at the head of the roadways leading up the western end of the Quebec Promontory. After a short standoff, he pulled his army back to Quebec. On the twenty-eighth, he left the city once more: "Half an hour after six the next morning, we marched out with all the force I could muster . . . and formed the army on the heights."

This army consisted of thirty-eight hundred soldiers, eighteen six- and twelve-pounder cannon, and two howitzers. Every soldier carried a pick or spade to construct earthwork fortifications. When they reached the site of Wolfe's battle line, Murray, wrote Malcolm Fraser, "ordered the whole to draw up in the line of battle two deep, and take up as much room as possible."

Fraser strongly approved of Murray's initial dispositions, which

> gave him all the advantage he could desire with such . . . [a numerically] inferior army and where, if the enemy ventured to attack him, he could use his artillery, on which was his chief dependence, to the best purpose: having a rising ground, where he might form his army and plant his cannon, so as to play on the enemy as they advanced for about four hundred or five hundred yards with round shot, and when they came within a proper distance the grapeshot must have cut them to pieces.

Then Murray changed his mind: "While the line was forming, I reconnoitered the enemy, and perceived their van busy throwing up redoubts, while their main body was yet on the march. I thought this the Lucky Minute [and] moved the whole in great order to attack them before they could have time to form."

Still in line of battle, British soldiers dropped their entrenching tools and began to make their way toward the French. Murray might have made a snap decision, but he took great care to ensure that his troops remained in a cohesive, disciplined formation. Fraser, no great admirer of his general's decision to abandon a strong position and attack, nonetheless conceded that Murray had "ordered . . . the whole army to advance slowly, dressing by the right."

BATTLE ON THE PLAINS OF ABRAHAM

Throughout the second Battle of the Plains of Abraham, generally known as the Battle of Sainte-Foy, both armies retained their cohesion and will to combat. The result was a three-hour bloodbath as French and British soldiers hurled themselves at one another and Lévis and Murray shifted battalions about the field, seeking an advantage.

The French had the larger army. Lévis reported that five thousand soldiers, half regulars, half militiamen, actually took part in the battle. The grenadiers and volunteers who had been with Bougainville at Cap-Rouge in 1759 were now present in the ranks. So were the three battalions of the *troupes de terre* that had served on the Lake Champlain frontier in the previous campaign. Native American warriors, on the other hand, not finding opportunities to employ their talents in a fast-moving battle of charges and countercharges, remained on the sidelines. Only three light field guns supported the troops.

The British had more artillery and more regulars on the field. But of Murray's thirty-eight hundred combatants, wrote Fraser, about one thousand "had that very day come voluntarily out of the hospitals; of these, about five hundred were employed in dragging the cannon, and five hundred more in reserve."

Both sides displayed skill, determination, and courage on a battlefield dominated by "low and swampy ground," where, wrote Knox, "our troops fought almost knee-deep in dissolving wreaths of snow and water." The British fought as hard and as well in 1760 as they had in 1759, under much more difficult conditions. The French, relieved of the structural flaws that had crippled their effort in 1759, performed superbly.

Over the winter, Lévis had organized the militia into three-company formations, each attached to a regular battalion and acting as skirmishers. Thus organized and deployed, they served so well that Malartic, who in 1759 had damned Canadians for opening fire prematurely, now praised their effectiveness: "The Canadians . . . who were in the intervals between or in front of the brigades fired for a long time and very well. They inflicted many casualties on the English."

Malartic himself was in the forefront of the fighting:

I was wounded by a grapeshot that hit me in the chest as I marched forward. The blow threw me down and knocked me out. When I regained consciousness, a sergeant and a soldier . . . were trying to pick me up. I begged them to let me die right there. As they lifted me up regardless, I felt something cold slide over my stomach. I opened my vest, which had been torn. The lower part of my left chest was as big as a fist and very black. I found the bloody grapeshot below my stomach. I was placed in the hands of a surgeon who opened the bruise with a dozen cuts from a scalpel.

. . .

In the end, the French prevailed and the British gave way. Some soldiers of the Forty-Third withdrew reluctantly. "The troops being ordered to fall back," wrote Knox, "a command they were hitherto unacquainted with . . . some of them cried out, *Damn it, what is falling back but retreating?*"

Other units began to come apart. "While we were on the retreat back to the town," wrote James Thompson, "the Highlanders . . . were got into great disorder, and had become more like a mob than regular soldiers."

For the piper who had remained in hiding during the charge in 1759, this breakdown represented a crucial social opportunity. British battalions were clusters of small communities of soldiers living and eating together, helping one another to endure the rigors of military service and, in this case, the rigors of the Canadian winter. Since September 13, the piper had lived outside this support system, shunned by his comrades.

Now, however, "as soon as the piper discovered that his men had scattered and were in disorder, he as soon recollected himself of the disgrace that still hung upon him, and he luckily bethought himself to give them a blast of his pipes. By the Lord Harry! this had the effect of stopping them short, and they soon allowed themselves to be formed into some sort of order."

Almost alone among the British, the piper had a good day on April 28: "For this opportune blast of his chanters [the reed pipes of a bagpipe] the piper gained back the forgiveness of the regiment, and was allowed to take his meals with his old messmates, as if nothing at all had happened."

When the British fled, the French let them go. "If," wrote Lapause, "our soldiers had not suffered from the cold, fatigue, the rain and snow, hunger above all, and the great number killed by the enemy artillery, a vigorous pursuit could have taken us into the city with our enemies."

Nonetheless, the French were in good spirits. For both regulars and militiamen, the victory represented redemption after the debacle of the previous engagement. The British agreed. "All the English officers," wrote Malartic, "readily admit that we took our revenge for September 13 on the 28th."

With Murray defeated and trapped in Quebec, Lévis's army looked forward to a successful siege and a triumphant defense of Canada in the coming campaign. "The English," wrote one officer of the *troupes de terre,* "were on the point of surrender . . . [W]e said that if our relief ships arrived first, Quebec would be taken and we would be saved."

THE WOUNDED AND THE DEAD

Every battle has its price. The French lost 266 killed and 773 wounded; the British, 292 killed, 837 wounded, and 53 taken prisoner.

Many of the wounded from both sides ended up in the Hôpital Général. Marie de la Visitation and her colleagues had watched the battle from the hospital. "The clash," she wrote, "occurred just outside Quebec, on the high ground opposite our house. There was not a cannon or musket shot that did not ring in our ears."

When the killing stopped, everything became much, much worse:

> It would take another pen than mine to portray the horrors we saw for the twenty-four hours taken up by the arrival of the wounded, the cries of the dying, and the anguish of their relatives . . . After setting up more than five hundred beds [for the wounded; they still had to find space for another five hundred casualties] . . . suffering unfortunates filled our barns and stables. We had hardly enough time to look after them all. There were seventy-two officers in our infirmaries, of whom thirty-three died. We saw nothing but amputated arms and legs.

None of this trauma was apparent to the patients who benefited from their care. When Malartic described his stay in the hospital, he wrote, "I arrived there at six o'clock. We were very well received by the sisters, and we found almost six hundred [wounded] there, as many English as French."

BRITISH COLLAPSE, BRITISH RESISTANCE

Defeat left the British army in 1760 as demoralized as the French army in 1759. When the French broke, they abandoned Quebec, seeking safety in flight. When the British collapsed, they pillaged the city, seeking oblivion in a three-day drunk. "Immense irregularities," wrote Knox, "are hourly committed by the soldiery, in breaking open store and dwelling houses to get at liquor: this seemingly the result of panic and despair, heightened by drunkenness."

Sunk in "lethargy," members of the garrison began to "harbour a thought of visiting France [as prisoners of war] or England [as repatriated prisoners], or of falling a sacrifice to a merciless scalping knife." Knox, for one, believed that for those three days, the French could have climbed over the walls and taken the city back from its drunken garrison: "Had they followed their blow [victory] on the 28th, 29th, or 30th, before the soldiers recollected themselves, I am strongly inclined to think . . . Québec would have reverted to its old masters."

Yet if the British feared defeat, they never considered surrender. Despite the temporary collapse of his army, Murray enjoyed two considerable advantages over Ramezay. First, help was at hand. The St. Lawrence River was open for navigation; he had already sent a ship carrying urgent requests for assistance to Louisbourg and Halifax. Writing to Amherst two days after the battle, Murray reported, "I am in hopes we shall not be reduced to extremities till the arrival of the fleet, which we expect daily."

Second, Ramezay had felt himself obliged to consider the opinions and welfare of a large civilian population; Murray didn't. He had, in fact, ordered all Canadians out of the city on April 21. "At ten o'clock this morning," wrote Knox, "a proclamation was fixed up at all public places, acquainting the inhabitants that the enemy are preparing to besiege us; that they must therefore quit the town, with their families and effects; and not presume to re-enter until further orders."

Canadian women cursed Murray as they left, shouting that the expulsion was a violation of the capitulation, which allowed them to remain in their homes, and that "the English are a people without honour."

THE FRENCH BESIEGE QUEBEC

After the battle, the French camped on the plains, occupied the Buttes-à-Neveu, and began to establish a parallel and batteries. The British bounced back from their demoralization, mounted additional cannon on the ramparts, and cannonaded the French siege works. On May 9, they experienced a very tense moment. "When," wrote James Miller, "the garrison were almost exhausted, by fatigue, intelligence was brought, that there were large vessels in the river, this increased our anxiety." Shortly thereafter, the tension broke.

"About eleven o'clock this forenoon," wrote Knox,

> we had the inconceivable satisfaction to behold the Lowestoft frigate sail up into the bason . . . The gladness of the troops is not to be expressed: both officers and soldiers mounted the parapets in the face of the enemy, and huzzaed, with their hats in the air, for almost an hour; the . . . circumjacent country for several miles, resounded with our shouts and the thunder of our artillery; for the gunners were so elated, that they did nothing but fire and load for a considerable time.

Undismayed, the French continued to work on their batteries. When two more British ships arrived on the fifteenth, however, Lévis finally gave up hope: "I very much fear that France has abandoned us . . . [The wind] has blown northeast for a long time . . . and nothing has arrived. We have done and are doing what we can. I think that the colony is lost."

On May 17, he lifted the siege and abandoned Quebec.

THE FRENCH CONVOY

Exactly one year after the first Battle of the Plains of Abraham, Jean-Nicolas Desandrouins, a French military engineer, discussed Lévis's siege of Quebec with Samuel Holland.

"Ah! One ship of the line," exclaimed Desandrouins, "and we would have taken the place."

"You're quite right," replied Holland.

The French battleship never came. France had already spent too much money and lost too many ships to be able to send more than a token convoy to Canada.

On April 10, one frigate and five transports had sailed from Bordeaux. They carried munitions, provisions, and four hundred soldiers, mostly former members of the Louisbourg garrison, but no heavy artillery. By the end of April, three of the ships had been lost to the British or the sea. The survivors pressed on until they seized several small British vessels in the Gulf of St. Lawrence and learned that they had lost the race to Quebec. Instead of following orders and sailing for Louisiana, the ships anchored in Baie-des-Chaleurs, where they were later captured by the Royal Navy.

THE FALL OF MONTREAL AND THE SURRENDER OF CANADA

The British spent most of the summer campaigning season making slow and ponderous preparations to capture Montreal. Canada's defenders watched passively. Under other circumstances, they could have mounted spoiling attacks to disrupt British offensives or taken advantage of Canada's interior lines of communication to concentrate in turn against British forces on the Lake Ontario, Lake Champlain, and Quebec frontiers. But the human and material resources that might have supported these operations had all been expended in April and May.

By mid-August, the British were attacking from all directions. Murray led four thousand troops up the St. Lawrence River. Three thousand more sailed down Lake Champlain. Amherst and an army of ten thousand crossed Lake Ontario to the upper St. Lawrence. The three armies overcame Canada's frontier outposts without difficulty and converged on Montreal.

Despite the absence of serious resistance on the part of the French field army, it took the British almost as much time to reach Montreal in 1760 as it had taken Wolfe to find his way up to the Plains of Abraham in 1759. When they finally arrived, Vaudreuil surrendered Montreal and the colony on September 8, bringing the Seven Years' War on the mainland of North America to an end. As the French capitulated, Native Americans took advantage of their status as independent combatants to negotiate first neutrality, then alliance, with the British.

Following the surrender of Montreal, those militiamen who were still in the field returned to their homes and prepared for life in a new Canada, a Canada that was garrisoned by foreign troops, ruled by a foreign governor, and subject to foreign laws. They were joined by many French regulars who slipped away into the countryside. Soldiers still in the ranks of the *troupes de la marine* and the *troupes de terre* were repatriated to France. The last remnants of Montcalm's army saw Quebec one more time on their way home, traveling aboard British vessels as prisoners of war.

VI

CONSEQUENCES

CHAPTER 34

The Road to Quebec

BATTLES IN HISTORY

Battles are the wild cards of human history. Violent, haphazard, and chaotic, they are the most random and unpredictable of human events, with regard to both their outcomes and their impact on the world.

When a battle begins, all bets are off. A supposedly inferior army can blunder its way to victory; an army with all the advantages can march blindly to defeat. Murphy's maxim that "anything that can go wrong, will, and at the worst possible time," rules the battlefield to a much greater extent than any general (who hopes to control events) or any historian (who hopes to understand them) would like to think.

The British victory on the Plains of Abraham turned, first, upon Wolfe's ability to overcome the geographic obstacle posed by the Quebec Promontory, which allowed his army to actually reach the plains and, second, upon a single order by Montcalm that effectively ceded command to his soldiers. These soldiers in turn made the thousands of individual decisions that determined the result of the battle. No one at 10:00 a.m., least of all the troops in the ranks of Montcalm's army, appears to have considered that this might happen. Half an hour later, the collapse of the French regular battalions was a historical fact.

. . .

Yet however complete a victory may be, battles change very little. Simply killing hundreds or thousands of people and leaving one side or another in control of a blood-soaked patch of ground is not in itself enough to change the course of history.

Battles are self-contained events whose outcomes depend upon their own internal dynamics, but each one occurs within a particular historical context. Most affect nothing more than the lives of participants and the course of a war. A few generate military results that interact with their environments to produce a future that would have been different if the battle had gone the other way. These futures, however, can be as random and unpredictable as battles themselves. Their significance becomes fully apparent only when examined against the background of centuries of history.

For those who thought about it at the time, the Battle of the Plains of Abraham was the climactic episode of an Anglo-French war for empire. The naval volunteer called Quebec "this hostile city, the . . . contested prize which is to decide the fate of a western world."

Viewed from a longer perspective, it was part of an infinitely greater process: the European occupation of the Americas and overrunning of a hemispheric Native American civilization. By contributing to the outcome of the Seven Years' War and the subsequent creation of Canada and the United States, the battle helped to determine the form that this occupation would take in North America. In so doing, it shaped and continues to shape the history of the world.

So if the history of the Battle of the Plains of Abraham begins with the formation of the Quebec Promontory, the history of its global impact begins with Native Americans and the world they made.

NATIVE AMERICAN CIVILIZATION

The greater part of the history of the Americas is Native American history. For over ten millennia, much of this history concerned a great civilization centered on Mesoamerica. When the Native Americans of that region invented agriculture, new sources of food supported significant population growth. This facilitated the rise of states and empires, including those established by the Olmecs, Toltecs, Mayas, and Aztecs.

These spectacular developments made Mesoamerica a source of new ideas for much of the Western Hemisphere. In northeastern North America, many bands of fishers and hunters assimilated Mesoamerican innovations and adapted them to suit their own egalitarian cultures. Most notably, the domestication of corn, beans, and squashes spread as far north as the St. Lawrence valley.

In the Southeast and the Mississippi valley, Native Americans combined indigenous and imported ideas to construct societies that more closely resembled the Mesoamerican model. They created chiefdoms, kingdoms, and cities featuring public squares, official religions, massive earthworks, flat-topped pyramids, and authoritarian rulers.

CONTACT AND CATASTROPHE

This civilization of authoritarian realms and egalitarian bands flourished for millennia until a massive, centuries-long catastrophe smashed it into fragments. In many regions, the cataclysm began with wave after wave of previously unknown diseases that destroyed entire families and communities. When populations collapsed, warfare spiraled out of control as nations fought to take prisoners to replace the dead, control trade, or simply to survive. Ecological disruption followed as imported plants and animals from Kentucky bluegrass and peach trees to brown rats and cattle displaced indigenous species.

Along with these infestations came human invaders bent on conquest, exploitation, and occupation. The French in the Northeast and the South, the British in the East and the North, the Spanish in the Southwest and the Southeast, and (in the late eighteenth century) the Russians in the Northwest all established permanent settlements on Native American territory.

Microscopic viruses and heavily armed Spaniards conquered the Mesoamerican heartland. French traders, clerics, and farmers established a colony in the St. Lawrence valley, where epidemics and war had swept away the Iroquoian population of the region. British settlers occupied an Atlantic coast dominated by abandoned farmland and empty towns.

. . .

By the end of the seventeenth century, transplanted societies and ecologies had created a series of enclaves along the Eastern Seaboard and the St. Lawrence River. From Canada to the Carolinas, French and British colonists lived and died amid Europeanized landscapes of farms, towns, ports, and cities. Colonial capitals featured impressive public buildings; settlers founded the Collège des Jésuites in Quebec and Harvard College in Boston in 1635 and 1636.

When Pehr Kalm's North American odyssey took him to Philadelphia, he observed that

> it will be easy to conceive why this city should rise so suddenly from nothing to such grandeur and perfection . . . Its fine appearance, good regulations, agreeable location, natural advantages, trade, riches, and power are by no means inferior to those of any, even of the most ancient, towns in Europe . . . Pennsylvania which was no better than a wilderness in the year 1681, and contained barely fifteen hundred [British] people, now vies with several kingdoms of Europe in the number of inhabitants.

In time, the colonists came to forget that they were invaders and forged new local identities. They became Canadians, Virginians, New Englanders, New Yorkers, Acadians, or Americans, without, in most cases, forsaking their primary allegiance as French or British subjects.

Yet the great epic of post-contact North America was not the founding of successful colonies, remarkable as that might have been, but the rebuilding of shattered Native American societies. Confronted with an ongoing human disaster, the survivors regrouped and carried on. They rode out the initial crisis of European contact, adapted new products and technologies to fit their needs, modified their economies to participate in a global trading system and take advantage of new crops and domestic animals, and formed new alliances with European powers and one another.

What they could not do was turn back the clock and expel the Europeans. The first European enclaves were hardly more than dots on the map, tiny in comparison with the territories controlled by Native Americans. Yet by the end of the seventeenth century, they were firmly established and too strong to be dislodged.

With Native Americans on the defensive and unable to roll back the European advance, the most pressing questions in North American geopolitics came to revolve around how far west the Europeans would go and how they would divide the continent between them. By the eighteenth century, this had become a matter of great concern for both Native Americans living on or near European settlement frontiers and the French and British Empires.

THE BRITISH AND THE FRENCH

England, France, the Netherlands, Portugal, Scotland, and Sweden all established settlement colonies in northeastern North America. By 1700, only the French and the British remained on their feet. Far from Europe, separated by hundreds of miles of Native American territory, neither power ever considered attempting to share the continent in peace.

Instead, conflict began almost as soon as there were enough settlers on the ground to fight. The French founded Port Royal in 1605 and Quebec in 1608. The British settled at Jamestown in 1607. An expedition from Virginia fired the first shots in the French-British war for America in 1613.

In that year, Samuel Argall, a sea captain employed by the Virginia Company, became Wolfe and Saunders's earliest predecessor. Sailing north from Jamestown to the coast of Maine, Argall attacked the Jesuit mission of Saint-Sauveur on Île des Monts Déserts. Pierre Biard, a slightly sarcastic Jesuit priest, witnessed the event: "The English ship came faster than an arrow . . . English flags flying & three trumpets and two drums making a raging noise."

French sailors called out a challenge. "The English did not reply in this manner, but . . . with great volleys of muskets and cannon," Biard wrote. "Captain Flory shouted 'fire the cannon, fire,' but the gunner wasn't there. Gilbert du Thet . . . hearing this cry & seeing no one obey, took the match & made us speak as loudly as the enemy. Regrettably, he didn't aim; if he had, perhaps [the result] would have been something more than just a loud noise."

The capture and destruction of Saint-Sauveur were only the beginning. Whenever France and Britain went to war in Europe, their colonies went to war in North America. As time passed, both the British and the French grew more and more afraid of what the other's colonies might mean for the balance of power between Britain and France in Europe and the world.

From small beginnings, British colonies in North America morphed into economic powerhouses, providing massive quantities of raw materials and enormous markets for British manufactured goods. "The English colonies in this part of the world," observed Kalm, "have increased so much in their number of inhabitants, and in their riches, that they almost vie with Old England." The American colonials, moreover, were not just prosperous; they were on the move, pushing farther into Native American territory.

Looking uneasily southward at British America, French strategists saw a swarming, acquisitive mass of humanity marching relentlessly forward with all of the awful inevitability of a horde of army ants, converting Native American homelands into productive units of the British Empire. They began to fear that if left unchecked, British settlers might very well expand across the Appalachians into the Mississippi valley and conquer Mexico and the French West Indies, thereby making the British Empire into an economic and military superpower strong enough to dominate Europe and the Western world. "One cannot express," warned Vaudreuil's father, Governor-General Philippe de Rigaud de Vaudreuil, in 1716, "to what point the power of England would increase if she seized the rest of North America and how formidable this power would become in Europe."

Canada might be formidable itself one day, but in the first half of the eighteenth century it was an economic deadweight for France. Caribbean sugar islands and the French share of the Newfoundland fishery were priceless national assets. Canadians bought only a small quantity of French manufactured goods, produced nothing in quantity but furs, for which demand in France was quite limited, and cost a great deal to defend and administer. Although Canada served as an anchor for a network of posts in Native American territory west of Montreal, Canadians occupied a tiny pocket of North America, consisting of a narrow ribbon along the St. Lawrence

River. Seventy thousand Canadians nonetheless alarmed some Britons and Americans almost as much as 1.2 million Americans alarmed the French.

For colonials like James Logan, a Philadelphia administrator and merchant, Canada's status as "a very cold and not very fruitful country" did not keep it from posing a serious threat to British America. The French occupation of the lower Mississippi valley in the eighteenth century only increased their fears. "Now they surround all the British dominions [and] . . . claim a country nearly equal to all Europe in extent."

The influential and well-connected Logan wrote a memoir on the French threat that reached the desk of a senior British cabinet minister in 1732. Echoing Vaudreuil, he warned of the dire consequences that could come from colonial expansion by a rival power: "It is manifest that if France could possess itself of these Dominions [British America] and thereby become masters of all their trade, their sugars, tobacco, rice, timber and naval stores, they would soon be an overmatch in naval strength to the rest of Europe and then be in a condition to prescribe laws to the whole."

DRAWING A LINE IN THE FOREST

Never strong enough to eliminate a potential threat by conquering the British colonies, the French attempted to confine British settlement to the Atlantic coast and preemptively occupy places where the British might settle farther inland. They began in 1701 and 1702 by founding outposts at Detroit and in Louisiana. Louis XIV described Louisiana as "a settlement at the mouth of the Mississippi . . . which has become an indispensable necessity to prevent the expansion by the English of Carolina and New York . . . into the lands between them and that river."

In so doing, however, the French had chosen to use their own colonies to challenge the British Empire in North America without at the same time maintaining a navy strong enough to defend these colonies. Instead, they fortified Louisbourg and Quebec, creating defended ports that could harbor French fleets but invited defeat in detail by British amphibious forces concentrating against each one in turn.

French attempts at containment, moreover, did not prevent the British from capturing Acadia in 1710, compelling the French to abandon their last outposts on Hudson Bay in 1713, and successfully besieging Louisbourg in 1745. Nor did they slow the expansion of the British settlement frontier, which, by the mid-eighteenth century, was poised to leap across the Appalachians to the Ohio valley.

Pennsylvania traders had been active in the Ohio valley since the 1720s, when they followed Native American migrants into the region. By the 1740s, their presence was causing French officials considerable concern, just as a new set of players made their appearance.

For the Virginia and English speculators of the Ohio Company, the Ohio valley represented a superb opportunity to make massive profits by selling off other people's property. They planned to push aside the local Native Americans (and Pennsylvanians) and change Native American homelands into European real estate that they could subdivide and sell to eager settlers.

As British Americans prepared to take a giant step toward the Mississippi valley and the French prepared to stop them, the worst fears of Logan and the elder Vaudreuil both seemed to be on the verge of coming true.

The French moved first. In 1753, an expedition from Canada built three forts at key points along the waterways linking Lake Erie and the Ohio River. In 1754, the Virginians built their own fort on the Ohio River, on the site of present-day Pittsburgh. A larger French expedition forced the Americans to withdraw and built Fort Duquesne on the site of the former Virginia outpost. When George Washington attempted to reclaim the region for Virginia, the French defeated his army, razed Fort Necessity, his improvised stronghold, and compelled him to withdraw back over the Appalachians.

The appearance of unwanted French forts and an uninvited French army within their territory profoundly displeased Ohio Native Americans. But if the French invasion annoyed them, British arrogance drove them to war. In 1755, Shingas, a leading Delaware chief in the region, approached a British general and asked about British intentions in the Ohio valley. He received a breathtakingly honest reply—"that the English should inhabit & inherit the land" and "that No Savage Should Inherit the Land."

Thoroughly nonplussed, most Ohio nations chose to temporarily tolerate the French as the lesser of two evils. They accepted French munitions and supplies to support attacks on British settlements and remained in the field until 1758, when they negotiated the Easton Treaty with British representatives.

Under the terms of the treaty, the Native Americans ceased their attacks, and the British agreed to keep their settlers east of the Appalachians. The British took advantage of this separate peace to send an army into the Ohio valley, forcing the French to demolish and abandon Fort Duquesne. Fort Pitt, built on the site of Fort Duquesne, grew into a town as British settlers ignored the Easton Treaty and swarmed across the mountains.

French attempts in the 1750s to stem the tide of British westward expansion failed dismally. Four years after they had expelled the Virginians from the Ohio valley, the British line of settlement swept across the Appalachians as if the French had never tried to get in their way.

For metropolitan France, this represented the disappointing failure of an imperial policy of containment. For the French of Canada, the situation was rather more serious. The original confrontation in the Ohio valley had touched off a war that spread across northeastern North America and around the world. In 1759, the fighting reached Canada when Saunders's fleet and Wolfe's army appeared before Quebec.

FROM THE OHIO VALLEY TO QUEBEC

In 1755, the British reacted to the construction of Fort Duquesne with a series of strikes against French outposts in territory claimed by Great Britain. The results of these expeditions ranged from the capture of Fort Beauséjour in Acadia and the subsequent expulsion of the Acadians to a shattering defeat at the hands of a Native American–French army at the Battle of the Monongahela in the Ohio valley.

Vaudreuil, who took office in 1755, quickly proved to be a dynamic, aggressive commander in chief. Over the next two years, he sent Montcalm to destroy Forts Oswego and William Henry before they could be used as bases for attacks on Canada. When a British army threatened Canada's Lake Champlain frontier in 1758, Vaudreuil's forces, again commanded by Montcalm, smashed it into fragments at the Battle of Carillon.

Yet none of these triumphs ever came close to threatening British America, whose strength lay in its coastal cities and countryside and its transatlantic link to Britain, not frontier forts and settlements. Every French victory only made British America stronger as a humiliated Britain responded to defeat by sending more troops, more ships, and more money to North America. As their resources increased and their regular army adapted to local conditions, British goals in North America changed from securing disputed territory to the invasion and conquest of Canada. With this shift in policy, the war in North America became a war for Quebec.

The French could only defend Canada and undertake operations in the interior for as long as supplies and reinforcements from France continued to arrive by way of Quebec. When they lost the city, they lost their Atlantic lifeline and with it the war in North America.

The question of whether the Battle of the Plains of Abraham would have any impact on history beyond determining the outcome of the Seven Years' War in North America remained unresolved for the next three years. Canadians like Marie de la Visitation continued to hope that a peace treaty would return Canada to France in exchange for concessions elsewhere. In that case, the battle would remain a minor historical footnote.

CHAPTER 35

The Battle of the Plains of Abraham and the History of the World

THE ROYAL PROCLAMATION AND THE TREATY OF PARIS

While the British occupied Canada, the global conflict kept on going. In North America, the Great Lakes and Ohio nations went to war against the British Empire. They had made peace with the British in good faith, expecting their new allies to hold up their side of the bargain. When the British began treating Native American homelands as if they were British possessions, the Native Americans struck back. In a single campaign in 1763, they captured every British post west of Lake Ontario except for Detroit and Fort Pitt.

Suitably chastened, the British, who had already issued the Royal Proclamation of 1763, negotiated a new peace in 1764. The first step toward Crown recognition of aboriginal title, the Royal Proclamation remains a key document for Native American land claims cases all across Canada.

More fortunate elsewhere, by the end of 1762 British forces had captured French colonies and outposts in India, Africa, and the West Indies, raided the coast of France, and landed in Germany to support their Prussian allies. As soon as Spain entered the war on the side of France, the British captured Manila and Havana, key Spanish ports on opposite sides of the globe. When a French expedition seized St. John's, Newfoundland, in 1762, British troops promptly recaptured the port after the Battle of Signal Hill.

Finally, the French and British governments decided that they had

had enough. Peace negotiations began in the fall of 1762; delegates concluded the Treaty of Paris on February 10, 1763. During the negotiations, the French had one last chance to try to get Canada back. They chose to trade Canada for Guadeloupe, a Caribbean sugar island, and pushed hard and successfully for access to the Newfoundland fisheries.

In both France and Britain, fireworks exploded overhead as cheering crowds celebrated the return of peace. British crowds applauded, among other triumphs, the Battle of the Plains of Abraham and the fall of Canada. French crowds seemed not to care.

With the signing of the Treaty of Paris, the Plains of Abraham became one of the great battles of world history. Under the terms of the treaty, France ceded all its possessions in northeastern North America to Britain. This included French claims to Native American territory east of the Mississippi.

The British agreed to respect the Catholicism of Canadians and gave French subjects eighteen months to depart for France if they desired. They ceded the islands of Saint-Pierre and Miquelon to France to serve as a base for French fishers and allowed the French to fish in the Gulf of St. Lawrence and dry their catch along part of the Newfoundland coast.

Britain returned Cuba and the Philippines to Spain; Spain ceded Florida to Britain and (under a separate agreement with France) received in exchange all "French" territory west of the Mississippi. This included the French colony of Louisiana and a vast tract of land belonging to Native Americans extending from the Gulf of Mexico to beyond what is now the Canadian-American border.

All of eastern North America from the Gulf of Mexico to Hudson Bay and the Atlantic to the Mississippi River now came under British sovereignty, at least as far as Europeans were concerned. The British occupation of Canada had become a conquest.

CATHOLIC FRANCOPHONES IN THE BRITISH EMPIRE

Each of the three French societies that had flourished in Canada, Acadia, and Louisbourg before the Seven Years' War experienced the conquest in its own way.

For Canadians, it was a calamity. Canada had been ripped away from France and forcibly converted into the province of Quebec, a minor component of Britain's North American empire. Within this province, the French of Canada began a long struggle for cultural survival as a Catholic, Francophone minority inside a Protestant, Anglophone empire.

Literate Canadians—the only ones who recorded their opinions—responded to news of the Treaty of Paris with a mix of sadness and rage. "One cannot," wrote Marie de la Visitation, "express the sorrow and bitterness that has seized every heart." She blamed the French, not the British, for the conquest. Canada, she declared, "would still be in our possession if Canadians, always victorious over the English, had been the only ones to defend it." With the signing of the treaty, France lost "an immense country whose value it never appreciated." But it had been Canadians who paid the price for French negligence and incompetence. "Our regrets . . . will last as long as our lives."

Some of the thirty-five hundred Canadians who emigrated after the conquest had their regrets as well. Ensign Antoine Bullau of the Montreal militia was one of those Canadians who "preferred to abandon the little they had, instead of living under foreign domination." Captain Louis-Frédéric Herbin of the *troupes de la marine* placed himself among "the officers of Canada [who] . . . abandoned their country to rejoin the white flag [of the Bourbons]."

Yet however loyal they might remain to France and the Bourbon monarchy, the exiles retained their provincial identity as Canadians. They called themselves Canadians in official correspondence and were referred to as such by the Ministry of Marine. Twenty years after the Treaty of Paris, the Quebec merchant who lost his entire inventory to fire during the bombardment continued to sign himself:

> Votre très humble & obéissent,
> Berthou-Dûbreüil,
> Canadien.

Among Acadians, already British subjects, the coming of peace marked the moment when the British stopped hunting them down like animals and permitted refugees and deportees to return home. With the sites of their former farms and settlements largely occupied by transplanted New Englanders, many Acadians chose to establish new communities on the south shore of the Gulf of St. Lawrence in what is now New Brunswick, Nova Scotia, and Prince Edward Island.

View of La Lor Ette in Canada, Inhabited by Catholic Indians. Britain's Red Ensign flies over Ouiharalihte's hometown of Lorette (Wendake), marking the presence of a new imperial power in Canada.

. . .

For former residents of Louisbourg, there was no homecoming and no renewal. They remained in France after the war. Once a flourishing North Atlantic port, Louisbourg became a forsaken ruin, plundered for building stone but otherwise ignored. While Montreal and Quebec ultimately took their place among the great cities of the world, a partially reconstructed Louisbourg is now a national historic site.

At least one Louisbourg resident damned the British in verse:

> I have lived for three years,
> In fear and torment.
> The English, crooked and treacherous,
> In spite of the terms of the treaties,
> Had sent into exile,
> All of our relatives from Grand-Pré [in Acadia].

On our island of Cape Breton,
In spite of this persecution,
[We] remained French subjects,
[In] the only corner of Acadia,
Where I could still hope,
To escape the enemy.

. . . So farewell, my dear Louisbourg,
I say good-bye to you forever.
. . . With a breaking heart I leave you,
You and your destroyers.

IMPERIAL AMERICA

For the world at large, the removal of a great power from the North American mainland was far more important than the people it left behind. National humiliation aside, France came out of the Seven Years' War in North America very well. The war had, in effect, downsized its expensive and unproductive land-based North American empire to a hugely valuable fishing station on the islands of Saint-Pierre and Miquelon. Moreover, Canada would prove to be far more dangerous to Britain as a British possession than it had ever been in the hands of the French.

Both local and transatlantic observers agreed that Britain's American colonies were nations in waiting. "I have been told by Englishmen," wrote Pehr Kalm, "and not only by such as were born in America but also by those who came from Europe, that the English colonies in North America, in the space of thirty or fifty years, would be able to form a state by themselves entirely independent of Old England."

The only obstacle in their path was Canada. Back in 1732, James Logan had confidently asserted that the American colonies would never lose their loyalty to the British Empire: "While Canada is so near, they cannot rebel." Kalm agreed: "As the whole country which lies along the seashore is unguarded, and on the land side is harassed by the French, these dangerous neighbours in times of war are sufficient to prevent the connection of the colonies from their mother country from being broken off."

The Battle of the Plains of Abraham changed all that. Under British control, Canada was just as close but no longer a threat. Some British soldiers, among them James Murray, had thought all along that a British Canada would be less a conquered colony than an incitement to American rebellion. In 1760, he confided his fears to Malartic, then awaiting repatriation to France.

"Do you think," asked Murray, "that we will give Canada back to you?"

"I am not," replied the French officer, "sufficiently familiar with high policy to see so far ahead."

"If we are wise, we won't keep it. New England needs a bridle to keep it under control, and we will give it one by not holding on to this country."

Murray's fears to the contrary, the British conquest of Canada did not in itself cause an American rebellion. Victory in the Seven Years' War produced a transatlantic outburst of triumphal pride in Britain and British America. Americans never felt more British than just before they tore the empire apart.

Emanuel Leutze, *Washington Crossing the Delaware.* "If we are wise, we won't keep it [Canada]. New England needs a bridle to keep it under control, and we will give it one by not holding on to this country." James Murray, 1759.

The Battle of the Plains of Abraham and subsequent fall of New France set the stage for the American Revolution.

Winning the Seven Years' War, however, had left the British government with a huge debt and more colonial interest groups than it could handle. Imposing taxes on the colonies to pay off war debts and support a North American garrison alienated many British colonials. So did attempts to accommodate non-British groups inside the empire by granting religious freedom and civil rights to Canadian Catholics and limiting western expansion to preserve the peace with Native Americans.

It soon became apparent that the British had chosen the worst possible time to antagonize their American colonists. With the French threat eliminated, the American colonies no longer needed British protection. With France humiliated in war and alarmed by the rising power of the British Empire, American rebels found a partner looking for a chance to cut Britain down to size and willing to support an American rebellion to do it.

Beginning in 1775, colonials from New England to Georgia who had come to see themselves as American rather than British rose up in rebellion against the Crown. Financed by French subsidies, equipped with French weapons, and assisted by French troops and warships, the American colonies won their independence and formed the United States of America. And this was only the beginning.

The French defeat in the Seven Years' War had cost Native Americans a proven ally whose principal goal in the region was keeping their land out of American hands. The American Revolution eliminated a British imperial authority that had tried to stand between American settlers and Native American homelands. The British remained occasional allies for Native Americans until the end of the War of 1812. After that, Native Americans faced the United States without the support of a European partner.

With the French and the British out of the way and Native American resistance crippled, American settlers and soldiers drove straight west for the Pacific. Along the way, they seized some of the richest territory in the world. As French strategists had predicted, Americans overran huge chunks of the former Spanish Empire, making California, Florida, and Texas into states and northern Mexico into the American Southwest.

In the course of the nineteenth century, Americans made their country into a power to be reckoned with. In the twentieth, it became a superpower. By the first decade of the twenty-first century, America was the most powerful nation in human history. From landing at Normandy to landing on the moon, every time the United States acts as a global power, the world reverberates to the echoes of the gunfire on the Plains of Abraham and the scratching of the pens that signed the Treaty of Paris.

CANADIAN EMPIRE

The consequences of the Seven Years' War did not end with the destruction of the French Empire in North America, the expulsion of the British from their traditional American colonies, and the creation of the United States. Almost unnoticed by the world at large, the Seven Years' War and the American Revolution created a second North American country.

In Canada, French- and English-speaking militiamen had joined with British regulars to defeat American rebels besieging Quebec City. In Nova Scotia, local Loyalists withstood a siege in Fort Cumberland and put down an incipient rebellion. The victorious colonies that had stood by the Crown united in 1867 to form the Dominion of Canada, a self-governing, federation within the British Empire.

The American Revolution provoked a demographic revolution in Canada. Prior to 1783, most Europeans in Canada spoke French; most of the territory outside the St. Lawrence valley and part of the Atlantic region was occupied and controlled by Native Americans. Following the revolution, tens of thousands of American Loyalists and Native American allies of the British sought sanctuary in what is now Canada. The arrival of the American refugees added a significant Anglophone component to Canada's European population. Reinforced by successive waves of immigrants from the United States and Britain, English speakers became a dominant majority in British North America.

This tidal wave of Anglophones represented an unmitigated disaster for Canada's Native Americans. Previous large-scale European settlements had been confined to the St. Lawrence valley and the Atlantic coast. Loyalist immigrants pushed the settlement frontier up the St. John River into the New Brunswick interior and past Montreal into what is now southern Ontario. Although peaceful, this migration nonetheless resulted in the transfer of huge blocks of territory from Native American to European control. It began a cycle of treaties and occupation of Native American territory that would not end until settlers moving westward from Montreal encountered settlers moving inland from the Pacific coast.

Canadian politicians took the land thus acquired from Native Americans and assembled a transcontinental federation out of the post–American Revolution British Empire in the east, the Hudson Bay drainage basin in the center, and British Columbia in the west.

Inside this transcontinental federation, Quebec became the heartland of a French Canadian population extending all the way across North America. For if New France had vanished, French Canada survived, trapped inside the British Empire. Within a generation of the conquest and the return to France of the officials and officers who had governed Canada, French Canadians produced new leaders who worked within the framework of the British parliamentary system to defend their language and culture. Strength of numbers, skilled political leadership, and partnerships with Anglophones won them a secure place within the new Canada. But they remained second-class citizens in their own country.

Until after World War II, most English-speaking Canadians saw themselves as British. The slogan on an 1898 Canadian postage stamp proudly proclaimed their membership—and ownership—of the British Empire: "We hold a vaster empire than has been." This was perhaps not surprising, given the language, culture, and history that they shared with British communities throughout that empire and the immense prestige and power of an empire that had bounced back from defeat in the American Revolution and gone on to seize vast territories in Asia, Africa, and Australia.

Seeing themselves as British did not prevent Anglophones from developing a strong parallel identity as Canadians. But they found it hard to simultaneously identify with British people around the world and French Canadians at home. Many harbored very strong anti-Francophone, anti-Catholic opinions. In 1936, George Drew, future premier of Ontario, leader of the opposition in Ottawa, and companion of the Order of Canada, neatly summed up the views of Anglophones of this persuasion regarding both the Battle of the Plains of Abraham and the role of Francophones in Canada: "It is not unfair to remind the French that they are a defeated race, and that their rights are rights only because of the tolerance of the English."

In the second half of the twentieth century, however, two competing groups of politicians sought to overturn the British conquest. While Québécois nationalists sought independence, a federalist coalition of Fran-

Britain and America triumphant. Viewed from the steps of Vaudreuil's former official residence in the Château Saint-Louis and illuminated by a cheerful sunrise, British troops parade in Quebec.

cophones and Anglophones embarked upon a sweeping program to make official Canada less British, more French, and ultimately more Canadian. Most notably, they replaced British symbols with Canadian icons, including the Maple Leaf flag, and compelled the federal government to function in both English and French, making both careers and public services equally available to Anglophones and Francophones.

At the same time, more and more Anglophones were coming to see themselves as Canadian citizens rather than British subjects and becoming more concerned about their relations with Francophones in Canada than with British people overseas. They discarded James Wolfe as a popular hero and generally supported measures that would make Canada as much a country for Francophones as it was for Anglophones.

Anglophone-Francophone tensions nonetheless remain. Canada still has two political parties, one provincial, one federal, dedicated to making Quebec an independent state. Québécois nationalism remains a powerful force, and the possibility remains that the contemporary Canada that was in part created by the Battle of the Plains of Abraham will one day be destroyed by it.

MORE THAN 250 YEARS LATER

Participants in the Battle of the Plains of Abraham fought for the French Empire, the British Empire, the Hurons, the Odawas, the Crees, or any one of a dozen other Native American nations. But the ultimate result of their battle was the division of the Native American lands of North America between two countries so large that they became empires in their own right.

As the European juggernaut rolled headlong across the continent, Native Americans neither accepted defeat nor quietly disappeared. In both Canada and the United States, Native Americans have adapted rather than submitted to the European presence, now reinforced by immigration from all around the world.

The two imperial states continue to dominate the continent. The United States remains an economic, cultural, and military colossus. Canada, against all odds, survives as a French- and English-speaking country.

More than 250 years after the event, the Battle of the Plains of Abraham continues to shape our lives and our world.

Acknowledgments

There's nothing like completing a manuscript to make you appreciate the family, friends, and colleagues you've been ignoring while you were writing it, because they're the ones you turn to for second opinions on your final draft. Tim Cook, Don MacLeod, and Glenn Ogden were kind enough to critique the entire manuscript. Peter Cook, Serge Durflinger, Xavier Gélinas, and Jason Ginn, equally kind, read chapters relating to their particular interests. Every one of their comments and suggestions made the manuscript significantly better.

Lara Andrews, Jane Naisbitt, and Catherine Woodcock, from the Canadian War Museum's Military History Research Centre, nobly endured an endless series of requests for interlibrary loans, each more obscure than the last.

I was fortunate enough to write this book while working at the Canadian War Museum. Dean Oliver (director of research and exhibitions) and Roger Sarty (formerly deputy director of the museum) have made CWM an exciting place to be a historian. Gifted and supportive colleagues like Dean, Roger, Martin Auger, Andrew Burtch, Tim Cook, Serge Durflinger, Lisa Leblanc, Amber Lloydlangston, Jeff Noakes, Glenn Ogden, and Patricia Grimshaw have made both my after-hours work on the Battle of the Plains of Abraham and developing exhibits at the museum much easier to survive. Many of the ideas in this book developed in conversation with Tim Cook, as we compared the experience of the Canadian Corps in World War I with that of the British, French, and Amerindian forces in 1759.

Rick Broadhead, a prince among literary agents, handled locating a very fine publisher and negotiating a contract with his usual superb competence. Vicky Wilson, Audrey Silverman, Ryan Smernoff, and the editorial team at Knopf have done a superb job of making this manuscript into a book.

Notes

PREFACE

xxx "New England": Malartic, *Journal des campagnes,* 331. The original text uses "bit" (*frein*) instead of "bridle."

CHAPTER 1
500,000 Years of History

3 One massive chunk: Quebec Geoscience Centre, "The Rocks of the Quebec City Area: A World Beneath Our Feet," http://www.cgq-qgc.ca/english/outreach/geotour/ ROCHES.htm; Mathieu and Kedl, *Plains of Abraham,* 19–23.

4 "the first world war": Churchill, *Age of Revolution,* 123.

4 A minor colony: Dechêne, *Le peuple, l'État et la guerre au Canada,* 423.

4 "Receiving supplies of men": "Considerations Offered by [?] upon a Scheme for Attacking Louisbourg & Quebec, 1757," in Pargellis, *Military Affairs in North America,* 295.

5 "The doing of this": Ibid.

5 "By going to Quebec": John Campbell, Fourth Earl of Loudoun, to John Campbell, Duke of Argyll, Jan. 9, 1757, in Gipson, *Victorious Years,* 91.

5 Perched atop the eastern tip: Stacey, *Quebec, 1759,* 43.

5 Throughout that time: Chartrand, *French Fortresses in North America,* 23.

CHAPTER 2
Sailing to Armageddon

6 Even before he arrived in Canada: Smith, *Journals of Ashley Bowen,* 8, 16, 54–57; Vickers, "Honest Tar," 534–42.

8 This surprisingly high percentage: Graves, "Appendix E: Order of Battle and Strength, British Army at Quebec, 1759," in Stacey, *Quebec, 1759,* 213–14; McCulloch, "With Wolfe at Quebec," 25.

8 One hundred and nineteen: Saunders lists thirty-four transports, seven ordnance vessels, and four victuallers as "English" compared with six ordnance vessels and sixty-eight transports (including sloops and schooners) that were "American." Saunders to William Pitt, June 6, 1759, Library and Archives Canada, Manuscript Group 11, Great Britain, Public Record Office, Colonial Office Papers, CO 5, Original Correspondence, Secretary of State, America and West Indies, vol. 51, fol. 31v, reel B-2113. See also Graves, "Appendix F: The Royal Navy at Quebec," in Stacey, *Quebec, 1759,* 221.

8 "in great want of seamen": Vice Admiral Saunders to James De Lancey, Esq., lieutenant governor of New York, and to Thomas Pownall, Esq., governor of Massachusetts Bay, March 10, 1759, copy of letter enclosed in Saunders to William Pitt, March 10, 1759, LAC, MG 11, CO 5, vol. 51, fol. 27, reel B-2113.

8 Two hundred and forty sailors: Saunders to William Pitt, June 6, 1759, fol. 31v.

8 More arrived: Philip Durell, Journal, entries of May 5, Aug. 13, Sept. 9, 1759, LAC, MG 12, vol. 3, fol. 226, 242v, 246v, reel B-19.

8 "the fleet and part of the army": Saunders to James De Lancey and Thomas Pownall, March 10, 1759.

9 Throughout the siege: See, for example, Durell, Journal, entry of Aug. 16, 1759, fol. 243v.

9 At least three African American teamsters: List prepared by Captain Matthew Leslie, assistant quartermaster general, ca. Oct. 24, 1759, LAC, MG 18-M, Northcliffe Collection, ser. 1: Monckton Papers, vol. 32, Quebec 1759, XV, reel C-366; Matthew Leslie, "Return of the Waggoners Employed on the Expedition Under General Wolfe," Oct. 24, 1759, ibid.

9 A floating herd: "Return of What Cattle Received from Boston Issued to the Army & What Remains, viz.," LAC, MG 18-M, ser. 1, vol. 32, Quebec 1759, XV, reel C-366.

9 "We have": Smith, *Journals of Ashley Bowen,* 57.

9 "He said to me": Ibid., 58.

10 "The last night": Ibid., 59.

10 Ten years later: Douglas, "Philip Durell."

10 "These prisoners": Wolfe to William Pitt, Nov. 1, 1758, LAC, MG 11, CO 5, vol. 53, fol. 204, reel B-220.

11 "a fleet at the Isle of Bic": James Wolfe, undated memorandum, in Bell, "An Exact and Faithful Copy of General Wolfe's Journal from the 13th May 1759 to the 16th of August 1759 (the Remainder of His Journal to Near the Day He Was Killed [13th Sept.] Was Destroyed by Himself Before the Battle), also Some Loose Hints and Part of a Journal of His Expedition to Gaspé Faithfully Copied from One of His Memorandum Books," LAC, MG 18-M, Northcliffe Collection, ser. 3: Separate Items in the Northcliffe Collection, Separate Items no. 24, Manuscript Quebec Journals, Captain Thomas Bell, vol. 6, reel C-370.

11 "At 12 this night": Smith, *Journals of Ashley Bowen,* 66, 67.

11 "The Master of her": Durell, Journal, entry of May 16, 1759, fol. 228.

11 "such quantities of ice": Durell, Journal, entries of April 8 and May 5, 1759, fols. 221, 226.

11 "We had therefore": Miller, "Memoirs of an Invalid," 25.

12 "give an account": Durell, Journal, entry of May 27, 1759, fol. 231.

12 On May 28: Hunter, "Biographical Memoir," 19; Durell, Journal, entry of May 28, 1759, fols. 231–231v.

13 Seven hundred and forty: Graham, "Sir Hovenden Walker," 660–61; "Report of ye Officers Soldiers &c Lost," Sept. 9, 1711, LAC, MG 11, CO 5, vol. 9, fol. 15, reel B-6171.

14 "the uncertainty & rapidity": "At a Consultation of Sea Officers Belonging to the Squadron Under the Command of Sir Hovenden Walker, Rear Admiral of the White, on Board Her Majesty's Ship the Windsor the 25th Day of August 1711 in the River of St. Laurence," LAC, MG 11, CO 5, vol. 9, fol. 66v, reel B-6171.

15 Cook subsequently published: Holland to John Graves Simcoe, Jan. 11, 1792, in Willis Chipman, "The Life and Times of Major Samuel Holland, Surveyor-General, 1764–1801," Ontario Historical Society, *Papers and Records* 21 (1924): 18–19; Hayes, *Histori-*

cal Atlas of Canada, 106–7; J. Thorpe, "Samuel Holland," in Halpenny, *Dictionary of Canadian Biography,* 5:425; Glyndwr Williams, "James Cook," in Halpenny, *Dictionary of Canadian Biography,* 4:163.

15   With the main body: Hunter, "Biographical Memoir," 20; Durell, Journal, entry of June 8, 1759, fol. 232v.

15   High professional standing: Whitely, "Sir Charles Saunders," 698–99.

16   "At 4 A.M. . . . sent pinnace": Smith, *Journals of Ashley Bowen,* 71.

16   "Mr. Cook would have me": Ibid., 84.

16   "We sent a boat": Ibid., 72.

16   "this island which": Coats, "A Private Journal of the Siege of Quebec," entry of Sept. 27, 1759, LAC, MG 18-N46, reel A-1221.

17   "As we halted": Knox, *Historical Journal,* 1:294.

18   "If, by accident": Wolfe to Amherst, March 6, 1759, LAC, MG 13, War Office Papers, WO 34, Amherst Papers, vol. 46b, fol. 293, reel B-2662.

CHAPTER 3

James Wolfe in Love and War

19   "Though I suppose": Wolfe to Henrietta Wolfe, Jan. 19, 1753, in Wilson, *James Wolfe,* 200.

20   When more senior officers: Harding, *Amphibious Warfare in the Eighteenth Century,* 182.

21   "Pushing on smartly": Wolfe to William Rickson, Nov. 5, 1757, LAC, MG 18-L5, James Wolfe Collection, Correspondence, Letters from General James Wolfe to Captain Wm. Rickson (Antiquaries' Miscellaneous Papers), Museum of the Society of Antiquaries, Edinburgh, Scotland, MS 2207, fols. 58–58v, reel A-1780.

21   "We lost the lucky moment": Wolfe to Edward Wolfe, Sept. 30, 1757, in Wilson, *James Wolfe,* 333.

21   Serving under Jeffery Amherst: Chartrand, *Louisbourg, 1758;* McLennan, *Louisbourg,* 236–93; Reid, *Wolfe,* 145–54.

21   "I can't help wishing": Wolfe to Lord George Sackville, Feb. 7, 1758, in Wilson, *James Wolfe,* 355.

CHAPTER 4

River Control, Fireships, Landing Craft, Bombardment

22   "was expected with 20 sail": Durell, Journal, entry of May 16, 1759, fol. 231.

22   The ships at each location: "Disposition of the Ships Under the Command of Vice Admiral Saunders in North America, 5th September, 1759," LAC, MG 11, CO 5, vol. 51, fols. 42–42v, reel B-2113.

23   "some frigates will always": Saunders to James De Lancey and Thomas Pownall, March 10, 1759, fol. 27.

23   To provide these services: Durell, Journal, entry of July 9, 1759, fol. 237.

23   Ships and convoys heading upstream: Ibid., entry of Aug. 13, 1759, fol. 242v.

23   *Eltham* resupplied any passing vessel: "During my stay in the River St. Lawrence," wrote Saunders, "I stationed the Eltham (one of the victuallers that came out with the Echo) at the Isle of Bic, under the protection of the Hind, to supply any of the cruizers that might be in want of provisions." Saunders to William Pitt, Nov. 24, 1759, LAC, MG 11,

CO 5, vol. 51, fol. 58, reel B-2113. See also Durell, Journal, entry of Oct. 19, 1759, fols. 250–250v.

23   "insult from the Indians": Durell, Journal, entry of July 9, 1759, fols. 237–237v.

23   When the troops moved upriver: Ibid., entry of June 24, 1759, fol. 235.

23   "to hinder any of the enemy": Ibid., entry of July 9, 1759, fol. 237v.

23   "At 1/2 past noon": Ibid., entry of July 20, 1759, fol. 239v.

24   On Thursday, July 12: Master's Log, HMS *Scarborough,* entry of July 12, 1759, LAC, MG 12, ADM 52, vol. 1022, fol. 36, reel C-12889.

24   British amphibious experts: Beatson, *Naval and Military Memoirs of Great Britain,* 2:167; Molyneux, *Conjunct Expeditions,* 211.

24   The boats came equipped: Harding, "Sailors and Gentlemen of Parade," 43–44; Syrett, "Methodology of British Amphibious Operations During the Seven Years' and American Wars," 272–73.

26   "Nothing could be more formidable": Knox, *Historical Journal,* 1:298.

27   "This night at 12 o'clock": Smith, *Journals of Ashley Bowen,* 76.

27   "I reckon": Wolfe to Walter Wolfe, May 17, 1759, in Wilson, *James Wolfe,* 428.

28   "We saw the town": Bell, "The First Part of My Quebeck Journal," May 27, 1759, LAC, MG 18-M, ser. 3, no. 24, reel C-370. Knox adds details. Wolfe, he wrote, "discovered the French army incamped on the north side of the river, their right extending close to Quebec, and their left towards the cataract of Montmorency; the ground which the French general has made choice of is high and strong by nature, with the village of Beauport in the center of their camp . . . to this post they are all employed in adding every kind of work, that art can invent, to render it impenetrable." Knox, *Historical Journal,* 1:295.

28   "a steep sandy precipice": Letter to "J.W.," Sept. 2, 1759, "Genuine Letters from a Volunteer in the British Service at Quebec. Published in Pamphlet Form in 1761, a Transcript of the Pamphlet in the British Museum Was Made by Permission of Mr. Fortescue," in Doughty and Parmelee, *Siege of Quebec,* 5:18–19.

29   "at 1 P.M. we saw": Smith, *Journals of Ashley Bowen,* 77.

29   "our longboat and pinnace": Ibid., 82.

29   "Our Masters Mate": Ibid.

29   "When I came into the camp": Ibid.

30   "I advanced towards him": Ibid., 83.

30   "their town is mostly built": John Campbell, Earl of Loudoun, to William Augustus, Duke of Cumberland, Oct. 2, 1756, in Pargellis, *Military Affairs in North America,* 236.

30   "be greatly assistant": "Considerations Offered by [?] upon a Scheme for Attacking Louisbourg & Quebec, 1757," 297.

30   "the lower town": Patrick Mackellar, "A Description of the Town of Quebeck Its Strength and Situation," in Pargellis, *Military Affairs in North America,* 413.

30   "set the Town on fire": Wolfe to Amherst, March 6, 1759, fol. 293.

30   "this hostile city": Letter to "J.W.," Sept. 2, 1759, 15–16.

31   Each expense magazine: Duffy, *Fire and Stone,* 113–18; Muller, *Attac and Defence of Fortified Places,* 38–41.

32   Packed with a highly flammable: Muller, *Treatise of Artillery,* 206.

32   "The 6th of July": Williamson to Thomas Hay, Earl of Kinnouille, August 10, 1759, LAC, MG 18-N21, George Williamson and Family Papers, reel A-573.

32   "At 9 General Wolfe": Smith, *Journals of Ashley Bowen,* 81.

32 "our shells at first": Adam Williamson, "Journal for 1759," LAC, MG 18-N21, reel A-573.

32 By late August: *Plan of the Town of Quebec,* LAC, National Map Collection, NMC 0011117.

32 A small army: Alex. Jno. Scott, Adjt. Rl. Artillery, "Return of the Detachment of the Royal Regiment of Artillery Camp at Pt. Levi August 27 1759," LAC, MG 18-M, vol. 21, Quebec vol. 4, reel C-366; Lieutenant Colonel Hector Boisrond, "Weekly Return of the Marines at the Camp at Point Levis, Augt. 27 1759," ibid.

32 "2498 thirteen inch shells": Williamson to the Board of Ordnance, Aug. 25, 1759, LAC, MG 18-N21, reel A-573; "Expenditure and Remain of Ammunition, Camp at Point Levy 18th August 1759," LAC, MG 18-M, vol. 21, Quebec vol. 4, reel C-366.

33 "At 1 A.M. the shells": Smith, *Journals of Ashley Bowen,* 90–91.

33 "I have seen Quebec": Letter to "J.W.," Sept. 2, 1759, 15.

33 "The Cathedral of Quebec": Coats, "Private Journal of the Siege of Quebec," entry of July 22, 1759.

33 "With Monckton and Townshend": Botwood, "Hot Stuff," 2.

34 "About 300 of their houses": Williamson to John Ligonier, Earl of Ligonier, Aug. 12, 1759, LAC, MG 18-N21, reel A-573.

34 "The place is so much burned": Williamson to Frederick, Sept. 2, 1759.

34 "We frequently set their town": Gibson to Charles Lawrence, Aug. 1, 1759, in Doughty and Parmelee, *Siege of Quebec,* 5:65.

34 "my present situation": Gibson to Gilbert White, Sept. 21, 1759, in Foster, "Quebec 1759," 221–22.

35 "no small Discovery": Ibid., 222.

35 "steal a detachment": Wolfe to Walter Wolfe, May 17, 1759, 428.

35 "The French": Master's Log, HMS *Squirrel,* July 20, 1759, LAC, MG 12, ADM 52, vol. 1043, fol. 12, reel C-12889.

35 "Perceiving that the enemy": Wolfe to William Pitt, Sept. 2, 1759, LAC, MG 11, CO 5, vol. 51, fol. 75, reel B-2113.

36 But instead of smashing: Knox, *Historical Journal,* 1:342–43.

CHAPTER 5

Defeat at Montmorency

37 A decisive battle would end: "It seems better," wrote Wolfe in his journal, "to receive the enemy superior in numbers, with the advantage of a small entrenchment, than to attack them behind their lines, with such a body of troops as can be landed at once, & by doing so put all to the hazard of one action." Bell, "Exact and Faithful Copy of General Wolfe's Journal," entry of June 29, 1759, 31.

38 "Two light armed transports": Hunter, "Biographical Memoir," 21–22.

38 "observed that the redoubt": Wolfe to William Pitt, Sept. 2, 1759, fol. 77.

38 "The boats of the Fleet": Hunter, "Biographical Memoir," 22.

38 "a shell falling so near": Letter to "J.W.," Sept. 2, 1759, 18; Coats, "Private Journal of the Siege of Quebec," entry of July 31, 1759.

38 These casualties included: *Rivington's New York Gazetteer,* May 5, 1774.

38 "My son": Williamson to Thomas Hay, Earl of Kinnouille, August 10, 1759.

39 "Our men were dreadfully exposed": Hunter, "Biographical Memoir," 22.

40 "The night had now": Ibid., 22–23.

40 "Sent the longboat.": Smith, ed., *The journals of Ashley Bowen*, p. 89.

40 "The enemy": Knox, *Historical Journal,* 2:2.

40 "to destroy the Harvest": Wolfe to Amherst, March 6, 1759, fol. 293.

40 "Here, we are entertained": Knox, *Historical Journal,* 1:292.

41 "I am apprehensive": Gibson to Gilbert White, Sept. 21, 1759, 222–23.

41 "I have been here": Letter of Alexander Murray, Aug. 29, 1759, in Wylly, "Letters of Colonel Alexander Murray," 213.

41 "I have": Wolfe to William Pitt, Sept. 2, 1759, fol. 83.

41 "our oars being all muffled": Hunter, "Biographical Memoir," 21.

42 Placed in command: Holmes to John Cleveland, March 21, 1758, in Beatson, *Naval and Military Memoirs of Great Britain,* 2:160–61; Corbett, *England in the Seven Years' War,* 1:234–51.

42 "We . . . endeavoured": Hunter, "Biographical Memoir," 21.

42 A few soldiers had to swim: Humphreys, "Rich Humphreys, His Journal," 50–51.

42 "that our landing was impracticable": "Journal of the Particular Transactions During the Siege of Quebec at Anchor Opposite the Island of Orleans, July 26th, 1759, by an Officer of Fraser's Regt.," in Doughty and Parmelee, *Siege of Quebec,* 5:178.

43 "About eight at night": Humphreys, "Rich Humphreys, His Journal," 52–53.

43 "We then": Hunter, "Biographical Memoir," 21.

43 The resistance continued: "Journal of the Particular Transactions," 179–80; Master's Log, HMS *Sutherland,* entry of Aug. 14, 1759, LAC, MG 12, ADM 52, vol. 720, reel C-12888.

43 "We then advanced still higher": Hunter, "Biographical Memoir," 21.

44 "We have seven hours": Wolfe to Robert Darcy, Earl of Holderness, Sept. 9, 1759, in Wilson, *James Wolfe,* 474.

45 "the Admiral also added": Hunter, "Biographical Memoir," 23.

45 "to send Wm. Hunter": Durell, Journal, entry of Sept. 6, 1759, fol. 246.

45 "a very flattering certificate": Hunter, "Biographical Memoir," 23.

45 "though my mind was buoyed up": Ibid.

45 "I observed a most tremendous sea": Ibid.

45 "I began to think": Ibid., 24.

CHAPTER 6

The Triumph of Geography

47 "the lucky moment of confusion": Wolfe to Walter Wolfe, Oct. 21, 1757, in Wilson, *James Wolfe,* 336.

48 "I wish I could": Wolfe to William Pitt, Sept. 2, 1759, fol. 72.

48 "the very going up": Wolfe to Amherst, Dec. 29, 1758, LAC, MG 13, WO 34, vol. 46b, fols. 289, 287, reel B-2662.

49 Promised twelve thousand troops: "Proposals for the Expedition to Canada," MG 18-M, Northcliffe Collection, ser. 1: Monckton Papers, vol. 20, Quebec 1759, vol. 3, Documents relating to the preparation of the expedition, reel C-366; James Wolfe, "Embarkation Return of His Majesty's Forces in the River St. Lawrence, Under the Command of Major General Wolfe," June 5, 1759, LAC, MG 11, CO 5, vol. 51, fols. 66v–67, reel B-2113.

49   "We have continued skirmishes": Wolfe to Robert Darcy, Earl of Holderness, Sept. 9, 1759, 473.

49   "We are greatly hurt": Gibson to Gilbert White, Sept. 21, 1759, 223.

50   "The troops on this side": Knox, *Historical Journal*, 2:2.

50   By the end of August: Isaac Barré, "State of the Troops," Aug. 24, 1759, LAC, MG 18-M, vol. 21, Quebec 1759, vol. 4, Documents relating to the expedition from the time of its sailing up the River St. Lawrence to the Battle of the Plains of Abraham, reel C-366; "Return of the Strength of the Army on the 13th September 1759 Before the Battle of Quebec," enclosed in Townshend to William Pitt, Sept. 20, 1759, LAC, MG 11, CO 5, vol. 51, fol. 102, reel B-2113.

50   "If," lamented Wolfe: Wolfe to Robert Darcy, Earl of Holderness, Sept. 9, 1759, 472.

51   "happy, if our efforts": Wolfe to Pitt, Sept. 2, 1759, fols. 84–85.

51   "No time shall be lost": Amherst to Thomas De Lancey, Aug. 5, 1759, LAC, MG 13, WO 34, vol. 30, fol. 65, reel B-2653.

51   "We shall remain here": Saunders to William Pitt, Sept. 5, 1759, LAC, MG 11, CO 5, vol. 51, fol. 39v, reel B-2113.

52   "this intelligence, otherwise pleasing": Humphreys, "Rich Humphreys, His Journal," 58–59.

52   "high and strong by nature": Knox, *Historical Journal*, 1:295.

52   "now became doubtful": Mackellar, "Journal," in Doughty and Parmelee, *Siege of Quebec,* 5:44.

52   "It is the general opinion": Williamson to Frederick, Sept. 2, 1759.

52   One of the couriers: Webster, *Journal of Jeffery Amherst*, 178.

CHAPTER 7
The Man Who Saved Canada

55   "We could," wrote Montcalm: "Journal des campagnes de M. le Marquis de Montcalm mis en ordre par M. Le Marquis de Lévis," LAC, MG 18-K8, Fonds Chevalier de Lévis, vol. 1, fol. 576, reel C-363.

55   "his mother's hasty departure": "Interrogatoire du S. Joseph Cadet prisonnier a la Bastille," Feb. 3, 4, and 6, 1761, LAC, MG 7-II, Fonds de la Bibliothèque de l'Arsenal, Archives de la Bastille: Prisonniers, vol. 12142 [Joseph-Michel Cadet], fols. 149, 148v–149, reel F-1104.

56   "sent him into the countryside": Ibid., fol. 149.

56   "although small in the beginning": Ibid., fol. 149v.

56   "Cadet was of . . . lowly birth": "Mémoire du Canada," 117.

56   By the early 1750s: For details regarding Cadet's early life and career, see Bosher, "Joseph-Michel Cadet," 123–24; Côté, *Joseph-Michel Cadet,* 35–48.

57   "Of all our enemies": Pierre de Rigaud de Vaudreuil, "Précis du plan des opérations générales de la campagne de 1759," April 1, 1759, LAC, MG 1, AC, C11A, Correspondance générale, Canada, vol. 104, fol. 48v, reel F-104.

57   While French–Native American armies: Côté, *Joseph-Michel Cadet,* 105–6; Lunn, "Agriculture and War in Canada," 123, 123n; Henri-Marie Dubreil de Pontbriand to Abbé de l'Isle Dieu, Oct. 30, 1757, LAC, MG 1, AC, C11A, 102, fols. 299–302, reel F-102; Dechêne, *Le partage des subsistances au Canada sous le régime français,* 146, 152.

57   "During . . . our captivity": Williamson, *French and Indian Cruelty*, 82.
58   "supplying provisions is an immense": "Mémoire du Canada," 127–28.
58   This gave him the exclusive right: Bosher, "Joseph-Michel Cadet," 124–25; Côté, *Joseph-Michel Cadet*, 77–85.
58   Cadet had large warehouses: Côté, *Joseph-Michel Cadet*, 94, 142, 378, 383.
58   "This huge number": "Mémoire du Canada," 127–28; Côté, *Joseph-Michel Cadet*, 94–96.
58   "Provisions of all kinds": Schuyler, "Intelligence from Colonel Peter Schuyler of the New Jersey Regiment," 141.
58   "I lack the words": Daine to Nicolas René Berryer, May 19, 1758, LAC, MG 1, AC, C11A, vol. 103, fols. 409v–410, reel F-103.
59   His associates in France: Côté, *Joseph-Michel Cadet*, 123.
59   Civilians had to be content: Cadet to Bigot, May 26, 1759, in Doughty and Parmelee, *Siege of Quebec*, 5:340–41; "Journal des campagnes de Montcalm," fol. 545.
59   "very good flour and beef": "Indian Lorette: The Story of Oui-ha-ra-lih-te."
59   "an English squadron coming": "Interrogatoire du S. Joseph Cadet prisonnier a la Bastille," Feb. 3, 4, and 6, 1761, fol. 151.
59   "His Majesty": Nicolas René Berryer to Vaudreuil and Bigot, Feb. 3, 1759, LAC, MG 1, AC, B, Lettres envoyées, vol. 109, fol. 411, reel F-313. See also Dull, *French Navy and the Seven Years' War*, 134–38.
60   "Canada would not run short": "Interrogatoire du S. Joseph Cadet prisonnier a la Bastille," Feb. 3, 4, and 6, 1761, fols. 151–151v.
60   "in fear of losing": Ibid., fol. 151v.
60   "Expecting that this number": Ibid.
60   He hired captains and sailors: Bosher, "Joseph-Michel Cadet," 125; Bosher, "Le ravitaillement de Québec en 1758."
60   Between May 10 and May 20: Panet, *Journal du siège de Québec*, 3–4.
60   The French navy sent: Dull, *French Navy and the Seven Years' War*, 143.
60   "You should not doubt": Panet, *Journal du siège de Québec*, 3.
60   With thirty thousand soldiers: Bigot Charles Louis Auguste Fouquet, Duc de Belle-Isle, Oct. 15, 1759, LAC, MG 4, Archives de la Guerre, A1, Correspondance générale, opérations militaire, vol. 3450, no. 103, fols. 15–16, reel F-724.
60   "General Wolfe is going": Nicolas René Berryer to Vaudreuil, Feb. 16, 1759, LAC, MG 1, AC, B, vol. 109, fol. 373, reel F-313.

CHAPTER 8
Soldiers and Shoe Brushes

61   "Our warehouses are empty": Fauteux, *Journal du siège de Québec*, 23.
62   There is no precise list: "Journal des campagnes de Montcalm," fol. 531; Bigot to Charles Louis Auguste Fouquet, Duc de Belle-Isle, Oct. 15, 1759, vol. 3450, fol. 15.
62   "Here is the sixth": Mathieu Valentin Jacques Miller to Marie-Joseph Miller, June 1759, Bibliothèque et Archives Nationales du Québec, Centre d'Archives de Montréal, Archives Judiciaires, pièces détachées, boite 1759–60, cited in Dechêne, *Le peuple, l'État et la guerre au Canada*, 394–95, 362n.
63   "such a competitive spirit": "Extrait d'un journal tenu à l'armée que commandoit feu M. de Montcalm Lieutenant g'n'al," LAC, MG 1, AC, C11A, vol. 104, fol. 169v, note in margin, reel F-104.

63   Some had to travel: "Mémoire du Canada," 152.

63   "I can perceive": Knox, *Historical Journal*, 1:311.

64   "The English search for laurels": Lortie, *Les textes poétiques*, 1:180.

64   "If Rigaud's troops": Ibid., 185.

64   The colonials included: Ibid., 145, 156, 164.

64   "Beaujeu with his military bearing": Ibid., 149–50.

65   "If you want to make a wonder": Ibid., 164.

65   As for their enemies: Ibid., 188, 163.

65   "The English are on our frontiers": Ibid., 152.

65   "The French like the English": Ibid., 180.

65   "They left their cannon": Ibid., 145.

65   "The singer of this song": Ibid., 163.

66   In wartime: Dechêne, *Le peuple, l'État et la guerre au Canada*, 293, 305, 363, 378–81.

66   Crown gunsmiths worked: Fauteux, *Journal du siège de Québec*, 20.

66   The Seven Nations might reside: Jan Grabowski, "Crime and Punishment: Sault-St. Louis, Lac des Deux-Montagnes, and French Justice, 1713–1735" (paper read at "Native Peoples and New France: Re-examining the Relationships, 1663–1763," McGill University, Feb. 15, 1992); Jan Grabowski, "Searching for the Common Ground: Natives and French in Montreal, 1700–1730" (paper read at the eighteenth annual meeting of the French Colonial Historical Society, McGill University, May 22, 1992); MacLeod, *Canadian Iroquois*, 1–36.

67   They now returned in force: MacLeod, "Microbes and Muskets."

67   This alliance linked them: Cook, "Vivre Comme Frères," 496–98; MacLeod, *Canadian Iroquois*, 155–56; White, *Middle Ground*, 142–85.

67   "The French & we are one": "Headquarters, Camp at the Great Carrying Place [Between the Hudson River and Lake George]," Aug. 21, 1755, "Minutes of Indian Affairs, 1755–1790," vol. 1822 [Indian Records, vol. 4], NAC, RG 10, reel C-1221, fol. 87; Druke, "Linking Arms."

67   "coming in order to help us": Gosselin, "Le journal de M. de Bougainville," 284.

67   "to defend the lands": Renaud d'Avène des Méloizes, "Journal militaire," 45. The western speakers added that they believed their own homelands to be comfortably beyond the reach of the British.

67   "Two thousand Englishmen": Lortie, *Les textes poétiques*, 1:145.

68   Overall, between 1,000 and 1,200: Panet, *Journal du siège de Québec*, 8; Fauteux, *Journal du siège de Québec*, 22; "Indian Lorette: Oui-ha-ra-lih-te, or Petit Etienne"; Récher, *Journal du siège de Québec*, 43; Vaudreuil to Nicolas René Berryer, Oct. 5, 1759, LAC, MG 1, AC, F3, Collection Moreau de Saint-Méry, vol. 15, fol. 272, reel F-391; Bigot to Nicolas René Berryer, Oct. 15, 1759, ibid., fol. 334v; "Memoire du Canada," 154, 155; Fauteux, *Journal du siège de Québec*, 50; Malartic, *Journal des campagnes*, 251; Courville, *Mémoires sur le Canada*, 161–62; Récher, *Journal du siège de Québec*, 17.

68   "they did not want to go": Fauteux, *Journal du siège de Québec*, 22.

68   Only a very few: Draper, ed., "Seventy-Two Years' Recollections of Wisconsin," 217–18.

68   "the French and Canadian Army": "Indian Lorette: Oui-ha-ra-lih-te, or Petit Etienne."

69   "I was to serve him": Grace, *History of the Life and Sufferings of Henry Grace*, 51, 52–53.

69   "I am reading": Montcalm to Marie-Thérèse-Charlotte de Lauris de Castellane, Feb. 8, 1756, cited in Chapais, *Le Marquis de Montcalm*, 41.

70   "The next day": Charlevoix, *Histoire et description générale de la Nouvelle France*, 3:119–21.

70 He owned an extensive library: Falgairolle, *A propos de Montcalm,* 5–9.

70 "the only place where the enemy": "Journal des campagnes de Montcalm," fol. 525.

70 "Work continues every day": Fauteux, *Journal du siège de Québec,* 22.

71 "It is generally the custom": Ibid., 15.

71 "The Sieur de Bougainville": *La gazette de France,* March 10, 1759, cited in Crèvecoeur, *Saint John de Crèvecoeur, sa vie et ses ouvrages,* 14.

71 Montcalm, perhaps suspecting: Crèvecoeur to Monckton, Oct. 20, 1759, LAC, MG 18-M, Northcliffe Collection, ser. 1: Monckton Papers, vol. 33, Letters addressed to General Monckton by French prisoners after the occupation of Quebec, reel C-366; Delisle, *Le régiment de La Sarre en Nouvelle-France,* 43; Allen and Asselineau, *St. John de Crèvecoeur,* xviii, 9–27.

72 "As much by courage": Unsigned memoir, Oct. 2, 1774, LAC, MG 2, Fonds de la Marine, C7, Dossiers individuels, vol. 17, "Barré, Jean," reel F-660.

72 "25 boats, all of his furniture": Unsigned memoir, Aug. 23, 1769, LAC, MG 2, C7, vol. 17, "Barré, Jean," reel F-660.

72 "found 2 bark canoes": "Journal des campagnes de Montcalm," fol. 528.

72 "that they regarded the capture": Panet, *Journal du siège de Québec,* 5.

72 "At the warehouse": Fauteux, *Journal du siège de Québec,* 16.

73 "I have always heard": Ibid., 15.

73 "But all the rest": Ibid., 18.

73 "There is so much work": Ibid., 23.

73 Less affluent residents: Ibid., 20; Récher, *Journal du siège de Québec,* 12.

73 In 1749, he became: Asselin, "Jean-Félix Récher."

74 The items he removed: Récher, *Journal du siège de Québec,* 24.

74 "proof that they": Fauteux, *Journal du siège de Québec,* 20.

74 "two of my little children": Ibid., 23.

74 "My wife left": Ibid., 24.

74 On June 30: Récher, *Journal du siège de Québec,* 8.

74 "People take everything": Fauteux, *Journal du siège de Québec,* 27, 28.

75 "It looked to me": Ibid., 31.

CHAPTER 9
City at War

76 "It's a chess match": Montcalm to Bourlamaque, July 20, 1759, LAC, MG 18-K9, Fonds François-Charles de Bourlamaque, vol. 1, "Lettres de Montcalm à Bourlamaque, 25 June 1756–22 September 1759," fol. 545, reel C-362.

76 "I suspect that the enemy": "Journal des campagnes de Montcalm," fol. 551.

76 "At 10:00 a.m.": Fauteux, *Journal du siège de Québec,* 38, 96n. Colas and Gauvreau were Jean Collet and Nicolas Gauvreau, *dit* Colas, a cooper. Jean-Baptiste Dufour was a merchant.

77 "It is maddening": Ibid., 39.

77 "The conduct of our generals": Ibid., 42.

77 These officials, in turn: Crowley, " 'Thunder Gusts,' " 23, 28.

77 "call militiamen who are about": "Journal des campagnes de Montcalm," fol. 545.

77 "The enemy": "Extrait d'un journal tenu à l'armée," fol. 177.

78 "Much is expected": Fauteux, *Journal du siège de Québec,* 36.

78 Around 9:00 that night: Ibid., 36.
78 "Equipped with all the artillery": Legardeur, *Relation de ce qui s'est passé au siège de Québec*, 3.
78 Thwarted by a royal edict: Roy, "Marie-Joseph LeGardeur de Repentigny."
78 "I did not return to the city gates": Récher, *Journal du siège de Québec*, 17–18.
79 "There, in a few words": Fauteux, *Journal du siège de Québec*, 36–37.
80 "This cloister, which is built": Kalm, *Travels in North America*, 2:454–55.
80 The nuns of the Hôtel-Dieu: Proulx, *Between France and New France*, 114.
80 So thanks to the Hôpital Général: D'Allaire, *L'Hôpital-Général de Québec*, 124–26; Saint-Félix, *Monseigneur de Saint-Vallier et l'Hôpital Général de Québec*, 325–29, 331, 334; Eccles, "French Forces in North America During the Seven Years' War," xviii.
80 Seven died in 1757: D'Allaire, *L'Hôpital-Général de Québec*, 124–25; Legardeur, *Relation de ce qui s'est passé au siège de Québec*, 1–3.
80 "was tended by a widow woman": King, *Narrative of Titus King of Northampton, Mass.*, 20.
81 "gripped by fear of the shells": Legardeur, *Relation de ce qui s'est passé au siège de Québec*, 4.
81 "The firebombs and red-hot shot": Ibid., 6.

CHAPTER 10
Bombardment and Fire

82 He counted missiles: Fauteux, *Journal du siège de Québec*, 49.
82 "At 10:00 a.m. the enemy": Ibid., 42.
82 "Since noon the shells": Ibid., 40.
82 "Throughout the night": Ibid., 43.
82 "Most of the bombs": Ibid., 54.
83 "the place being no longer": Ibid., 38.
83 "the cannonballs and shells began": Ibid., 43.
83 The newcomers included: Ibid., 44.
84 "five shells and a firebomb": Ibid., 55.
84 "A bomb fell and razed": Ibid., 40.
84 "I truly cannot understand": Ibid.
84 Her refusal to allow: Saint-Félix, *Monseigneur de Saint-Vallier et l'Hôpital Général de Québec*, 627.
85 "because of the excessive danger": Récher, *Journal du siège de Québec*, 19–20.
85 "surprised and alarmed many people": Ibid., 21–22.
85 "which completely surprised us": Ibid., 33.
86 Whether as a result: Eccles, *French in North America*, 161; Lachance, *Vivre à la ville en Nouvelle-France*, 183–89; Moogk, *Building a House in New France*, 50–59, 119–20; Roy, "La protection contre le feu à Québec sous le régime français."
87 "seeing the fire break out": Récher, *Journal du siège de Québec*, 19.
87 "Some spark, some cinder, blown by the wind": Ibid., 23–24.
87 "During that fire": Ibid., 24.
87 A year later: Frenière, "Jean-Claude Panet."
88 "That same day": Panet, *Journal du siège de Québec*, 18.
88 "It is indeed heartrending": Fauteux, *Journal du siège de Québec*, 39.

88 "unfortunate Canadian merchant": Berthou-Dûbreüil to Charles Eugène Gabriel de La Croix, May 26, 1783, LAC, MG 1, AC, E, Dossiers personnels, vol. 28, "Berthou-Dûbreüil (Le Sieur)," reel F-812.

89 Their efforts provided: Eccles, *French in North America*, 161; Lachance, *Vivre à la ville en Nouvelle-France*, 183–89; Moogk, *Building a House in New France*, 50–59.

89 "It was first discovered": Pote, "Remarkable Occurrences from the Year 1745 to 1748," 122.

89 "I had orders to go": "Mémoire du Sr. Levasseur fils ecrivan de la marine et des classes," July 15, 1766, LAC, MG 2, C7, vol. 184, "Le Vasseur dit le fils, fils de René Nicolas," reel F-796.

89 "caught fire immediately": Fauteux, *Journal du siège de Québec*, 56.

89 "kept the fire from spreading": Panet, *Journal du siège de Québec*, 19–20.

90 "Two cannonballs passed": Ibid., 20.

90 With the civil population: Ibid., 14.

90 "the robbery that occurs": Fauteux, *Journal du siège de Québec*, 44.

91 "Their trial began": Récher, *Journal du siège de Québec*, 26. See also Panet, *Journal du siège de Québec*, 15; Fauteux, *Journal du siège de Québec*, 46–47.

91 "burglars continued to rob": Récher, *Journal du siège de Québec*, 36.

91 "the English, following": Panet, *Journal du siège de Québec*, 21.

91 "I saw the first frigate": Ibid., 16, 17.

91 "never dared attempt": Legardeur, *Relation de ce qui s'est passé au siège de Québec*, 7.

92 "People truly fear": Fauteux, *Journal du siège de Québec*, 49.

CHAPTER II
The Governor, the General, and Just a Hint of Scandal

94 "humane and generous": Howe, "Captivity and Sufferings of Mrs. Jemima Howe," 95.

94 This mobility allowed: Eccles, "Pierre de Rigaud de Vaudreuil de Cavagnial, Marquis de Vaudreuil," 662–74.

94 "I saw the English standards": Eastburn, *Faithful Narrative*, 168–69.

95 "Vaudreuil under whose command": Lortie, *Les textes poétiques*, 1:169.

95 "We celebrate the great Vaudreuil": Ibid., 170.

97 Promoted to *maréchal de camp*: Eccles, "Louis-Joseph de Montcalm, Marquis de Montcalm." Montcalm nominally began his military career in 1721 when, at nine years old, he received an ensign's commission, but he did not actually serve in the army until 1732.

97 "From a laurel tree cut a palm": Lortie, *Les textes poétiques*, 1:167.

97 "Like Alexander he is small": Ibid., 161.

97 "Farewell, my heart": Montcalm to Angélique-Louise de Montcalm, April 16, 1757, Dominion du Canada, in *Rapport sur les Archives Publiques pour l'année 1929*, 56.

97 "When will I see": Montcalm to Angélique-Louise de Montcalm, Oct. 27, 1758, in *Rapport sur les Archives Publiques pour l'année 1929*, 76.

98 "I am no further advanced": Montcalm to Bourlamaque, June 16, 1757, LAC, MG 18-K9, vol. 1, fol. 109, reel C-362.

98 "Bougainville told me": Montcalm to Angélique-Louise de Montcalm, May 16, 1759, in *Rapport sur les Archives Publiques pour l'année 1929*, 81. For Montcalm, see Eccles, "Louis-Joseph de Montcalm, Marquis de Montcalm."

98 "the governor-general's desire": Lapause, "Mémoire et réflexions politiques et militaires sur la guerre du Canada depuis 1746 jusqu'à 1760," 150.

98   "thought that the government": Ibid. For Montcalm at the siege of Oswego, see MacLeod, "French Siege of Oswego in 1756," and MacLeod, "Canadians Against the French."

98   "M. le Marquis de Montcalm reserved": Vaudreuil to Nicolas René Berryer, July 28, 1758, LAC, MG 1, AC, F3, vol. 15, fols. 119v, 121v, 122, reel F-391.

99   "say loudly that M. de Vaudreuil": Montcalm to Doreil, July 24, 1758, paraphrased in letter of Doreil, July 28, 1758, in Roy, "Lettres de Doreil," 138.

99   "I will completely compromise": Vaudreuil to Nicolas René Berryer, Aug. 4, 1758, LAC, MG 1, AC, C11A, vol. 103, fols. 145–146v, reel F-103.

99   "You have come": "Paroles des Iroquois, Nepissingues, Algonkins, Abenakis, et Mississagués de 30 juillet, 1758," enclosed in ibid., fol. 159. For Native American leaders encountering Montcalm at Fort Carillon, see MacLeod, *Canadian Iroquois and the Seven Years' War,* 120–28.

99   Vaudreuil concluded by supporting: Montcalm to Nicolas René Berryer, Aug. 3, 1758, LAC, MG 1, AC, C11A, vol. 103, fol. 124v, reel F-103.

99   "I consider, my lord": Vaudreuil to Nicolas René Berryer, Aug. 4, 1758, fol. 151.

100   As such, he assumed: Eccles, "Louis-Joseph de Montcalm, Marquis de Montcalm," 464.

100   "in order to prepare with him": Nicolas René Berryer to Vaudreuil, Feb. 16, 1759, fol. 373.

100   "The Marquis de Vaudreuil": "Journal des campagnes de Montcalm," fol. 537.

100   "The indecision of the field marshal": Ibid., fols. 545, 539, 533, 529.

CHAPTER 12
Wheat and War

101   "determine with the Marquis de Montcalm": Nicolas René Berryer to Vaudreuil, Feb. 16, 1759, fol. 374.

101   "The Marquis de Vaudreuil": "Journal des campagnes de Montcalm," fol. 528.

101   "Our enemies will not": Lévis to Charles Louis Auguste Fouquet, Duc de Belle-Isle, May 17, 1759 [2], LAC, MG 4, AG, A1, vol. 3450, no. 64, fol. 2, reel F-724.

102   "Here is Canada": "Journal des campagnes de Montcalm," fol. 476.

102   "preserve in France and Canada": "Mémoire premièrement sur la position des Anglois et des François dans l'Amérique septentrionale; secondement sur ce qu'il est absolument nécessaire d'y envoy, pour qu'on puisse au moins tenter de s'y défendre," LAC, MG 4, AG, A1, vol. 3405, no. 217, fol. 8, reel F-665.

102   "the retreat of the ten thousand": Ibid., fol. 7.

102   To provision that retreat: "Extrait d'un journal tenu à l'armée," fol. 169, note in margin.

102   "every possible measure": "Journal des campagnes de Montcalm," fol. 531.

103   Instead, he assembled: "Extrait d'un journal tenu à l'armée," fols. 187–187v; Fauteux, *Journal du siège de Québec,* 48.

104   The army had been down: Montreuil to Bougainville, Aug. 17, 1759, in Doughty and Parmelee, *Siege of Quebec,* 4:49.

104   Its surface was plain dirt: Miquelon, *New France from 1701 to 1744,* 193; Sanfaçon, "La construction du premier chemin Québec-Montréal et le problème des corvées," 4–8.

104   The carts were coming apart: "Extrait d'un journal tenu à l'armée," fols. 187–187v.

104   As soon as the boats: Bigot to Bougainville, Aug. 17, 1759, in Doughty and Parmelee, *Siege of Quebec,* 4:51; Montreuil to Bougainville, Aug. 24, 1759, in ibid., 66; Vaudreuil to Bougainville, Aug. 24, 1759, in ibid., 67.

105 In Canada as in France: Eccles, *French in North America*, 135.

105 The Montreal government: Harris, *Seigneurial System in Early Canada*, 15–16.

106 "saw about twenty vessels": James Johnson, "Narrative of James Johnson," 86–87. The definition for "brigantine" is from Falconer and Burney, *Universal Dictionary of the Marine*, 58.

106 "I see nothing": Rigaud de Vaudreuil to Nicolas René Berryer, Oct. 28, 1759, LAC, MG 1, AC, CIIA, vol. 104, fols. 97–97v, reel F-104.

106 "There were moreover": "Mémoire du Canada," 162.

106 "It is absolutely necessary": Vaudreuil to Lévis, Aug. 26, 1759, "Lettres du marquis de Vaudreuil à Lévis, 1756–1760," LAC, MG 18-K8, vol. 5, no. 60, reel C-364.

107 "Already we see our heroes": "1756," in Casgrain, *Collection de manuscrits contenant lettres, mémoires et autres documents historiques*, 4:42.

107 Parish priests frequently: Jaenen, *Role of the Church in New France*, 72–73, 95–119.

107 "I have asked them": Rigaud de Vaudreuil to Nicolas René Berryer, Oct. 28, 1759, fol. 97v.

107 "the most just": Ibid.

107 "take, in cooperation": "Mémoire du Canada," 162.

108 In August, Rigaud: Ibid., 160, 162.

108 "wrote to all of the priests": Ibid., 163.

108 He reminded Rigaud: Courville, *Mémoires sur le Canada*, 160.

108 "encouraged the women": "Journal des campagnes de Lévis au Canada, 1756–1760," LAC, MG 18-K8, vol. 12, fol. 152, reel C-365.

108 Normally, millers sifted: Vaudreuil to Lévis, Aug. 18, 1759, "Lettres du marquis de Vaudreuil à Lévis, 1756–1760," LAC, MG 18-K8, vol. 5, no. 58, reel C-363.

108 "the battles waged": Courville, *Mémoires sur le Canada*, 158.

CHAPTER 13
Alarms in the Night

110 "This movement alerted": Panet, *Journal du siège de Québec*, 23.

110 Magnan was Jean-Baptiste-Paschal Magnan: Bonnault, "Le Canada militaire," 288.

111 "We in the city": Fauteux, *Journal du siège de Québec*, 28.

111 Two thousand troops: Récher, *Journal du siège de Québec*, 44–45.

111 "in practice": Fauteux, *Journal du siège de Québec*, 44.

111 Two had been captured: Ibid., 43–44; "Extrait d'un journal tenu à l'armée," fols. 182–182v.

111 The alarm sounded: Fauteux, *Journal du siège de Québec*, 51; Récher, *Journal du siège de Québec*, 29.

111 It turned out to have come: Panet, *Journal du siège de Québec*, 19.

112 Lieutenant Colonel Félicien de Bernetz: Ibid., 22.

112 "Beauport," he complained: Fauteux, *Journal du siège de Québec*, 41.

112 "I don't know just now": Ibid., 42.

112 "This place is naturally fortified": Ibid., 34.

112 A roadway from Lower Town: *Plan of the Town of Quebec*.

113 "has a lot of ground": Fauteux, *Journal du siège de Québec*, 59.

CHAPTER 14

The Last Convoy to Quebec

114   "Monday morning": Récher, *Journal du siège de Québec,* 41.

114   "General Wolfe seems to have lost": "Mémoire du Canada," 165.

114   According to a British engineer: Panet, *Journal du siège de Québec,* 23.

114   "This news": Récher, *Journal du siège de Québec,* 42.

115   The colonial administration: Montcalm to Lévis, Sept. 9, 1759, "Lettres de Montcalm à Lévis, 1756–1759," LAC, MG 18-K8, vol. 6, no. 152, reel C-364; Récher, *Journal du siège de Québec,* 40.

115   Frequent, heavy rains: Bigot to Lévis, Sept. 11, 1759, LAC, MG 18-K8, vol. 8, no. 43, reel C-364; "Extrait d'un journal tenu à l'armée," fol. 193.

115   "all the countryside": Bigot to Lévis, Sept. 8, 1759, LAC, MG 18-K8, vol. 8, no. 42, reel C-364.

115   "the habitants found their wheat": Panet, *Journal du siège de Québec,* 23.

115   These cutbacks were just enough: Cadet also made cash payments to the regulars to compensate for their reduced rations. "Journal des campagnes de Montcalm," fol. 560; Malartic, *Journal des campagnes,* 275.

116   On August 28: Cadet to Bougainville, Aug. 29, 1759, in Doughty and Parmelee, *Siege of Quebec,* 4:78.

116   They had saved their cargo: Vaudreuil to Bougainville, Aug. 31, 1759, in Doughty and Parmelee, *Siege of Quebec,* 4:81; Vaudreuil to Bougainville, Aug. 31, 1759 [2], in ibid., 82.

116   In the first days: "Extrait d'un journal tenu à l'armée," fol. 195v.

116   "Would it not be possible": Vaudreuil to Bougainville, n.d., around Aug. 31 or Sept. 1, 1759, in Doughty and Parmelee, *Siege of Quebec,* 6:83.

116   "Beauport is constantly guarded": Fauteux, *Journal du siège de Québec,* 63.

116   The discovery on September 2: "Extrait d'un journal tenu à l'armée," fol. 195v.

116   At Beauport, the army: Panet, *Journal du siège de Québec,* 22–23; "Extrait d'un journal tenu à l'armée," fols. 195v–196.

117   The sentry fired: Récher, *Journal du siège de Québec,* 41.

117   This touched off: "Extrait d'un journal tenu à l'armée," fols. 197–197v; Récher, *Journal du siège de Québec,* 42.

117   The French stood to arms: "Extrait d'un journal tenu à l'armée," fols. 197–197v; "Journal des campagnes de Montcalm," fol. 569.

117   Five detachments of regulars: Panet, *Journal du siège de Québec,* 24.

117   "They have made marches": Ibid.

117   "the enemy continues to cannonade": Fauteux, *Journal du siège de Québec,* 64.

117   On the seventh: "Journal des campagnes de Montcalm," fol. 570.

117   The battalions at Beauport: Ibid.

117   "M. Devergor": Fauteux, *Journal du siège de Québec,* 64.

118   On the ninth: "Journal des campagnes de Montcalm," fol. 570.

118   On the morning of September 10: Cadet to Bougainville, Sept. 9, 1759, in Doughty and Parmelee, *Siege of Quebec,* 4:115, 116.

118   "several officers, wearing many colors": Luc-Angélique Remigny to Bougainville, Sept. 11, 1759, in Doughty and Parmelee, *Siege of Quebec,* 4:121.

118   "These buoys have caused": "Journal des campagnes de Montcalm," fol. 572.

118   "but I always fear": Fauteux, *Journal du siège de Québec,* 64.

118   "I calculated that our troops": "Journal des campagnes de Montcalm," fol. 572.

118 If all went well: Olson et al., "Perfect Tide, Ideal Moon," 966.

119 "As it is important": Vaudreuil to Bougainville, Aug. 23, 1759, in Doughty and Parmelee, *Siege of Quebec*, 4:66.

119 "The necessity of having": Vaudreuil to Nicolas René Berryer, Oct. 5, 1759, LAC, MG 1, AC, F3, vol. 15, fol. 285v, reel F-391.

119 "I will have to send carts": Cadet to Bougainville, Sept. 12, 1759, in Doughty and Parmelee, *Siege of Quebec*, 4:126.

119 "must be challenged": Malartic, *Journal des campagnes*, 283.

119 "On the twelfth, he received orders": Unsigned memoir to Étienne François, Duc de Choiseul, LAC, MG 1, AC, E, vol. 143, "Dossier Dupont du Chambon de Vergor, Louis," reel F-614.

119 "The ships had not moved": Fauteux, *Journal du siège de Québec*, 65.

119 "The twelfth of September": Bernier to Charles Louis Auguste Fouquet, Duc de Belle-Isle, Oct. 15, 1759, LAC, MG 4, AG, A1, vol. 3540, no. 102 bis, fol. 1, reel F-724.

120 "I repeated often to Johnstone": Johnstone, "Memoirs of a French Officer," 204.

120 "the city then made": "Journal des campagnes de Montcalm," fol. 572.

120 "We did not doubt": Ibid.

120 "I began to have more quietness": Johnstone, "Memoirs of a French Officer," 204.

121 "This Canadian": "Journal des campagnes de Montcalm," fol. 573.

121 "to march to the vicinity": "Journal des campagnes de Lévis," vol. 12, fol. 163.

121 Montreuil ordered these troops: Ibid.

CHAPTER 15

The Anse au Foulon

125 "The extreme heat": Wolfe to Robert Darcy, Earl of Holderness, Sept. 9, 1759, 474.

125 "I am sensible": Wolfe to Saunders, Aug. 30, 1759, *Gentleman's Magazine and Historical Chronicle* 71, pt. 1 (June 1801): 508.

125 "my plan of quitting": Wolfe to Henrietta Wolfe, Aug. 31, 1759, in Wilson, *James Wolfe*, 469.

126 "I know perfectly well": Seward, "Drossiana. Number CII," 170.

126 "supposing (as I have very little hope of)": Wolfe to Saunders, Aug. 30, 1759, 509.

126 Too sick to lead: Knox, *Historical Journal*, 2:30; Wolfe to Saunders, Aug. 30, 1759, 509.

126 "I found myself so ill": Wolfe to William Pitt, Sept. 2, 1759, fols. 81–82.

126 "Every step he takes": Gibson to Charles Lawrence, Aug. 1, 1759, 65.

126 "threatened [him] with": Bell, "An Exact and Faithful Copy of General Wolfe's Journal," entry of July 7, 1759.

126 "The first, in action": "Account of Quebec Campaign, June–September 1759," pt. 1, LAC, MG 18-D4, Arthur Dobbs Fonds, fol. 1, reel A-652.

126 "General Wolfe's health": Townshend to Charlotte Townshend, Sept. 6, 1759, in Doughty and Parmelee, *Siege of Quebec*, 5:194–95.

126 "I wish his [Wolfe's] friends": Murray to Townshend, Oct. 5, 1759, LAC, MG 18-M, Northcliffe Collection, ser. 3: Separate items in the Northcliffe Collection, vol. 12, "Miscellaneous Documents Relating to the Campaign Against Quebec in 1759 and the Battle of Sillery on 28 April 1760," reel C-370.

127 "When we establish ourselves": Monckton, Townshend, and Murray to Wolfe, Sept. 12, 1759, LAC, MG 18-M, ser. 2, vol. 12, fol. 41, reel C-369.

127 There was, in fact: C. J. J. Bond, "Roads Above Quebec" (map), in Stacey, *Quebec, 1759,* 65.

127 By August 31: Knox, *Historical Journal,* 2:36.

127 "I have acquiesced": Wolfe to William Pitt, Sept. 2, 1759, fol. 82.

127 "The generals seem to think": Wolfe to Saunders, Aug. 30, 1759, 509.

128 "to burn all the country": Wolfe to Monckton, Aug. 22, 1759, in Wilson, *James Wolfe,* 465.

128 "that country . . . is totally": Wolfe to Saunders, Aug. 30, 1759, 509.

128 "to act in conjuncture": Durell, Journal, entries of Sept. 3, 7, and 8, 1759, fols. 245v, 246, 246–246v.

128 Under the command: Stacey, "George Scott."

129 In 1758, he took part: Charters and Sutherland, "Joseph Goreham."

129 The light infantry were elite regulars: Brumwell, *Redcoats,* 228–36; McCulloch and Todish, *British Light Infantryman of the Seven Years' War,* 7, 10–11.

129 Rangers at Quebec: Chartrand and Rickman, *Colonial American Troops,* 30 (plate F), 45.

129 Their jackets had: May and Embleton, *Wolfe's Army,* 30 (plate F), 46.

129 "a firelock, cutlass": Durell, Journal, entry of July 20, 1759, fol. 239v; Rodger, *Wooden World,* 64–65.

129 One day later: Master's Log, HMS *Zephyr,* entry of Sept. 7, 1759, LAC, MG 12, ADM 52, vol. 1117, reel C-12890; Scott, "Report of a Tour to the South Shore of the River St. Lawrence," LAC, MG 18-M, entry of Sept. 6, 1759, reel C-366.

129 "saluted Admiral Durell": Master's Log, HMS *Trent,* entry of Sept. 7, 1759, LAC, MG 12, ADM 52, vol. 1073, fol. 41, reel C-12890.

129 "The country this side": Perry, *Recollections of an Old Soldier,* 26.

130 The forty-four hundred regulars: "Return of the Strength of the Army on the 13th September 1759 Before the Battle of Quebec."

130 "At 2 am our First Lieutenant": Smith, *Journals of Ashley Bowen,* 95.

130 "fresh gales with hard rain": Master's Log, HMS *Hunter,* entries of Sept. 6, 7, 8, 1759, LAC, MG 12, ADM 52, vol. 894, reel C-12888.

131 "I am so far recovered": Wolfe to Robert Darcy, Earl of Holderness, Sept. 9, 1759, 475.

131 "During this interval": "Account of Quebec Campaign, June–September 1759," pt. 3, fol. 3.

132 "Opened a cask of pork": Master's Log, HMS *Eurus,* entry of Sept. 9, 1759, LAC, MG 12, ADM 52, vol. 847, fol. 21, reel C-12888.

132 "The people": Perry, *Recollections of an Old Soldier,* 26–27.

132 "We marched a little distance": Ibid., 28; Scott, "Report of a Tour to the South Shore of the River St. Lawrence," entry of Sept. 9, 1759.

132 "At the landing of the troops": Master's Log, HMS *Zephyr,* entry of Sept. 9, 1759, fol. 20.

133 "They [the French] seem to have neglected": Townshend, "Diary of Proceeding up the River St. Lawrence," entry of July 18, LAC, MG 18-M, ser. 2, vol. 9, reel C-369.

133 "has been with me": Wolfe to Richmond, July 28, 1758, in Whitworth, "Some Unpublished Wolfe Letters," 84.

133 "went towards Etchemin River": Holland to John Graves Simcoe, June 10, 1792, LAC, MG 23-HI1, ser. 5, file 24, no. 18, fol. 1, reel A-606.

133 "the movements made": Ibid., fol. 2.

133 "that [the Foulon]": Ibid.

134 "to show them the places": "Account of Quebec Campaign, June–September 1759," pt. 3, fol. 3.

134 "The place is called Toulon": Mackellar, "Journal," 48–49.

134 "[We] marched off": Perry, *Recollections of an Old Soldier,* 28–29.

134 "landed the seamen": Master's Log, HMS *Zephyr,* entry of Sept. 10, 1759, fol. 20.

135 "The troops will land": "General Wolfe's Orders, Sutherland Septr 11th," 1759, LAC, MG 18-M, Northcliffe Collection, ser. 3: Separate items in the Northcliffe Collection, Separate Items No. 23, fol. 195, reel C-370.

135 "that the French Generals": Knox, *Historical Journal,* 2:66.

135 "the strongest country": Wolfe to Robert Darcy, Earl of Holderness, Sept. 9, 1759, 472.

135 "a wall of masonry": Patrick Mackellar, "A Description of the Town of Quebec in Canada, Accompanied with a Plan," LAC, MG 18-M, ser. 2, vol. 6, fols. 4, 6, reel C-369.

135 "The defences are inconsiderable": Wolfe to Robert Darcy, Earl of Holderness, Sept. 9, 1759, 472.

135 "Their plan of defence": Bell, "Exact and Faithful Copy of General Wolfe's Journal," fol. 47.

136 "a numerous body of armed men": Wolfe to Robert Darcy, Earl of Holderness, Sept. 9, 1759, 472.

136 On the morning of the twelfth: "Account of Quebec Campaign, June–September 1759," pt. 3, fol. 5.

136 "officer of note": Holland to John Graves Simcoe, June 10, 1792, fol. 2.

136 "After he [Monckton] was gone": "Account of Quebec Campaign, June–September 1759," pt. 3, fol. 5.

136 Chads, an amphibious expert: Wolfe to Saunders, Aug. 30, 1759, 509.

136 "made many frivolous objections": "Account of Quebec Campaign, June–September 1759," pt. 3, fols. 4–6.

137 "the most hazardous & difficult": Letter of Charles Holmes, Sept. 18, 1759, in Doughty and Parmelee, *Siege of Quebec,* 4:295, 296.

137 "the place or places": Monckton, Townshend, and Murray to Wolfe, Sept. 12, 1759.

137 "My reason for desiring": Wolfe to Monckton, Townshend, [and Murray?], Sept. 12, 1759, LAC, MG 18-M, ser. 2, vol. 1, "Major General James Wolfe's Instructions to His Brigadiers Concerning the Battle of Quebec on 13 September 1759 with Two Autograph Letters from him (1) to Brigadier General Monckton (2) to Brigadier General Townshend," reel c-369.

CHAPTER 16

Standing on Guard

138 "This cove": Lapause, "Itinéraire de ma route," 95.

138 Quickly reinforced: "Relation du siège de Québec publiée par les François," LAC, MG 4, A1, vol. 3540, no. 74 bis, fols. 17–18, reel F-724; Malartic, "Journal des mouvemens qu'a fait le regt de Béarn, 1758–1759," LAC, MG 4, AG, A1, vol. 3540, no. 128, fols. 47–48, reel F-724; Récher, *Journal du siège de Québec,* 20–21.

139 A few hours later: Vaudreuil to Nicolas René Berryer, Oct. 5, 1759, fols. 275v–276; "Relation du siège de Québec publiée par les François," fols. 17–18; "Journal des campagnes de Montcalm," fol. 552; Récher, *Journal du siège de Québec,* 21.

139 The battery went into action: Knox, *Historical Journal,* 1:342–43; Master's Log, HMS *Squirrel,* entry of July 20, 1759, fol. 12.

140 When he briefly returned: Taillemite, "Louis-Antoine de Bougainville."

140 "I was then detached": "Note probablement dictée par Bougainville lui-même," Sept. 21, 1759, in Doughty and Parmelee, *Siege of Quebec,* 4:139.

140 The Canadians attached: Vaudreuil to Bougainville, Sept. 6, 1759, in Doughty and Parmelee, *Siege of Quebec,* 4:99–100; Bougainville, "Note probablement dictée par Bougainville lui-même," 140.

141 Thirty soldiers from the Languedoc: Vaudreuil to Bougainville, Sept. 5, 1759, in Doughty and Parmelee, *Siege of Quebec,* 4:99.

141 Born in France, Douglas: Henderson, "Francois-Prosper de Douglas, Chevalier de Douglas."

141 The remainder stood ready: Holland to John Graves Simcoe, June 10, 1792, fol. 4.

141 On September 2, 1759: "Etat des services du M. Dupont du Chambon de Vergor," LAC, MG 1, AC, E, vol. 143, reel F-614; Pothier, "Louis Du Pont Duchambon de Vergor."

141 Then both Vergor and Douglas joined their lookouts": "Etat des services de Vergor"; Vaudreuil to Nicolas René Berryer, Oct. 5, 1759, fol. 285v.

CHAPTER 17
Ashore in the Dark

142 At 9:00 p.m., the first: "General Wolfe's Orders, Sutherland Septr 11th," fol. 192; Master's Log, HMS *Sutherland,* entry of Sept. 13, 1759.

142 "The night of the 12th": Williamson to George Bellford, Dec. 10, 1759, LAC, MG 18-N21, reel A-573.

143 "our grand aim": Letter of Holmes, Sept. 18, 1759, 297.

143 "Admiral made a signal": Smith, *Journals of Ashley Bowen,* 96.

143 "to draw the attention": Townshend to William Pitt, Sept. 20, 1759, fol. 69.

143 "make a false alarm": Holland to John Graves Simcoe, June 10, 1792, fol. 4.

143 "At 2AM": Master's Log, HMS *Seahorse,* entry of Sept. 13, 1759, LAC, MG 12, ADM 52, vol. 1028, reel C-12889.

143 "Now was the time": Coats, "Private Journal of the Siege of Quebec," entry of Sept. 12, 1759.

144 Behind the light infantry: "General Wolfe's Orders, Sutherland Septr 11th," fols. 191, 192. A ship's longboat could carry forty armed soldiers, a ship's cutter fifteen.

144 Their tents and other equipment: Ibid., fols. 193–94; John Johnson, "Memoirs of the Siege of Quebec and Total Reduction of Canada in 1759 and 1760," LAC, MG 18-N18, "Siege of Quebec 1759 Collection," vol. 3, fol. 40.

144 "No officer must attempt": "General Wolfe's Orders, Sutherland Septr 11th," fol. 192.

144 It took half an hour: Master's Log, HMS *Seahorse,* entry of Sept. 13, 1759; letter of Holmes, Sept. 18, 1759, 296.

144 "as being known to General Wolfe": Williamson to Bellford, Dec. 10, 1759.

144 "on board the armed sloops": "General Wolfe's Orders, Sutherland Septr 11th," fol. 194.

144 "keep an eye on the enemy's motions": Letter of Holmes, Sept. 18, 1759, 296.

144 "Should any accident occasion": Orders of Charles Holmes, Sept. 12, 1759, LAC, MG 18-M, ser. 3, no. 25, Order book of Captain James Smith, reel C-370.

145 The boats reached a maximum: Olson et al., "Perfect Tide, Ideal Moon," 960–62.

146 Aboard HMS *Hunter*: Vaudreuil to Nicolas René Berryer, Oct. 5, 1759, fol. 285v; Renaud d'Avène des Méloizes, "Journal militaire," 74.

146 Captain Simon Fraser: "Account of Quebec Campaign, June–September 1759," pt. 3, fol. 7.

146 "The shores of the river": Kalm, *Travels in North America,* 2:424.

146 "foot of the eminence": Gordon Skelly, Journal, 1759, in Graves, "Anse au Foulon, 1759," 71; Olson et al., "Perfect Tide, Ideal Moon," 966.

146 "seven minutes past four": DeLaune, flyleaf inscription in his copy of Bland's *Treatise of Military Discipline.* Edward Coats noted, "At 4 we landed the troops about two miles from Quebec." Coats, "Private Journal of the Siege of Quebec," entry of Sept. 13, 1759.

146 "the heat [speed] of the tide": "Account of Quebec Campaign, June–September 1759," pt. 3, fol. 4.

147 "were obliged to pull": Saunders to William Pitt, Sept. 21, 1759, LAC, MG 11, CO 5, vol. 51, fol. 45, reel B-2113.

147 "with incredible difficulty": Coats, "Private Journal of the Siege of Quebec," entry of Sept. 13, 1759.

148 Although still on the "wrong" side: Knox, *Historical Journal,* 2:67.

148 "By the time we had run": Skelly, Journal, 1759, 71.

148 "In the boat where I was": Knox, *Historical Journal,* 2:68n.

148 "which I deemed invaluable": Holland to John Graves Simcoe, June 10, 1792, fol. 4.

149 "Whilst our people": Skelly, Journal, 71.

CHAPTER 18
Night Battle

150 "Who goes there": Renaud d'Avène des Méloizes, "Journal militaire," 74.

150 Douglas allowed the boats: Vaudreuil to Nicolas René Berryer, Oct. 5, 1759, fol. 285v.

150 As the Canadians fired: "Etat des services de Vergor"; Bernetz to Vaudreuil, Sept. 13, 1759, LAC, MG 1, AC, F3, vol. 15, fol. 333, reel F-391.

151 Moments later, muskets fired: Skelly, Journal, 71. See also "Etat des services de Vergor"; Bernetz to Vaudreuil, Sept. 13, 1759, fol. 333; Knox, *Historical Journal,* 2:68n.

151 Vergor's first reaction: Holland to John Graves Simcoe, June 10, 1792, fol. 4.

151 They wounded the lieutenant: Fauteux, "Relation du siège de Québec," 17; "Journal of the Particular Transactions," 187–88; Mackellar, "Journal," 50.

151 "The remainder": Mackellar, "Journal," 50.

152 "came up to him": Knox, *Historical Journal,* 2:68n.

152 With the sentries out of the way: Townshend to William Pitt, Sept. 28, 1759, LAC, MG 11, CO 5, vol. 51, fol. 90, reel B-2113; Knox, *Historical Journal,* 2:68, 68n; "Journal of the Particular Transactions," 187–88; Mackellar, "Journal," 50; *Short Authentic Account of the Expedition Against Quebec,* 27.

152 "Presently we were apprised": Skelly, Journal, 71.

153 Reunited, the light infantry charged: Fauteux, "Relation du siège de Québec," 17; "Journal of the Particular Transactions," 187–88; Mackellar, "Journal," 50.

153 They completed their ascent: *Short Authentic Account of the Expedition Against Quebec,* 27.

153 "In less than a quarter": DeLaune, flyleaf inscription in his copy of Bland, *Treatise of Military Discipline.*

153 "Some of our boats": Mackellar, "Journal," 50.

153 "until he had an opportunity": Henry Caldwell to Murray, Nov. 1, 1772, LAC, MG 18-L4, Jeffery Amherst, 1st Baron Amherst and Family Fonds, ser. 1: Military Career:

National Archives of Canada series, vol. 4, packet 28: Miscellaneous, 1759–72, fols. 122–23. Barré, telling the story afterward, stressed "that it was notorious to every body who had any the least knowledge of Mr. Wolfe's wishes, and intentions that campaign that they were most ardently bent on bringing the enemy to an action, on anything like equal terms, & that his ordering him to stop the landing, could only be a temporary measure 'till he learned the enemy's force in the neighbourhood of the landing place."

154 "highly pleased with the measures": "Account of Quebec Campaign, June–September 1759," pt. 3, fols. 7–8.

154 "You may be assured": Wolfe to Walter Wolfe, May 19, 1759, in Wilson, *James Wolfe,* 429.

154 "towed on shore": Holland to John Graves Simcoe, June 10, 1792, fol. 4.

155 Troops working under his supervision: Ibid.

155 "a convenient road": Gardiner, *Memoirs of the Siege of Quebec,* 26.

155 "This grand enterprise": Knox, *Historical Journal,* 2:68.

156 At 7:00 a.m., the ships anchored: Master's Log, HMS *Lowestoft,* entry of Sept. 13, 1759, LAC, MG 12, ADM 52, vol. 926, reel C-12889.

156 "The flat bottomed boats": Orders of Holmes, Sept. 12, 1759.

156 "fired several shot over us": Master's Log, HMS *Seahorse,* entry of Sept. 13, 1759.

156 "had several shot fired at us": Master's Log, HMS *Squirrel,* entry of Sept. 13, 1759.

156 Howe's light infantry: Townshend to William Pitt, Sept. 28, 1759, fol. 90v; Mackellar, "Journal," 51; "Journal of the Particular Transactions," 188; Master's Log, HMS *Seahorse,* entries of Sept. 12–13, 1759; James Murray, "Journal of the Expedition Against Quebec in the Year One Thousand Seven Hundred and Fifty Nine and from the Surrender Being the 18th Day of Sepr 1759 to the 17th May 1760, Also a Journal Resum'd from the 18th May to the 17th Sepr Following . . . ," LAC, MG 23-GII1, James Murray Collection, ser. 4, vol. 1, fol. 30, reel C-2225.

156 "Famishing with cold": Knox, *Historical Journal,* 2:80.

157 Boats could now cross: Olson et al., "Perfect Tide, Ideal Moon," 967.

157 Sailors loaded the French: "Etat des services de Vergor"; Fauteux, "Relation du siège de Québec," 17.

157 One hundred and sixty-five: Scott, "Report of a Tour to the South Shore of the River St. Lawrence," entries of Sept. 9, 10, 11, and 12, 1759.

157 "The main party marched up": Perry, *Recollections of an Old Soldier,* 29–30.

158 "We marched from the church": "Jeremiah Pearson His Book 1759," entry of Sept. 11, 1759, LAC, MG 18-N43, box 2.

158 "the regulars and seamen": Master's Log, HMS *Zephyr,* entry of Sept. 11, 1759, fol. 20.

158 "made the signal": Ibid., entries of Sept. 11 and 12, 1759, fols. 20, 21.

158 "I swear to you": Montcalm to Vaudreuil, n.d., enclosed in Vaudreuil to Nicolas René Berryer, Oct. 5, 1759, fol. 327.

158 "We don't have to believe": Montcalm to Vaudreuil, July 29, 1759, LAC, MG 1, AC, F3, vol. 15, fols. 326–326v, reel F-391.

159 "The slope near [the road]": Lapause, "Itinéraire de ma route," 95.

160 "according to the French manner": "Account of the Quebec Campaign," pt. 3, LAC, MG 18, D 1, fol. 7, reel A-652.

CHAPTER 19

The Plains of Abraham

161 "to Genl. Wolfe": Holland to John Graves Simcoe, June 10, 1792, fol. 4.

162 "As one walks westward": Bouchette, *Description topographique de la province du Bas Canada,* 482–83.

162 "Almost all the grass": Kalm, *Travels in North America,* 2:458.

162 The standing wheat: Ibid., 458–59; Knox, *Historical Journal,* 2:70.

162 A clump of trees: Jefferys, *Correct Plan of the Environs of Quebec,* LAC, NMC 54105; Knox, *Historical Journal,* 2:70.

162 Two prominent hedges: *Plan of the Town of Quebec.*

162 Two shallow rainwater ponds: Mackellar, "Plan of the Battle Fought on the 28th of April 1760 upon the Heights of Abraham near Quebec, Between the British Troops Garrison'd in That Place and the French Army That Come to Besiege It," 1760, LAC, NMC 14081.

162 "a well of mineral waters": Kalm, *Travels in North America,* 2:471.

163 South of the road: Jefferys, *Correct Plan of the Environs of Quebec.*

163 French officers describing: "Journal des campagnes de Lévis au Canada," vol. 12, fol. 165; "Extrait d'un journal tenu à l'armée," fol. 247v.

164 "A messenger from the Foulon": Bernetz to Vaudreuil, Sept. 13, 1759, fol. 333.

164 Moving quickly, they expelled: Mackellar, "Journal," 51.

164 "The General did me the honour": Henderson to his uncle, Oct. 7, 1759, in Archbold, "Letter Describing the Death of General Wolfe," 763.

165 "and recommended me strongly": Ibid., 762.

165 The third wave crossed: Mackellar, "Journal," 52.

165 Along with the infantry: Williamson to Lord George Sackville, Sept. 20, 1759, LAC, MG 18-N21, George Williamson and Family Fonds, reel A-573.

165 "the boats came for us": Williamson to Bellford, Dec. 10, 1759.

165 Macleod took charge: Adam Williamson, "Journal for 1759."

165 "We prepared": Williamson to the Board of Ordnance, Sept. 20, 1759, LAC, MG 18-N21, reel A-573.

166 "ordered . . . to go": Magnan to Étienne François, Duc de Choiseul, ca. 1764, LAC, MG 1, AC, E, vol. 296, "Magnan (Jean Baptiste), Officier au Canada, 1764," reel F-868.

166 Magnan's mission was quickly: Fauteux, *Journal du siège de Québec,* 64.

166 A second detachment: Mackellar, "Journal," 51.

167 "forced by a vigorous resistance": Magnan to Étienne François, Duc de Choiseul, ca. 1764.

167 "the Canadians . . . fired vigorously": Fauteux, *Journal du siège de Québec,* 65.

167 "traded fire with the enemy": Ibid., 65, 106n.

167 "in spite of all the efforts": Fauteux, "Relation du siège de Québec," 17.

167 "he [Magnan] . . . fortunately joined him": Magnan to Étienne François, Duc de Choiseul, ca. 1764.

167 "the strongest position": "Journal des campagnes de Lévis au Canada," vol. 11, fols. 163–64.

167 "to support the Guyenne battalion": Pierre Marcel, "Journal abrégé de la campagne de 1759 en Canada par M. [Pierre]M** [Marcel]," in Doughty and Parmelee, *Siege of Quebec,* 5:296.

167 "the Canadians from the different governments": Ibid.

168 Montreuil appeared and stopped: "Journal des campagnes de Montcalm," fol. 573.

168 When musket shots at daybreak: "Etat des services du Sr. Charles Deschamps de Boishébert, Capitaine chevalier de St. Louis, cy devant commandant à l'Acadie," LAC, MG 1, AC, E, vol. 36, "Dossier Charles Deschamps de Boishébert," reel F-818.

169 "to speed up the arrival": Ibid., C11E.

169 "caused him to lose": Ibid.

169 As Bernier fled: LeMoine, *L'album du touriste*, 299. Scott's forces reached L'Islet on September 16.

169 "the boats returned": Master's Log, HMS *Zephyr*, entry of Sept. 13, 1759, fol. 21.

169 "they had only burned": Fraser to Townshend, Sept. 13, 1759, LAC, MG 18-L7, George Townshend, 1st Marquess Townshend Collection, "Military Papers," reel A-931.

169 "Thurs the 13th": Scott, "Report of a Tour to the South Shore of the River St. Lawrence," entry of Sept. 13, 1759.

169 "We marched along": "Jeremiah Pearson His Book 1759," entry of Sept. 13, 1759.

170 "I never saw him": Malartic to Bourlamaque, Sept. 28, 1759, LAC, MG 18, K9, Bourlamaque Papers, vol. 4, "Lettres Variarum," 215.

170 With the decisive moment: See chapters 21 and 26.

CHAPTER 20

Preparing for Battle

171 Taking charge, Montcalm approved: Jérome de Foligné, "Journal des faits arrivé à l'armée de Québec capital dans l'Amérique septentrional pendant la campagne de l'année 1759," LAC, MG 1, AC, C11A, vol. 104, fol. 289v, reel F-104; Magnan to Étienne François, Duc de Choiseul, ca. 1764.

172 While Montcalm waited: Draper, "Seventy-Two Years' Recollections of Wisconsin," 217–18.

172 "The fire of Musketry": "Indian Lorette: Oui-ha-ra-lihte, or Petit Etienne."

172 "Know that the Frenchman": Abenaki speaker, probably Moxus or Atecouando, meeting with Massachusetts delegates at Casco in 1703. Letter of Sabastien Rasles, Oct. 12, 1723, in *Lettres édifiantes et curieuses écrites des missions étrangères*, 204.

173 Native Americans made: MacLeod, *Canadian Iroquois and the Seven Years' War*, 19–36.

173 "never to expose": Desandrouins, "Recueil et journal des choses principales qui me sont arrives, et de celles qui m'ont le plus frappes, depuis mon départ de France," in Gabriel, *Le maréchal de camp Desandrouins*, 35.

173 "My grand father": "Indian Lorette: Oui-ha-ra-lih-te, or Petit Etienne."

173 "without any path": "Journal des campagnes de Montcalm," fol. 573.

174 "that fired straight down": Ibid.

174 "served [at the Battle of the Plains of Abraham]": Vaudreuil Nicolas René Berryer, Sept. 19, 1760, LAC, MG 1, AC, E, vol. 137, "Gallet, François," reel F-830.

174 "ordered me to withdraw": "Journal des campagnes de Montcalm," fol. 573.

174 "asked the soldiers": Malartic, *Journal des campagnes*, 285.

174 "The entire army": Marcel, "Journal abrégé de la campagne de 1759," 297.

174 "I can well recollect": LeMoine, *Scot in New France*, 28–29.

175 "De Gere used to say": Draper, "Seventy-Two Years' Recollections of Wisconsin," 218.

176 "About 6 o'clock": "Account of Quebec Campaign, June–September 1759," pt. 3, fol. 8.

176 "what galled us most": Knox, *Historical Journal*, 2:70. Knox describes the French as having "got some cannon to play on us, with round and canister-shot."

176 "ordered us all to lie flat": John Johnson, "Memoirs of the Siege of Quebec," 3:41–42.

176 "showed his intention": Townshend to William Pitt, Sept. 20, 1759, fol. 90v.

176 Wolfe responded by deploying: Ibid.

176 "where with the grenadier company": Holland to John Graves Simcoe, June 10, 1792, fol. 4.

176 "the houses into which": "Brigadier General Townshend's Draft of His Despatch Concerning the Operations Resulting in the Capitulation of Quebec in 1759," LAC, MG 18-M, ser. 2, vol. 3, p. 3, reel C-369.

177 "erect a redoubt": Holland to John Graves Simcoe, June 10, 1792, fol. 4.

CHAPTER 21
Montcalm's Decision

178 "This happened slowly": Vaudreuil to Nicolas René Berryer, Oct. 5, 1759, fol. 286v.

178 "I wrote to M. de Montcalm": Ibid., fols. 286v–287.

178 He sent the order: Ibid., fol. 287; Fauteux, *Journal du siège de Québec*, 66.

179 After the battle, Townshend reported: These included 1 major general, 3 brigadiers, 11 staff officers, 6 lieutenant colonels, 4 majors, 47 captains, 104 lieutenants, 69 ensigns, 1 surgeon and 1 surgeon's mate, 239 sergeants, 83 drummers, 3,826 rank and file, along with 1 colonel, 1 captain, 4 subalterns, and 40 gunners of the Royal Artillery. "Return of the Strength of the Army on the 13th September 1759 Before the Battle of Quebec."

179 Arrayed in two lines: *Journal of the Expedition up the River St. Lawrence*, 4:58.

180 But instead of coats: Chartrand, *Wolfe's Army*, 30 (plate E), 31 (plate F), 46–47; Reid and Chappell, *18th Century Highlanders*, 27 (plate C), 36–37.

180 "I hope it will": Wolfe to Henrietta Wolfe, Oct. 24, 1756, in Wilson, *James Wolfe*, 304–5.

180 Lovat, who played: Brumwell, *Redcoats*, 69–84, 268–70; McCulloch, *Sons of the Mountains*, 2:81–82.

181 La Sarre, Languedoc, Béarn: Malartic, "Journal des mouvemens qu'a fait le regt de Béarn," fols. 80–81; "Mémoire de la campagne de 1759 [presumé de M. de Joannes, major de Québec]," LAC, MG 4, AG, A1, vol. 3540, no. 99, fol. 15, reel F-724.

181 "were placed to the right": Marcel, "Journal abrégé de la campagne de 1759," 296.

181 Captain Louis-Frédéric Herbin: "Précis de ce qui s'est passé: La campagne de 1759 en Canada, [envoyé par M. Bernier]," LAC, MG 4, AG, A1, vol. 3540, no. 90, fol. 5, F-724; "Etat des services du Sr. Herbin depuis son entrée dans le corps des cadets à l'aiguillette jusqu'à la reforme de régiment de recrue," LAC, MG 2, C7, vol. 141, "Herbin, Louis-Frédéric," reel F-780; Vaudreuil to Nicolas René Berryer, Oct. 5, 1759, fol. 287v.

181 This matches Lévis's estimate: "The French Line," enclosed in Townshend to William Pitt, Sept. 20, 1759, fols. 101–101v; "Journal des campagnes de Lévis au Canada," vol. 11, fol. 164; Vaudreuil to Nicolas René Berryer, Oct. 5, 1759, fol. 287; Bigot to Nicolas René Berryer, Oct. 15, 1759, LAC, MG 1, AC, F3, vol. 15, fol. 337v, reel F-391.

181 Wolfe's deployment of troops: "French Line."

182 With his army in position: Mackellar, "Journal," 52.

182 "making every platoon": Wolfe, "Dover Castle," 1754, in *General Wolfe's Instructions to Young Officers*, 35.

183 "The officers to inform": Wolfe, "Instruction for the 20th Regiment (in Case the French Land) Given by Lieutenant-Colonel Wolfe at Canterbury," Dec. 15, 1755, in ibid., 49.

183 "On the very morning": DeLaune flyleaf inscription, in his copy of Bland, *Treatise of Military Discipline.*

183 "Our orders were positively": John Johnson, "Memoirs of the Siege of Quebec," 3:44.

184 "At the Battle": Thompson, "Anecdote of Wolfe's Army—1760—Quebec," "Journal of James Thompson Sr. 1783–84," no. 24, James Thompson Fonds, 1758–1867, LAC, MG 23 K2, Journals, military papers, and family papers, fol. 80, reel M-2312.

184 "Gen. Wolfe . . . sent orders": Skelly, Journal, 1759, 72.

185 "Such was their impetuosity": Letter to "J.W.," Sept. 20, 1759, in Doughty and Parmelee, *Siege of Quebec*, 5:24.

185 "On the return of the sailors": "Articles of Intelligence from the Other Daily Papers of Yesterday," *Gazetteer* (London), April 9, 1762, Canadian War Museum, CWM 1975-0228-002 58F 35.1.

185 "while concealing their movement": Marcel, "Journal abrégé de la campagne de 1759," 297.

186 "certain defeat if he waited": Montreuil to Charles Louis Auguste Fouquet, Duc de Belle-Isle, Sept. 22, 1759, LAC, MG 4, AG, A1, vol. 3540, no. 98, fol. 2, reel F-724.

186 Montcalm had faith: "Journal des campagnes de Montcalm," fol. 573.

186 "old men or boys": Montcalm to Bougainville, July 15, 1759, in Doughty and Parmelee, *Siege of Quebec*, 4:4.

186 He sent orders: Bigot to Charles Louis Auguste Fouquet, Duc de Belle-Isle, Oct. 15, 1759, vol. 3450, fols. 103–7.

186 "I stopped for a moment": "Journal des campagnes de Montcalm," fol. 574.

187 "He [Montcalm] left without": Ibid.

187 "Although I regarded": Montreuil to Charles Louis Auguste Fouquet, Duc de Belle-Isle, Sept. 22, 1759, fol. 2.

187 At 10:00 a.m., the last soldier: "Extrait d'un journal tenu à l'armée," fol. 201v.

187 "I sent all the officers": Johnstone, "Memoirs of a French Officer," p. 209.

188 A light breeze blew: Master's Log, HMS *Lowestoft,* entry of Sept. 13, 1759; Master's Log, HMS *Seahorse,* entry of Sept. 13, 1759; Knox, *Historical Journal,* 2:71.

CHAPTER 22

The French Charge

189 "I was at the cannon": "Journal des campagnes de Montcalm," fol. 574.

189 "Canada will fall": Montcalm to Charles Louis Auguste Fouquet, Duc de Belle-Isle, April 12, 1759, LAC, MG 1, AC, C11A, vol. 104, fol. 159v, reel F-104.

190 "The *troupes de terre*": Montreuil to Charles Louis Auguste Fouquet, Duc de Belle-Isle, March 19, 1759, LAC, MG 4, AG, A1, vol. 3450, no. 36, fol. 2, reel F-724.

190 "I have never seen": Montgay to Charles Louis Auguste Fouquet, Duc de Belle-Isle, May 17, 1759, LAC, MG 4, AG, A1, vol. 3450, no. 63, fol. 3, reel F-724.

190 "Fear nothing, my dear friend": Lortie, *Les textes poétiques,* 1:154.

190 "the troops marched eagerly": Malartic, "Journal des mouvemens qu'a fait le regt de Béarn," fol. 80. Montreuil used almost the same words. "Les troupes s'approchrent [the British line] de bonne grace." Montreuil to Lévis, Sept. 15, 1759, "Lettres adressées à Lévis, 1756–1760," LAC, MG 18-K8, vol. 9, no. 62, reel C-364.

190 "the troops displayed": Lapause, "Canada—relations de la campagne 1759," enclosed in Lapause to Charles Louis Auguste Fouquet, Duc de Belle-Isle, Nov. 10, 1759, LAC, MG 4, AG, A1, vol. 3450, no. 111, fol. 14, reel F-724.

190   "After the action began": Mackellar, "Journal," 52.
190   This placed him just: McCulloch, "With Wolfe at Quebec," 24–25.
190   "the General came": Henderson to his uncle, Oct. 7, 1759, 763.
191   "much too fast": Malartic to Bourlamaque, Sept. 28, 1759, 214.
191   "Our troops": "Extrait d'un journal tenu à l'armée," fol. 201v.
191   "the majors shout": Saxe, *Mes rêveries*, 36.
191   The southern cluster contained: "French Line."
191   "we hadn't gone twenty steps": Malartic to Bourlamaque, Sept. 28, 1759, 214.
191   No one was heading: Knox, *Historical Journal*, 2:70.
192   "a day that I'd like to forget": Malartic to Bourlamaque, Sept. 28, 1759, 213.
192   "The enemy had": Knox, *Historical Journal*, 2:69–70.
192   "About ten o'clock": Ibid., 70.
192   "we advanced very slowly": Letter of Alexander Murray, Sept. 20, 1759, in Wylly, "Letters of Colonel Alexander Murray," 216.
192   "We were saluted": Coats, "Private Journal of the Siege of Quebec," entry of Sept. 13, 1759.
193   "in advancing towards the enemy": Bland, *Treatise of Military Discipline*, 80.
193   "The third and last attack": Wolfe to Edward Wolfe, July 4, 1743, in Wilson, *James Wolfe*, 37.
194   "the Canadians of the second rank": Malartic, "Journal des mouvemens qu'a fait le regt de Béarn," fols. 80–81.
194   Twentieth-century tests: Krenn, Kalaus, and Hall, "Material Culture and Military History," 101.
194   "I have," he wrote: Greener, *Gun*, 219.
194   "Their front began": Mackellar, "Journal," 53.
194   "firing obliquely": Knox, *Historical Journal*, 2:70.
194   "owing to the enemy's firing": *Accurate and Authentic Journal of the Siege of Quebec*, 41.
195   As the battle lines clashed: Foligné, "Journal des faits," fol. 289v; Mackellar, "Journal," 52–53; Townshend to William Pitt, Sept. 20, 1759, fol. 90v.
195   "whilst I was preparing": Holland to John Graves Simcoe, June 10, 1792, fol. 4.
196   "Returning from these campaigns": Vaudreuil to Nicolas René Berryer, Nov. 26, 1775, LAC, MG 1, AC, E, vol. 135, "Domas, François," reel F-826.
196   This was all very well: Gosselin, "Le recensement du gouvernement de Québec en 1762."
196   "The power of the infantry": Lévis, "Instructions concernant les dispositions et ordre de bataille que doivent suivre tous les troupes," in "Journal des campagnes de Lévis au Canada," vol. 12, fol. 195.
197   A British witness described: Robert Macpherson to Andrew Macpherson, Sept. 16, 1759, in McCulloch, *Sons of the Mountains*, 1:185; *Journal of the Expedition up the River St. Lawrence*, 4:21; Malcolm Fraser, *Extract from a Manuscript Journal*, 23.

CHAPTER 23
Firefight

198   Between thirty and forty yards: Townshend to William Pitt, Sept. 20, 1759, fol. 91; Robert Macpherson to Andrew Macpherson, Sept. 16, 1759, 186.
198   "looking at one another": Robert Macpherson to Andrew Macpherson, Sept. 16, 1759, 186.
199   "At last," wrote Macpherson: Ibid.

199 "The oblique fire of the enemy": Knox, *Historical Journal,* 2:71n. In Knox's text, the quotation reads, "The forty-third and forty-seventh regiments, in the center, being little affected by the oblique fire of the enemy . . ."

199 "Their first fire": Malcolm Fraser, *Extract from a Manuscript Journal,* 21.

199 "The regiment": Knox, *Historical Journal,* 1:237.

199 "The method we were ordered": Ibid., 331–32, 331n.

199 "As they came nearer": Mackenzie, "Journal of Operations, 1757–1765," LAC, MG 23-K34, Frederick Mackenzie Collection, vol. 3.

199 "as remarkable": Knox, *Historical Journal,* 2:71n.

200 "We . . . continued firing": Malcolm Fraser, *Extract from a Manuscript Journal,* 21.

200 "4 or 5 General Discharges": Robert Macpherson to Andrew Macpherson, Sept. 16, 1759, 186.

200 "about a quarter of an hour": *Journal of the Expedition up the River St. Lawrence,* 4:21.

200 "Our firing": Marcel, "Journal abrégé de la campagne de 1759," 298.

201 "A leaden ball": Robins, *New Principles of Gunnery,* 79–80.

201 Tests on an early-eighteenth-century flintlock: Krenn, Kalaus, and Hall, "Material Culture and Military History," 104.

201 "When a leaden bullet": Robins, *New Principles of Gunnery,* 94.

201 "I have fired at a body": Greener, *Gun,* 222.

201 "I was hit by two musket balls": Boucherville to Nicolas René, May 5, 1761, LAC, MG 2, C7, vol. 39, "Boucherville, Amable de," reel F-676.

201 "his wounds, one in the stomach": Unsigned memoir, Sept. 15, 1763, LAC, MG 2, C7, vol. 78, "Cuisy d'Argenteuil," reel F-565.

202 "Two musket balls": "Etat des services du Herbin."

202 "his left thigh": Memoir to Nicolas René Berryer, ca. 1762, LAC, MG 1, AC, E, vol. 242, "La Chevrotière (François de), enseigne des troupes du Canada," reel F-645.

202 "My Epitaph": Lortie, *Les textes poétiques,* 1:190.

203 "We fired our cannon": Williamson to Sackville, Sept. 20, 1759.

204 "delivering and receiving": Joannès, "Mémoire de la campagne de 1759," fol. 16.

204 "most of our soldiers": Malartic, "Journal des mouvemens qu'a fait le regt de Béarn," fol. 81.

204 "Heavier enemy fire": "Principaux evenems de la campagne 1759 jusqu'à la prise de Québec," LAC, MG 4, AG, A1, vol. 3540, no. 85, fol. 6, reel F-724.

204 "Our right [north]": "Canada—relations de la campagne 1759," fol. 16.

204 "a rout, which I dare say": Foligné, "Journal des faits," fol. 290.

204 "to cure their madness": Johnstone, "Memoirs of a French Officer," 222.

204 Marcel referred to: Marcel, "Journal abrégé de la campagne de 1759," 298; Foligné, "Journal des faits," fol. 290.

204 "Nothing . . . could stop": Marcel, "Journal abrégé de la campagne de 1759," 298.

204 "we hardly had time": "Principaux evenems de la campagne 1759 jusqu'à la prise de Québec."

205 Three years later: Anderson, *A People's Army,* 144; Gipson, *Years of Defeat,* 127–28, 133.

CHAPTER 24
Dying Generals

206 "the fire slackening": Malcolm Fraser, *Extract from a Manuscript Journal,* 21.

206 "By the time the cloud": Knox, *Historical Journal,* 2:71.

206 "gave them a full fire": Mackenzie, "Journal of Operations, 1757–1765."

206 "at the head of Bragg's": Townshend to Pitt, Sept. 20, 1759, fol. 91.

207 "commanded the 800 Canadians": "Etat des services du Herbin."

207 "courage and resolution": Henderson to his uncle, Oct. 7, 1759, 762.

207 "was scarce a moment": Ibid., 763.

207 "He first received a musket ball": *Gentleman's Magazine,* 1759, 556.

207 "When the General received": Henderson to his uncle, Oct. 7, 1759, 763.

207 "I assisted in supporting": Holland to John Graves Simcoe, June 10, 1792, fol. 4.

208 "and found his shirt": Henderson to his uncle, Oct. 7, 1759, 763.

208 "The dear General": Holland to John Graves Simcoe, June 10, 1792, fols. 4–5.

208 "body was brought down": Skelly, Journal, 1759, 72.

208 By 11:00 a.m.: Master's Log, HMS *Lowestoft,* entry of Sept. 13, 1759.

209 "drove them [the French]": Williamson to Sackville, Sept. 20, 1759.

209 "General Montcalm was killed": Williamson to the Board of Ordnance, Sept. 20, 1759.

209 "as fast as their legs": "Journal des campagnes de Montcalm," fol. 574.

209 Montcalm had been riding: Bigot to Charles Louis Auguste Fouquet, Duc de Belle-Isle, Oct. 15, 1759, vol. 3450, fols. 8–9.

210 "Sir, Obliged to surrender": Montcalm to Wolfe, Sept. 13, 1759, LAC, MG 18-M, Northcliffe Collection, ser. 2: Townshend Papers, vol. 2, "A Letter Signed by Louis Joseph de Saint-Veran, Marquis de Montcalm, Concerning the Capitulation of Quebec, Written on 13th September, 1759, Shortly Before His Death," reel C-369.

210 Montcalm passed the night: Marcel to Lévis, Sept. 14, 1759, LAC, MG 18-K8, Fonds Chevalier de Lévis, vol. 6, "Lettres du Marquis de Montcalm au chevalier de Lévis," no. 154, reel C-364; Johnstone, "Memoirs of a French Officer," fol. 112.

210 "At 8:00 p.m., M. le Marquis": Foligné, "Journal des faits," fol. 291.

210 "Gen. Monckton . . . upon his first taking": Henderson to his uncle, Oct. 7, 1759, 763.

210 "I hear no confirmation": Murray to Manie Murray, Quebec, Sept. 28, 1759, in Wylly, "Letters of Colonel Alexander Murray," 218, 219.

211 "You know my situation": Marcel to Lévis, Sept. 14, 1759.

CHAPTER 25
The British Charge

213 "I here saw": "Indian Lorette: Oui-ha-ra-lih-te, or Petit Etienne."

213 "Highlanders rushed in": *Journal of the Expedition up the River St. Lawrence,* 4:54.

213 "had one of his cheeks": Thompson, "Anecdote of Wolfe's Army, Quebec, 1760 (by a Volunteer)," no. 23, LAC, MG 23 K2, fol. 80, reel M-2312.

213 "The bullet and bayonet": Letter to "J.W.," Sept. 20, 1759, 23.

214 "When our lines advanced": Thompson, "Anecdote of Wolfe's Army—1760—Quebec," no. 24, fols. 80–81.

214 "In advancing, we passed over": Malcolm Fraser, *Extract from a Manuscript Journal,* 21.

214 "lay there as thick as a flock": Thompson, "Anecdote of Wolfe's Army, Quebec, 1760," no. 23, fol. 80.

214 "When the French gave": Ibid.

215 "He immediately": Letter of Captain Calcraft, Sept. 20, 1759, in Doughty and Parmelee, *Siege of Quebec,* 6:146.

215 Only then did he allow: Thomson, *Memoirs of the Life and Gallant Exploits of the Old Highlander, Donald Macleod,* 88.

215 "they pursued them": Robert Macpherson to Andrew Macpherson, Sept. 16, 1759, 186. See also Malcolm Fraser, *Extract from a Manuscript Journal,* 22.

215 "Colonel Williamson pursued": Adam Williamson, "Journal for 1759."

215 Along the way: Robert Macpherson to Andrew Macpherson, Sept. 16, 1759, 186.

216 "I can remember the Scotch Highlanders": LeMoine, *Scot in New France,* 29.

217 "Several of my Grenadiers' bayonets": Murray to Manie Murray, Sept. 28, 1759, 216.

217 The British pulled back: Knox, *Historical Journal,* 2:71.

217 The Fifty-Eighth advanced: Ibid.

217 "Every man, exerted himself": John Johnson, "Memoirs of the Siege of Quebec," 3:44–45.

217 "We followed them": Mackenzie, "Journal of Operations, 1757–1765."

217 "I was carried off.": Johnstone, "Memoirs of a French Officer," fol. 214.

218 He ordered the gunners: "Journal des campagnes de Montcalm," fol. 574.

218 "Taking me for a general": Johnstone, "Memoirs of a French Officer," fol. 214.

218 "I escaped their terrible fire": Ibid.fol.

218 "the enemies right & a body": Townshend to William Pitt, Sept. 20, 1759, fol. 91v.

CHAPTER 26
The Canadians Strike Back

220 "At the action": Charest to Louis François, Marquis de Monteynard, ca. 1772, LAC, MG I, AC, E, vol. 68, "Charest, Étienne," fol. 49v, reel F-820; Roland-J. Auger, "Étienne Charest."

220 "Only the regulars collapsed": "Extrait d'un journal tenu à l'armée," fol. 248.

221 "What an idea": "Journal des campagnes de Montcalm," fol. 575.

221 "pursued them into the Sainte-Louis suburb": Vaudreuil to Nicolas René Berryer, Oct. 5, 1759, fol. 287v.

221 "The Canadians were more attentive": Ibid. See also "Journal des campagnes de Lévis au Canada," vol. II, fol. 166.

221 "On September 13, 1759": Albergati-Vezza to Étienne François, Duc de Choiseul, 1764, LAC, MG I, AC, E, vol. 2, "François-Marie Balthazara, Marquis d'Albergati-Vezza," reel F-810.

221 "forced the enemy left": Vaudreuil to Nicolas René Berryer, Oct. 5, 1759, fol. 287v.

222 "From moment to moment": Ibid.

222 "When the Highlanders": Robert Macpherson to Andrew Macpherson, Sept. 16, 1759, 186.

223 For the first time: Ibid.; Malcolm Fraser, *Extract from a Manuscript Journal,* 22.

223 "killed and wounded a great many": Ibid.

224 "wheeled . . . to the left": Knox, *Historical Journal,* 2:71.

224 "It was at this time": Malcolm Fraser, *Extract from a Manuscript Journal,* 22.

224 "incredible rage and despair": Johnstone, "Memoirs of a French Officer," fol. 210.

224 Quebec's suburbs and refugee camps: Joannès to Vaudreuil, Sept. 16, 1759, LAC, MG I, AC, F3, vol. 15, fol. 314v, reel F-391.

224 "On that day": Bernier to Nicolas René Berryer, Sept. 21, 1759, LAC, MG I, AC, CIIA, vol. 104, fol. 337v, reel F-104.

225 He died of his wounds: Bronze, *Les morts de la guerre de Sept Ans au Cimitière de l'Hôpital-Générale de Québec,* 103; "Acte d'inhumation d'Augustin Cadet (21 septembre

1759)," in "Les héros de 1759 et de 1760 inhumés au Cimetière de l'Hôpital Général de Québec," 252.

225 "I used it that day": Bernier to Nicolas René Berryer, Oct. 15, 1759, fol. 3.

225 "We saw," wrote Marie de la Visitation: Legardeur, *Relation de ce qui s'est passé au siège de Québec,* 9.

225 When they attempted: Jefferys, *Authentic Plan of the River St. Lawrence from Sillery to the Fall of Montmorency.*

225 "Captain Thomas Ross": Malcolm Fraser, *Extract from a Manuscript Journal,* 22–23.

225 Two or three shots: Fauteux, *Journal du siège de Québec,* 66, 107v.

226 At about the same time: "Account of Quebec Campaign, June–September 1759," pt. 3 fol. 9; Malartic, "Journal des mouvemens qu'a fait le regt de Béarn," fol. 81.

226 Vaudreuil estimated that: Vaudreuil to Nicolas René Berryer, Oct. 5, 1759, fol. 288. French officer casualties broke down to four senior officers, twenty-six junior officers of the *troupes de terre,* and fourteen junior officers of the *troupes de la marine.*

226 As for the British: "Return of the Killed, Wounded, and Missing at the Battle of Quebec, September the 13th 1759," enclosed in Townshend to William Pitt, Sept. 20, fol. 97.

226 "At 4 [a.m.] . . . heard": Master's Log, HMS *Captain,* entry of Sept. 13, 1759, LAC, MG 12, ADM 52, vol. 819, fol. 27, reel C-1288.

227 "If we give him": "Journal des campagnes de Montcalm," fol. 574.

227 Yet as the campaign opened: Nicolai, "Different Kind of Courage," 67.

228 Conventional wisdom held: Muir, *Tactics and the Experience of Battle in the Age of Napoleon,* 75.

229 "The example of the bravest": Johnstone, "Memoirs of a French Officer," 209–10.

CHAPTER 27
After the Battle

230 The battalions Monckton had led: Holland to John Graves Simcoe, June 10, 1792, fol. 5.

230 "I had myself": Monckton to William Pitt, Sept. 15, 1759, LAC, MG 11, CO 5, vol. 51, fol. 88, reel B-2113.

230 By 10:30 a.m.: Master's Log, HMS *Lowestoft,* entry of Sept. 13, 1759.

231 Further inquiry established: *Short Authentic Account of the Expedition Against Quebec,* 32.

231 "the pursuit had put part": Townshend to William Pitt, Sept. 20, fol. 91v.

231 "pursuing the enemy": *Journal of the Expedition up the River St. Lawrence,* 4:55.

231 "You will not I flatter myself": Townshend to William Pitt, Sept. 20, 1759, fol. 91v.

231 The French lost forty: Vaudreuil to Nicolas René Berryer, Oct. 5, 1759, fol. 288; Marcel, "Journal abrégé de la campagne de 1759," 297.

231 "having learned after having": "Journal des campagnes de Lévis au Canada," vol. 11, fol. 166.

232 "A man allowed himself": Bougainville to Bourlamaque, Sept. 18, 1759, LAC, MG 18-K9, vol. 1, fol. 605, reel c-363.

232 "Our men had nothing": Thompson, "Anecdote of Wolfe's Army, Quebec, 1760," no. 23, fol. 80.

232 Only a privileged few: "Return of the Strength of the Army on the 13th September 1759 Before the Battle of Quebec."

232   Eleanor Job, thirty-six years old: Ward, *Battle for Quebec, 1759,* 40.

233   Women in eighteenth-century armies: James Alexander Browne, *England's Artillery-men,* 26.

233   "Happy in escaping unhurt": Letter to "J.W.," Sept. 20, 1759, 23–24.

233   "I had almost forgot": Murray to Manie Murray, Sept. 20, 1759, in Wylly, "Letters of Colonel Alexander Murray," 217.

234   "Hunger getting the better": LeMoine, *Scot in New France,* 28.

CHAPTER 28
Besieging Quebec

237   To prepare for the counterattack: Vaudreuil to Nicolas René Berryer, Oct. 5, 1759, fol. 288v.

237   "he thought that they could": Bigot to Nicolas René Berryer, Oct. 15, 1759, vol. 15, fol. 339.

237   "unanimously rejected": "Copie du Conseil de guerre tenu le 13 7bre chés M. le Mis de Vaudreuil," LAC, MG 1, AC, F3, vol. 15, fol. 324, reel F-391.

237   "a victorious army": Ibid., fols. 324–324v.

238   Vaudreuil and Bigot argued: Vaudreuil to Nicolas René Berryer, Oct. 5, 1759, fol. 288v; Bigot to Nicolas René Berryer, Oct. 15, 1759, vol. 15, fol. 339.

238   "If I had attacked": Vaudreuil to Nicolas René Berryer, Oct. 5, 1759, fol. 288v.

239   They received orders: "Journal des campagnes de Montcalm," fol. 575.

239   "The disorder": Malartic, "Journal des mouvemens qu'a fait le regt de Béarn," fols. 82; Malartic, *Journal des campagnes,* 287.

239   "The French soldier": "Journal des campagnes de Montcalm," fol. 576.

239   "It was . . . not a retreat": Johnstone, "Memoirs of a French Officer," 19.

239   "We hastened to the Village": "Indian Lorette: The Story of Oui-ha-ra-lih-te."

240   They did not, however: Townshend, a skilled artist, also produced a fine watercolor portrait of Wolfe and valuable, if unflattering, sketches of an Amerindian warrior and an Amerindian family. His sketches, paintings, and caricatures remain a priceless visual record of the Quebec campaign.

240   In 1758, with a new commander in chief: Stacey, "George Townshend," 822–5.

241   "As I have not heard": Saunders to Townshend, Sept. 13, 1759, in Townshend, *Military Life of Field-Marshal George, First Marquess Townshend,* 243.

241   "I am doing the best": Townshend to Monckton, Sept. 14, 1759, "Seven Letters from General Townshend to General Monckton, 14–25 September 1759," LAC, MG 18-M, ser. 1, vol. 31, Quebec XIV, reel C-366.

242   "During the nine years": Ramezay, "Détail de mes services depuis 1720 jusqu'en 1759," LAC, MG 1, AC, C11A, vol. 104, fol. 320v, reel F-104.

242   "greatly troubled": Ramezay to Vaudreuil, Sept. 18, 1759, LAC, MG 1, AC, F3, vol. 15, fol. 312v, reel F-391.

242   To hold Quebec: Marcel, "Journal abrégé de la campagne de 1759," 298–99.

242   "I did not have": Ramezay, "Mémoire du Sieur de Ramezay, chevalier de l'ordre Royal et Militaire de Saint Louis c'y devant commandant à Quebec au sujet de la redittion de cette ville, Article Deux: Mémoire de la conduitte que j'ay ténu pendant le siege de Quebec et dans la redittion de cette place," LAC, MG 1, AC, C11A, vol. 104, fols. 323–323v, reel F-104.

242   "during the siege": Ibid., fol. 323v.

242 "Everyone acquainted with the colony": Ibid., fol. 321v.

242 "I dared to hope": Ibid., fol. 322v.

242 Most important, in the context of a war: Vaudreuil, "Mémoire pour servir d'instruction de M. de Ramezai commandant à Quebec," Sept. 13, 1759, LAC, MG 1, AC, F3, vol. 15, fol. 320, reel F-391.

243 Already hard-pressed: Joannès to Vaudreuil, Sept. 16, 1759, fol. 314v.

243 "To be deserted so quickly": Ramezay, "Mémoire du Sieur de Ramezay," fol. 323.

243 "abandoned the city": Ibid., fol. 322.

243 "we saw the tents": Ibid., fol. 323.

244 A veteran of three sieges: Taillemite, "Louis-Thomas Jacau de Fiedmont."

244 Fiedmont's waterfront artillery: Knox, *Historical Journal,* 2:72.

244 "During the battle": Foligné, "Journal des faits," fol. 290v.

244 The bombardment continued: Ibid., fol. 291.

245 "was immediately tried": Knox, *Historical Journal,* 2:72.

245 "Brigadier Townshend went": Ibid., 76.

246 "Although we lacked": Legardeur, *Relation de ce qui s'est passé au siège de Québec,* 9, 10.

CHAPTER 29

Townshend's Siege

247 One step followed another: For the socially uncertain, Muller even included a section on etiquette for surrenders. This covered delicate issues ranging from how to open negotiations and draft articles of capitulation to the precise order in which a defeated garrison marched out of a fortress. Muller, *Attac and Defence of Fortified Places,* 197–205.

248 If the defenders had a band: Duffy, *Fire and Stone,* 101–53; Muller, *Attac and Defence of Fortified Places,* 7–129.

248 "there are several knolls": Montresor to James Gabriel Montresor, Oct. 18, 1759, in Doughty and Parmelee, *Siege of Quebec,* 4:333.

249 "At 9 all the longboats": Master's Log, HMS *Stirling Castle,* entry of Sept. 14, 1759, LAC, MG 12, ADM 52, vol. 1046, reel C-12889.

249 "some hundred sailors": Letter of Calcraft, Sept. 20, 1759, 145.

249 Calcraft might smile: Knox, *Historical Journal,* 2:83.

249 On the Plains of Abraham: Ibid., 78.

249 Attempting to rein them in: General Monckton's Orderly Book, August 4, 1759, entry of Sept. 14, 1759, LAC, MG 18-M, ser. 1, vol. 23, reel C-366. Monckton's copies of the day's orders are more detailed than Townshend's. See "Brigadier General Townshend's General Orders, 26 June–10 October 1759," entry of Sept. 14, 1759, LAC, MG 18-M, ser. 2, vol. 8, reel C-369.

250 Townshend ignored Montcalm's attempt: Saunders to Townshend, Sept. 15, 1759, LAC, MG 18-L7, "Military Papers," reel A-931.

250 "burning & destroying": Master's Log, HMS *Zephyr,* entry of Sept. 14, 1759, fol. 21.

250 "marched from the River Ouelle": Scott, "Report of a Tour to the South Shore of the River St. Lawrence," entry of Sept. 14, 1759.

250 "We marcht all day": "Jeremiah Pearson His Book 1759."

250 "They could hardly believe": Ramezay, "Mémoire du Sieur de Ramezay," fol. 323v.

251 "Is there not therefore": "À messieurs les commandant et officiers majors de la ville de Québec," LAC, MG 1, AC, C11A, vol. 104, fols. 332, 332v, reel F-104.

251 Of the fifty-nine men: The French stormed Fort Bull on March 27, 1756. Gaspard-Joseph Chaussegros de Léry, "Journal de la campagne d'hiver," 392.

251 "mostly older married men": Ramezay, "Mémoire du Sieur de Ramezay," fol. 323v.

251 Instead, they shifted: "À messieurs les commandant et officiers majors de la ville de Québec," fols. 332, 332v.

252 "In this request": Ramezay, "Mémoire du Sieur de Ramezay," fols. 323v–324.

252 "to discuss the means": Council minutes, Sept. 15, 1759, LAC, MG 1, AC, C11A, vol. 104, fols. 333, reel F-104.

252 "We warn M. de Ramezay": Vaudreuil, "Mémoire pour servir d'instruction de M. de Ramezai commandant à Quebec."

252 "In view of the complete lack": Council minutes, Sept. 15, 1759, fol. 333v.

252 "to reduce the ration again": Ibid., fol. 334.

252 "Considering the instructions": Ibid., fol. 334v.

253 "We run [*sic*] along": Johnstone, "Memoirs of a French Officer," 221.

253 "whose manners everyone": "Extrait d'un journal tenu à l'armée," fol. 252.

253 "We marched the whole night": "Indian Lorette: The Story of Oui-ha-ra-lih-te."

253 He passed on the news: Lévis to Charles Louis Auguste Fouquet, Duc de Belle-Isle, Nov. 1, 1759, LAC, MG 18-K8, vol. 2, "Lettres de Monsieur le marquis de Lévis concernant la guerre du Canada, 1756–1762," fol. 288, reel C-364.

254 By the end of the day: Vaudreuil to Bougainville, Sept. 16, 1759, in Doughty and Parmelee, *Siege of Quebec*, 4:128.

254 "By tomorrow I hope": Cadet to Bougainville, Sept. 16, 1759, in Doughty and Parmelee, *Siege of Quebec*, 4:129.

254 "that the army had reassembled": Vaudreuil to Nicolas René Berryer, Oct. 5, 1759, fol. 289.

254 On June 20: Vaudreuil to Nicolas René Berryer, Nov. 10, 1759, LAC, MG 2, C7, vol. 24, "Belcourt, Le sieur de, Thisbé," reel F-661.

254 "Their light cavalry": Knox, *Historical Journal*, 2:361.

254 "I will not hide from you": Joannès to Vaudreuil, Sept. 16, 1759, fols. 314v–315.

255 "Monsieur de Ramesay, who commands": Knox, *Historical Journal*, 2:79–80.

255 Lacking his own batteries: Townshend, "Diary of Proceeding up the River St. Lawrence," entry of Sept. 15, 1759.

255 The Royal Navy came under fire: Knox, *Historical Journal*, 2:80.

256 "At 7 1 flat bottomed boat": Master's Log, HMS *Stirling Castle*, entry of Sept. 15, 1759.

256 "he said he . . . was afraid": Knox, *Historical Journal*, 2:80.

256 This redoubt covered: Montresor to James Gabriel Montresor, Oct. 18, 1759, 333; Knox, *Historical Journal*, 2:81.

256 At four o'clock that afternoon: Scott, "Report of a Tour to the South Shore of the River St. Lawrence," entry of Sept. 15, 1759.

256 "We lay still today": "Jeremiah Pearson His Book 1759."

256 "to embark the troops": Master's Log, HMS *Zephyr*, entry of Sept. 15, 1759, fol. 21.

256 "the south shore fired a shot": Ibid., entry of Sept. 16, 1759, fol. 22.

257 Among the latter: Ramezay, "Mémoire du Sieur de Ramezay," fol. 324v.

257 On September 15: Knox, *Historical Journal*, 2:80.

257 Elsewhere on the city wall: Townshend, "Diary of Proceeding up the River St. Lawrence," entry of Sept. 15, 1759; Knox, *Historical Journal*, 2:80.

257 "opened in such rugged ground": Foligné, "Journal des faits," fol. 291v.

257 Shot and shells flew: Knox, *Historical Journal*, 2:82.

257 Belcourt, who appears to have remained: Joannès to Vaudreuil, Sept. 16, 1759, fol. 314.

257 "to find out what was going on": Ramezay, "Mémoire du Sieur de Ramezay," fol. 324v.

257 "I spoke," wrote Joannès: Joannès to Vaudreuil, Sept. 16, 1759, fol. 314v.

258 "They told me": Ramezay, "Mémoire du Sieur de Ramezay," fol. 324v.

258 "The tools," wrote Townshend: Townshend, "Diary of Proceeding up the River St. Lawrence," entry of Sept. 16, 1759.

258 On the return journey: Master's Log, HMS *Stirling Castle,* entry of Sept. 16, 1759.

258 "he announced an advance": Malartic, *Journal des campagnes,* 289.

258 "If," wrote Lévis: Lévis to Nicolas René Berryer, Nov. 10, 1759, LAC, MG 1, AC, F3, vol. 15, fol. 370v, reel F-391.

259 "I will carry 100 quintals": Rochebeaucourt to Bougainville, Sept. 17, 1759, in Doughty and Parmelee, *Siege of Quebec,* 4:131.

259 "that the army was marching": "Journal des campagnes de Lévis au Canada," vol. 11, fol. 169.

259 Once inside Quebec: Vaudreuil to Bougainville, Sept. 17, 1759, in Doughty and Parmelee, *Siege of Quebec,* 4:130; "Note: Probablement dictée par Bougainville lui-même," 140–41.

CHAPTER 30

Ramezay's Surrender

260 "threatened to do nothing": Joannès, "Mémoire de la campagne de 1759," fol. 10.

260 "According to the English officers": Foligné, "Journal des faits," fol. 291v.

260 "I found myself abandoned": Ramezay to Vaudreuil, Sept. 18, 1759, fols. 306–306v.

261 Ramezay agreed: Joannès, "Mémoire de la campagne de 1759," fols. 19–20.

261 "Nothing could be better": Bernetz to Bougainville, Sept. 17, 1759, in Doughty and Parmelee, *Siege of Quebec,* 4:131.

261 Finding cannon that were unattended: Foligné, "Journal des faits," fol. 291v.

261 Finally, lookouts reported: Ramezay, "Mémoire du Sieur de Ramezay," fols. 323v, 324v; Ramezay to Vaudreuil, Sept. 19, 1759, LAC, MG 1, AC, F3, vol. 15, fols. 306–306v, reel F-391.

262 "made people think": Foligné, "Journal des faits," fol. 291v.

262 "so that when the enemy enters": Ramezay, "Mémoire du Sieur de Ramezay," fol. 325.

262 "if the army had not abandoned them": Ibid., fol. 324v.

263 But at that instant: Joannès, "Mémoire de la campagne de 1759," fol. 20.

263 "That officer, who has no experience": Ibid., fol. 10.

263 French wounded and those who cared for them: "Articles de la capitulation demandée par M. de Ramezai Lieutenant pour le Roi commandant la haute & bas ville de Quebec, chevalier de l'ordre Royal & Militaire de St. Louis à Son Excellence Monsieur le General des troupes de Sa. Majesté Britannique," Sept. 18, 1759, LAC, MG 1, AC, C11A, vol. 104, fols. 315–16.

264 Ramezay agreed to the change: Ramezay to Vaudreuil, Sept. 18, 1759, fol. 306v; Joannès, "Mémoire de la campagne de 1759," fol. 20; Ramezay, "Mémoire du Sieur de Ramezay," fol. 325.

264 "18 to 20 sacks": Ramezay, "Mémoire du Sieur de Ramezay," fol. 325v.

264 "It hadn't dared to face": Ibid.

264 "M. de Ramezay": Rochebeaucourt to Vaudreuil, Sept. 18, 1759, LAC, MG 1, AC, F3, vol. 15, fol. 316, reel F-391.

264 "My Dear Friend, I arrived": Rochebeaucourt to Bougainville, Sept. 17, 1759, 133.

265 "The enemy," wrote Knox: Knox, *Historical Journal,* 2:83.

265 "At noon," wrote the master: Master's Log, HMS *Stirling Castle,* entry of Sept. 17, 1759.

265 "moved seven of the best": Letter of Holmes, Sept. 18, 1759, 299.

265 Townshend sent for Saunders: Knox, *Historical Journal,* 2:83.

265 "have signified their intention": Ibid., 84.

265 That night, British engineers: Montresor to James Gabriel Montresor, Oct. 18, 1759, 333.

265 "marched up to the east part": Scott, "Report of a Tour to the South Shore of the River St. Lawrence," entry of Sept. 16, 1759.

266 "the tide preventing the vessels": Ibid., entry of Sept. 17, 1759.

267 "The enemy surrendered": Williamson to the Board of Ordnance, Sept. 20, 1759; Foligné, "Journal des faits," fol. 292.

267 From there, they fanned out: "Brigadier General Townshend's General Orders, 26 June–10 October 1759," entry of Sept. 18, 1759.

267 "You can not conceive": Murray to Manie Murray, Sept. 28, 1759, 218.

267 "with a large body of seamen": Knox, *Historical Journal,* 2:85.

267 "At 3 P.M. we had": Smith, *Journals of Ashley Bowen,* 97.

267 "The capital of Canada": "Brigadier General Townshend's General Orders, 26 June–10 October 1759," entry of Sept. 18, 1759.

268 When Belcourt withdrew: Vaudreuil to Nicolas René Berryer, Nov. 10, 1759.

268 "all of them": Johnstone, "Memoirs of a French Officer," fol.222.

268 Carrying rations for two days: Malartic, *Journal des campagnes,* 289.

268 "Upon this news": Lévis to Charles Louis Auguste Fouquet, Duc de Belle-Isle, Nov. 10, 1759, fol. 371v.

269 "I have nothing but misfortunes": "Journal des campagnes de Montcalm," fol. 572.

270 "I lived here, at the French King's table": Knox, *Historical Journal,* 2:171–72.

270 "We hoped in vain": Legardeur, *Relation de ce qui s'est passé au siège de Québec,* 22.

270 "One day as I was driving": Grace, *History of the Life and Sufferings of Henry Grace,* 54.

CHAPTER 31
Occupied Canada

273 "The town is much more": Williamson to the Board of Ordnance, Sept. 20, 1759.

273 "The havoc is not to be conceived": Knox, *Historical Journal,* 2:94.

273 "I have the pleasure": Letter to "J.W.," Sept. 20, 1759, 24.

274 "General Monckton . . . is so far recovered": Townshend to Amherst, Sept. 26, 1759, in Townshend, *The Military Life of Field-Marshal George, First Marquess Townshend,* 245.

274 The following spring: Steele, "Robert Monckton."

274 "several houses & cellars": Monckton's Orderly Book, August 4, 1759, entry of Oct. 1, 1759.

274 A soldier of the Fortieth: Ibid., entry of Oct. 5, 1759.

274 "notorious robbery on the house": Knox, *Historical Journal,* 2:207–8.

275 "some of the female inhabitants": Ibid., 113.

275 "The general desires": Monckton's Orderly Book, August 4, 1759, entry of Oct. 1, 1759.

275 "a Serjeant and eleven men": Knox, *Historical Journal,* 2:176.

275 "great quantity of black cattle": Ibid., 94.

275 "Upon the whole": Scott, "Report of a Tour to the South Shore of the River St. Lawrence," entry of Sept. 19, 1759.

275 "Today," wrote Pearson: "Jeremiah Pearson His Book 1759."

276 "It was truly surprising": Perry, *Recollections of an Old Soldier,* 31–32.

276 It speaks volumes: "Return of What Cattle Received from Boston Issued to the Army & What Remains, viz."

276 HMS *Captain* and *Neptune:* Durell, Journal, entry of Sept. 22, 1759, fol. 247v. Durell's entry refers only to ships under his direct command, but Saunders presumably ordered the entire fleet to contribute.

276 "the water of the town": Monckton's Orderly Book, August 4, 1759, entry of Oct. 15, 1759.

277 While their comrades: Knox, *Historical Journal,* 2:104.

277 "cart-house and a stable": Ibid., 168.

277 "I'm quartered in a house": Montresor to James Gabriel Montresor, Oct. 18, 1759, 331.

277 "This once splendid city": Spavens, *Narrative of William Spavens,* 133–34.

277 Monckton began by ordering: Monckton's Orderly Book August 4, 1759, entries of Oct. 9 and 14, 1759.

277 French scouts observed: Knox, *Historical Journal,* 2:101, 112, 115.

278 "I am providing": Montresor to James Gabriel Montresor, Oct. 18, 1759, 332.

278 "It is recommended": Monckton's Orderly Book, August 4, 1759, entry of Oct. 3, 1759.

278 "I hope," he wrote: Townshend to Bougainville, Sept. 22, 1759, in Doughty and Parmelee, *Siege of Quebec,* 4:136.

278 "were indeed rendered": Knox, *Historical Journal,* 2:154.

278 Monckton ordered their battalion: Monckton's Orderly Book, August 4, 1759, entry of Oct. 21, 1759.

279 But the exodus continued: Foligné, "Journal des faits," fol. 293v.

279 "the townspeople and inhabitants": Ibid.

279 Men assembled in their militia companies: Those who had not already handed in their muskets to the French authorities surrendered their arms. Murray, "Journal of the Expedition Against Quebec," fol. 48.

279 "The men stand": Knox, *Historical Journal,* 2:354.

279 "I solemnly promise": "Form of Oath Administered to the Canadians Subdued by His Britannick Majesty's Troops in the River St. Lawrence 1759," LAC, MG 11, CO 5, vol. 57, pt. 3, fol. 79, reel B-2171.

279 "It was on that day": Foligné, "Journal des faits," fol. 293v.

279 "But," asked Foligné: Ibid.

280 Carved by the Canadian sculptor: French Royal Arms, 1727, Canadian War Museum, CWM 19940024-001.

280 "This trophy was taken": Trophy Mount for French Royal Arms, ca. 1759, Canadian War Museum, CWM 19670139-001.

280 In 1917, the Royal Navy: The British returned a second set of arms, taken by James Murray, to Quebec City in 1925. It is now part of the collection of the Musée de la Civilisation. Pothier, "Royal Arms of France and Its Ancillary Artifacts."

280 "From what I could learn": Holland to John Graves Simcoe, June 10, 1792, fol. 4.

280 "It was reported in Canada": Johnstone, "Memoirs of a French Officer," fol. 212n.

280 "I was not responsible": Bougainville to Townshend, Sept. 24, 1759, LAC, MG 18-L7, George Townshend, 1st Marquess Townshend Collection, "Military Papers," reel A-931; Bougainville to Townshend, ca. Sept. 1759, ibid.

281 Along with the troops: Knox, *Historical Journal,* 2:100–104.

281 The ships raised anchor: Foligné, "Journal des faits," fols. 293v–294v.

281   "It was our miserable fate": Ibid., fol. 294.

282   Shortly thereafter, Durell appeared: Durell, Journal, entry of Oct. 19, 1759, fols. 250–250v.

282   "Our sailors willingly": Foligné, "Journal des faits," fol. 294.

282   "at four o'clock": Ibid., fol. 294v.

282   They would not return: Durell, Journal, entries of Sept. 22 and 24, 1759, fols. 247v, 248; Laberge and Hébert, "Les prisonniers de la bataille des Plains d'Abraham," 257–64.

282   "I have some good news": Smith, *Journals of Ashley Bowen,* 100.

283   On October 18: Knox, *Historical Journal,* 2:175.

283   "As it has been thought": Monckton's Orderly Book, August 4, 1759, entry of Oct. 19, 1759.

284   Two weeks later: Knox, *Historical Journal,* 2:179.

284   As for Ashley Bowen: Smith, ed., *The journals of Ashley,* pp. 100, 101, 104.

284   "I came over the ferry": Smith, *Journals of Ashley Bowen,* 100, 101, 104.

284   Command of the Quebec garrison: G. P. Browne, "James Murray," 569–70.

284   American rangers instructed: Knox, *Historical Journal,* 2:234.

284   "A severe winter, now commenced": Miller, "Memoirs of an Invalid," Centre for Kentish Studies, U1350/Z9A, 31–33.

285   "The fatigues of the winter": Ibid.

CHAPTER 32
Canadian Winter

286   "to-day I saw about twenty": Knox, *Historical Journal,* 2:102.

286   British officers maintained: Ibid., 171–74.

286   "enticing our men to desert": Ibid., 208–9, 210.

287   "The English . . . have taken": Henri-Marie Dubreil de Pontbriand, "Description imparfaitte de la misère du Canada," enclosed in Pontbriand to Nicolas René Berryer, Nov. 5, 1759, LAC, MG 1, AC, C11A, vol. 104, fols. 368v, 369, reel F-104.

287   "a suitable reward": Knox, *Historical Journal,* 2:167.

287   Other betrayals followed: MacLeod, "Treason at Quebec."

287   "The English," wrote Marie de la Visitation: Legardeur, *Relation de ce qui s'est passé au siège de Québec,* 14.

288   "Every measure": Murray, "Journal of the Expedition Against Quebec," fol. 65.

288   "This search": Ibid., fol. 75.

288   Canadians nonetheless continued: Ibid., fol. 59; Knox, *Historical Journal,* 2:244.

288   When their patients were: Legardeur, *Relation de ce qui s'est passé au siège de Québec,* 16.

288   At the same time: Murray, "Journal of the Expedition Against Quebec," fols. 77–78. For an example of a report by French agents in Quebec, see "Journal des campagnes de Lévis au Canada," vol. 12, fol. 192.

288   "a Frenchman is taken up": Knox, *Historical Journal,* 2:245.

288   They were careful: Murray, "Journal of the Expedition Against Quebec," fol. 71.

289   "the boatmen of Point Levi": Ibid., fol. 72.

289   "joined our patrols": Legardeur, *Relation de ce qui s'est passé au siège de Québec,* 14.

289   "burned a parish": Knox, *Historical Journal,* 2:209.

289   "proclamations are every-where dispersed": Ibid., 209–10.

289   "An unfortunate Canadian": Ibid., 203–4.

289   "that they had never seen": Legardeur, *Relation de ce qui s'est passé au siège de Québec,* 14.

CHAPTER 33

The Second Battle of the Plains of Abraham

291 Following his accession: Eccles, "François (François-Gaston) de Lévis, Duc de Lévis," 477–82.

291 To create the first: "Journal des campagnes de Lévis au Canada," vol. 12, fol. 206.

291 None of the heavier guns: Ibid., fols. 190, 227.

291 With French resources steadily: "Instruction pour MM. les officers des troupes de la marine, 1760," in Casgrain, *Lettres et pièces militaires,* 231; "Journal des campagnes de Lévis au Canada," vol. 12, fols. 190–91.

291 At the end of the 1759 campaign: Lévis to Charles Louis Auguste Fouquet, Duc de Belle-Isle, Nov. 1, 1759, 295–96.

292 In his orders: Vaudreuil, "Ordonnance du gouverneur général," April 16, 1760 [1], in Casgrain, *Lettres et pièces militaires,* 224; Vaudreuil to Savard, April 16, 1760, in ibid., 230.

292 On March 28, one of these agents: MacLeod, "Treason at Quebec," 55–56.

292 "My plan of defense": Murray to William Pitt, May 25, 1760, LAC, MG 11, CO 5, vol. 64, fol. 20, reel B-2175.

292 "Half an hour after six": Ibid., fol. 20v.

293 Every soldier carried: Knox, *Historical Journal,* 2:292.

293 "ordered the whole": Malcolm Fraser, *Extract from a Manuscript Journal,* 30.

293 "gave him all the advantage": Ibid., 33–34.

293 "While the line was forming": Murray, "Journal of the Expedition Against Quebec," fol. 96.

293 "ordered . . . the whole army": Malcolm Fraser, *Extract from a Manuscript Journal,* 30–31.

294 The French had the larger army: "Journal des campagnes de Lévis au Canada," vol. 12, fol. 215.

294 "had that very day": Malcolm Fraser, *Extract from a Manuscript Journal,* 32.

294 "low and swampy ground": Knox, *Historical Journal,* 2:294.

294 Over the winter: Each of these units detached a captain to command the militia serving with it and three lieutenants to command the companies. Militia officers and sergeants served as lieutenants. In action, "elles marchant en avant et chercheront à s'emparer des situations les plus avantageuses pour approcher au plus près et faire feu sur l'ennemi et le suivre de près, s'il se replie." If compelled to withdraw themselves, they fell back into the intervals between bodies of regulars. Lévis, "Instructions concernant l'ordre dans lequel les milices attachées à chaque bataillon seront formées pour camper et servir pendant la campagne," fols. 200–201.

294 "The Canadians . . . who were": Malartic, *Journal des campagnes,* 319.

294 "I was wounded by a grapeshot": Ibid., 318.

295 "The troops being ordered": Knox, *Historical Journal,* 2:294–95.

295 "While we were on": Thompson, "Anecdote of Wolfe's Army, Quebec, 1760," no. 23, fol. 81.

295 "as soon as the piper": Ibid., fol. 82.

295 "If," wrote Lapause: Lapause, "En 1760," 159.

295 "All the English officers": Malartic to Lévis, May 17, 1760, LAC, MG 18-K8, vol. 11, fol. 363, reel C-364.

296 "The English," wrote one officer: Pouchot, *Mémoires sur la dernière guerre de l'Amérique septentrionale,* 2:168.

296 The French lost: "Etat général des officiers et soldats tués ou morts de leurs blessures ou blessés à la bataille du 28 avril, au siège de Québec," in "Journal des campagnes de Lévis au Canada," vol. 12, fol. 217; Murray, "A Return of the Number Kill'd, Wounded, Prisoners, etc. from the 27th April to the 24th May 1760," enclosed in Murray to William Pitt, May 25, 1760.

296 "The clash": Legardeur, *Relation de ce qui s'est passé au siège de Québec,* 19, 20–21.

296 "I arrived there": Malartic, *Journal des campagnes,* 319.

296 "Immense irregularities": Knox, *Historical Journal,* 2:298, 301.

297 "I am in hopes": Murray to Amherst, April 30, 1760, LAC, MG 11, CO 5, vol. 64, fol. 16, reel B-2175.

297 "At ten o'clock this morning": Knox, *Historical Journal,* 2:285, 288.

297 After the battle: Lapause, "Mémoire et observations sur mon voyage en Canada," 113.

298 "When," wrote James Miller: Miller, "Memoirs of an Invalid," 40–41.

298 "About eleven o'clock": Knox, *Historical Journal,* 2:309–10.

298 "I very much fear": Lévis to Bigot, May 15, 1760, LAC, MG 18-K8, vol. 11, fol. 361–62, reel C-364.

298 "Ah! One ship of the line": Desandrouins, "Conversation que j'ay eue avec le Sr. Holland capitaine au 2e bataillon de Royal Américain, faisant fonction d'ingénieur en chef, pendant le siège de Québec, le 13 septembre 1760, en présence du Sr. Vanbrane, ancien otage Anglais," in Gabriel, *Le maréchal de camp Desandrouins,* 326.

298 France had already: Dull, *French Navy and the Seven Years' War,* 173–75.

299 Instead of following orders: Beattie and Pothier, *The Battle of the Restigouche,* 12–14.

299 As the French capitulated: MacLeod, *Canadian Iroquois and the Seven Years' War,* 154–90.

CHAPTER 34

The Road to Quebec

304 "this hostile city": Letter to "J.W.," Sept. 2, 1759, 15.

306 "it will be easy": Kalm, *Travels in North America,* 1:33.

307 Sailing north from Jamestown: Squires, "Sir Samuel Argall," 67–9.

307 "The English did not reply": Biard, "Nostre prinse par les anglois," 278, 280.

308 "The English colonies": Kalm, *Travels in North America,* 1:139.

308 They began to fear: Eccles, "Role of the American Colonies in Eighteenth Century French Foreign Policy," 164–65.

308 "One cannot express": Rigaud de Vaudreuil, "Mémoire de M. de Vaudreuil au Duc d'Orleans, Regen du Royaume," 292.

309 Seventy thousand Canadians: Dechêne, *Le peuple, l'État et la guerre au Canada,* 423; Dull, *French Navy and the Seven Years' War,* 26.

309 "a very cold": Logan, "Of the State of the British Plantations in America," 117–18, 113.

309 Never strong enough: Eccles, "Role of the American Colonies in Eighteenth Century French Foreign Policy," 164–65.

309 "a settlement at the mouth": "Mémoire du Roy à Callière et Champigny," Versailles, May 31, 1701, LAC, MG 1, AC, B, vol. 22, fol. 231v, reel F-201.

309 Instead, they fortified: Dull, *French Navy and the Seven Years' War,* 9–14; Eccles,

"French Imperial Policy for the Great Lakes Basin," 37; Pritchard, *In Search of Empire*, xxi.

310 When George Washington: MacLeod, *Canadian Iroquois and the Seven Years' War*, 37–50.

310 "that the English should inhabit": Bond, "Captivity of Charles Stuart," 63.

CHAPTER 35
The Battle of the Plains of Abraham and the History of the World

314 They ceded the islands: "Definitive Treaty of Peace and Alliance Between Great Britain, France, and Spain, Concluded at Paris, with the Separate Articles Thereunto Belonging," Feb. 10, 1763, in Shortt and Doughty, *Documents Relating to the Constitutional History of Canada*, 1:97–112.

315 "One cannot": Marie de la Visitation to Étienne François, Duc de Choiseul, Sept. 27, 1763, in O'Reilly, *Monseigneur de Saint-Vallier et L'Hôpital Général de Québec*, 374–75.

315 Some of the thirty-five hundred: Larin, "Les Canadiens passés en France à la conquête," 146, 150. A further five hundred Canadians departed between 1754 and 1758. These figures did not include the thousands of French soldiers, administrators, and merchants who returned to France in 1759 and 1760.

315 "preferred to abandon": Unsigned memoir, March 4, 1765, "Bullau, Antoine," LAC, MG 1, AC, E. vol. 56, reel F-819.

315 "the officers of Canada": Unsigned memoir, ca. 1776, LAC, MG 2, C7, vol. 141, "Herbin, Louis-Frédéric," reel F-780.

315 "Votre très humble & obéissent": Berthou-Dûbreüil to Charles Eugène Gabriel de La Croix, Marquis de Castries, May 26, 1783.

316 "I have lived for three years": Lortie, *Les textes poétiques*, 1:188–89.

317 "I have been told": Kalm, *Travels in North America*, 1:139–40.

317 "While Canada is so near": Logan, "Of the State of the British Plantations in America," 128.

317 "As the whole country": Kalm, *Travels in North America*, 1:140.

318 "Do you think": Malartic, *Journal des campagnes*, 331. The original text uses "bit" (*frein*) instead of "bridle."

321 "We hold a vaster empire": Designed by Warren L. Green, Based on a map by George Robert Parkin, "Canadian Imperial Stamp, XMAS 1898, 'We Hold a Vaster Empire Than Has Been,'" Dec. 7, 1898, LAC, Canadian Postal Archives, POSTAL 0083, http://data4.collectionscanada.ca/netacgi/nph-brs?s1=0083&l=20&d=POST&p=1&u=http%3A%2F%2Fwww.collectionscanada.ca%2Farchivianet%2F020117%2F02011703 0103_e.html&r=1&f=G&SECT3=POST.

321 "It is not unfair": "French Defeated Race Is Col. Drew's Reminder," *Toronto Star*, Nov. 28, 1936, LAC, MG 32, C3, George Drew Papers, vol. 57, file 517A, "French Canadians—'Defeated Race'—Correspondence, Memoranda, Clippings, Affidavits of Witnesses re Alleged Statements Made at the East Hastings By-Election."

Bibliography

ARCHIVAL SOURCES: LIBRARY AND ARCHIVES CANADA

MG 1 Archives des Colonies

B, Lettres Envoyées

Vol. 22 [1700–1701], reel F-201.
Vol. 109 [1759], reel F-313.

C11A, Correspondance Générale, Canada

Vol. 102 [1757], reel F-102.
Vol. 103 [1758], reel F-103.
Vol. 104 [1759], reel F-104.

E, Dossiers Personnels

Vol. 2, "François-Marie Balthazara, Marquis d'Albergati-Vezza," reel F-810.
Vol. 28, "Berthou-Dûbreüil (Le Sieur)," reel F-812.
Vol. 36, "Dossier Charles Deschamps de Boishébert," reel-F818.
Vol. 56, "Bullau, Antoine," reel F-819.
Vol. 68, "Charest, Étienne," reel F-820.
Vol. 135, "Domas, François," reel F-826.
Vol. 137, "Gallet, François," reel F-830.
Vol. 143, "Du Pont du Chambon de Vergor, Louis," reel F-614.
Vol. 242, "La Chevrotière (François de), enseigne des troupes du Canada," reel F-645.
Vol. 296, "Magnan (Jean-Baptiste), Officier au Canada, 1764," reel F-868.

F3, Collection Moreau de Saint-Méry

Vol. 15, reel F-391.

MG 2 Fonds de la Marine
Série C7, Dossiers Individuels

Vol. 17, "Barré, Jean," reel F-660.
Vol. 24, "Belcourt, Le sieur de, Thisbé," reel F-661.
Vol. 39, "Boucherville, Amable de," reel F-676.
Vol. 78, "Cuisy d'Argenteuil," reel F-565.
Vol. 141, "Herbin, Louis-Frédéric," reel F-780.
Vol. 184, "Le Vasseur dit le fils, fils de René Nicolas," reel F-796.

MG 4 Archives de la Guerre
A1, Correspondance Générale, Opérations Militaire

Vol. 3405, reel F-665.
Vol. 3540, reel F-724.

MG 4-A Bibliothèque du Ministère de la Guerre

Johnstone, James. "Memoirs of a French Officer: A Military, Critical, and Philosophical History of the Pretender's Expedition on Scotland in the Year 1745; of the Canadian War
Until the Capitulation of Montreal for the Colony in 1760; and the Siege of Louisbourg
in the Year 1758. With an Exact and Impartial Account of the Hostilities Committed in
Acadia and Cape Breton Before the Declaration of War," reel F-734.

MG 7-11 Fonds de la Bibliothèque de l'Arsenal, Archives de la Bastille

Prisonniers, vol. 12142 [Joseph-Michel Cadet], reel F-1104.

MG 11 Great Britain, Public Record Office, Colonial Office Papers
CO 5 Original Correspondence, Secretary of State, America and West Indies

Vol. 9, reel B-6171.
Vol. 51, reel B-2113.
Vol. 53, reel B-220.

MG 12 Great Britain, Public Record Office, Admiralty Papers
ADM 50, Admiral's Journals

Vol. 3, reel b-19 [Philip Durell, Journal].
ADM 52, Master's Logs

Vol. 720, HMS *Sutherland,* reel C-12888.
Vol. 819, HMS *Captain,* reel C-12888.
Vol. 847, HMS *Eurus,* reel C-12888.
Vol. 894, HMS *Hunter,* reel C-12888.
Vol. 926, HMS *Lowestoft,* reel C-12889.
Vol. 1028, HMS *Seahorse,* reel C-12889.
Vol. 1043, HMS *Squirrel,* reel C-12889.
Vol. 1046, HMS *Stirling Castle,* reel C-12889.
Vol. 1073, HMS *Trent,* reel C-12890.
Vol. 1117, HM Sloop *Zephyr,* reel C-12890.

MG 13 Great Britain, Public Record Office, War Office Papers
WO 34, Amherst Papers

Vol. 30, reel B-2653.
Vol. 39, reel B-2657.
Vol. 46b, reel B-2662.

MG 18-D4 Arthur Dobbs Fonds

"Account of Quebec Campaign, June–September 1759," reel A-652.

MG 18-K8, Fonds Chevalier de Lévis

Vol. 1, "Journal des campagnes de Mr le Marquis de Montcalm mis en ordre par M. Le Mar-
quis de Lévis," reel C-363.
Vol. 5, "Lettres du Marquis de Vaudreuil à Lévis, 1756–1760," reel C-363 and C-364.
Vol. 6, "Lettres de Montcalm à Lévis, 1756–1759," reel C-364.
Vol. 8, "Lettres de Bigot à Lévis, 1756–1760," reel C-364.

Vol. 9, "Lettres adressées à Lévis, 1756–1760," reel C-364.

Vol. 12, "Journal des campagnes de Lévis au Canada, 1756–1760," reel C-365.

MG 18-K9 Fonds François-Charles de Bourlamaque

Vol. 1, "Lettres de Montcalm à Bourlamaque, 25 June 1756–22 September 1759," reel C-362.

Vol. 4, "Lettres Variarum," 215.

MG 18-L4, Jeffery Amherst, 1st Baron Amherst and Family Fonds

Series 1: Military Career, vol. 4, packet 28: Miscellaneous 1759–72.

MG 18-L7, George Townshend, 1st Marquess Townshend Collection

"Military Papers," reel A-931.

MG 18-L5 James Wolfe Collection

Correspondence, Letters from General James Wolfe to Captain Wm. Rickson (Antiquaries' Miscellaneous Papers), Museum of the Society of Antiquaries, Edinburgh, Scotland, MS 2207, reel A-1780.

MG 18-M Northcliffe Collection

Series 1: Monckton Papers

Vol. 20, Quebec 1759, vol. 3, Documents relating to the preparation of the expedition, reel C-366.

Vol. 21, Quebec 1759, vol. 4, Documents relating to the expedition from the time of its sailing up the river St. Lawrence to the Battle of the Plains of Abraham, reel C-366.

Vol. 23, Quebec 1759, vol. 6, General Monckton's Orderly Book, August 4, 1759, reel C-366.

Vol. 33, Letters addressed to General Monckton by French prisoners after the occupation of Quebec, reel C-366.

Vol. 31, Quebec 14, "Seven Letters from General Townshend to General Monckton, 14–25 September 1759," reel C-366.

Vol. 32, Quebec 15, "Documents Relating to Quebec After Its Capture up to the Time of General Monckton's Departure for New York. With a Return of the Officers Killed, Wounded, etc. at the Battle of St. Foy on the 28th April 1760," reel C-366.

Series 2: George Townshend Papers

Vol. 1, "Major General James Wolfe's Instructions to His Brigadiers Concerning the Battle of Quebec on 13 September 1759 with Two Autograph Letters from Him (1) to Brigadier General Monckton (2) to Brigadier General Townshend," reel C-369.

Vol. 2, "A Letter Signed by Louis Joseph de Saint-Veran, Marquis de Montcalm, Concerning the Capitulation of Quebec, Written on 13th September, 1759, Shortly Before His Death," reel C-369.

Vol. 3, "Brigadier General Townshend's Draft of His Despatch Concerning the Operations Resulting in the Capitulation of Quebec in 1759," reel C-369.

Vol. 6, Patrick Mackellar, "A Description of the Town of Quebec in Canada, Accompanied with a Plan," reel C-369.

Vol. 9, "Diary of Proceeding up the River St. Lawrence," reel C-369.

Vol. 12, "Miscellaneous Documents Relating to the Campaign Against Quebec in 1759 and the Battle of Sillery on 28 April 1760," reel C-370.

Series 3: Separate Items in the Northcliffe Collection
Separate Items No. 23, General Wolfe's Orders
Separate Items No. 24, Manuscript Quebec Journals, Captain Thomas Bell

Vol. 3, Thomas Bell, "The First Part of My Quebeck Journal," reel C-370.

Vol. 6, Thomas Bell, ed., "An Exact and Faithful Copy of General Wolfe's Journal from the 13th May 1759 to the 16th of August 1759 (the Remainder of His Journal to near the Day He Was Killed [13th Sept.] Was Destroyed by Himself Before the Battle), Also Some Loose Hints and Part of a Journal of His Expedition to Gaspé Faithfully Copied from One of His Memorandum Books," reel C-370.

Separate Items No. 25, Order Book of James Smith
Order book of James Smith, reel C-370.

MG 18-N18 Siege of Quebec 1759 Collection
Vol. 3, John Johnson, "Memoirs of the Siege of Quebec and Total Reduction of Canada in 1759 and 1760, by John Johnson, Clerk and Quartermaster Serjeant, Fifty Eighth Regiment."
Vol. 4, *A Journal of the Expedition up the River St. Lawrence: Containing a True and Most Particular Account of the Fleet and Army Under the Command of Admiral Saunders and General Wolfe, from the Time of Their Embarkation at Louisbourg 'til After the Surrender of Quebek,* by the Sergeant-Major of Gen. Hopson's Grenadiers. Boston: Printed and Sold by Fowle and Draper at Their Printer-Office in Marlborough Street, 1759.

MG 18-N21 George Williamson and Family Papers
Williamson Family Papers, reel A-573.

MG 18-N43 Diary Kept by Jeremiah Pearson
Jeremiah Pearson His Book 1759, box 2.

MG 18-N46 Edward Coats, a Private Journal of the Siege of Quebec
Edward Coats, "A Private Journal of the Siege of Quebec with a Description of the Town Commencing the 16th of February 1759 (Being the Day of Our Departure from England) and Ending the 18th of September Following the Day of Capitulation of the Town," reel A-1221.

MG 23-A2 William Pitt, 1st Earl of Chatham Fonds
Chatham Manuscripts, vol. 2, bundle 50.

MG 23-HI1 John Graves Simcoe Fonds
Series 5, 1765–1860, file 24, no. 18, reel A-606.

MG 23 K2 James Thompson Fonds
Journals, military papers, and family papers, "Journals of James Thompson, Sr., 1783–84," reel M-2312.

MG 23-K34 Frederick Mackenzie Collection
Vol. 3, "Journal of Operations, 1757–1765."

MG 32, C3, George Drew Papers
Vol. 57, file 517A, "French Canadians—'Defeated Race'—Correspondence, Memoranda, Clippings, Affidavits of Witnesses re Alleged Statements Made at the East Hastings By-Election."

RG 10, Records Relating to Indian Affairs
Series A. Administrative Records of the Imperial Government, 1667–1864; Subseries 2. Records of the Superintendent's Office, 1755–1830; Minutes of Indian Affairs, 1755–90, vol. 1822, reel C-1221.

National Map Collection, Library and Archives Canada

Jefferys, Thomas. *An Authentic Plan of the River St. Lawrence from Sillery to the Fall of Montmorency with the Operations of the Siege of Quebec Under the Command of Vice-Adml. Saunders & Gen. Wolfe down to the 5 Sepr. 1759. Drawn by a Captain in His Majesty Navy.* 1759–60. NMC 97970.

——. *A Correct Plan of the Environs of Quebec, and of the Battle Fought on the 13th September, 1759: Together with a Particular Detail of the French Lines and Batteries, and Also of the Encampments, Batteries, and Attacks of the British Army, and the Investiture of That City Under the Command of Vice Admiral Saunders, Major General Wolfe, Brigadier General Monckton, and Brigadier General Townsend. Drawn from the Original Surveys Taken by the Engineers of the Army.* London: Thomas Jefferys, ca.1760. NMC 54105.

Mackellar, Patrick. *Plan of the Battle Fought on the 28th of April 1760 upon the Heights of Abraham near Quebec, Between the British Troops Garrison'd in That Place and the French Army That Come to Besiege It.* 1760. NMC 14081.

Plan of the Town of Quebec, the Capital of Canada in North America, with the Bason and a Part of the Adjacent Country Shewing the Principal Encampments and Works of the British Army Commanded by Major General Wolfe, and Those of the French Army Commanded by Lieut General the Marquis of Montcalm, During the Siege of That Place in 1759. NMC 0011117.

ARCHIVAL SOURCES: OTHER ARCHIVES AND LIBRARIES
British Library

Humphreys, Richard. "Rich Humphreys, His Journal, Commencing Cork May 1757 with Its Continuation." Blechynden Papers, vol. 85, Add. MSS 45662, British Library.

Centre for Kentish Studies

Miller, James. "Memoirs of an Invalid," CKS, U1350/Z9A.

George Metcalf Archival Collection, Military History Research Centre,
Canadian War Museum

"Articles of Intelligence from the Other Daily Papers of Yesterday." *London Gazetteer,* April 9, 1762. CWM 1975-0228-002 58F 35.1.

Webster Library Collection, Archives and Research Library, New Brunswick Museum

DeLaune, William. Flyleaf inscription. In Humphrey Bland, *A Treatise of Military Discipline: In Which Is Laid Down and Explained the Duty of the Officer and Soldier, Thro' the Several Branches of the Service.* 6th ed. London: John and Paul Knapton, Sam. Birt, T. Longman, and T. Shewell, 1746. LC 355 B64, AN 2926.

PRINTED PRIMARY SOURCES

An Accurate and Authentic Journal of the Siege of Quebec, 1759. By a Gentleman in an Eminent Station on the Spot. London: J. Robinson, 1759.

Archbold, W. A. J. "A Letter Describing the Death of General Wolfe." *English Historical Review* 12, no. 48 (1897): 762–63.

Biard, Pierre. "Nostre prinse par les anglois." In *The Jesuit Relations and Allied Documents: Travels and Explorations of the Jesuit Missionaries in New France, 1610–1791: The Original French, Latin, and Italian Texts, with English Translations and Notes.* Vol. 3, *Acadia, 1611–1616,* edited and translated by Reuben Gold Thwaites, 274–83. Cleveland: Burrows Brothers, 1897.

Bland, Humphrey. *A Treatise of Military Discipline: In Which Is Laid Down and Explained the Duty of the Officer and Soldier, Through the Seveaal [sic] Branches of the Service*. London: printed for S. Buckley, 1727.

Bond, Beverly W. "The Captivity of Charles Stuart, 1755–1757." *Mississippi Valley Historical Review* 13, no. 1 (June 1926): 58–81.

Bosher, John F. "Le ravitaillement de Québec en 1758: Quelques documents." *Histoire Sociale—Social History* 5, no. 9 (April 1972): 79–85.

Botwood, Ned. "Hot Stuff." *Rivington's New York Gazetteer*, May 5, 1774, 2.

Bouchette, Joseph. *Description topographique de la province du Bas Canada: Avec des remarques sur le Haut Canada et sur les relations des deux provinces avec les Etats Unis de l'Amérique*. London: W. Faden, 1815.

Canada, Public Archives. *Rapport sur les Archives Publiques pour l'année 1929*. Ottawa: F. A. Acland, 1930.

Casgrain, H.-R., ed. *Collection de manuscrits contenant lettres, mémoires et autres documents historiques relatifs à l'histoire de la Nouvelle-France, recueillis aux archives de la province de Québec ou copiés à l'étranger*. Vol. 4. Quebec: A. Coté, 1884.

———. *Collection des manuscrits du maréchal de Lévis*. 12 vols. Montreal and Quebec, 1889–95. Vol. 5, *Lettres de M. de Bourlamaque au maréchal de Lévis*. Quebec: L.-J. Demers & Frère, 1891.

———. *Collection des manuscrits du maréchal de Lévis*. Vol. 4, *Lettres et pièces militaires, instructions, ordres, mémoires, plans de campagne et de défense, 1756–1760*. Quebec: L.-J. Demers & Frère, 1891.

Charlevoix, Pierre-François-Xavier de. *Histoire et description générale de la Nouvelle France, avec le journal historique d'un voyage fait par ordre du roi dans l'Amérique septentrionnale*. Vols. 3 and 4. Paris: Rollin Fils, 1744.

Chaussegros de Léry, Gaspard-Joseph. "Journal de la campagne d'hiver, du 13 février au neuf avril 1756." Edited by Amédée Gosselin. *Rapport de l'archiviste de la province de Québec* (1926–27): 372–94.

Courville, Louis-Léonard Aumasson de. *Mémoires sur le Canada, depuis 1749 jusqu'à 1760*. Quebec: T. Cary, 1838.

Doughty, Arthur George, and G. W. Parmelee. *The Siege of Quebec and the Battle of the Plains of Abraham*. Vols. 4–6. Quebec: Dussault & Proulx, 1901.

Draper, Lyman C., ed. "Seventy-Two Years' Recollections of Wisconsin, by Augustin Grignon, of Butte des Morts, Winnebago County." *Third Annual Report and Collections of the State Historical Society of Wisconsin, for the Year 1856*. Vol. 3, 195–295. Madison: Calkins & Webb, Printers, 1857.

Eastburn, Robert. *A Faithful Narrative, of the Many Dangers and Sufferings, as Well as Wonderful Deliverances of Robert Eastburn, During His Late Captivity Among the Indians: Together with Some Remarks upon the Country of Canada, and the Religion, and Policy of Its Inhabitants; the Whole Intermixed with Devout Reflections*. Philadelphia: William Dunlap, 1758. Reprinted in *Held Captive by Indians: Selected Narratives, 1642–1836*, edited by Richard Vanderbeets, 151–76. Knoxville: University of Tennessee Press, 1973.

Falgairolle, Prosper, ed. *A propos de Montcalm: Notes et documents inédits*. Nimes: Imprimerie générale, 1910.

Fauteux, Aegidius, ed. *Journal du siège de Québec du 10 mai au 18 septembre 1759*. Quebec, 1922.

———. "Relation du siège de Québec." *Rapport de l'archiviste de la province de Québec* (1937–38): 4–20.

Foster, Paul G. M., ed. "Quebec 1759: James Gibson, Naval Chaplain, Writes to the Naturalist Gilbert White." *Journal for the Society of Army Historical Research* 64, no. 260 (Winter 1986): 218–23.

Fraser, Malcolm. *Extract from a Manuscript Journal, Relating to the Siege of Quebec in 1759, Kept by Colonel Malcolm Fraser, Then Lieutenant of the 78th (Fraser's Highlanders) and Serving in That Campaign.* Quebec: Literary and Historical Society, 1866.

Gabriel, Charles Nicolas. *Le maréchal de camp Desandrouins, 1729–1792: Guerre du Canada, 1756–1760; Guerre de l'indépendance américaine, 1780–1782.* Verdun, Quebec: Renvé-Lallemant, 1887.

Gardiner, Richard, ed. *Memoirs of the Siege of Quebec, . . . from the Journal of a French Officer on Board the* Chezine *Frigate, Taken by His Majesty's Ship* Rippon. London: printed for R. & J. Dodsley, 1761.

Gosselin, Amédée, ed. "Le journal de M. de Bougainville." *Rapport de l'archiviste de la province de Québec* (1923–24): 202–93.

———. "Le recensement du gouvernement de Québec en 1762." *Rapport de l'archiviste de la province de Québec* (1925–26): 1–143.

Grace, Henry. *The History of the Life and Sufferings of Henry Grace, of Basingstoke in the County of Southampton, Being a Narrative of the Hardships He Underwent During Several Years Captivity Among the Savages in North America,.* Reading, U.K.: printed for the author, 1764. Reprinted New York and London: Garland, 1977.

Graves, Donald E. "The Anse au Foulon, 1759: Some New Theories and Some New Evidence." *Northern Mariner* 14, no. 4 (Oct. 2004): 61–72.

Howe, Jemima. "The Captivity and Sufferings of Mrs. Jemima Howe, Taken Prisoner by the Indians at Bridgman's Fort, in the Present Town of Vernon, Vt. Communicated to Dr. Belknap by the Rev. Bunker Gay, 1755." In *North Country Captives: Selected Narratives of Indian Captivities from Vermont and New Hampshire,* edited by Colin G. Calloway, 89–99. Hanover, N.H.: University Press of New England, 1992.

Hunter, William. "Biographical Memoir of Lieutenant William Hunter, of Greenwich Hospital: An Intimate Friend of the Poet Falconer." *Naval Chronicle* 13 (Jan.–July 1805): 1–45.

"Indian Lorette: Oui-ha-ra-lih-te, or Petit Etienne, the Oldest of the Chiefs of the Council of the Village." *Star and Commercial Advertiser/L'etoile et journal du commerce,* Feb. 13, 1828.

"Indian Lorette: The Story of Oui-ha-ra-lih-te or Petite Etienne, the Old Chief,—Continued." *Star and Commercial Advertiser/ L'etoile et journal du commerce,* Feb. 27, 1828.

Johnson, James. "Narrative of James Johnson." In *North Country Captives: Selected Narratives of Indian Captivities from Vermont and New Hampshire,* edited by Colin G. Calloway, 85–87. Hanover, N.H.: University Press of New England, 1992.

Johnson, Susanna. "A Narrative of the Captivity of Mrs. [Susanna] Johnson. Notices of the Willard Family." In *Indian Narratives: Containing a Correct and Interesting History of the Indian Wars, from the Landing of Our Pilgrim Fathers, 1620, to Gen. Wayne's Victory, 1794: To Which Is Added a Correct Account of the Capture and Sufferings of Mrs. Johnson, Zadock Steele, and Others, and Also a Thrilling Account of the Burning of Royalton,* 128–82. Claremont, N.H.: Tracy and Bros., 1854.

A Journal of the Siege of Quebec: To Which Is Annexed a Correct Plan of the Environs of Quebec and of the Battle Fought on the 13th September, 1759: . . . Engraved by Thomas Jefferys, Geographer to His Majesty. Ca. 1759.

Kalm, Pehr. *Peter Kalm's Travels in North America: The English Version of 1770.* Edited by Adolph B. Benson. New York: Dover, 1966.

King, Titus. *Narrative of Titus King of Northampton, Mass.: A Prisoner of the Indians in Canada, 1755–1758.* Vol. 109 of *The Garland Library of Narratives of North American Indian Captivities,* edited by Wilcomb E. Washburn. New York: Garland, 1977.

Knox, John. *An Historical Journal of the Campaigns in North America for the Years 1757, 1758, 1759, and 1760.* London: printed for the author and sold by W. Johnston, in Ludgate-Street, and J. Dodsley, in Pall-Mall, 1769.

Lapause de Margon, Jean-Guillaume Plantavit de. "En 1760." *Rapport de l'archiviste de la province de Québec* (1933–34): 158–60.

———. "Itinéraire de ma route," *Rapport de l'archiviste de la province de Québec* (1933–34), 95–97.

———. "Mémoire et observations sur mon voyage en Canada." *Rapport de l'archiviste de la province de Québec* (1931–32): 3–125.

———. "Mémoire et réflexions politiques et militaires sur la guerre du Canada depuis 1746 jusqu'à 1760." *Rapport de l'archiviste de la province de Québec* (1933–34): 147–60.

———. "Mémoire sur l'état de la nouvelle-France (1757)." *Rapport de l'archiviste de la province de Québec* (1923–24): 42–70.

———. "Milices du Canada: Inconvénients dans la constitution de ces milices qui empêchent leur utilité; moyens d'en tirer parti, la campagne prochaine." Jan. 1759. *Rapport de l'archiviste de la province de Québec* (1923–24): 29–31.

Legardeur de Repentigny, Marie-Joseph, Soeur Marie de la Visitation. *Relation de ce qui s'est passé au siège de Québec, et de la prise du Canada; par une religieuse de l'Hôpital Général de Québec: Adressé à une communauté de son ordre en France.* Quebec: Bureau du Mercury, 1855.

LeMoine, James MacPherson. *The Scot in New France: An Ethnological Study. Inaugural Address, Lecture Season 1880–81, Read Before the Literary and Historical Society of Quebec, 29th November, 1880,* 28–29. Montreal: Dawson Brothers, 1881.

Lettres édifiantes et curieuses écrites des missions étrangères. Nouvelle Édition. Mémoires d'Amérique. Tome sixième. Paris: J. G. Merigot le Jeune, 1781.

Little, Charles Herbert, ed. *Despatches of Rear-Admiral Philip Durell, 1758–1759, and Rear-Admiral Lord Colville, 1759–1761.* Halifax: Maritime Museum of Canada, 1958.

Logan, James. "Of the State of the British Plantations in America, a Memorial." In "A Quaker Imperialist's View of the British Colonies in America, 1732," edited by Joseph E. Johnson. *Pennsylvania Magazine of History and Biography* 60, no. 2 (April 1936): 97–130.

Lortie, Jeanne d'Arc. *Les textes poétiques du Canada français, 1606–1867.* Vol. 1, *1606–1806.* With Pierre Savard and Paul Wyczynski. Montreal: Fides, 1987.

Malartic, Anne-Joseph-Hippolyte de Maurès de. *Journal des campagnes au Canada de 1755 à 1760.* Paris: Plon, 1890.

"Mémoire du Canada." *Rapport de l'archiviste de la province de Québec* (1924–25): 94–198.

Molyneux, Thomas More. *Conjunct Expeditions; or, Expeditions That Have Been Carried on Jointly by the Fleet and Army. With a Commentary on a Littoral War.* London: R. & J. Dodsley, 1759.

Muller, John. *The Attac and Defence of Fortified Places.* 2nd ed. London: J. Millan, 1757.

———. *A Treatise of Artillery.* 3rd ed. London: John Millan, 1780.

Panet, Jean Claude. *Journal du siège de Québec en 1759.* Montreal: Eusèbe Senécal, 1866.

Pargellis, Stanley McCrory, ed. *Military Affairs in North America, 1748–1765: Selected Docu-*

ments *from the Cumberland Papers in Windsor Castle.* New York: D. Appleton–Century, 1936.

Parscau du Plessix, Louis-Guillaume de. "Journal de la campagne de *la Sauvage,* frégate du roy, armée au port de Brest, au mois de mars, 1756 (écrit pour ma dame)." *Rapport de l'archiviste de la province de Québec* (1928–29): 211–26.

Perry, David. *Recollections of an Old Soldier:.* Windsor, Vt.: Republican & Yeoman Printing Office, 1822. Reprinted Cottonport, La.: Polyanthos Press, 1971.

Pote, William. "Remarkable Occurrences from the Year 1745 to 1748, During the Far Greater Part of Which Time I Was a Prisoner in the Hands of the French and Spaniards; Transcrib'd from by Private Notes in Rhode Island Anno 1748." In *The Journal of Captain William Pote Jr. During His Captivity in the French and Indian War from May, 1745, to August, 1747.* New York: Dodd, Mead, 1896.

Pouchot, Pierre. *Mémoires sur la dernière guerre de l'Amérique septentrionale, entre la France et l'Angleterre, suivis d'observations dont plusieurs sont relatives au théâtre actuel de la guerre & de nouveaux détails sur les moeurs & les usages des sauvages, avec des cartes topographiques.* Yverdon, Switzerland, 1781.

Récher, Jean-Félix. *Journal de siège de Québec en 1759.* Quebec: Société Historique de Québec, Université Laval, 1959.

Renaud d'Avène des Méloizes, Nicolas. "Journal militaire tenu par Nicolas Renaud d'Avène des Méloizes, Cher, Seigneur de Neuville, au Canada, du 8 mai 1759 au 21 novembre de la même année. Il était alors capitaine aide-major aux troupes détachées de la marine." *Rapport de l'archiviste de la province de Québec* (1928–29): 29–86.

Rigaud de Vaudreuil, Philippe de. "Mémoire de M. de Vaudreuil au Duc d'Orleans, Régent du royaume." Feb. 1716. *Rapport de l'archiviste de la province de Québec* (1947–48): 291–95.

Roy, Antoine, ed. "Lettres de Doreil." *Rapport de l'archiviste de la province de Québec* (1944–45): 3–171.

Saxe, Maurice de. *Mes rêveries: Ouvrage posthume de Maurice Comte de Saxe, Duc de Curlande et de Sémigalle, maréchal général des armées de sa majesté trés-Chrétienne: Augmenté d'une histoire abrégée de sa vie, & de différentes pièces qui y ont rapport, par Monsieur L'abbé Pérau.* Vol. 1. Amsterdam and Leipzig: Arkstée et Merkus, 1757.

Schuyler, Peter. "Intelligence from Colonel Peter Schuyler of the New Jersey Regiment, Taken at Oswego, and Now a Prisoner at Quebec: Sent by Joseph Morse, Who Left That Place October 4, 1757." In *Colonial Captivities, Marches, and Journeys,* edited by Isabel M. Calder, 140–42. New York: Macmillan, 1935.

Seward, William. "Drossiana. Number CII. Anecdotes of Illustrious and Extraordinary Persons, Perhaps Not Generally Known." *European Magazine,* March 1798, 168–72.

A Short Authentic Account of the Expedition Against Quebec in the Year 1759, Under Command of Major-General James Wolfe, by a Volunteer upon That Expedition. Quebec: Middleton & Dawson, 1872.

Shortt, Adam, and Arthur G. Doughty, eds. *Documents Relating to the Constitutional History of Canada, 1759–1791.* Vol. 1. Ottawa: King's Printer, 1918.

Smith, Philip Chadwick Foster, ed. *The Journals of Ashley Bowen (1728–1813) of Marblehead.* Boston: Peabody Museum of Salem in cooperation with the Colonial Society of Massachusetts, 1973.

Spavens, William. *The Narrative of William Spavens, a Chatham Pensioner, Written by Himself: A Unique Lower Deck View of the Navy of the Seven Years War.* Louth: R. Sheardown, 1796. Reprinted London: Chatham, 1988.

Thomson, William, ed. *Memoirs of the Life and Gallant Exploits of the Old Highlander, Donald Macleod: Who Having Returned, Wounded with the Corpse of General Wolfe, from Quebec, Was Admitted an Out-Pensioner of Chelsea Hospital in 1759; and Is Now in the CIII.d Year of His Age*. London: Peterborough-House Press, 1791.

Webster, J. Clarence, ed. *The Journal of Jeffery Amherst: Recording the Military Career of General Amherst in America from 1758 to 1763*. Toronto: Ryerson Press, 1931.

Whitworth, R. H., ed. "Some Unpublished Wolfe Letters, 1755–1758." *Journal of the Society for Army Historical Research* 53, no. 214 (Summer 1975): 65–86.

Williamson, Peter. *French and Indian Cruelty; Exemplified in the Life and Various Vicissitudes of Fortune of Peter Williamson*. Glasgow: J. Bryce and D. Patterson, 1758.

Wolfe, James. *Letter to Charles Saunders, Aug. 30, 1759, Gentleman's Magazine and Historical Chronicle* (June 1801).

———. *General Wolfe's Instructions to Young Officers*. London: J. Millan, 1768.

Wylly, Harold Carmichael, ed. "The Letters of Colonel Alexander Murray, 1742–59." *1926 Regimental Annual. The Sherwood Foresters, Nottinghamshire and Derbyshire Regiment*, 181–220. London: Swan Sonnenschein, 1927.

SECONDARY SOURCES

Allen, Gay Wilson, and Roger Asselineau. *St. John de Crèvecoeur: The Life of an American Farmer*. New York: Viking, 1987.

Anderson, Fred. *A People's Army: Massachusetts Soldiers and Society in the Seven Years' War*. Chapel Hill: University of North Carolina Press, 1984.

Andrès, Bernard. "D'une mère patrie à la patrie canadienne: Archéologie du patriote au XVIIe siècle." *Voir et images* 26, no. 3 (78) (Spring 2001): 478–97.

Asselin, Jean-Pierre. "Jean-Félix Récher." In Halpenny, *Dictionary of Canadian Biography*, 3:545–47.

Audet, Bernard. *Se nourrir au quotidien en Nouvelle-France*. Sainte-Foy: GID, 2001.

Auger, Martin. "On the Brink of Civil War: The Canadian Government and the Suppression of the 1918 Quebec Easter Riots." *Canadian Historical Review* 89, no. 4 (Dec. 2008).

Auger, Roland-J. "Étienne Charest." In Halpenny, *Dictionary of Canadian Biography*, 4:140–41.

Axtell, James. "The White Indians." In *The Invasion Within: The Contest of Cultures in Colonial North America*, edited by James Axtell, 302–27. New York: Oxford University Press, 1985.

Beatson, Robert. *Naval and Military Memoirs of Great Britain, from 1727 to 1783*. Vol. 2. London: printed for Longman, Hurst, Rees and Orme, W. J. Richardson, A. Constable, A. Brown, 1804.

Beattie, Judith, and Bernard Pothier. *The battle of the Restigouche*. Ottawa: Parks Canada, 1996.

Beaulieu, Alain. "Les Hurons et la conquête: Un nouvel éclairage sur le 'traité Murray.'" *Récherches amérindiennes au Québec* 30, no. 3 (2000): 53–63.

Bonnault, Claude de. "Le Canada militaire: État provisoire des officiers de milice de 1641 à 1760." *Rapport de l'archiviste de la province de Québec* (1949–51): 261–527.

Bosher, John F. "Joseph-Michel Cadet." In Halpenny, *Dictionary of Canadian Biography*, 4:123–28.

Bronze, Jean-Yves. *Les morts de la guerre de Sept Ans au Cimitière de l'Hôpital-Générale de Québec*. Quebec: Les Presses de l'Université Laval, 2001.

Browne, G. P. "James Murray." In Halpenny, *Dictionary of Canadian Biography,* 4:569–78.

Browne, James Alexander. *England's Artillerymen: An Historical Narrative of the Services of the Royal Artillery, from the Formation of the Regiment to the Amalgamation of the Royal and Indian Artilleries in 1862.* London: Hall, Smart and Allen, 1865.

Brumwell, Stephen. *Redcoats: The British Soldier and War in the Americas, 1755–1763.* Cambridge, U.K.: Cambridge University Press, 2002.

Casgrain, P.-B. "Le moulin à vent et la maison de Borgia lors de la bataille des plaines d'Abraham." *Bulletin des recherches historiques* 6, no. 2 (Feb. 1900): 37–41.

Chapais, Thomas. *Le Marquis de Montcalm (1712–1759).* Quebec: J.-P. Garneau, 1911.

Charters, David A., and Stuart R. J. Sutherland. "Joseph Goreham." In Halpenny, *Dictionary of Canadian Biography,* 4:308–10.

Chartrand, René. *Canadian Military Heritage.* Vol. 1, *1000–1754.* Montreal: Art Global, 1993.

———. *French Fortresses in North America, 1535–1763: Québec, Montréal, Louisbourg, and New Orleans.* New York: Osprey, 2005.

———. *Louisbourg, 1758: Wolfe's First Siege.* Oxford: Osprey, 2000.

Chartrand, René, and David Rickman. *Colonial American Troops, 1610–1773 (3).* London: Osprey, 2003.

Churchill, Winston. *A History of the English Speaking Peoples.* Vol. 3, *The Age of Revolution.* London: Cassell, 1957.

Conway, Stephen. *War, State, and Society in Mid-eighteenth-century Britain and Ireland.* Oxford: Oxford University Press, 2006.

Cook, Peter. "Vivre Comme Frères: Native-French Alliances in the St. Lawrence Valley, 1535–1667." Ph.D. thesis, McGill University, 2008.

Corbett, Julian S. *England in the Seven Years' War: A Study in Combined Strategy.* 2nd ed., vol. 1. London: Longmans, Green, 1918.

Côté, André. *Joseph-Michel Cadet, 1719–1781, négociant et munitionnaire du roi en Nouvelle-France.* Sillery: Septentrion, 1998.

Crèvecoeur, Robert St. John de. *Saint John de Crèvecoeur, sa vie et ses ouvrages (1735–1813) avec les portraits de Crèvecoeur et de la comtesse d'Houdetot, gravés d'après des miniatures du temps.* Paris: Librairie des Bibliophiles, 1883.

Crowley, Terence. "'Thunder Gusts': Popular Disturbances in Early French Canada." *Canadian Historical Association, Historical Papers* (1979): 11–32.

D'Allaire, Micheline. *L'Hôpital-Général de Québec, 1692–1764.* Montreal: Fides, 1971.

Dechêne, Louise. *Le partage des subsistances au Canada sous le régime français.* Montreal: Boréal, 1994.

———. *Le peuple, l'État et la guerre au Canada sous le Régime français.* Montreal: Boréal, 2008.

Delisle, Joël. *Le régiment de La Sarre en Nouvelle-France, 1756–1760.* L'Assomption, Quebec: J. Delisle, 2000.

Dempsey, Hugh A. *Big Bear: The End of Freedom.* Vancouver: Douglas & McIntyre, 1984.

Dickason, Olive P. *Canada's Native Americans: A History of Founding Peoples from Earliest Times.* Toronto: McClelland & Stewart, 1992.

Douglas, W. A. B. "Philip Durell." In Halpenny, *Dictionary of Canadian Biography,* 3:208–10.

Druke, Mary A. "Linking Arms: The Structure of Iroquois Intertribal Diplomacy." In *Beyond the Covenant Chain: The Iroquois and Their Neighbors in Indian North America, 1600–1800,* edited by Daniel K. Richter and James H. Merrell, 29–35. Syracuse, N.Y.: Syracuse University Press, 1987.

Duffy, Christopher. *Fire and Stone: The Science of Fortress Warfare, 1660–1860*. New York: Hippocrene Books, 1974.

———. *The Military Experience in the Age of Reason*. New York: Atheneum, 1998.

Dull, Jonathan R. *The French Navy and the Seven Years' War*. Lincoln: University of Nebraska Press, 2005.

———. "Great Power Confrontation or Clash of Cultures? France's War Against Britain and Its Antecedents." In *Cultures in Conflict: The Seven Years' War in North America*, edited by Warren R. Hofstra, 61–77. Lanham, Md.: Rowman & Littlefield, 2007.

Durflinger, Serge. "Canada's Easter Riot: Views and Consequences of Quebec's Anti-conscription Riots, 1918." Paper read at the Western Front Association Annual Conference, State University of New York at Plattsburgh, Aug. 6–8, 2004.

Eccles, W. J. "François (François-Gaston) de Lévis, Duc de Lévis." In Halpenny, *Dictionary of Canadian Biography*, 4:477–82.

———. "The French Forces in North America During the Seven Years' War." In Halpenny, *Dictionary of Canadian Biography*, 3:xv–xxiii.

———. "French Imperial Policy for the Great Lakes Basin." In *The Sixty Years' War for the Great Lakes, 1754–1814*, edited by David Curtis Skaggs and Larry L. Nelson, 21–41. East Lansing: Michigan State University Press, 2001.

———. *The French in North America, 1500–1783*. Markham, Ont.: Fitzhenry & Whiteside, 1998.

———. "Louis-Joseph de Montcalm, Marquis de Montcalm." In Halpenny, *Dictionary of Canadian Biography*, 3:458–69.

———. "Pierre de Rigaud de Vaudreuil de Cavagnial, Marquis de Vaudreuil." In Halpenny, *Dictionary of Canadian Biography*, 4:660–74.

———. "The Role of the American Colonies in Eighteenth Century French Foreign Policy." In *Atti del I Congresso Internazionale de Storia Americana, Genova, 29 Maggio 1976*, 164–73. Genoa: Tilgher, 1978.

Elting, John Robert. *Swords Around a Throne: Napoleon's Grande Armée*. New York: Free Press, 1988.

Falconer, William, and William Burney. *A Universal Dictionary of the Marine Being a Copious Explanation of the Technical Terms and Phrases Usually Employed in the Construction, Equipment, Machinery, Movements, and Military, as Well as Naval, Operations of Ships . . . to Which Is Annexed: A Vocabulary of French Sea-Phrases and Terms of Art*. Rev. ed. London: T. Cadell and W. Davies, 1815.

Fraser, Graham. *Sorry, I Don't Speak French: Confronting the Canadian Crisis That Won't Go Away*. Toronto: McClelland & Stewart, 2006.

Frenière, André. "Jean-Claude Panet." In Halpenny, *Dictionary of Canadian Biography*, 4:601–3.

Gibbon, John. *The Artillerist's Manual, Compiled from Various Sources, and Adapted to the Service of the United States*. New York: D. Van Nostrand, 1860. Reprinted Glendale, N.Y.: Benchmark, 1970.

Gipson, Lawrence Henry. *The British Empire Before the American Revolution*. Vol. 7, *The Great War for the Empire: The Victorious Years, 1758–1760*. New York: Alfred A. Knopf, 1949.

———. *The British Empire Before the American Revolution*. Vol. 6, *The Great War for the Empire: The Years of Defeat, 1754–1757*. New York: Alfred A. Knopf, 1946.

Graham, Gerald S. "Sir Hovenden Walker." In *Dictionary of Canadian Biography*. Vol. 2, *1701 to 1740*, edited by David M. Hayne, 658–62. Toronto: University of Toronto Press, 1969.

Greener, William. *The Gun; or, A Treatise on the Various Descriptions of Small Fire-Arms.* London: Longman, Rees, Orme, Brown, Green, and Longman; Edinburgh: Cadell, 1835. Reprinted as *The Gun 1834.* Forest Grove, Ore.: Normount Technical Publications, 1971.

Halpenny, Francess G., ed. *Dictionary of Canadian Biography.* Vol. 5, *1801–1821.* Toronto: University of Toronto Press, 1983.

———. *Dictionary of Canadian Biography.* Vol. 4, *1771 to 1800.* Toronto: University of Toronto Press, 1979.

———. *Dictionary of Canadian Biography.* Vol. 3, *1741 to 1770.* Toronto: University of Toronto Press, 1974.

Harding, Richard. *Amphibious Warfare in the Eighteenth Century: The British Expedition to the West Indies, 1740–1742.* Woodbridge, Suffolk: Royal Historical Society, 1991.

———. "Sailors and Gentlemen of Parade: Some Professional and Technical Problems Concerning the Conduct of Combined Operations in the Eighteenth Century." *Historical Journal* 32, no. 1 (1989): 35–55.

Harris, Richard Colebrook. *The Seigneurial System in Early Canada: A Geographical Study.* Montreal and Kingston: McGill-Queen's University Press, 1984.

———, ed. *Historical Atlas of Canada.* Vol. 1, *From the Beginning to 1800.* Toronto: University of Toronto Press, 1987.

Hayes, Derek. *Historical Atlas of Canada: Canada's History Illustrated with Original Maps.* Vancouver: Douglas & McIntyre, 2002.

Henderson, Susan W. "Francois-Prosper de Douglas, Chevalier de Douglas." In Halpenny, *Dictionary of Canadian Biography,* 4:224–25.

Jaenen, Cornelius J. *The Role of the Church in New France.* Toronto: McGraw-Hill Ryerson, 1976.

Jennings, Francis. *Founders of America: From the Earliest Migrations to the Present.* New York: W. W. Norton, 1994.

Krenn, Peter, Paul Kalaus, and Bert Hall. "Material Culture and Military History: Test-Firing Early Modern Small Arms." *Material History Review* 42 (Fall 1995): 101–9.

Laberge, Alain, and Yves Hébert. "Les prisonniers de la bataille des Plains d'Abraham." *Bulletin des recherches historiques* 32, no. 5 (May 1926): 257–64.

Lachance, André. *Vivre à la ville en Nouvelle-France.* Outremont: Libre Expression, 2004.

Larin, Robert. "Les Canadiens passés en France à la conquête (1754–1770)." In *Mémoires de Nouvelle-France: De France en Nouvelle-France,* edited by Philippe Joutard, Thomas Wien, and Didier Poton, 145–51. Rennes: Presses Universitaires de Rennes, 2005.

Lavery, Brian. *Nelson's Navy: The Ships, Men, and Organization, 1793–1815.* Annapolis, Md.: Naval Institute Press, 2003.

LeMoine, James MacPherson. *L'album du touriste: Archéologie, histoire, littérature, sport.* Quebec: Augustin Côté, 1872.

León-Portilla, Miguel. "Men of Maize." In *America in 1492: The World of the Indian Peoples Before the Arrival of Columbus,* edited by Alvin M. Josephy, 147–75. New York: Vintage Books, 1991.

"Les héros de 1759 et de 1760 inhumés au Cimetière de l'Hôpital Général de Québec." *Rapport de l'archiviste de la province de Québec* (1920–21): 247–96.

Lunn, Jean. "Agriculture and War in Canada, 1740–1760." *Canadian Historical Review* 16, no. 2 (June 1935): 123–36.

MacLeod, D. Peter. *The Canadian Iroquois and the Seven Years' War.* Toronto: Dundurn Press and the Canadian War Museum, 1996.

———. "The Canadians Against the French: The Struggle for Control of the Expedition to Oswego in 1756." *Ontario History* 80, no. 2 (June 1988): 143–57.

———. "The French Siege of Oswego in 1756: Inland Naval Warfare in North America." *American Neptune* 49, no. 4 (Fall 1989): 262–71.

———. "Microbes and Muskets: Smallpox and the Participation of the Amerindian Allies of New France in the Seven Years' War." *Ethnohistory* 39, no. 1 (Winter 1992): 42–64.

———. "Treason at Quebec: British Espionage in Canada During the Winter of 1759–1760." *Canadian Military History* 2, no. 1 (Spring 1993): 49–62.

Mann, Charles C. *1491: New Revelations of the Americas Before Columbus.* New York: Vintage Books, 2005.

Mathieu, Jacques, and Eugen Kedl, eds. *The Plains of Abraham: The Search for the Ideal.* Translated by Kathe Roth. Sillery: Septentrion, 1993.

May, Robin, and Gerry Embleton. *Wolfe's Army.* London: Osprey, 1997.

McCulloch, Ian Macpherson. *Sons of the Mountains: The Highland Regiments in the French and Indian War, 1756–1767.* Toronto: Robin Brass Studio, 2006.

———. "With Wolfe at Quebec: Who Fought at the Plains of Abraham?" *Beaver* 72, no. 2 (April/May 1992): 19–25.

McCulloch, Ian Macpherson, and Tim J. Todish. *British Light Infantryman of the Seven Years' War, North America, 1757–1763.* Wellingborough: Osprey, 2004.

McLennan, J. S. *Louisbourg: From Its Foundation to Its Fall, 1713–1758.* London: Macmillan, 1919.

Miquelon, Dale. *New France, 1701–1744: A Supplement to Europe.* Toronto: McClelland & Stewart, 1987.

Moogk, Peter N. *Building a House in New France: An Account of the Perplexities of Client and Craftsmen in Early Canada.* Toronto: McClelland & Stewart, 1977.

Muir, Rory. *Tactics and the Experience of Battle in the Age of Napoleon.* New Haven, Conn.: Yale University Press, 1998.

Nicolai, Martin L. "A Different Kind of Courage: The French Military and the Canadian Irregular Soldier During the Seven Years' War." *Canadian Historical Review* 70, no. 1 (1989): 55–75.

Noël, Jan. "Besieged but Connected: Survival Strategies at a Quebec Convent." Canadian Catholic Historical Association, *Historical Studies* 67 (2001): 27–41.

———. "Caste and Clientage in an Eighteenth-Century Quebec Convent." *Canadian Historical Review* 82, no. 3 (Sept. 2001): 465–90.

Olson, Donald W., William D. Liddle, Russell L. Doescher, Leah M. Behrends, Tammy D. Silakowski, and François-Jacques Saucier. "Perfect Tide, Ideal Moon: An Unappreciated Aspect of Wolfe's Generalship at Québec, 1759." *William and Mary Quarterly,* 3rd ser., 59, no. 4 (Oct. 2002): 957–74.

Pariseau, Jean. "Jean-Baptiste-Nicolas-Roch de Ramezay." In Halpenny, *Dictionary of Canadian Biography,* 4:650–653.

Parker, Geoffrey. *The Military Revolution: Military Innovation and the Rise of the West, 1500–1800.* Cambridge, U.K.: Cambridge University Press, 1988.

Pothier, Bernard. "Louis Du Pont Duchambon de Vergor." In Halpenny, *Dictionary of Canadian Biography,* 4:249–51.

———. "The Royal Arms of France and Its Ancillary Artifacts." *Canadian Military History* 7, no. 2 (Spring 1998): 56–64.

Pritchard, James. *In Search of Empire: The French in the Americas, 1670–1730.* Cambridge, U.K.: Cambridge University Press, 2004.

Proulx, Gille. *Between France and New France: Life Aboard the Tall Sailing Ships.* Toronto: Dundurn Press, 1984.

Provencher, Jean. *Québec sous la loi des mesures de guerre 1918.* Trois-Rivières: Boréal Express, 1971.

Reid, Stuart. *Wolfe: The Career of General James Wolfe from Culloden to Quebec.* Rockville Centre, N.Y.: Sarpedon, 2000.

Reid, Stuart, and Mike Chappell. *18th Century Highlanders.* London: Osprey, 1993.

Robins, Benjamin. *New Principles of Gunnery: Containing the Determination of the Force of Gun-Powder, and an Investigation of the Difference in the Resisting Power of the Air to Swift and Slow Motions.* London: printed for J. Nourse, 1742.

Rodger, N. A. M. *The Command of the Ocean: A Naval History of Britain, 1649–1815.* London: W. W. Norton, 2004.

———. *The Wooden World: An Anatomy of the Georgian Navy.* Annapolis, Md.: Naval Institute Press, 1986.

Ross, Lester A. *Archaeological Metrology: English, French, American, and Canadian Systems of Weights and Measures for North American Historical Archaeology.* Ottawa: National Historic Parks and Sites Branch, Parks Canada, 1983.

Rothenberg, Gunther E. *The Art of Warfare in the Age of Napoleon.* Bloomington: Indiana University Press, 1978.

Roy, Pierre-Georges. "Marie-Joseph LeGardeur de Repentigny." *Bulletin des recherches historiques* 53, no. 8 (Aug. 1947): 230–31.

———. "La protection contre le feu à Québec sous le régime français." *Bulletin des recherches historiques* 30, no. 5 (May 1924): 129–40.

Saint-Félix, Soeur. *Monseigneur de Saint-Vallier et l'Hôpital Général de Québec: Histoire du Monastère de Notre-Dame des Anges, religieuses hospitalières de la Miséricorde de Jésus, ordre de Saint-Augustin.* Quebec: C. Darveau, 1882.

Sanfaçon, Roland. "La construction du premier chemin Québec-Montréal et le problème des corvées (1706–1737)," *Revue d'histoire de l'Amérique française* 12, no. 1 (June 1958): 3–29.

Séguin, Rhéal. "Quebec City's 400th Anniversary: A Birthday Visit by the Queen? Quebeckers Are Not Amused." *Globe and Mail,* May 14, 2007, A1.

Squires, W. Austin. "Sir Samuel Argall." In *Dictionary of Canadian Biography.* Vol. 1, *1000–1700,* edited by George W. Brown, 67–69. Toronto: University of Toronto Press, 1966.

Stacey, C. P. "George Scott." In Halpenny, *Dictionary of Canadian Biography,* 3:589–90.

———. "George Townshend, 4th Viscount and 1st Marquess Townshend." In Halpenny, *Dictionary of Canadian Biography,* 5:822–25.

———. *Quebec, 1759: The Siege and the Battle.* Rev. ed. Edited by Donald E. Graves. Toronto: Robin Brass Studio, 2002.

Steele, Ian K. "Robert Monckton." In Halpenny, *Dictionary of Canadian Biography,* 4:540–42.

Stephenson, Robert Scott. *Clash of Empires: The British, French, and Indian War, 1754–1763.* Pittsburgh: Senator John Heinz Pittsburgh Regional History Center, 2005.

Syrett, David. "The Methodology of British Amphibious Operations During the Seven Years' and American Wars." *Mariner's Mirror* 58, no. 3 (Aug. 1972): 269–80.

Taillemite, Étienne. "Louis-Antoine de Bougainville." In Halpenny, *Dictionary of Canadian Biography,* 5:102–6.

———. "Louis-Thomas Jacau de Fiedmont." In Halpenny, *Dictionary of Canadian Biography,* 4:382–83.

Townshend, Charles Vere Ferrers. *The Military Life of Field-Marshal George, First Marquess Townshend, 1724–1807, Who Took Part in the Battles of Dettingen 1743, Fontenoy 1745,*

Culloden 1746, Laffeldt 1747, & in the Capture of Quebec 1759: From Family Documents Not Hitherto Published. London: John Murray, 1901.

Vickers, Daniel. "An Honest Tar: Ashley Bowen of Marblehead," *New England Quarterly* 69, no. 4 (Dec. 1996): 531–53.

Ward, Matthew C. *The Battle for Quebec, 1759.* Brimscombe Port: Tempus, 2005.

White, Richard. *The Middle Ground: Indians, Empires, and Republics in the Great Lakes Region, 1650–1815.* New York: Cambridge University Press, 1991.

Whitely, William H. "Sir Charles Saunders." In Halpenny, *Dictionary of Canadian Biography,* 4:698–702.

Wilson, Beckles. *The Life and Letters of James Wolfe.* London: W. Heinemann, 1909.

Zoltvany, Yves F. "Claude de Ramezay." In *Dictionary of Canadian Biography.* Vol. 2, *1701 to 1740,* edited by David M. Hayne, 545–49. Toronto: University of Toronto Press, 1969.

CANADIAN WAR MUSEUM ARTIFACTS

French Royal Arms, 1727, CWM 19940024-001.

Trophy Mount for French Royal Arms, ca. 1759, CWM 19670139-001.

Index

Page numbers in *italics* refer to illustrations.

ILLUSTRATION CREDITS

A NOTE ON THE TYPE

This book was set in Adobe Garamond. Designed for the Adobe Corporation by Robert Slimbach, the fonts are based on types first cut by Claude Garamond (ca. 1480–1561). Garamond was a pupil of Geoffroy Tory and is believed to have followed the Venetian models, although he introduced a number of important differences, and it is to him that we owe the letter we now know as "old style." He gave to his letters a certain elegance and feeling of movement that won their creator an immediate reputation and the patronage of Francis I of France.

Composed by North Market Street Graphics,
Lancaster, Pennsylvania

Printed and bound by Berryville Graphics,
Berryville, Virginia

Designed by Soonyoung Kwon

the Right Honourable WILLIAM PITT Esqr.
One of His Majesties most Honourable Privy Council
AND PRINCIPAL SECRETARY OF STATE &c

This Plan is most Humbly Inscribed
By his most Obliged and
most Obedient Humble Servt.
Ths. Jefferys

...ES of QUEBEC.
No. of Gus. Mortrs.
.... 9 .. 0
Barbette .. 28 .. 5
.... 7 .. 0
over the
thro Pickets 2 .. 0
y no G. mounted 0
at the upper
sines yard .. 3 .. 0
t the lower
s yard .. 3 .. 0
.... 10 .. 0
ry .... 10 .. 0
.... 57 ..
13 .. 0

R. St. CHARLES

Larrey R.

FRENCH INCAMPMEN...

Notre Dame des Anges

Place of Arms to Defend the Head of the Bridge

Batteries of 3 Gun. Each

New Battery of...

The Place where a Feint was made by the Boats of the Fleet during the whole night, whilst the Troops landed at Sille...

les Batures de Beauport a Shoal Dry a...

Hospital General

Bridge of Boats

Two Hulks to defend the River & Fords each 8 Guns on one side

A Battery of 4 Guns to Defend the Boom

Buoys that deceiv'd the Enemy & to which the Boats Moored that protec-ted the Fleet from the Rafts of Fire Stages.

THE LITTLE R.

FRENCH BATTERY &c

CHM...

a French Wreck

TH...

AM...

LOWER

TOWN

Stores

ADMIRAL

HOLMES'S

DIVISION

Cape Diamond

Point des Peres

Road from St. Nicholas

RIVER St. LAURENCE

Redoubt

FRIGAT...

St. Joseph

BRIG. GENL. MONCTENS CAMP

Road to...

An AUTHENTIC PLAN
of the
RIVER St. LAURENCE
from
Sillery, to the Fall of Montmorenci,
with the Operations of the
SIEGE of QUEBEC
under the Command of
Vice-Adml. Saunders & Major Genl. Wolfe
down to the 5. Sepr. 1759.
Drawn by a CAPTAIN in his Majesties Navy

British Miles